Familienunternehmen und KMU

Reihe herausgegeben von
Andreas Hack, Bern, Schweiz
Andrea Calabrò, Witten, Deutschland
Thomas Zellweger, St. Gallen, Schweiz
Franz W. Kellermanns, Charlotte, USA
Hermann Frank, Wien, Österreich
Marcel Hülsbeck, Witten, Deutschland

AF823320

Sowohl Familienunternehmen als auch kleine und mittlere Unternehmen (KMU) zeichnen sich durch eine Reihe spezifischer Besonderheiten aus, die ihnen im Marktumfeld einen klaren Wettbewerbsvorteil bieten aber auch zu besonderen Risiken führen können. Die vorliegende Schriftenreihe präsentiert wissenschaftliche Arbeiten, die einen empirischen und theoretischen Beitrag zur Erkundung dieser Besonderheiten und deren Auswirkungen auf die betriebswirtschaftliche Praxis leisten. Übergeordnetes Ziel ist es, die Theorieentwicklung des Managements von Familienunternehmen und KMU voranzutreiben.

Both Family Firms and Small and Medium Sized Enterprises (SME) feature a number of distinct behaviors and characteristics which could provide them with a competitive advantage in the market but could also lead to certain risks. The scientific series at hand presents research which provides an empirical and theoretical contribution to the investigation on these specific characteristics and their impact on business practice. The overall aim of this series is to advance the development of theory in the areas of family firm and SME management.

Weitere Bände in der Reihe http://www.springer.com/series/11570

Carola Normann-Tschampel

Value-Based Management in Mittelstand

The Relevance to Strategic Decision-Making, Objectives, and Attitudes

Springer Gabler

Carola Normann-Tschampel
Engelsbrand, Germany

Dissertation, University of Chester, 2019

ISSN 2520-1174 ISSN 2520-1182 (electronic)
Familienunternehmen und KMU
ISBN 978-3-658-29227-0 ISBN 978-3-658-29228-7 (eBook)
https://doi.org/10.1007/978-3-658-29228-7

© Springer Fachmedien Wiesbaden GmbH, part of Springer Nature 2020
This work is subject to copyright. All rights are reserved by the Publisher, whether the whole or part of the material is concerned, specifically the rights of translation, reprinting, reuse of illustrations, recitation, broadcasting, reproduction on microfilms or in any other physical way, and transmission or information storage and retrieval, electronic adaptation, computer software, or by similar or dissimilar methodology now known or hereafter developed.
The use of general descriptive names, registered names, trademarks, service marks, etc. in this publication does not imply, even in the absence of a specific statement, that such names are exempt from the relevant protective laws and regulations and therefore free for general use.
The publisher, the authors and the editors are safe to assume that the advice and information in this book are believed to be true and accurate at the date of publication. Neither the publisher nor the authors or the editors give a warranty, expressed or implied, with respect to the material contained herein or for any errors or omissions that may have been made. The publisher remains neutral with regard to jurisdictional claims in published maps and institutional affiliations.

This Springer Gabler imprint is published by the registered company Springer Fachmedien Wiesbaden GmbH part of Springer Nature.
The registered company address is: Abraham-Lincoln-Str. 46, 65189 Wiesbaden, Germany

Acknowledgements

The completion of my doctoral thesis would not have been successful without the support of a number of people. I am very grateful to everyone who has supported me and given me strength in the last years.

I am very thankful to my supervisors Prof. Peter Stokes and Dr. Neil Moore. Their extensive and quick feedback as well as the insightful discussions we had have been a very valuable contribution to my thesis. I am also very thankful for their patience and encouragement in the last years. I would also like to thank Prof. Bernd Britzelmaier for the suggestion to write this doctoral thesis and his advice throughout the research project. Additonally, I am thankful to Prof. Erich Riess who has been supporting my academic and personal development for many years. I am very grateful to the interviewees for their participation in my empirical study and for providing unique insights into management practices in Mittelstand. This has been absolutely essential for the thesis. Furthermore, I would like to thank my examiners Prof. Paul Manning and Dr. Max Visser for their valuable advice in the final stages of my thesis.

I would also like to thank my family and friends for their patience and support. I am particularly grateful for the immeasurable help of my father, who always provided a sympathetic ear when I needed someone to talk to. He has been an inexhaustive source of professional advice as well as encouragement. The exchange I had with other doctoral students has been a valuable source of ideas and motivation. In particular, I would like to thank Berta and Antje for the comprehensive and thorough exchange on our doctoral theses. Thanks also to Celia, Patrick and Henry for discussing ideas and providing input to my work. Thanks also to my mother, my brothers, my close friends Bettina, Irina, Nadine and Sabine and everyone else who encouraged me in writing my doctoral thesis. Finally, I am most grateful to my husband, Benjamin, for his love and patience. I am infinitely grateful that we share the joy and challenges of our lives.

Acknowledgements

The completion of my doctoral thesis would not have been successful without the support of a great many people. I am very grateful to everyone who has supported me.

I am very thankful to my supervisors [illegible]

Table of contents

Detailed table of contents

List of figures

All figures are own diagrams. Where other sources than this research have been used this is made evident either in the title of the diagram (e.g. Figure 3) or in the diagram (e.g. Figure 10).

Abbreviations

BSC	Balanced Scorecard
CEO	Chief executive officer
CFO	Chief financial officer
CVA	Cash Value Added
DCF	Discounted cash flow
EM	Amendment to the abbreviation for the interviewees that are not owner-managers but external managers or authorised representatives
EVA	Economic Value Added
ext.	external
FCNE	Family-centred non-economic
F-PEC	Family Influence on Power, Experience and Culture scale
I-x	Interviewee number x
IRR	Internal rate of return
KPI	Key performance indicator
NPV	Net present value
OBJ	Objectives
OM	Owner-manager
R	Researcher
RoI	Return on Investment
RQ	Research question
SDM	Strategic decision-making
SEW	Socioemotional wealth
SME	Small- and medium-sized entity
VBM	Value-based management

Abstract

This study aims to understand the relevance of value-based management (VBM) in three specifically identified areas of management (strategic decision-making, objectives, attitudes) in German Mittelstand (broadly related to small- and medium-sized entities). VBM seeks to orientate all management activities towards the increase of the monetary company value.

The review of literature on VBM in Mittelstand identifies three key topics – applicability of VBM, proposals for an adaptation of VBM and the empirical analysis of VBM's application in management practice. The review also shows a gap that is crucial to the development of VBM in Mittelstand: On the one hand, there is a consensus on the applicability of VBM in Mittelstand and there are proposals for an application of VBM in Mittelstand which consider its characteristics. On the other hand, empirical studies show little application of VBM in Mittelstand management practice. However, there are differences and gaps in the existing empirical insights i.e. little insights related to decision-making and with regard to owner-managers' attitudes. Consequently, this empirical study uses a specific focus and research approach to gain further understanding regarding existing gaps in empirical insights as well as the overall research gap.

The research approach involves taking an interpretive stance and conducting semi-structured interviews with owner-managers of 28 companies from manufacturing Mittelstand in Baden-Württemberg, Germany.

The findings show that VBM is of minimal relevance for strategic decision-making. This includes different aspects such as limited application of the net present value method and other VBM management tools. Little relevance of VBM is found in objectives. However, from a holistic analysis, different nuances with regard to economic and non-economic objectives are found. Beyond this, the findings identify not only differences in the attitudes towards VBM but also differences in the understandings of VBM. In this respect, there is a considerable divergence to extant understanding in literature.

Overall, it is concluded that VBM is of minimal relevance in all three areas of Mittelstand management. Thus, the research supports the existing empirical insights through a specific focus and approach. The findings as a whole imply a theory-practice gap.

This research contributes to the body of knowledge by gaining a more in-depth as well as open understanding of the relevance of VBM in the management of Mittelstand. The research addresses gaps in empirical insights. It considers different aspects and adds a new perspective on objectives which responds to existing rationales in the literature. The understanding gained from taking an interpretive stance towards owner-managers' practical experience also provides a valuable basis to further address the overall research gap. In this respect the understanding generated might be a basis for an intensified dialogue between researchers and owner-managers in Mittelstand.

1 Introduction

1.1 Background of the research

Small- and medium-sized entities (SMEs) are a worldwide phenomenon. In Germany, a related, but slightly different sort of company is crucial for the economy, Mittelstand.[1] Mittelstand is distinct, as there is a unity of ownership and management. Consequently, the single owners of a company have a significant influence on its management. The crucial role of Mittelstand for the German economy becomes evident, as a characteristic in 95% of German companies (Haunschild & Wolter, 2010). Beyond the numerical importance, many positive effects are related to Mittelstand, such as its societal role and its stabilizing effect on the economy (Welter, Levering, & May-Strobl, 2016). As an employer, Mittelstand is "as important as never before" (translated from KfW Bankengruppe, 2017, p. 1). The importance of Mittelstand is also reflected in the view expressed by the current Minister of Economics, Peter Altmaier:

> "Economic growth in Germany depends, to a very large degree, on Mittelstand doing well." (translated from Bundesministerium für Wirtschaft und Energie, 2018)

Thus, it still seems valid to regard German Mittelstand as "the backbone of the nation and driver of stabile growth and employment" (translated from Schauf, 2009, p. 28).

However, Mittelstand faces various challenges. German Mittelstand is pressured more and more by globalisation and its consequences (Schauf, 2009). Furthermore, Mittelstand needs to deal with increased innovation, competition, digitalisation and demographic change (Astor, Rammer, Klaus, & Klose, 2016). In this environment, the strategic orientation is a decisive competitive advantage because it ensures the existence of the company in the long run (Steinhübel, 2006). However, management of Mittelstand is often highly involved in daily business (Krol, 2009b). Besides the limited resources of Mittelstand, this is seen as a reason for the negligence of strategic and formal planning (Piontkowski, 2009). Also, less staff are usually available for the support of management than in larger companies (Schomaker & Günther, 2006). Furthermore, information and communication technology and thus also the documentation (Arbeitskreis "Wertorientierte Führung in mittelständischen Unternehmen" der Schmalenbach-Gesellschaft für Betriebswirtschaft e.V., 2003a) and the possibilities for planning and control systems are much more limited than in larger companies (Schomaker & Günther, 2006). Overall, a great number of mittelständische companies suffer from a lack of capacity and competency with regard to strategic management (Astor et al., 2016). This is the greatest obstacle to the development of Mittelstand (Astor et al., 2016). Thus, there is a need for "higher professionalisation in management" (translated from Schauf, 2009, p. 28).

[1] Mittelstand is regarded as distinct phenomenon and different to small- and medium-sized entities. There is no equivalent English term. Thus, the German term Mittelstand and its adjective mittelständisch(e) will be used in this thesis.

© Springer Fachmedien Wiesbaden GmbH, part of Springer Nature 2020
C. Normann-Tschampel, *Value-Based Management in Mittelstand*, Familienunternehmen und KMU, https://doi.org/10.1007/978-3-658-29228-7_1

Value-based management (VBM) is a topic that has been widely discussed since the publication of Rappaport's (1986) reference work "Creating Shareholder Value". The fundamental aspect of VBM is focusing management activities on the increase of the monetary company value in the long run (Becker, Ulrich, & Ebner, 2010b; Golsner, 2012; Gonschorek, 2009a, 2015b, 2016c; Günther, 2014a, 2015b; Krol, 2009c; Lehmann, 2012; Tappe, 2009; Wenzel, 2014). Therefore, VBM helps to secure the existence and survivability of a company in the long run (Becker et al., 2010b; Gonschorek, 2015b, 2016c; Krol, 2009c; Lehmann, 2012; Tappe, 2009; Wenzel, 2014). VBM has gained importance and is nowadays seen as one of the key management philosophies (Britzelmaier, 2013). In large, listed companies VBM is an established management concept (Gonschorek, 2009a, 2015b, 2016c; Lehmann, 2012).

Given the significance of VBM as a management approach, the importance of Mittelstand for the German economy and its specific challenges of management, suggests considering VBM as a management approach for Mittelstand itself. Against the background of the extensive and long-standing academic debate on VBM in large, listed companies, it is astonishing that academic interest in VBM in Mittelstand only emerged around the turn of the century and increased in the last ten years (see section 2.3).

1.2 Research gap, objective and questions

As the literature review will show VBM in Mittelstand still seems to be an emerging field of research (see section 2.3). However, the field has moved beyond focusing on whether VBM is applicable in the context of Mittelstand. In this respect, potential benefits and hurdles of VBM in the context of Mittelstand are being addressed. Against this background there is an agreement that VBM is applicable and beneficial for Mittelstand. There is also the common demand to adjust VBM to Mittelstand's characteristics. This is met by existing proposals for an application of VBM in Mittelstand. While central aspects have thus already been explored, there remains a crucial research gap. Incipient empirical research in the last years, shows that the consensus in literature is in contrast to the minimal application of VBM in Mittelstand's management practice. In this research project, the **aim of research** is to understand the relevance of VBM in selected areas of management in Mittelstand. A more in-depth understanding of the application of VBM in Mittelstand shall contribute to the body of knowledge by gaining additional insights regarding the research gap. The following overall research question guides the study:

> In what way is VBM relevant for specifically identified areas of management in Mittelstand (i.e. strategic decision-making, objectives, attitudes)?

The empirical investigation is based upon the following supplementary research questions:

1. What management tools are used in strategic decision-making in Mittelstand, and in which ways are these tools relevant for strategic decision-making?
2. How is VBM reflected in the use of management tools in strategic decision-making in Mittelstand?
3. What are the objectives of Mittelstand?

4. How is VBM reflected in the objectives of Mittelstand?
5. What are Mittelstands' attitudes towards VBM?

It is regarded as crucial, to gain an in-depth understanding of the phenomenon given its complexity and the existing research gap. Thus, the research focuses on selected areas of management and takes an interpretive stance (see chapter 3).

1.3 Structure of the thesis

Chapter 1 introduces Mittelstand and value-based management as a background for the research as well as the research objective and research questions that shall address the research gap. Chapter 2 provides a brief literature review of Mittelstand and value-based management as well as an in-depth review of literature on value-based management in Mittelstand. Furthermore, existing empirical results will be presented for selected areas of management that will be focused on in the empirical investigation. Chapter 3 then outlines the methodological considerations in designing the empirical study. Beyond this, details about the research methods applied will be given. In chapter 4 the findings in relation to the three specifically identified areas of management will be described and discussed. Finally, chapter 5 summarises the results and the contribution to the body of knowledge and names limitations and avenues for further research.

2 Literature review

The literature review will cover different topics to provide a basis for the empirical study. Firstly, section 2.1 will outline different facets of Mittelstand as specific phenomenon to be researched. Secondly, a brief introduction to value-based management will be provided in section 2.2. With this background, section 2.3 gives an in-depth review of literature on value-based management in Mittelstand. In this section, the understanding of value-based management will be delineated. Furthermore key topics in the field of research will be outlined and research gaps identified. Finally, section 2.4 adresses the specifically identified areas of management that will be researched in the empirical study.

2.1 Mittelstand

2.1.1 Aim and approach of the section

Mittelstand is a particular phenomenon in the German economy. This phenomenon will be approached in the following. This includes delineating definitions of Mittelstand as much as possible from that of small- and medium-sized entities and family businesses (subsection 2.1.2). Furthermore, characteristics of Mittelstand shall be illustrated (subsection 2.1.3) and the importance for the German economy will be outlined (subsection 2.1.4).

2.1.2 Delineation of Mittelstand towards related phenomena

2.1.2.1 Difficulties and criteria used in defining Mittelstand and related phenomena

This subsection contours the definition of Mittelstand. First of all it must be acknowledged that there is no generally accepted definition of Mittelstand (Becker & Ulrich, 2015b; Tappe, 2009; Walther, 2004). In addition different terms are used in this context (Becker & Ulrich, 2015b; Tappe, 2009). Further difficulties arise as the terms are used in parallel and partly interchangeably (Becker & Ulrich, 2009a). According to Becker and Ulrich (2015b) it is difficult to develop a unique definition for a phenomenon as complex and heterogeneous as Mittelstand. To nevertheless approach the phenomenon it helps to draw upon a distinction of different criteria used for definitional issues in this context.

In research on Mittelstand it is common to distinguish between quantitative and qualitative definition criteria (Reinemann & Ludwig, 2015). Furthermore, there is a partly combined or parallel use of qualitative and quantitative criteria (Reinemann & Ludwig, 2015). Often, small- and medium-sized entities are defined by using quantitative criteria, while in definitions of Mittelstand and family businesses there is a tendency to use qualitative criteria (Becker & Ulrich, 2009a, 2015b). On this basis the following outline will briefly present common definitions of small- and medium-sized entities. Then, aspects included in definitions of Mittelstand will be outlined to derive the definition of Mittelstand used in this research project. This will be followed by a brief delineation towards common ways of defining family businesses.

© Springer Fachmedien Wiesbaden GmbH, part of Springer Nature 2020
C. Normann-Tschampel, *Value-Based Management in Mittelstand*,
Familienunternehmen und KMU, https://doi.org/10.1007/978-3-658-29228-7_2

2.1.2.2 Small- and medium-sized entities

Common quantitative criteria for defining SMEs are a company's number of employees and annual turnover (Becker & Ulrich, 2015b; Kosmider, 1994 according to Becker & Ulrich, 2009a; Legenhausen, 1998; Schlüchtermann & Pointner, 2004; Ulrich, 2011). Alternatively, the balance sheet total is used (Ihlau, Duscha, & Gödecke, 2013 and Schön, 2012 according to Becker & Ulrich, 2015b). A definition of SMEs adopted by the European Commission, initially in 1996, has been widely applied in the European Union (European Commission, 2005, 2015). In January 2005 a new definition was adopted by the European Union to reflect the economic development (European Commission, 2005, 2015). This definition is important due to its relevance for support programs for companies (Becker & Ulrich, 2015b). In German-speaking regions the most common definition of SMEs is that of the Institut für Mittelstandsforschung Bonn (Becker & Ulrich, 2015b). To portray the specifics of German SMEs the Institut für Mittelstandsforschung Bonn (2018b) uses a higher threshold for the number of employees than the European Commission (20.5.2003). These two definitions are summarised in Figure 1.

Figure 1: Most common definitions of SMEs[2]

Institution providing definition (column), criteria included in the definition (line)	**Institut für Mittelstandsforschung Bonn**	**European Commission**
Number of employees	Less than 500	Less than 250
Turnover (per year)	Less than 50 million Euros	Less than 50 million Euros and/or
Balance sheet total (per year)		Less than 43 million Euros

In addition to SMEs there is often reference to Mittelstand in Germany. Despite the SME definition by the Institut für Mittelstandsforschung Bonn (2018b) accounting for the specifics of German SMEs, researchers regard it necessary to use a separate definition for Mittelstand. In this respect, Becker and Ulrich (2015b) criticise that there is often the impression that the quantitative criteria adequately reflects Mittelstand's qualitative characteristics. Reinemann and Ludwig (2015) also express that quantitative definitions fall short of Mittelstand and demand using qualitative criteria. These will be looked at in the following.

2.1.2.3 Mittelstand

There is a demand to use qualitative criteria in defining Mittelstand as quantitative criteria are not sufficient to reflect Mittelstand's characteristics (Becker & Ulrich, 2015b; Reinemann & Ludwig, 2015). A variety of qualitative criteria are used to de-

[2] Based on Institut für Mittelstandsforschung Bonn (2018b) and European Commission (20.5.2003). In addition to fulfilling the quantitative thresholds that are displayed, companies are only regarded as SMEs according to definition of the European Commission (20.5.2003) when they are autonomous. This is only given when a limit of 25 % holding is not exceeded (European Commission (20.5.2003)).

fine Mittelstand (Becker & Ulrich, 2009a). Hausch (2004) has identified the following as most common qualitative criteria:

- Unity of ownership and management[3]
- Orientation of management towards individual person(s)
- Economic and legal independence of the company
- Limited size

The common criteria are also referred to in recent overviews (Becker & Ulrich, 2009a, 2015b) and reflect in definitions used in researching VBM in Mittelstand as well as in two common definitions of Mittelstand (Becker, Fischer, Staffel, & Ulrich, 2008; Gonschorek, 2009a; Institut für Mittelstandsforschung Bonn, 2018b; Khadjavi, 2005; Krol, 2009c; Tappe, 2009).

Against this background these definitions are analysed to decide on the definition to be applied (for the definitions and the analysis of the criteria included see Appendices-Figure 1). In line with these definitions, unity of ownership and management is at the heart of the definition, in a modified form however. The resulting definition is shown in Figure 2. Its specifics will be briefly commented in the following.

Figure 2: Definition of Mittelstand in this thesis

Mittelständische companies are companies

- where single natural persons or family members hold at least 50 % of the shares (directly or indirectly) and
- have a significant influence on the management of the company (directly or indirectly) and
- that are legally and economically independent from corporate groups.

In line with the definitions analysed, a **broader view of unity of ownership and management** is used that refers to a significant influence of owners on the management. For the specific formulation the reasonings of Becker, and Fischer et al. (2008) and Gonschorek (2009a) are considered. Gonschorek (2009a) explicitly includes companies that are managed by external manager(s) and those managed by owner(s) and external manager(s) as long as the owners execute a significant influence. This influence can be executed **either directly as part of the management board or indirectly by a majority vote in the meeting of shareholders and/or supervisory board.** Becker, and Fischer et al.'s (2008) definition also includes externally managed companies. This broader definition is valuable for the research at hand as one driver of the application of VBM is that it can help to reduce costs related to information asymmetries resulting from a principal-agent-relationship (for details see subsection 2.2.2). As Tappe (2009) notes the principal-agent-problem is less relevant when there is unity of ownership and management. When external managers are involved, the principal-agent-problem might be more relevant than for owner-managed companies. Thus, externally-managed companies are regarded as

[3] In line with common linguistic use in recent literature on Mittelstand and VBM in Mittelstand (e.g. Institut für Mittelstandsforschung Bonn (2018b); Khadjavi (2005); Reinemann and Ludwig (2015); Tappe (2009)) the following two characteristics separately listed by Hausch (2004) are combined: the company is firstly owned by an owner who bears responsibility and risk and is secondly managed by the owner. While not making this explicit this is similarly done by Becker and Ulrich (2009a, 2015b).

Mittelstand in this thesis as long as there is a significant influence by the owners on the management of the company. Another aspect of Gonschorek's (2009a) reasoning shall be followed. He states that the owners as individual natural persons or family members need to be known by name but does not explicitly define a specific limit to the number of owners.

Beyond the significant influence on the management of the company, empirical studies and common definitions of Mittelstand do not include further aspects that relate to the **orientation of management towards individual person(s)**. Thus, this additional element is not included in the definition underlying this work.

In relation to **economic and legal independence of the company** a more specific formulation is used in the style of Khadjavi (2005). He particularises that mittelständische companies shall not be a branch of a company and shall not be dependent upon a parent company or a network of companies. Gonschorek (2009a) argues that this common criterion is difficult as there are owner-managed companies which are divided into several companies due to considerations with regard to tax and public funding. Under consideration of this rationale the definition at hand refers to economic and legal independence from corporate groups.

There is partly reference to a **limited size of a company** in form of quantitative criteria. According to Becker and Ulrich (2015b) this use of quantitative criteria must be questioned. Overall, quantitative criteria are regarded as not sufficient to define Mittelstand and are thus not included in the definition. Nevertheless, it might be possible to use quantitative criteria as supplementary criteria to aid in selecting participants for the empirical study.[4] The definition of Mittelstand shall be briefly delineated towards definitions of family businesses.

2.1.2.4 Family businesses

There is reference to a similar phenomenon as for defining Mittelstand when defining family businesses. There are different approaches to define family business (Brockhaus, 1994, Chua, Chrisman, & Sharma, 1999 Leyherr, 2000, Litz, 1995 and Neubauer, 1992 according to Hausch, 2004; Hausch, 2004 according to Becker and Ulrich (2015b); Klein, 2010 according to Reinemann & Ludwig, 2015). Generally speaking, family businesses are companies that are influenced by a family (Bornheim, 2000 according to Hausch, 2004). This **influence of the family** has to be be specified further (Hausch, 2004). According to Reinemann and Ludwig (2015), there are approaches that define family businesses in a broader or a narrower sense in relation to the influence of the owner family. Broader definitions consider the family's influence in strategic matters by a majority of votes, while narrower definitions demand the family being involved in the management of the company (Astrachan & Shanker, 2003 and Welge & Witt, 2013 according to Reinemann & Ludwig, 2015). Furthermore, more sophisticated approaches to defining family businesses such as the F-PEC scale are frequently referred to (Becker & Ulrich, 2009a, 2015b; Reinemann & Ludwig, 2015). The F-PEC scale considers power,

[4] Such an approach is used by Hausch (2004) and in a number of the empirical studies on VBM in Mittelstand (e.g. Krol (2009c); Piontkowski (2009); Tappe (2009)).

experience and culture as important dimensions of family influence (Klein, Astrachan, & Smyrnios, 2005).

The definition of family businesses by the Institut für Mittelstandsforschung Bonn (2018a) is one example for a narrower definition of family businesses. The Institut für Mittelstandsforschung Bonn (2018a) regards all companies as family businesses when up to two natural persons or their family members hold at least 50 % of the shares and are part of the management of the company. Thus, the Institut für Mittelstandsforschung Bonn (2018a) regards Mittelstand and family businesses as synonyms. This example shows that when using narrower definitions of family businesses there is **proximity or even identity of definitions of Mittelstand and family businesses** (Reinemann & Ludwig, 2015). On this basis, Reinemann and Ludwig (2015) conclude that family business research can provide insights that are valuable in relation to Mittelstand. A definite distinction of Mittelstand and family businesses is regarded as difficult (Becker & Ulrich, 2015b; Reinemann & Ludwig, 2015). The proximity of Mittelstand and family businesses is acknowledged, in that the definition of Mittelstand underlying this work includes companies held by individual persons as well as those held by family members. Within the definition of Mittelstand, a differentiation of companies held and/or managed by single owner-manager(s) and those held and/or managed by family members might nevertheless be valuable to account for potential influences of an owner family.

Overall, this subsection showed that there is a large overlap of Mittelstand with family businesses and SMEs and that a definite distinction seems to be difficult. Mittelstand as a phenomenon will be further illustrated by looking at its characteristics in the following.

2.1.3 Characteristics of Mittelstand

Mittelstand is regarded as a distinct phenomenon due to its qualitative characteristics. Some key characteristics have already been addressed in defining Mittelstand. Beyond this, additional characteristics that are often addressed shall be outlined in the following.

The **orientation of management towards individual person(s)** involves several aspects. Usually the owner-manager is the sole decision maker and has a high level of self-reliance and independency (Becker, Staffel, & Ulrich, 2009). In contrast to large businesses where different bodies are responsible for taking decisions and controlling them, the owner-manager can immediately take operative and strategic decisions (Reinemann & Ludwig, 2015). Therefore, he is of major importance for the company (Krol, 2007a; Reinemann & Ludwig, 2015) and has a high influence on the management of the company (Hausch, 2004; Piontkowski, 2009). This company structure which is focused on the owner-manager results in positive characteristics as having a high adaptability and flexibility but also in negative characteristics (Piontkowski, 2009). Resulting from the endeavour to sustain their own decision-making power, owner-managers tend to use all internal sources of financing before considering external sources (Reinemann & Ludwig, 2015). While this availability of 'patient capital' can result in a long-term focus in taking decisions, it can also limit the possibilities for investment (Reinemann & Ludwig, 2015). Furthermore, there is a high dependency upon the owner-manager, which results in specific challenges in the case of succession (Reinemann & Ludwig, 2015). Beyond this, the owner-manager usually has a technical background and has only limited knowledge on management tools (Krol, 2009c). Given that a lot of activities are carried out by the owner-manager, there is a threat of a too patriarchal management by an owner-manager not qualified enough (Krol, 2009c). Furthermore, the management in Mittelstand is often highly involved in daily business (Krol, 2009c). Additionally, there is an overload of work and limited management capacities (Reinemann & Ludwig, 2015). This is seen as a reason for the negligence of strategic and formal planning that can be observed among Mittelstand (Piontkowski, 2009).

Another characteristic of Mittelstand is **personal relationships** with employees, customers and suppliers that often exist for a long time (Schomaker & Günther, 2006). These relationships are much more important for the company's success than in larger companies (Arbeitskreis "Wertorientierte Führung in mittelständischen Unternehmen" der Schmalenbach-Gesellschaft für Betriebswirtschaft e.V., 2003a). Due to flat hierarchies and less formal structures, there is closer contact between management and employees which results in a sense of responsibility for the employees and a positive working atmosphere (Reinemann & Ludwig, 2015). Based on informal and personal contacts, there is also often a close cooperation in regional networks along value chains (Reinemann & Ludwig, 2015). Furthermore, mittelständische companies are usually strongly dependent upon financing by a house bank, which can be seen as an important stakeholder of the company (Krol, 2007a). Additionally, Mittelstand is interested in a close and long-term relationship with the house bank (Reinemann & Ludwig, 2015).

Limited resources are another characteristic of mittelständische companies. Usually, less staff is available for the support of management than in large companies (Schomaker & Günther, 2006). Beside this, information and communication technology and also documentation are much more limited than in large companies (Arbeitskreis "Wertorientierte Führung in mittelständischen Unternehmen" der Schmalenbach-Gesellschaft für Betriebswirtschaft e.V., 2003a, p. 525). Consequently, possibilities for planning and control systems are much more constrained than in large companies (Schomaker & Günther, 2006). This can result in disadvantages for management in comparison with large companies (Schomaker & Günther, 2006).

This raises concerns as **Mittelstand faces various challenges**. German Mittelstand is being more and more pressured by globalisation and its consequences (Schauf, 2009). Globalisation and technological advances lead to increased competitive pressure (Astor et al., 2016). In this context a recent empirical study finds that Mittelstand is losing ground on an international level, which is particularly related to a tenacious weakness in demand outside Europe (KfW Bankengruppe, 2017). Beyond globalisation other trends, such as increasing innovation competition, digitalisation and demographic change, will shape Mittelstand's business environment now and in the years to come (Astor et al., 2016). A recent empirical study finds that these can partly be used by Mittelstand to maintain its success (Astor et al., 2016). However, there are increasing signs that the success model might face a crisis if certain challenges are not adequately addressed (Astor et al., 2016). One aspect that raises concerns is that there is a lack of perception and willingness to critically question one's own structures and processes in Mittelstand, especially in the context of digitalisation (Astor et al., 2016). Additionally, multiple challenges are accompanied by a lack of strategic capacity and competency in a multitude of mittelständische companies (Astor et al., 2016). Management in Mittelstand is often highly involved in daily business (Krol, 2009b). Medium- and long-term questions are neglected (Astor et al., 2016). Given the tendency of decreasing returns, the strategic deficit is both a potential explanation as well as an area where activity is crucially needed (Astor et al., 2016). In the environment of globalisation and other challenges, the strategic orientation is a decisive comparative advantage because it ensures the existence of the company in the long run (Steinhübel, 2006). Given recent multiple changes, additional impulses are needed that serve to protect the competitiveness of Mittelstand in the long run (Astor et al., 2016). Besides financing, the lack of strategic competencies is one of the greatest obstacles in the development of Mittelstand (Astor et al., 2016). Thus, there's a need for "higher professionalisation in management" (translated from Schauf, 2009, p. 28). Nowadays, it is discussed if VBM is an approach that could improve the management of Mittelstand and help Mittelstand to face these challenges. This discussion is especially important given Mittelstand's role for the Germany economy which will be illustrated in the following.

2.1.4 Role of Mittelstand in Germany

The definition of Mittelstand has implications for evaluating its significance. Official statistics only provide insufficient data for the qualitative criteria that are used to define Mittelstand, such as the unity of ownership and management (Haunschild & Wolter, 2010; Institut für Mittelstandsforschung Bonn, 2018a). Against this background the empirical insights of Haunschild and Wolter (2010) into the **significance of Mittelstand** are especially valuable. Haunschild and Wolter (2010) use a specific approach to determine the significance of Mittelstand in 2006 on the basis of data from official statistics and a commercial database.[5] Key results are shown in Figure 3. These include 95,3 % of all German companies being mittelständische companies. Beyond this, Mittelstand employs the majority of employees that are subject to social insurance contribution and generates a large part of the turnover of German companies. Additionally, Mittelstand is the predominant type of company for all economic sectors (Haunschild & Wolter, 2010).

[5] For details on the database and the approach taken see Haunschild and Wolter (2010, pp. 5–10). In the empirical study Mittelstand is defined according to the definition of the Institut für Mittelstandsforschung Bonn (2018a), which focuses on unity of ownership and management and treats Mittelstand and family businesses as synonyms (Institut für Mittelstandsforschung Bonn (2018a); Haunschild and Wolter (2010)).

Figure 3: Percentage of Mittelstand in Germany according to Haunschild and Wolter (2010, p. 26)

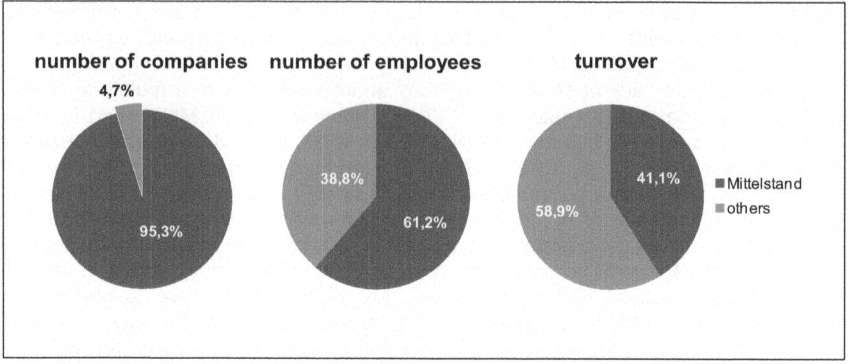

Thus, Mittelstand is of considerable importance for the German economy (Haunschild & Wolter, 2010). Furthermore, Haunschild and Wolter (2010) find that there are mittelständische companies in all size ranges. It is emphasised that mittelständische companies are not per se small companies. Nevertheless, the results show that the share of Mittelstand companies is higher for the size ranges that represent small and medium-sized companies than for large companies.[6] The results are also compared to a former study with the similar objective. A direct comparison to the results of Wolter and Hauser (2001) is not possible due to a refinement of the database and the research (Haunschild & Wolter, 2010). However, there are indications that the importance of Mittelstand for the German economy is stable (Haunschild & Wolter, 2010).

While the empirical results of Haunschild and Wolter (2010) show Mittelstand's significant role for the German economy, the data is not very recent. As the vast majority of SMEs belongs to Mittelstand, recent data on SMEs can be used to further evaluate the significance of Mittelstand (a similar reasoning is applied by Institut für Mittelstandsforschung Bonn, 2018a). Data on SMEs in Germany and Baden-Württemberg for 2015 indicates that Mittelstand is still of crucial importance (based on Statistisches Bundesamt Deutschland; Statistisches Landesamt Baden-Württemberg (2018a), for details see Appendices-Figure 2).

The importance of Mittelstand for Germany is not only evident in numerical terms but also in **its economic and societal role**. The positive development of the German economy is accredited to the specific characteristics of Mittelstand (Reinemann & Ludwig, 2015). This includes that resulting from its characteristics, Mittelstand has a stabilizing effect on employment, especially as mittelständische companies dismiss less personnel in times of recession (Welter et al., 2016). Furthermore, Mittel-

[6] For companies with a turnover of less than 1 Million Euro 97 % of the companies are Mittelstand (for the data see Haunschild and Wolter (2010, p. 15)). When looking at the companies with a turnover of 10 to 50 million Euro, which is the upper threshold for SMEs according to the definition of the Institut für Mittelstandsforschung Bonn (2018b) 60 % are still mittelständische companies. The percentage of Mittelstand for large companies with more than 50 Million Euro turnover is still 34 %.

stand combines highly innovative capabilities with an international market perspective and social responsibility (Astor et al., 2016). Mittelstand is also a crucial factor in achieving goals of economic policy such as economic growth (Welter & Lasch, 2008). This reflects in the view expressed by the current Minister of Economics Peter Altmaier:

> "Economic growth in Germany depends, to a very large degree, on Mittelstand doing well." (translated from Bundesministerium für Wirtschaft und Energie, 2018)"

In this respect, mittelständische companies currently present themselves in "top form" (translated from KfW Bankengruppe, 2017, p. 1) which includes the highest increase of turnover in the last 5 years, a good level of profitability and the highest level of productivity in the last 8 years.

Besides a number of economic roles, Mittelstand also has societal functions (Welter et al., 2016). These include its role as an employer in general as well as in vocational training (KfW Bankengruppe, 2017; Welter et al., 2016). As an employer, Mittelstand is as important as never before and was solely responsible for the increase in employment in Germany in 2016 (KfW Bankengruppe, 2017). Furthermore, Mittelstand reflects the fundamental values of the German social order and mirrors desirable behaviour in terms of the market economy (Welter et al., 2016). Thus, it is of high importance to maintain Germany's social market economy (Welter et al., 2016).

Overall, it still seems to be accurate to regard German Mittelstand as "the backbone of the nation and driver of stabile growth and employment" (translated from Schauf, 2009, p. 28). This also becomes evident from Mittelstand being regarded as a crucial element in the success of the German economy (Astor et al., 2016). According to Reinemann and Ludwig (2015), Mittelstand has even developed into the "brand essence" (translated from Reinemann & Ludwig, 2015, p. 38) of the German economy at the latest since the economic and financial crisis. Despite challenges, the "success model Mittelstand" (translated from Astor et al., 2016, p. 4) is definitely not drawing to a close. Mittelstand has still much potential for a competitive and future-oriented economy and society (Welter et al., 2016). Consequently it is regarded important to research Mittelstand. The following subsection will address key characteristics of this field of research.

2.1.5 Summary of the section

This section has illustrated Mittelstand as a phenomenon to be researched in different ways. Firstly, difficulties have been found in defining and differentiating Mittelstand, SMEs and family businesses (see subsection 2.1.2). This involves that there is no generally accepted definition for all these terms. There is a tendency to define SMEs with the use of quantitative criteria while Mittelstand and family businesses are defined using qualitative criteria. The definition of Mittelstand for this thesis has been presented (see subsection 2.1.2.3) based on an analysis of common characteristics included in definitions of Mittelstand. An attempt to delineate Mittelstand towards SMEs and family businesses has shown that there is a large overlap and that a clear distinction is difficult. In line with Reinemann and Ludwig's (2015) reasoning, this thesis will refer to literature on SMEs and family businesses to amend the literature specifically focusing on Mittelstand where it is appropriate.

Secondly, Mittelstand has further been illustrated by addressing key characteristics (see subsection 2.1.3). Resulting from the orientation of management towards individual persons the owner-manager is of crucial importance. Additionally, there are personal relationships with stakeholders. Due to limited resources there can be disadvantages in management in comparison to large, listed companies. This raises concerns given that Mittelstand faces challenges resulting from globalisation and its consequences as well as other recent trends. In this context the strategic orientation is regarded as decisive. However, there often is a strategic deficit. From this results a demand for higher professionalisation of management. This demand is especially important given the significance of Mittelstand for Germany.

Thirdly, the significant importance of Mittelstand for the economy in Germany has been addressed (see subsection 2.1.4). The subsection also briefly outlined facets of the economic and societal role of Mittelstand for the German economy. Overall this can still be summarised as Mittelstand being "the backbone of the nation and driver of stabile growth and employment" (translated from Schauf, 2009, p. 9).

Against the background of characteristics and challenges of Mittelstand and its importance for the German economy, it is regarded as valuable to research management in Mittelstand. Becker and Ulrich (2009a) also express the hope that management research finally pays the attention to Mittelstand that it has deserved for a long time due to its economic importance. Given this demand, one aspect of management that can be researched in the context of Mittelstand is value-based management. This management approach will be introduced in the following subsection.

2.2 Introduction to value-based management

2.2.1 Aim and approach of the section

This section shall provide a short introduction into value-based management. This includes an outline of its key idea as well as its origins and related benefits (subsection 2.2.2). Additionally, the significance of VBM as a management approach among German companies is addressed (subsection 2.2.3). This serves as background for reviewing the literature on VBM in Mittelstand in the following section.

2.2.2 Introduction to value-based management and its origin

Value-based management seeks to orient all activities in a company towards the objective **to increase the company value for the owners** (Britzelmaier, 2013; Firk, Schmidt, & Wolff, 2016; Weber, Bramsemann, Heineke, & Hirsch, 2017). Value-based metrics are a key feature of VBM for aligning corporate action holistically with value creation (Firk, Schrapp, & Wolff, 2016).

The **origin of VBM lies in the development of the shareholder value approach** in the 1980s (Britzelmaier, 2013; Firk, Schmidt et al., 2016; Gonschorek, 2009a, 2015b; Krol, 2009c; Tappe, 2009; Weber et al., 2017; Wenzel, 2014). In this context, there is often reference to "Creating Shareholder Value" by Rappaport (1986). For Rappaport (1986, p. 12) the rationale for why management should pursue the fundamental objective to increase the shareholder value is "comparatively straightforward". Management involves balancing the interests of different corporate constituencies. This includes financial relationships and a company must "satisfy the financial claims of its constituents" (Rappaport, 1986, p. 12). Otherwise its existence is threatened. Thus, a company must be focused on enhancing its ability to generate cash. Consequently, according to the shareholder value approach, the economic value of investments has to be evaluated "by discounting forecasted cash flows by the cost of capital" (Rappaport, 1986, p. 12).

The shareholder value approach emerged in the context of a debate on traditional measures of economic performance and changes on the capital market. Its emergence was additionally supported by other factors e.g. the takeover wave during the 1980s. The shareholder value approach responded to this context by introducing performance measures that are oriented towards the capital market by integrating established concepts of financing and capital market theory with strategic management (for this paragraph see Britzelmaier, 2013; Gonschorek, 2009a, 2015b; Günther, 2015b; Krol, 2009c; Tappe, 2009; Wenzel, 2014).

Beyond Rappaport (1986) other authors also argue that VBM has **positive effects on management** in general and financial management in specific. VBM is assumed to have positive effects on performance as it enables managers to develop and implement strategies that create value (Firk, Schrapp et al., 2016). In addition, VBM contributes to securing the financing and thus the long-term existence of the company by emphasising that managers need to consider financial claims (Blume, 2016; Firk, Schmidt et al., 2016). The consideration of the expectations of the capital market can lead to more realistic planning, improved decision-making and improved results (Weber et al., 2017). Managers are sensitised to the need to earn a risk-adequate return as an economic condition for the development of the company (Blume, 2016; Weber et al., 2017). Thus, VBM facilitates using capital efficiently (Blume, 2016). There also seems to be empirical support for this reasoning. On the basis of reviewing empirical studies Blume (2016) finds indications that one fundamental way in that VBM improves performance is its contribution to efficient capital management.

Additionally, Blume's (2016) findings support the argument that VBM is positive in relation to **information asymmetries** that can exist in a company. This reasoning is also repeatedly addressed as an advantage of VBM. Firk, and Schmidt et al. (2016) address VBM being a management tool that can counteract information asymmetries within the company and between owners and managers. According to principal-agent-theory such information asymmetries typically arise when there is a principal-agent relationship (Britzelmaier, 2013). In this context, VBM is beneficial as it enables aligning the interests of a manager or other persons acting as agents to the interests of the owners or other persons acting as principals (Britzelmaier, 2013; Firk, Schrapp et al., 2016). VBM performance measures can give employees clarity on how they have to act in line with the company objective (Weber et al., 2017). As VBM metrics consider costs of capital as a benchmark for performance and decision-making, the shareholders' costs to monitor management's activities are de-

creased (Blume, 2016). Blume's (2016) results indicate that VBM's effect to reduce monitoring costs in case of a principal-agent-situation is another fundamental way in which VBM contributes to an improved performance.
Together with other factors such as an increased globalisation, in general and on capital markets, these advantages of VBM led to an increasing implementation of VBM (Firk, Schmidt et al., 2016). However, it is also noted that there has been criticism of VBM and that the implementation effort is repeatedly addressed as a barrier to using VBM (Blume, 2016; Britzelmaier, 2013; Firk, Schmidt et al., 2016; Weber et al., 2017).[7]

Since the emergence of the shareholder value approach, which uses the discounted cash flow (DCF) method **different value-based metrics have been developed** by management consultants (Blume, 2016; Britzelmaier, 2013; Weber et al., 2017). Economic Value Added (EVA) and Cash Value Added (CVA) are regarded as the most common ones (Firk, Schmidt et al., 2016; Weber et al., 2017). This also becomes evident from reviews of empirical studies which show that EVA is by far the most often used in German companies (Britzelmaier, 2013; Weber et al., 2017). VBM metrics are regarded as crucial to focus all activities on the increase of the company value (Weber et al., 2017). The overall objective only becomes the guiding principle when it is operationalised with periodic performance measures (Weber et al., 2017). Thus periodic performance measures are the cornerstone and necessary condition for VBM (Firk, Schmidt et al., 2016). Additionally, the objective to increase the company value should be considered in other areas of management. In this respect, there is reference to target planning and the integration into a company's management, compensation and communication systems (Firk, Schmidt et al., 2016; Weber et al., 2017). A consistent implementation of VBM enables companies' activities and decisions being consistently focused on the increase of the company value (Firk, Schmidt et al., 2016). While originating from the shareholder value approach, the term value-based management or equivalent German terms are nowadays more commonly used in Germany (Lehmann, 2012). This is also evident from the titles of recent literature on VBM in general and specifically VBM in Mittelstand.[8]

2.2.3 Significance to management practice in Germany

Several authors comment on the current significance of VBM in Germany drawing upon results from empirical studies (Blume, 2016; Britzelmaier, 2013; Firk, Schmidt et al., 2016). According to Firk, and Schmidt et al. (2016) today's management prac-

[7] The drivers and hurdles of VBM as well as the understanding of VBM in the context of Mittelstand will be looked at in more depth in section 2.3.

[8] There is reference to different terms being used as synonyms in this context (Lehmann (2012), Wenzel (2014)). Many of the slightly different German terms used in the titles can be translated as value-based management ("Wertorientiertes Management", "wertorientierte Unternehmensführung" or "unternehmenswertorientierte Führung" used by Becker, Ulrich, and Ebner (2010b), Britzelmaier (2013), Gonschorek (2009a, 2015b, 2016c), Günther (2014a), Krol (2009c), Lehmann (2012) and Tappe (2009)). Furthermore, there is use of the English term value-based management (e.g. Blume (2016); Firk, Schrapp, and Wolff (2016)). In addition, the terms "value management" ("Wertmanagement") and "value-oriented (management) control" ("Wertorientierte (Unternehmens-)Steuerung") are used by some authors (e.g. Golsner (2012); Günther (2015b); Firk, Schmidt, and Wolff (2016); Weber, Bramsemann, Heineke, and Hirsch (2017); Wenzel (2014).

tice can hardly be visualised without VBM. They refer to a recent empirical study that shows the share of European companies that use VBM increased from 2005 to 2010. Other authors refer to a broader basis of empirical studies. Britzelmaier (2013) names 11 empirical studies that analyse the diffusion and application of VBM among listed companies in Germany. Among others, he finds a dominance of EVA in the studies published from 2000 to 2012. Furthermore, all these studies show that a large part of the companies is committed to VBM. Thus, Britzelmaier (2013) concludes that VBM has developed into an important topic in listed companies and regards VBM as one of the key management philosophies.

Weber et al. (2017) similarly state that VBM has won recognition in large German companies. Furthermore, they conclude that the continuing demand for a long time shows that VBM cannot only be a management fad. This view is based on an analysis of empirical findings on the diffusion and aspects of the implementation of VBM. Weber et al. (2017) draw upon 16 empirical studies mostly focusing on listed companies in Germany. These were published between 2002 and 2013 and are amended by additional results from other European countries. One finding from this analysis is that the diffusion of VBM is still growing. Furthermore, the majority of large German corporations communicates the increase of the company value as a high priority objective (for this paragraph see Weber et al., 2017). Blume (2016, p. 554) also sees a necessity to discuss "whether value-based management is an old-fashioned management practice from the 1990s or a tailor-made management practice to manage organizations successfully". Thus, he conducts a literature review to gain insights into VBM's role for managing firms successfully. This includes a systematic identification of empirical studies on VBM from 29 highly-ranked English- and German-speaking journals from 2000 to 2012. On the basis of the empirical studies identified, he additionally considers the empirical studies these refer to. In total, he analyses 56 empirical studies. On the basis of analysing these empirical studies he concludes that "the idea of VBM is not outdated" (Blume, 2016, p. 581). Furthermore, he generates insights into contextual factors influencing VBM and organisational performance (for this paragraph see Blume, 2016).

A recent empirical study also supports the significance of VBM in Germany. Firk, and Schrapp et al. (2016, p. 51) find that on average 69 % of German companies in a sample of the large listed companies in the Unites States and 16 Western European countries apply VBM. Overall, this shows that VBM is an established management concept nowadays for large, listed companies. This view is shared by other authors (Gonschorek, 2009a, 2015b, 2016c; Lehmann, 2012).

While VBM has **largely won recognition in large, listed companies in Germany one still cannot infer a "sweeping success"** (translated from Weber et al., 2017, p. 291) of VBM. In addition to Weber et al.'s (2017) reasoning for this view, other empirical results and views expressed justify a more differentiated opinion of VBM.

Firstly, Weber et al. (2017) and Britzelmaier (2013) point towards empirical indications that VBM is more commonly used in Germany than in other countries. Firk, and Schrapp et al.'s (2016) recent empirical study supports this. They find that Germany is, with a noticeable gap, the country with the highest average use of VBM.

Secondly, Weber et al.'s (2017) comparison of empirical results related to the implementation of VBM shows that the commitment to VBM in the first instance, goes seldom beyond the use of a VBM key performance indicator. In comparison to the normative-theoretical views on the implementation of VBM it is implemented in a simplified form in management practice. Until today these implementation gaps are rather the norm than the exception. However, these implementation gaps are decreasing. Overall this implies for Weber et al. (2017) that despite the diffusion of VBM still increasing, there has not been a „revolutionary replacement" (translated from Weber et al., 2017, p. 300) of traditional management concepts by VBM.

Thirdly, empirical evidence on the advantageousness of an implementation of VBM has to be considered. In this respect, Firk, and Schmidt et al. (2016) point towards two recent empirical studies that, in their view, provide robust indications of an advantageousness of VBM. The empirical study of Firk, and Schrapp et al. (2016) also finds VBM to be related to a higher performance. In this respect, their assumption based on previous empirical studies is confirmed. In his comprehensive review of 56 empirical studies Blume (2016) also finds that VBM has, on average, positive performance effects. However, he concludes that VBM is a "valuable management practice to manage organizations successfully in certain circumstances" (Blume, 2016, p. 581). He addresses that this includes companies that encounter comparatively stronger agency conflicts. This indicates that the empirical studies analysed by Blume (2016) do not provide universally valid evidence for a positive effect of VBM on performance. Weber et al. (2017) also point out that there is not yet definite evidence on VBM's effect on company performance. A variety of empirical studies on VBM's potential exists, but there is no consistent body of knowledge due to inconsistencies. They mention that this might be the case as empirical studies are often based on publicly available data and do not consider the level to which VBM is implemented (Weber et al., 2017). Firk, and Schrapp et al. (2016) also refer to mixed empirical evidence on VBM's effect on performance and a respective debate in academia and practice. However, based on referring to a categorisation of existing empirical studies, they mainly consider a selection of empirical studies. Based on these studies they assume that VBM has a positive effect on performance, which is then empirically confirmed (Firk, Schrapp et al., 2016). Overall, this implies that VBM might have positive effects on company's performance. However, these effects are not consistently confirmed by empirical studies.

2.2.4 Summary of the section

This section has illustrated the origin of VBM, its key idea and potential benefits of its application (see subsection 2.2.2). Furthermore, the most important aspects that influenced its emergence and the development until today have been mentioned. A key feature of VBM are VBM performance metrics such as EVA and CVA.

Additionally, the section has shown that VBM is a well-established management approach nowadays in listed companies in Germany (see subsection 2.2.3). However, implementation gaps can also be seen and there is not yet consistent empirical evidence on its effect on performance.

Overall, this results in the following conclusion. VBM's orientation of all company activities towards the objective to increase the company value is regarded as an important management approach. Weber et al.'s (2017) view that VBM has a number of advantages which justify an application of VBM is shared. However, VBM should not be overestimated as there are some weaknesses which have not yet been adequately resolved (similarly concluded by Weber et al., 2017). In fact, VBM has not „revolutionarily replaced“ (translated from Weber et al., 2017, p. 300) traditional management approaches but has been established as a management concept that is used by companies depending on their individual situation and needs (similarly concluded by Weber et al., 2017). Given VBM's significance as a management approach, it is beneficial to consider its application. This consideration cannot only be valuable for large listed companies but also for Mittelstand. Considering VBM for Mittelstand is a necessity due to the significance of VBM, the importance of Mittelstand and the demand for a higher professionalisation of management. In this context, there are even comments that the potential benefits of VBM are higher for Mittelstand (Weber et al., 2017). While the focus of VBM literature has been on large, listed companies, VBM in the context of Mittelstand is increasingly addressed.[9] Based on this introduction to VBM, the following chapter will analyse the literature focusing on VBM in Mittelstand in-depth.

2.3 Value-based management in Mittelstand

2.3.1 Aim and approach of the section

The aim of the section is threefold:

- An overview of the body of knowledge on VBM in Mittelstand is given.
- Existing research gaps shall be highlighted.
- It shall be illustrated how this research project addresses existing research gaps.

To achieve this aim a literature search has been conducted to identify literature with a focus on VBM in Mittelstand.[10] In this literature search synonyms for both terms have been considered.[11] The relevant literature[12] identified from this search is ana-

---

[9] This becomes evident e.g. from Weber et al. (2017) and Britzelmaier (2013) commenting on VBM's relevance in the context in Mittelstand in their recent publications on VBM in general. Firk, and Schrapp et al. (2016) also indicate that the performance effects of VBM in small- and medium-sized entities are a valuable avenue for future research.

[10] To gain a broad understanding of the topic, not only literature related to Mittelstand in a narrow sense is considered but also literature referring to related phenomena such as SMEs or family businesses (see next footnote with details on the search terms used). For readability the text nevertheless refers to "VBM in Mittelstand".

[11] The literature search included German and English terms that are used in relation to VBM (value-based management, shareholder value (management), value(-)orient(at)ed management, Economic Value (Added)/EVA, Cash Value Added/CVA, Discounted Cash flow/DCF, Wertmanagement, Wertsteigerung, wertorientierte Unternehmensführung, wert-orientiertes Management, wertorientierte (Unternehmens)Steuerung, wertschöpfungs-orientiertes Controlling). These have been searched for in combination with German and English terms that are related to Mittelstand (small business(es), small- and medium-sized entity/entities/companies/enterprise, SME, family firm, family business(es), Mittelstand, kleine und mittlere (Unternehmen), kleine und mittelständische (Unternehmen), KMU, Familienunternehmen, eigentümergeführt). Different German and English databases have been used for searching literature.

lysed for the topics that are addressed, as well as for the approach taken. A table listing the approach and the key topics in each of the contributions is shown in Appendices-Figure 3. The topics repeatedly addressed can be related to three themes. Firstly, the outline of drivers and hurdles of VBM in Mittelstand as well as its applicability in Mittelstand. The second topic is the adaptation of VBM concepts to the characteristics of mittelständische companies. Thirdly, there is a focus on an empirical analysis of different aspects related to VBM in Mittelstand.

These three themes are approached differently in the literature. Partly, the authors only draw conclusions on the basis of literature and partly, the conclusions result from an empirical analysis. It can be observed that earlier works are more often based on drawing conclusions from literature. From 2005 onwards there is a growing number of empirical studies, with a peak that includes three doctoral theses analysing VBM in Mittelstand in 2009. Despite the recent tendency towards empirical research, the topic is still addressed by drawing conclusions from literature. Overall, VBM in Mittelstand still seems to be an emerging field of research. This view results firstly from the limited number of empirical studies focusing on VBM in Mittelstand, which is lower than expected given the importance of VBM and Mittelstand (for details see subsections 2.1.4 and 2.2.3). In addition, the empirical studies are not based on a common understanding of Mittelstand and look at different kinds of companies in the context of Mittelstand e.g. small businesses or family businesses. On the basis of this overall impression of the field of research the following subsections give an overview of the existing body of knowledge.

This shall be based on an outline of the understanding of value-based management in the context of Mittelstand (subsection 2.3.2). This includes deriving a working definition of VBM for this thesis. Then, the insights gained from the literature review in relation to the three key topics are outlined. This starts with looking at drivers, hurdles and the applicability of VBM in Mittelstand (subsection 2.3.3) and is followed by addressing views on how VBM can be adapted to characteristics of mittelständische companies and applied by them (subsection 2.3.4). Additionally, an overview of empirical insights into the application of VBM in Mittelstand is given (subsection 2.3.5). Finally, the review of relevant literature on VBM in Mittelstand is summarised and it is derived how the research project will address key research gaps in the existing body of knowledge (subsection 2.3.6).

[12] Some of the literature is regarded as not relevant and is not considered in the overview of the body of knowledge. On the one hand, this includes literature which addresses VBM in Mittelstand but does not include an adequate literature review. An example is Mäkeläinen and Roztocki (15.08.1998) which addresses why EVA can be useful for SMEs and illustrate how they can apply it. However, it is not made evident on what basis these conclusions are drawn. On the other hand, part of the German literature on VBM in Mittelstand is not considered. A considerable amount of German literature on VBM in Mittelstand draws conclusions from literature. This literature is only regarded as relevant when it has been published after 2010, as it is assumed that this literature reflects the current body of knowledge. Such German contributions published before 2010 are only included when they are repeatedly addressed in recent contributions and can thus be regarded as seminal works despite not including an empirical analysis of the topic. An example is Achleitner and Bassen (2000). While Achleitner and Bassen (2000) only draw conclusions from literature, the approach presented is still frequently referred to in recent literature on VBM in Mittelstand and thus considered as relevant.

2.3.2 Delineation of the understanding of value-based management

This subsection shall deepen the initial understanding of VBM that has been illustrated by the introduction to VBM and its origin in subsection 2.2.2. The aim is to develop an understanding of VBM for this thesis.

2.3.2.1 Understanding of value-based management

The **systematic analysis of the understanding addressed in relevant literature** has been conducted as follows. All relevant literature has been analysed with regard to how the understanding of VBM is addressed. Firstly, sections specifically addressing the understanding of VBM or the fundamentals of VBM have been identified. In these sections, the aspects referred to in relation to the understanding of VBM have then been analysed. The detailed results of the analysis are displayed in Appendices-Figure 4. The aspects related to will be outlined in the following.[13]

At the heart of VBM is **focusing management on the company value** (Becker et al., 2010b; Golsner, 2012; Gonschorek, 2009a, 2015b, 2016c; Günther, 2014a, 2015b; Krol, 2009c; Lehmann, 2012; Tappe, 2009; Wenzel, 2014). The company value is understood in a monetary or economic sense (Becker et al., 2010b; Gonschorek, 2015b, 2016c; Günther, 2015b; Krol, 2009c; Lehmann, 2012), more precisely as net present value (NPV) of future cash flow for the owners of a company (Golsner, 2012; Gonschorek, 2009a; Günther, 2014a; Tappe, 2009; Wenzel, 2014). Thus, the company value is determined by discounting these cash flow (Golsner, 2012; Günther, 2014a; Wenzel, 2014). The focus on the monetary company value is expressed by all relevant authors.

In different ways, the relevant authors articulate that **management shall holistically focus on this monetary company value** (Becker et al., 2010b; Golsner, 2012; Gonschorek, 2009a, 2015b, 2016c; Günther, 2014a, 2015b; Krol, 2009c; Lehmann, 2012; Tappe, 2009; Wenzel, 2014). This becomes evident from distinct references to VBM as "a holistic framework for the manifold tasks in a company" (translated from Lehmann, 2012, p. 4) or "a holistic management concept, in that all elements and systems of management are formed and coordinated in a value-oriented manner" (translated from Tappe, 2009, p. 69). This is also explicitly referred to in a similar way by other authors (Becker et al., 2010b; Gonschorek, 2009a, 2015b, 2016c). In addition, this is hinted at more indirectly by authors stating that the operative and strategic orientation of the company shall be oriented towards the company value (Gonschorek, 2009a, 2015b, 2016c; Lehmann, 2012; Wenzel, 2014) or by similar references that express all management activities shall be focused on the company value (Golsner, 2012; Günther, 2015b; Krol, 2009c; Lehmann, 2012). Only in two cases is there a rather feeble hint towards understanding VBM as a holistic management approach as VBM is referred to as "(an approach for) corporate management" (translated from Becker, Staffel, & Ulrich, 2010, p. 222; Krol, 2009c, p. 56). In line with understanding VBM as a holistic management approach, the majority of relevant authors states that VBM shall also be the basis for

[13] This partly includes the use of direct quotes. Direct quotes from German literature are translated into English for readability. The translation shall reflect the original meaning as closely as possible.

decision-making within the company (Gonschorek, 2009a, 2015b, 2016c; Günther, 2014a, 2015b; Krol, 2009c; Lehmann, 2012; Tappe, 2009; Wenzel, 2014). VBM offers guiding principles for managerial decisions (Gonschorek, 2009a; Lehmann, 2012) and provides improved support for decisions (Günther, 2014a, 2015b). It is emphasised that all decisions shall be consistently oriented towards the basic idea of VBM (Gonschorek, 2015b, 2016c; Tappe, 2009). This shall include strategic as well as operative decisions (Gonschorek, 2016c; Wenzel, 2014). It is interesting to note that in relevant literature, there seems to be a widespread consensus on VBM as a holistic management approach that refers to all management activities and decisions.

Mutual agreement can also be found for another aspect in relation to VBM. The majority of authors expresses that in VBM **the emphasis is on the interests of the owners** (Becker et al., 2010b; Gonschorek, 2009a, 2015b, 2016c; Günther, 2015b; Krol, 2009c; Lehmann, 2012; Tappe, 2009; Wenzel, 2014). A common way in which this is articulated is by stating that the focus of VBM is on the value for the owners, which is fundamentally based on the cash flow to the owners (Gonschorek, 2009a; Günther, 2015b; Krol, 2009c; Lehmann, 2012; Wenzel, 2014). Other authors express this by saying that the shareholders and owners are regarded as a key stakeholder group or that there is an emphasis on their interests (Gonschorek, 2015b, 2016c, 2016c; Lehmann, 2012; Tappe, 2009; Wenzel, 2014).

A majority of authors also illustrates under which conditions the company value is positively influenced. An increase of the company value is only achieved when the **rate of return does not only exceed costs of capital but also the expected interest on equity capital** (Becker et al., 2010b; Golsner, 2012; Gonschorek, 2009a, 2015b, 2016c; Günther, 2014a, 2015b; Krol, 2009c; Lehmann, 2012).

Furthermore, the majority of authors addresses the role of other stakeholders than the owners of the company. In this respect, it is stated that it is **necessary to consider the interests of these other stakeholders** (Becker et al., 2010b; Gonschorek, 2009a, 2015b, 2016c; Günther, 2014a; Krol, 2009c; Lehmann, 2012; Tappe, 2009; Wenzel, 2014). Only then, an increase of the company value can be achieved (Gonschorek, 2009a, 2015b, 2016c; Günther, 2014a; Lehmann, 2012). Thus, "a trade-off" (translated from Wenzel, 2014, p. 28) or balance, with regard to interests of other stakeholders, is necessary (Gonschorek, 2016c). A few authors also add that VBM is beneficial for other stakeholders as well (Becker et al., 2010b; Krol, 2009c).

While the authors agree in their emphasis of VBM as a holistic management concept which focuses on the monetary value for the owners there is a slight **difference** with regard to another aspect. Some authors express that the focus should be on an **increase or growth of the company value** (Becker et al., 2010b; Golsner, 2012; Gonschorek, 2015b; Krol, 2009c; Lehmann, 2012). A similar idea is evident from reference to a creation of value (Günther, 2014a, 2015b). However, Gonschorek (2009a) goes beyond an increase of the company value and includes a **maximisation of value** in his definition of VBM. A third group of authors addresses **increase and maximisation** and does not express a preference for one of them (Gonschorek, 2016c; Tappe, 2009; Wenzel, 2014) In this respect Krol (2009c) argues that a company does not necessarily need to focus on a maximisation of the company value but can also focus on securing the value or achieving a certain minimum value. This depends on the risk aversion of the owner(s). In line with this reasoning and VBM's emphasis on the interests of the owner(s), the broader view of focusing on an increase of the company value shall be part of the definition of VBM underlying this work. This can, but does not necessarily need to, be a maximisation of the company value.

A further aspect is that all relevant authors emphasise the **long-term focus** of VBM (Becker et al., 2010b; Golsner, 2012; Gonschorek, 2009a, 2015b, 2016c; Günther, 2014a, 2015b; Krol, 2009c; Lehmann, 2012; Tappe, 2009; Wenzel, 2014). It is specified that this means that the company value shall be increased or maximised in the long term and ongoing (Becker et al., 2010b; Golsner, 2012; Gonschorek, 2009a, 2015b, 2016c; Günther, 2014a; Krol, 2009c; Lehmann, 2012; Tappe, 2009; Wenzel, 2014). Krol (2009c) emphasises this by stating that the long-term focus is the "substantial element of value-based management" (translated from Krol, 2009c, p. 58). In this respect some authors also stress that VBM helps to secure the existence or survivability of a company in the long run (Becker et al., 2010b; Gonschorek, 2015b, 2016c; Krol, 2009c; Lehmann, 2012; Tappe, 2009; Wenzel, 2014).

Beyond outlining aspects referred to in relation to the understanding of VBM it **has to be criticised that not all authors outline their understanding of VBM to an adequate extent**. There are authors that address the understanding of VBM extensively (Gonschorek, 2009a; Krol, 2009c; Lehmann, 2012; Tappe, 2009; Wenzel, 2014). It is valuable that some authors do not only address the understanding of VBM on a general level but clearly explicate the understanding underlying their work (Becker et al., 2010b; Golsner, 2012; Gonschorek, 2009a; Lehmann, 2012; Tappe, 2009). Unfortunately, the understanding of VBM is sometimes only addressed briefly (Becker et al., 2010b; Gonschorek, 2015b, 2016c; Günther, 2014a). Fortunately, the illustration of aspects related to VBM allows us to gain some insights into the understanding of VBM in these cases and in cases where the understanding of VBM is not addressed at all (Günther, 2015b). However, it still has to be criticised that these authors do not make their understanding of VBM explicit with an adequate clarity and/or to an adequate extent.

The systematic analysis of the relevant literature shows that a **consensus regarding the understanding of VBM seems to exist**. The understanding underlying this work shall include the aspects commonly related to. The only aspect where there are different views is whether the focus shall be on an increase or a maximisation of the company value. In relation to this, the understanding underlying this work follows Krol's (2009c) reasoning in favour of focusing on an increase of the company value. This work is thus grounded on the following understanding:

> Value-based management is a holistic management approach that focuses on the objective to increase the monetary company value for the owners of a company in the long run. This is done under consideration of interests of other stakeholders and includes decisions taken in a company. A key element of measuring the creation of value is that costs of debt and equity capital are considered. It is supposed that VBM helps to secure the existence of a company.

The first sentence of this definition reflects the core focus of VBM. This is amended by aspects that are repeatedly addressed in relation to this understanding. It has to be noted that these aspects are addressed by a majority but not always all relevant authors. Despite the consensus on the understanding of VBM found in relevant literature, the relevant literature also refers to the existence of other views.

2.3.2.2 Demarcation towards other understandings of value and related debates

The previous subsection showed that the understanding of VBM in the literature on VBM in Mittelstand is based upon a unanimously agreed understanding of value as monetary value of the company. This is understood as net present value of future cash flow. However, the relevant literature also acknowledges that other understandings of value exist.[14] These will be addressed to demarcate VBM to other views. In addition, the related debates shall be signified. It has to be emphasised that a holistic overview of different understandings of value that exist, is beyond the scope of this work.

Two different themes can be identified in the literature on VBM in Mittelstand which are related to differing views and debates on VBM and its implications for company objectives:

- Existence of concepts of "value" other than the monetary understanding underlying VBM.
- Existence of stakeholders other than VBM's focus on the owners.

These themes are not clearly separated themes but are understood as related to each other.

In relation to the understanding of "value" there is repeated reference to the **existence of other values** such as ethical values, humanistic principles and ecological values (Becker et al., 2010b; Gonschorek, 2016c; Günther, 2014a; Krol, 2009c; Lehmann, 2012; Tappe, 2009). It is emphasised that other such understandings of value reflect in meta-economic or non-monetary objectives that exist in mittelständische companies (Becker et al., 2010b; Günther, 2015b; Krol, 2009c; Tappe, 2009). It is said that there is a debate on the compatibility of these different understandings of value with VBM (Gonschorek, 2016c).

Beyond this, the relevant literature acknowledges that there is **criticism of the orientation of value-based management towards the owners** of the company. Critics have the view that other stakeholders are neglected and that VBM can involve unfair hardness towards these stakeholders. The critics thus demand that the interests of these stakeholders are also considered. In response to this criticism the stakeholder value approach has been developed (for this paragraph see Gonschorek, 2009a, 2015b, 2016c; Krol, 2009c; Lehmann, 2012; Tappe, 2009).

[14] This becomes evident in two ways. The authors partly directly state that different understandings exist (Krol (2009c, p. 59); Tappe (2009, p. 68); Becker et al. (2010b, p. 115)). In addition, this becomes evident from authors referring to different understandings in their outline of the understanding of VBM.

Some authors also address the **attitudes towards VBM.** In this respect two different views can be identified. On the one hand, it is expressed that society, parts of society and/or mittelständische companies refuse the concept which they understand as a one-sided focus on short-term profit maximisation at the expense of other stakeholders (Becker et al., 2010b; Gonschorek, 2015b; Günther, 2014a, 2015b; Krol, 2009c; Lehmann, 2012). On the other hand, there is the position that mittelständische companies have a positive attitude towards VBM and relate it to economic benefits (Gonschorek, 2015b; Krol, 2009c).[15]

This shows that authors in the field of VBM in Mittelstand acknowledge the existence of other understandings of value and other stakeholders as well as the differing views related to this. However, there still is a consensus on the understanding of VBM in the relevant literature. Regarding the themes addressed and their consequences for the objectives in mittelständische companies, two points are made in the relevant literature:

- Value-based management is valuable as a counterpart to meta-economic objectives in mittelständische companies (Günther, 2015b).
- In the long run the principles of value-based management are not in contrast with the interests of stakeholders (Gonschorek, 2009a; Krol, 2009c; Lehmann, 2012; Tappe, 2009).

2.3.3 Drivers, hurdles and applicability of value-based management in Mittelstand

A key topic in the literature on VBM in Mittelstand is why Mittelstand should apply VBM. In the following an overview of key drivers of VBM in Mittelstand as well as the main hurdles identified in the relevant literature will be given. Then, the stance the relevant authors take towards an application of VBM in Mittelstand will be pictured.

2.3.3.1 Key drivers

From the body of knowledge the following five key drivers of VBM in Mittelstand have been identified:

- VBM overcomes shortcomings of traditional performance measures
- VBM is beneficial in the context of company objectives in Mittelstand
- VBM is valuable to improve the management of Mittelstand in light of many challenges
- VBM can improve Mittelstand's financing situation
- VBM is beneficial in relation to the succession problem in Mittelstand

These will be briefly outlined in the following.[16]

[15] It needs to be acknowledged that these two different positions are usually not addressed on the basis of immediate empirical insights but on the basis of reference to other literature. Only Krol (2009c) refers to this on the basis of empirical insights gained from a questionnaire.

[16] More extensive and in-depth outlines of drivers of VBM in Mittelstand can especially be found in Gonschorek (2009a, pp. 47–67) and Krol (2009c, pp. 89–127).

A benefit of applying VBM is that value-based performance measures **overcome shortcomings of profit-oriented performance measures**. The criticism of profit-oriented performance measures such as "Return on Investment" or "Return on Sales" was one of the factors that promoted the development of the Shareholder Value Approach. In contrast to profit-oriented performance measures, value-based performance measures overcome the lack of displaying risks by considering risk-adjusted costs of capital. One of the other shortcomings that is overcome, is the focus on the past as VBM looks at future cash flow. In doing this, VBM enables an improved decision-making and is thus advantageous for all kinds of companies (for this paragraph see Günther, 2014a, 2015b).

Furthermore, the application of VBM is regarded as **beneficial in the context of objectives in Mittelstand**. This is because VBM enables a long-term and sustainable economic development, which is in accordance with mittelständische company objectives (Gonschorek, 2015b, 2016c; Krol, 2009c; Lehmann, 2012). However, some authors also state that the key objective to increase the company value can be in conflict with non-economic objectives that play a role in Mittelstand (Gonschorek, 2015b; Lehmann, 2012). When there is an emphasis on non-economic objectives there is the threat that economic objectives are neglected, which can in extreme cases threaten the existence of the company (Krol, 2009c). Given this potential conflict of aims, VBM is still regarded as beneficial (Krol, 2009c; Lehmann, 2012). This is because authors partly regard VBM as a valuable opposite pole to meta-economic objectives (Krol, 2009c; Piontkowski, 2009). Other authors put forward the argument that non-economic objectives, resulting from the interests of other shareholders, and the objective to increase the company value for the owners are not in conflict in the long run (Gonschorek, 2009a; Krol, 2009c; Lehmann, 2012; Tappe, 2009). It can be noted that there are different arguments in relation to the advantageousness of VBM in light of company objectives in Mittelstand. Overall, several authors in the relevant body of literature sum up their considerations in relation to objectives of mittelständische companies concluding that VBM is beneficial for Mittelstand (Arbeitskreis "Wertorientierte Führung in mittelständischen Unternehmen" der Schmalenbach-Gesellschaft für Betriebswirtschaft e.V., 2004b; Krol, 2009c; Wenzel, 2014).

Several authors express the opinion that VBM is advantageous for Mittelstand to **improve the management** in light of challenges for management. In this context different aspects and contexts are addressed. One topic is that management faces challenges due to increased globalisation (Gonschorek, 2009a; Wenzel, 2014). Authors also argue for the application of VBM as they see a need for a higher professionalisation in management (Wenzel, 2014). There is also the view that the lack of strategic awareness in Mittelstand can be addressed with VBM (Lehmann, 2012). VBM is also regarded as beneficial in light of a deterioration of a company's business performance and the general weakness of profitability in Mittelstand (Gonschorek, 2009a; Wenzel, 2014). VBM improves the management of a company among others because it enables better management decisions (Krol, 2009c; Lehmann, 2012). These different reasons are named in the context of arguing for VBM as a tool to improve the management of Mittelstand in general. Other reasons are related to financing.

It is also argued for the use of VBM to **improve the financing situation in Mittelstand**. This is regarded as important because of the need to strengthen the equity capital in mittelständische companies that often have a weak equity basis (Gonschorek, 2009a; Krol, 2009c). Securing a good financial situation is also seen as crucial because the value of the company usually forms the majority of the wealth of owners of mittelständische companies (Günther, 2014a; Wenzel, 2014). Given this, there are two ways in which VBM contributes to improving the financing situation. Firstly, VBM improves the access to debt capital. Due to changed regulations for banks, companies need to fulfil higher standards for getting debt capital (Gonschorek, 2009a; Krol, 2009c; Wenzel, 2014). VBM helps to fulfil these standards especially as it has positive effects on the rating of a company (Krol, 2009c). Secondly, VBM improves the financing situation with regard to other forms of financing. In this respect there is a positive effect of VBM in the context of the increasing importance of modern forms of financing (Gonschorek, 2015b; Günther, 2014a; Krol, 2009c) and increased possibilities on the capital market (Gonschorek, 2009a; Wenzel, 2014). Overall, relevant authors regard VBM as beneficial for the financing of Mittelstand independent of whether this is debt financing from banks or other forms of financing.

Another key driver of VBM in Mittelstand is its **advantageousness in the context of successions**. This is especially evident in case of selling the company, where the company value is of crucial importance and thus a management oriented towards an increase of the company value has clear advantages (Gonschorek, 2009a; Krol, 2009c; Lehmann, 2012; Wenzel, 2014). However, VBM is also advantageous for a succession plan that involves external managers (Gonschorek, 2015b; Krol, 2009c; Lehmann, 2012). In this context, VBM can help to reduce a conflict of interest resulting from the arising principal-agent-relationship (Günther, 2014a; Krol, 2009c; Wenzel, 2014). VBM is also deemed beneficial in addressing other multi-layered challenges related to succession, which shall not be addressed in this concise overview (for a comprehensive outline see Krol, 2009c, pp. 115–121). Apart from these key drivers that speak in favour of an application of VBM in Mittelstand potential hurdles need to be considered.

2.3.3.2 Main hurdles

While the body of knowledge on VBM in Mittelstand comprises of a multitude of drivers and benefits of VBM in Mittelstand it also identifies hurdles. In this respect, the lack of resources is identified as a main hurdle from the relevant literature.[17]

The general **lack of resources** in Mittelstand makes an implementation of VBM difficult (Gonschorek, 2009a; Günther, 2014a; Lehmann, 2012; Martens & Bluhm, 2007). There is a lack of time to deal with new management tools in general and VBM in specific (Gonschorek, 2009a; Krol, 2009c). This is also related to the absence of a controlling department in Mittelstand (Becker et al., 2010b; Gonschorek, 2009a, 2015b; Krol, 2009c). In addition authors identify a lack of business expertise as a hurdle to the application of VBM (Gonschorek, 2015b; Krol, 2009c; Wenzel,

[17] For a more extensive outline of barriers to the implementation of VBM see Krol (2009c, pp. 128–132).

2014). Furthermore, there can be difficulties implementing VBM in relation to a lack of information needed for the determination of VBM performance measures (Becker et al., 2010b; Krol, 2009c; Lehmann, 2012; Martens & Bluhm, 2007).

Beyond this key hurdle Krol (2009c) additionally refers to hurdles related to the **owner-managers view on VBM**. Given that the implementation of new management tools includes costs, it is necessary that the owner-manager recognises the benefit of those new management tools. Otherwise he will not strive for applying new management tools. This can be difficult given the addressed lack of expertise and time to deal with new management tools. In addition, there might be reservations towards VBM resulting from a different understanding of VBM and a negative attitude towards VBM (for this paragraph see Becker et al., 2010b; Krol, 2009c). Given the drivers and hurdles of VBM in Mittelstand it is interesting to have a look at the general assessment of the applicability of VBM in Mittelstand.

2.3.3.3 Stance towards applicability of VBM in Mittelstand

The question of whether VBM as a well-established concept in large listed companies can be transferred to mittelständische companies is a key topic of many early contributions on VBM in Mittelstand (examples are Achleitner & Bassen, 2000; Bea & Thissen, 1997; Becker, 2000). However, this question is still a key topic in recent literature on VBM in Mittelstand. The applicability of VBM in Mittelstand and the related topics of drivers, hurdles and success factors are for example addressed extensively in some dissertations (Gonschorek, 2009a; Krol, 2009c; Lehmann, 2012; Tappe, 2009; Wenzel, 2014). The applicability of VBM in Mittelstand thus seems to be an ongoing theme in the relevant literature.

This is interesting as there seems to be a **strong consensus that the application of VBM in Mittelstand is advantageous**. All relevant authors make clear that they regard the application of VBM as being beneficial for Mittelstand (Becker et al., 2010b; Gonschorek, 2009a, 2015b, 2016c; Günther, 2014a, 2015b; Krol, 2009c; Lehmann, 2012; Martens & Bluhm, 2007; Wenzel, 2014). In this context VBM is regarded as "indispensable" (translated from Wenzel, 2014, p. 232) and "a useful management tool" (translated from Gonschorek, 2009a, p. 68). Günther (2015b) states very concisely that the question of whether VBM is also an appropriate management approach for Mittelstand can "definitely be answered with "yes"" (translated from Günther, 2015b, p. 221). It is also concluded that VBM is transferable to Mittelstand and/or will gain importance in the future (Martens & Bluhm, 2007; Tappe, 2009). Even authors that initially question the applicability of VBM in Mittelstand, finally join the consensus of its advantageousness. Wenzel (2014) had "fundamental doubts" (translated from Wenzel, 2014, p. 2) regarding the usefulness of VBM for large family businesses from the results of a case study. The strong difference of his impression to the existing view in literature motivated him to focus on VBM in large family businesses in his dissertation (Wenzel, 2014). Finally, he concludes that VBM is "indispensable" (translated from Wenzel, 2014, p. 232). Despite a careful analysis of the relevant literature no authors could be identified whose overall assessment on the applicability of VBM in Mittelstand was negative.

In addition to the consensus on the applicability of VBM a consensus exists regarding the **necessity to adapt VBM to characteristics of mittelständische companies**. The notion that it is necessary to adapt VBM to Mittelstand partly becomes evident from direct statements (Günther, 2015b, pp. 485, 493; Martens & Bluhm, 2007, p. 18). Other authors address this more indirectly by referring to how adaptations of VBM to Mittelstand shall or can be done or by stating that it is necessary to address this further (Becker et al., 2010b; Gonschorek, 2009a; Krol, 2009c; Lehmann, 2012; Wenzel, 2014).

The views regarding the necessity to adapt VBM to Mittelstand tie in with the addressed drivers and hurdles and will be addressed in the following before referring to specific proposals how Mittelstand can apply VBM in subsection 2.3.4. Based on the lack of resource, some authors demand pragmatic or resource-friendly forms of VBM (Becker et al., 2010b; Krol, 2009c; Martens & Bluhm, 2007). Krol (2009c) emphasises that an adequate cost-benefit relation of VBM in Mittelstand shall thus be ensured (Krol, 2009c). In addition, VBM for Mittelstand has to be comprehensible (Becker et al., 2010b; Günther, 2015b; Krol, 2009c; Lehmann, 2012). It is also pointed out that the individual situation of a company has to be considered in the form VBM takes (Gonschorek, 2015b; Tappe, 2009). A comprehensive and detailed literature review on requirements for VBM in Mittelstand and the respective empirical findings are presented by Lehmann (2012).

On the basis of the dominant view that VBM has to be adapted to characteristics of mittelständische companies, identified proposals for the use of VBM in Mittelstand will be presented in the next subsection.

2.3.4 Adaptation of value-based management to mittelständische characteristics

Going beyond the question of whether VBM is applicable to Mittelstand, another key topic in the relevant literature is how VBM can be applied in Mittelstand. Proposals and comments on this can already be found in the early contributions in the field and are still made in the recent literature. An overview is given by first outlining the approaches for a holistic value-based management of a mittelständische company and secondly picturing how VBM can support decisions in Mittelstand.

In relation to a **holistic value-based management of a mittelständische company** the relevant literature addresses different aspects and frequently refers to three proposals. Several authors emphasise that a prerequisite for a holistic VBM of a mittelständische company is a good understanding of the company's business model (for the rest of this paragraph see Becker, Ulrich, & Ebner, 2010a; Gonschorek, 2015b; Günther, 2015b). If this is not already given, it is important to deal with it when beginning to implement a holistic VBM for the company. In doing this, a SWOT analysis or an analysis along the lines of the four dimensions of a Balanced Scorecard (BSC) can be valuable.[18]

[18] An example for an analysis of a company's respective general situation and especially the situation regarding managerial accounting on the basis of the dimensions of a BSC can be found in Becker, Ulrich, and Ebner (2010a).

One approach for a holistic value-based management is the **approach developed by the Arbeitskreis "Wertorientierte Führung in mittelständischen Unternehmen" der Schmalenbach-Gesellschaft für Betriebswirtschaft e.V.**.[19] This working group consists of several experts from academia and business practice and describes its approach in several publications (Arbeitskreis "Wertorientierte Führung in mittelständischen Unternehmen" der Schmalenbach-Gesellschaft für Betriebswirtschaft e.V., 2003a, 2004b, 2006; Schomaker & Günther, 2006). The approach shall account for characteristics of Mittelstand by simplifying existing VBM tools to a necessary degree without falsifying them (Arbeitskreis "Wertorientierte Führung in mittelständischen Unternehmen" der Schmalenbach-Gesellschaft für Betriebswirtschaft e.V., 2003a). The proposed approach is a modular concept which allows implementation in a gradual manner as well as the use of parts of the approach. There are three core modules – VBM instruments of control, a VBM system of targets and a VBM system of incentives. The instruments of control include non-monetary as well as monetary key performance indicators (KPIs). The non-monetary KPIs can be displayed in a simplified BSC and consider internal as well as external value drivers. With regard to the monetary KPIs it is outlined how different measures such as EVA, CVA and Free-cash-flow can be derived for mittelständische companies. There is no general commitment to one of those measures but it is emphasised that a companys' specifics shall be considered in the selection of a measure. The system of targets and the system of incentives shall be designed accordingly. The three core modules shall also be embedded in the general framework for the management of the company, which includes the business strategy as well as the communication with stakeholders and an active and ongoing adaptation to the business environment (for this paragraph see Arbeitskreis "Wertorientierte Führung in mittelständischen Unternehmen" der Schmalenbach-Gesellschaft für Betriebswirtschaft e.V., 2003a).

The advantages of this approach are its modular structure and the consideration of mittelständische characteristics to enable its application in Mittelstand practice. A disadvantage is that early stages of the implementation of the approach are only addressed briefly. Furthermore, it is criticised that there is no detailed outline of the determination of the costs of capital (these views are shared by Lehmann, 2012). Beyond this, the approach seems to be developed on the basis of the experience of the members of the working group. Therefore although the business practice experience of the group members as well as from academia helps, there has not been an empirical analysis of requirements of such an approach.

The **approach of Achleitner and Bassen (2000)** proposes the use of Economic Profit as a VBM performance measure (Achleitner & Bassen, 2000). While differing in the proposal of a VBM performance measure, the approach is similar to that of the Arbeitskreis in addressing the identification of value drivers and a VBM system of incentives (this is also addressed by Lehmann, 2012; Tappe, 2009). In addition to those elements, Achleitner and Bassen (2000) propose to establish an advisory and control board, which includes people that have experience with VBM. Furthermore, there is a company valuation on the basis of the DCF method considering specifics of Mittelstand (for this paragraph see Achleitner & Bassen, 2000).

[19] For readability the abbreviation Arbeitskreis will be used in the outline.

Overall, it must be criticised that despite the adaptation to Mittelstand's characteristics, the approach is still rather complex (this view is shared by Lehmann, 2012). Furthermore, the approach is developed on the basis of a brief literature review and does not consider requirements derived from an empirical analysis.

In contrast to the two approaches outlined previously, the **approach proposed by Khadjavi (2005)** is derived on the basis of an empirical study. From a case study encompassing three mittelständische companies, he derives requirements for a VBM approach adapted to Mittelstand. The proposed approach shall enable a holistic VBM of a company under consideration of its objectives and resources. Khadjavi (2005) addresses the system of objectives more extensively and presents alternatives for the form of the VBM company objective on the basis of its extent and time-related coverage.[20] On this basis he proposes a modified DCF-approach and Total Business Return as a measure for the value creation in a period. For operational control he uses CVA and value-driver trees that show the relation of CVA and the identified crucial resources of the company (for this paragraph see Khadjavi, 2005).

In doing this Khadjavi (2005) considers fewer elements of a VBM management approach but addresses the system of targets, VBM performance measures and value-driver trees in more depth than the other approaches. While an advantage of this approach is its empirical foundation, a disadvantage is its complexity (this critique is shared by Lehmann, 2012). In addition, there is little reference to prerequisites and ways of implementation (this critique is shared by Tappe, 2009).

The **overview of existing approaches to a holistic VBM** has shown that core elements of these approaches are a system of objectives, key performance indicators, value drivers and a system of incentives. The BSC is referred to as a useful management tool in this context. In relation to KPIs there is reference to different VBM key figures. Rappaport's (1986) original DCF method is addressed as well as EVA, CVA, Economic Profit, Total Business Return and Free-Cash-flow. These proposals and their presentation in several publications give mittelständische companies a point of reference for the application of VBM as a holistic management approach. However, a continued examination in the relevant literature is regarded as beneficial to further develop these approaches (this view is shared by Lehmann, 2012).

In addition, the relevant literature addresses how VBM can be used as a **basis for decisions in the company**. The use of VBM in decision-making is regarded as a crucial aspect of its implementation by some authors (Copeland, Koller, & Murrin, 1996 according Wenzel, 2014). Based on an outline of the basic economic view of VBM, Günther (2015b) outlines how a multitude of VBM tools can be used for decision-making with regard to a single business or a portfolio of businesses (Günther, 2015b). The basic economic view of VBM can either be used for a static analysis with focus on a single period or for a dynamic, long-term analysis of several periods.

[20] This includes aiming at a preservation of the company value, satisfying the expected increase of the company value and a maximisation of the company value. Each of these objectives can be specified in the short and in the long run.

For the analysis of a single period, independent of which specific measure is chosen, the following conditions apply:

Return on capital > costs of capital

Or

Excess return (e.g. EVA, CVA) > 0

When a multi-year business plan exists, there is the possibility to analyse value-creation in a dynamic view on the basis of the following basic economic view:

Company value > capital invested

In relation to examples of decision-making for single businesses, Günther (2015b) gives an overview of the following tools that consider this basic economic view of VBM:

- Valuation of a business strategy regarding its value creation
- Break-even analysis for strategies, investments or projects on the basis of discounted cash flow
- Deriving value and risk drivers for single businesses
- Comparison of planned/actual data of the value creation of business plans and monetary analysis of deviations
- Risk evaluation of a business and a link to the risk management
- Cash-flow based short- or long-term profit and loss accounts along the lines of a cash flow statement
- Real options valuation

In addition he mentions the following possibilities as examples for decisions related to a portfolio of businesses:

- Evaluation of the value contribution of single businesses in relation to the whole portfolio
- Comparison of short-term, static value creation with the long-term, dynamic value creation of the businesses of a portfolio
- Analysis of matrix views related to value drivers
- Analysing the matrix of market shares and market growths from a VBM perspective

Unfortunately, Günther (2015b) only mentions these tools briefly and does not further outline or discuss possibilities to apply them in Mittelstand. Based on the consensus identified in the relevant literature regarding the lack of resources and the resulting requirement for simple approaches formulated by some authours (Arbeitskreis "Wertorientierte Führung in mittelständischen Unternehmen" der Schmalenbach-Gesellschaft für Betriebswirtschaft e.V., 2003a; Lehmann, 2012), there is slight doubt whether some of the more complicated tools such as real options valuation can be applied by Mittelstand without further explanation. Furthermore, the use of VBM as a basis for decisions as one aspect of the application of VBM in mittelständische companies is addressed to a lower extent than holistic VBM of mittelständische companies.

2.3.5 Empirical analysis of value-based management in Mittelstand

Given the consensus on the applicability of VBM in Mittelstand and the existence of proposals how VBM can be applied in Mittelstand it is not surprising that another key topic in the relevant literature is the empirical analysis of VBM in Mittelstand.

The insights gained will be synthesised in the following. As a background, subsection 2.3.5.1 will give an overview of the empirical studies.

2.3.5.1 Overview of empirical studies focusing on VBM in Mittelstand

From the literature search, several empirical studies focusing on VBM in Mittelstand or similar companies have been identified. These are analysed for the topics that are empirically analysed and the respective research approach (see table in Appendices-Figure 5).[21] With regard to the key topic, two perspectives can be identified. These will be addressed in the following.

On the one hand, empirical studies look at **different aspects of the application of VBM inside Mittelstand companies** (Bluhm & Martens, 2009; Golsner, 2012; Gonschorek, 2009a; Khadjavi, 2005; Krol, 2009c; Lehmann, 2012; Mafirowanda, 2015; Piontkowski, 2009; Roztocki & Needy, 1999; Tappe, 2009; Wenzel, 2014).[22] This is based on qualitative or quantitative primary data acquired from companies by interviews, in case studies or surveys. Some of the studies go beyond an empirical analysis of the application and additionally look at related aspects (Golsner, 2012; Gonschorek, 2009a; Krol, 2009c; Tappe, 2009; Wenzel, 2014). An example for this is Gonschorek (2009a), who first analyses different aspects of the status of application of VBM in German Mittelstand and then empirically identifies influencing factors that promote or constrain the use of VBM methods. In addition to such an empirical analysis of influencing factors of the application of VBM, there is an empirical analysis of success factors, organisational factors and the economic benefit of VBM in Mittelstand. This shows that the studies assigned to this group, primarily look at VBM for Mittelstand from the perspective of applying VBM as a management approach inside a company. While the analysis partly includes a comparison of different companies the question of whether the application of VBM results in an improved value creation in comparison to other companies is mostly omitted.[23] Taking this perspective in the empirical analysis of VBM in Mittelstand will be addressed as the **"internal application perspective"** in the following.

On the other hand, empirical studies focus on analysing the **companies' value creation from an outside perspective** (Bahri, St-Pierre, & Sakka, 2011; Dixit, 2011; Nathani, Rathod, & Rohira, 2016; Oliveira, 2014; Print & Reynolds, 2011). These empirical studies are all based on quantitative, secondary data and compare the value creation of different companies. For example Print and Reynolds (2011)

[21] Partly, results of one empirical study are addressed in several publications (see overview of the literature on VBM in Mittelstand in Appendices-Figure 3). When this is the case this subsection and Appendices-Figure 5 build upon the publication that reports the approach and findings most holistically. This means for example that the dissertation of Khadjavi (2005) is looked at and not the presentation of an overview of the findings in Khadjavi and Volery (2009).

[22] Except for the study of Lehmann (2012), all studies yield insights into different aspects of the application of VBM. Lehmann (2012) is nevertheless assigned to this perspective as its focus on an adaptation of VBM concepts to mittelständische characteristics is related to the other studies' focus on application of VBM concepts in Mittelstand.

[23] Exceptions are Krol (2009c) and Wenzel (2014). Among other aspects, their empirical studies touch upon the economic benefit of an application of VBM in Mittelstand (for details see subsection 2.3.5.4). Still, their approach is different to the empirical studies that are assigned to the "outside value creation perspective".

compare the performance of UK family-controlled businesses to that of comparable non-family-controlled businesses from a shareholder value perspective. Partly, the studies include analysing influences on value creation. An example is Nathani et al. (2016) who analyse the impact of corporate social responsibility practices on EVA in Indian family businesses. Similar to this empirical study, others also have a strong emphasis on other topics. All these studies are based on quantitative, secondary data and do not provide insights into whether the companies apply VBM as a management approach or not. The VBM perspective is, in these studies, used as a benchmark to evaluate the performance of the companies. Thus, this perspective will be related to as the **"outside value creation perspective"** in the following.[24]

Beyond recognising that VBM in Mittelstand is approached from two different perspectives, the analysis of the empirical studies shows that there are **considerable differences in the kinds of companies looked at**. In addition to studies focusing on Mittelstand or mittelständische companies (Golsner, 2012; Gonschorek, 2009a; Khadjavi, 2005; Krol, 2009c; Lehmann, 2012; Piontkowski, 2009; Tappe, 2009) there are several studies looking at VBM in small businesses or small- and medium-sized entities (Bahri et al., 2011; Bluhm & Martens, 2009; Mafirowanda, 2015; Oliveira, 2014; Roztocki & Needy, 1999). Other studies focus on family businesses or family-controlled businesses (Dixit, 2011; Nathani et al., 2016; Print & Reynolds, 2011; Wenzel, 2014). This seems to reflect the difficulties in delineating Mittelstand from related phenomena (for details see subsection 2.1.2). In addition to the limited number of empirical studies in the context of VBM in Mittelstand, this is regarded as an indication that VBM in Mittelstand is still an emerging field of research.

All empirical studies focusing on Mittelstand defined in a similar manner as in the thesis at hand, apply the "internal application perspective". This perspective seems to be more relevant in relation to Mittelstand in a narrower sense. As this thesis takes a similar perspective on VBM in Mittelstand the following subsections will outline the **key topics addressed by the empirical studies taking the "internal application perspective"**. These include

- the analysis of the application of VBM,
- the analysis of influencing and success factors and
- the analysis of the economic benefit of the application of VBM.

These will be outlined in the following.

2.3.5.2 Application of VBM in Mittelstand

In relation to the application of VBM the empirical **studies look at different aspects**. It is regarded as valuable to display these findings along the dimensions of a framework Krol (2009c, p. 68) uses to systemise VBM performance indicators and management tools. The resulting framework is shown in Figure 4. Krol (2009c) uses two different levels. One level refers to performance indicators that reflect a

[24] Bahri, St-Pierre, and Sakka (2011) is slightly different from the other empirical studies assigned to this perspective. Similar to the other empirical studies the empirical study has an "outside value creation perspective" by analysing the influence of business practices on performance measured by EVA. However, it goes beyond this outside perspective by proposing a performance measurement and management system for SMEs based on EVA. Thus, there is also an element of the „internal application perspective“ on VBM.

definition of the company objective in the sense of VBM. The other level refers to the implementation and control of strategies to achieve this objective. Given the insights gained on tools proposed to apply VBM in Mittelstand this is modified in the following way to be used as a framework to display the findings on the application of VBM. When taking a more general view the two levels identified by Krol (2009c) can be formulated as questions. These ask whether the company's purpose is in line with VBM and whether the company's actions are in line with VBM. The question of whether the company's purpose is related to whether VBM reflects in findings on the content of objectives and also in findings on attitudes towards VBM. The question of whether a company's actions are in line with VBM can be analysed in relation to the two broad areas of application that have been identified – the application of a holistic VBM management of the company and the application in context of decisions (see chapter 2.3.4). The findings in relation to these areas of application are outlined in the following before analysing the findings that are related to whether the purpose of Mittelstand is in line with VBM.

Figure 4: Framework to display findings on application of VBM

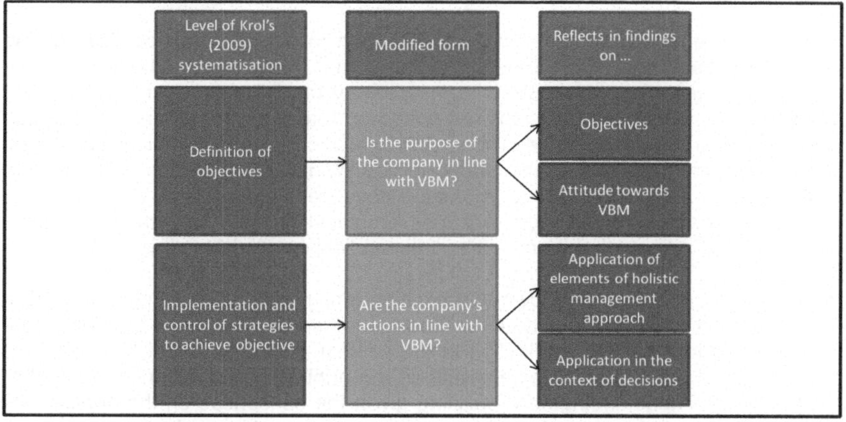

The empirical studies that analyse the **application of a holistic value-based business management** analyse several aspects. This often includes an analysis of management control (Gonschorek, 2009a; Krol, 2009c), the incentive system (Gonschorek, 2009a; Piontkowski, 2009; Tappe, 2009; Wenzel, 2014) and communication (Gonschorek, 2009a; Krol, 2009c).[25]

All these areas of management are included in Gonschorek's (2009a) empirical analysis. Subsequently, Gonschorek (2009a) concludes that the management in Mittelstand is not universally focused on an increase of the company value. According to the findings, this is especially the case for smaller businesses (Gonschorek, 2009a). Krol (2009c) also concludes that the application of management tools and methods of investment appraisal that are usually regarded as oriented towards an

[25] In line with the framework to display findings the analysis of objectives is addressed later in this subsection.

increase of the company value is comparatively rare. The conclusions of Piontkowski (2009) and Wenzel (2014) go in a similar direction. Piontkowski (2009) finds an underdeveloped application of VBM. Wenzel (2014) concludes that there is predominantly no systematic implementation of VBM. A low application of VBM is also reflected in the superficial insights gained by Roztocki and Needy (1999), who find that none of the six small manufacturing companies in the sample uses EVA. This is also supported by Bluhm and Martens (2009) who conclude that the tools advised for VBM are only used by a minority of the firms. However, results of Martens and Bluhm (2007) show that these gained importance in comparison to the empirical findings presented by Gonschorek and Günther (2006a).[26] Only Tappe's (2009) conclusion points towards mittelständische companies acting partly in a certain manner that supports an increase of the company value. However, this is formulated in a cautious manner. Thus, despite the empirical studies looking at different elements of the application of a holistic VBM in Mittelstand, they find that VBM is only applied to a small extent. This is also expressed by other relevant literature, which points to the findings of others to support this view (Becker et al., 2010b; Gonschorek, 2015b, 2016c; Günther, 2014a, 2015b; Martens & Bluhm, 2007).

Some of the empirical studies briefly touch upon the **application of VBM in the context of decisions**. Krol (2009c) concludes that the use of methods of investment appraisal in line with VBM is comparatively rare. Piontkowski (2009) briefly mentions that investment decisions are based on return or the net present value to a lesser extent than experience. Tappe (2009) also concludes that decision-making is not value-oriented. This is also supported by Wenzel (2014) who concludes that neither operative nor strategic decisions are consistently focused on an increase of the company value. While there are less empirical findings regarding decisions, these findings indicate that there is also little application of VBM in this context.

Previous paragraphs have shown that existing empirical studies suggest that VBM is only applied to a minimal extent for the management of the company. There are similar indications for the application in the context of decisions but this has, until now, not been addressed as extensively as the application for the management of the company. These findings are puzzling given the consensus on the applicability that has been found in the relevant literature and the existence of proposals on the application of VBM in Mittelstand. It is thus interesting to look at whether the empirical findings regarding objectives suggest that VBM is in line with the purpose of Mittelstand or not. This will be looked at in the following.

With regard to the **importance of the increase of the company value as an objective for mittelständische companies** there are differing findings. Some authors, in relevant literature, conclude that the increase of the company value is of high importance in mittelständische companies (Gonschorek, 2009a; Krol, 2009c). This is supported by other empirical studies who focus on Mittelstand but not specifically on VBM (Achleitner, Bock, Braun, Schraml, & Welter, 2010; PricewaterhouseCoopers AG Wirtschaftsprüfungsgesellschaft, 2014; Schlepphorst & Schlömer-Laufen, 2016). However, a few authors also conclude that the increase of

[26] Bluhm and Martens (2009) replicate the initial empirical findings of the doctoral dissertation of Gonschorek (2009a). These are presented in Gonschorek and Günther (2006a).

the company value is not very important in mittelständische companies. Tappe (2009) finds that the focus is rather on healthy growth. From the interviews with large family businesses Wenzel (2014) finds that the increase of the company value is very seldom an explicit company objective. Mafirowanda (2015) also finds that none of the interviewees refers to the goal of increasing the company value. These differing views also reflect in Khadjavi's (2005) case study, where one company is primarily oriented towards a maximum shareholder value in line with the VBM approach while another focuses on handing over a well-operating company. Based on the differing findings regarding objectives, there is still a puzzling situation. The low importance of the increase of the company objective that is found in some empirical studies might be a reason for the minimal application of VBM. In contrast to this reasoning, several studies suggest that the objective to increase the company value is of high importance. On the basis of these results one would expect a higher application of VBM.

In this respect it is also interesting to have a look at the empirical indications with regard to the **attitudes towards VBM**. If these suggest a negative attitude towards VBM it could explain the little application which seems puzzling on the basis of the views expressed in relevant literature. An indication that supports this reasoning is Gonschorek's (2009a) conclusion that particularly smaller companies have not yet dealt much with VBM and have reservations towards its application. However, Krol's (2009c) conclusions point in a different direction regarding the attitude towards VBM. He finds that entrepreneurs relate potential benefits to an increased value orientation and are open towards defining company success in a value-oriented manner. On this basis he concludes that the lack of application of VBM is less related to a refusal of the concept but more towards a lack of knowledge and tools (Krol, 2009c). Wenzel (2014) finds evidence for both views. On the one hand he finds cases where the owner has been the key driver of an implementation of VBM. On the other hand, he finds that some owner families refuse the application of VBM (Wenzel, 2014). Given these differing findings there is no distinct evidence to evaluate whether there is a positive or negative attitude towards VBM. In addition, there are very little empirical results regarding the attitudes towards VBM. Thus, the findings regarding the attitudes towards VBM also do not help to clarify the puzzling situation found. Thus, a closer look at the findings in relation to influencing and success factors will be taken in the following.

2.3.5.3 Influencing and success factors

Part of the empirical studies analyses **influencing and success factors** of VBM in Mittelstand. The empirical analysis of factors influencing the application of VBM in Mittelstand includes an analysis of the form these take and their influence on the application of VBM (Gonschorek, 2009a; Krol, 2009c; Tappe, 2009; Wenzel, 2014). With regard to the influence, it is looked at whether these factors have a positive or negative influence on the application of VBM. In addition, there is partly reference to the strength of the influence (Gonschorek, 2009a; Krol, 2009c). In contrast, Golsner (2012) and Tappe (2009) focus on success factors.[27]

Overall, the findings indicate that **internal influencing factors are of great significance**. Gonschorek (2009a) and Wenzel (2014) conclude that the application of VBM is primarily determined by internal influencing factors. While Krol (2009c) does not address this aspect directly, the factors with the strongest total effect he identifies are also internal factors. He finds the strongest **positive effects on VBM** resulting from the

- use of complex strategic management tools, that are not VBM management tools,
- the importance of controlling and
- the formalisation of decision-making (Krol, 2009c).

This is partly supported by Gonschorek (2009a), who finds the application of formal and complex management tools having a positive influence on the application of VBM. He also finds the knowledge on VBM being a supporting factor. In his view these factors are closely related to whether management controlling is designed as an independent department. Wenzel's (2014) findings are especially interesting. His approach is different to that of Gonschorek (2009a) and Krol (2009c) as he does not analyse influencing factors identified from literature on the basis of questionnaires but identifies influencing factors on the basis of interviews. While he does not look at the strength of the influence, it is interesting to note that the majority of the factors identified have a positive effect on VBM. His findings add to those of Gonschorek (2009a) and Krol (2009c) in finding that the company's culture and the managers and owners of the company often influence the implementation of VBM positively.

Wenzel (2014) emphasises the **key importance of the management and owners for the application of VBM**. This is supported by Golsner (2012) who concludes that the owner and/or top management of a company is of specific importance for the implementation of VBM. In this respect Wenzel (2014) observes two ways of influence. Firstly, he finds that top management and especially the entrepreneur are a key stimulus for the implementation of VBM. Golsner (2012) also finds that the owners and/or managers can support the continuous application of VBM in the company by their behaviour. However, Wenzel (2014) also finds a critical stance or even an explicit refusal of VBM among owners and/or managers. This indicates that the significant influence of the owners and managers in Mittelstand **can either have a positive or a negative effect on the application of VBM**. This is supported by Tappe's (2009) observation that the fulfilment of requirements for VBM seems to be more dependent upon the personal attitude of the entrepreneur towards VBM than on the size of the company.

Gonschorek's (2009a) conclusion in relation to **impeding factors** goes in a similar direction. He concludes that the sparse application of VBM is a consequence of Mit-

[27] Tappe (2009) derives requirements on the form critical success factors need to take from literature. He then analyses the form these factors take empirically. Golsner (2012) formulates requirements for an effective VBM in relation to organisational factors and analyses these based on a single case study. Both empirical studies result in findings on the form different factors in a company need to take as a basis for VBM.

telstand not having dealt with the content and possibilities of VBM. This in turn is because controlling is primarily done by the accounting department. The employees there do not have the know-how and time to deal with VBM. Thus, Gonschorek (2009a) concludes that a key hurdle that needs to be addressed is the awareness for the importance of management control. In this respect he demands more research to further understand the specifics of management in Mittelstand and for more mutual communication of research and Mittelstand (Gonschorek, 2009a).

Krol (2009c) also identifies factors that impede the application of VBM. However, the lower number of negative factors also has a lower strength than the positive factors. Krol (2009c) concludes that given the little application of VBM in Mittelstand, further inhibiting factors beyond the factors included in his analysis must exist. Thus, he demands future researchers uncover and examine those factors in order to consider them in the further developing of VBM management concepts for Mittelstand. This demand is partly addressed by Wenzel (2014), whose empirical study also identifies additional inhibiting factors. He finds technical problems, the complexity of key figures, the success of a company and the entrepreneurial management style as inhibiting factors. However, as Wenzel (2014) does not look at the strength of these factors it is unclear whether their effect goes beyond the significant positive effects of internal factors found by Gonschorek (2009a) and Krol (2009c).

Overall, the existing insights into influencing and success factors cannot explain the little application of VBM in Mittelstand, as mostly positive influences are identified. Thus, further insights into influencing factors, especially impeding factors are valuable. Given the indications for their key importance further insights into the role of the attitude and behaviour of owners and managers is beneficial.

2.3.5.4 Economic benefit

There has also been an effort to analyse the **economic effect of an application of VBM in Mittelstand empirically.** This is an additional research question by Krol (2009c) and Wenzel (2014). However, in comparison to other aspects there are few empirical insights. The reason for this can be the difficulties related to the empirical analysis of this aspect that are addressed by Wenzel (2014). For privately owned businesses there is no data on the development of the share price. This can therefore not be used to picture the performance effects of VBM. Consequently, the analysis can only be based upon the interviewees' assessment of the development of the company value (Wenzel, 2014). Krol (2009c) also analyses the effect of VBM on the basis of the respondents' assessment of the companies' performance.

The significance of Wenzel's (2014) findings is limited, as this aspect could only be analysed for the four companies that apply VBM (partly or fully). From the interviews he partly finds an indirect positive effect on the company value by a reduction of the capital invested, which is a key value driver. For the other two cases no such effect is found (Wenzel, 2014). Thus, it is difficult to derive conclusions on the economic effect of an application of VBM.

On the basis of questionnaires, Krol (2009c) looks at the population as a whole and additionally at differences between smaller and larger mittelständische companies. He analyses the economic effect not only for the application of VBM management tools but also for the consideration of core principles of VBM. He finds a positive effect for the application of VBM. He concludes that there is a positive effect of VBM especially for smaller mittelständische companies. This positive effect is especially high for the consideration of risks, which is a core principle of VBM. Thus, he derives the view that not only an explicit use of VBM management tools has a positive effect on a company's performance but also the consideration of VBM's core principles (Krol, 2009c). Still, there is a lack of empirical insights that provide evidence on an economic benefit of the application of VBM.

2.3.6 Summary of the section: Key topics and gaps in the field of research

In the following the insights gained from the review of the relevant literature will be summarised. On this basis the gaps identified in the body of knowledge and how these will be addressed in this research project are outlined.

From an **analysis of the topics addressed and the approaches applied in relevant literature** it has been found that there are three recurrent themes (see subsection 2.3.1). In addition to looking at those three themes it has been looked at the understanding of VBM.

Insights have been gained from relevant literature in relation to the **understanding of VBM** (see Figure 5 and subsection 2.3.2). Value-based management is fundamentally understood as focusing the management of a company on the objective of an increase of the monetary company value. In relation to this understanding, it is emphasised that VBM is a holistic management approach which includes decision-making, has a long-term focus and considers the interests of stakeholders. Given the existence of different views and related debates it is interesting that there is little debate on this understanding in the relevant literature.

Figure 5: Understanding of value-based management

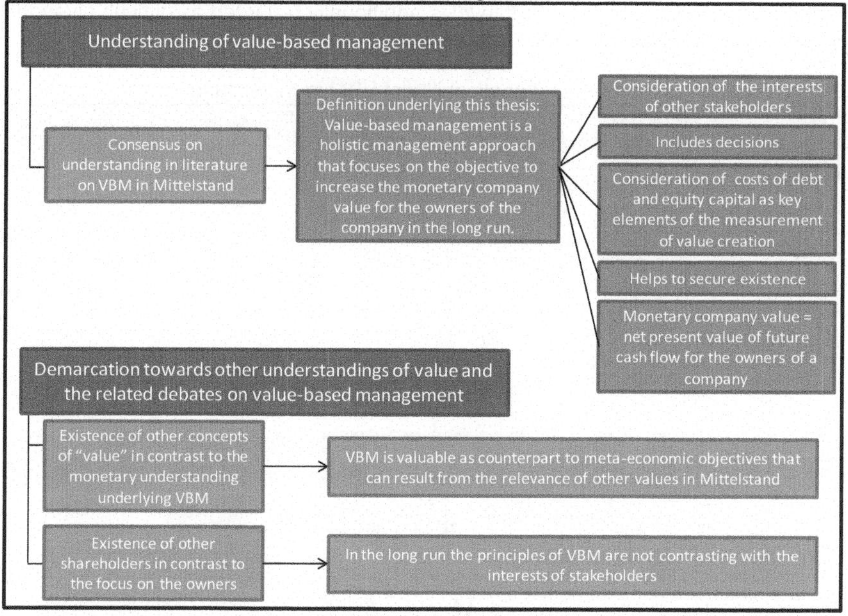

A key topic addressed in the relevant literature is the transferability of VBM to Mittelstand. This is related to **drivers and hurdles of VBM in Mittelstand and its applicability** (see Figure 6 and subsection 2.3.3). In this respect there is the general advantage of VBM overcoming weaknesses of profit-oriented performance indicators. In addition, key drivers of VBM that are especially relevant in Mittelstand are identified. These include a positive effect in relation to objectives of mittelständische companies, an improvement of management in light of challenges Mittelstand faces, an improvement of Mittelstand's financing situation and a number of positive effects in the context of succession. A main hurdle is the lack of resources in Mittelstand. In addition, some authors identify a potential hurdle resulting from the owner-manager's view on the costs and benefits of an implementation of VBM as well as his attitude towards VBM. In relation to the applicability of VBM in Mittelstand there is a consensus in two ways. On the one hand, all relevant authors make clear that they regard VBM as beneficial for Mittelstand. On the other hand, there is the agreement that VBM must be adapted to mittelständische characteristics.

On this basis the reasoning for applying VBM in Mittelstand and for the necessity for adaptation are persuasive. However, there is a shortcoming that limits the value of this reasoning. There is reference to the need to consider the individual situation of a company and ensure an adequate cost-benefit ratio in the adaptation of VBM in Mittelstand. This legitimate demand results in the view that the applicability of VBM in Mittelstand needs, at first, to be judged on the level of individual companies and can only subsequently be evaluated on the level of Mittelstand in general. However, the existing body of knowledge regards VBM as applicable for Mittelstand in general. This evaluation on a general level is additionally regarded as difficult given the heterogeneity of Mittelstand (see section 2.1).

Figure 6: Drivers, hurdles and applicability of VBM in Mittelstand

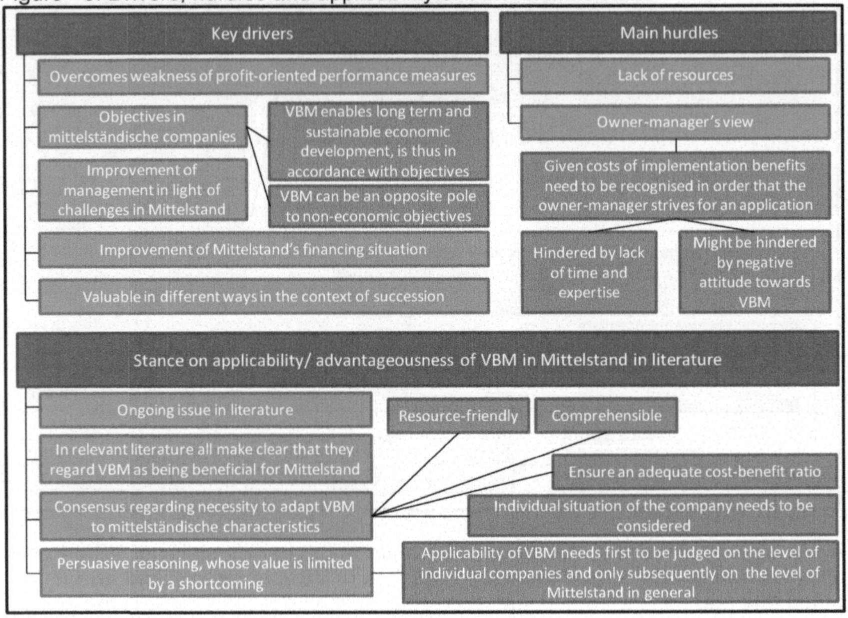

Furthermore, the relevant literature addresses **proposals how VBM can be adapted to the characteristics of Mittelstand** (see Figure 7 and subsection 2.3.4). This includes proposals how Mittelstand can apply a holistic value-based management. Additionally, it is described how the basic economic view of VBM can reflect in decision-making.

Figure 7: Proposals for the application of VBM in Mittelstand

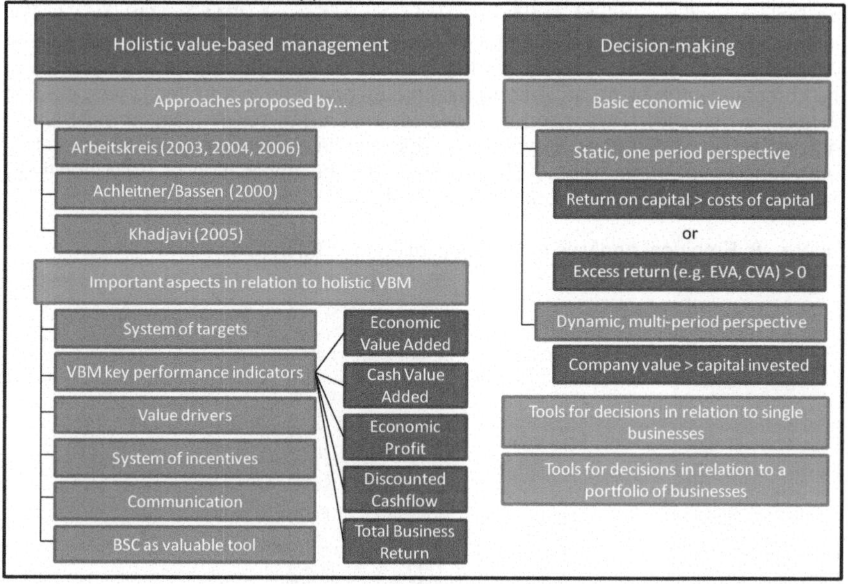

Another key topic in the relevant literature is the **empirical analysis of VBM in Mittelstand** and similar companies (see Figure 8 and subsection 2.3.5). These have been analysed for the key focus of the empirical analysis and the research approach. This has shown that VBM in Mittelstand is addressed from two perspectives which have been labelled as "internal application perspective" and "outside value creation perspective". The studies focusing on Mittelstand similar to the study at hand apply the "internal application perspective". Those empirical studies look at

- the application of VBM in Mittelstand,
- influencing and success factors and
- its economic benefit.

In relation to the application of VBM in Mittelstand it has been decided to structure the overview of the findings according to dimensions modified from the two levels Krol (2009c) uses to systemise VBM management tools. One level covers empirical findings on objectives and attitudes to evaluate whether VBM is in line with the purpose in Mittelstand. On the level of the question whether Mittelstands' actions are in line with VBM, this encompasses empirical findings regarding the application of elements of a holistic VBM and the application in the context of decisions.

The review has shown that the empirical findings indicate little relevance of VBM. Regarding the holistic management approach, several empirical studies, which refer to different elements of such an approach, show this. In relation to decision-making there are fewer findings which show a similar tendency. This is puzzling given the consensus on the applicability and advantageousness of VBM in Mittelstand and the proposals for an adaptation to Mittelstand. It has been looked at the findings regarding objectives and attitudes towards VBM as well as those regarding influencing factors as these might explain the low application of VBM in Mittelstand. The findings differ regarding the question of whether VBM is in line with the purpose in Mittelstand. In relation to objectives the findings range from finding the increase of the company value being an important company objective to that this is very seldom an explicit objective. Regarding attitudes towards VBM, fewer insights exist which indicate similar differences. Beyond this, research into influencing and success factors found several internal factors that influence the application of VBM positively but only a few factors that impede the application of VBM.

Figure 8: Empirical analysis of the application of VBM in Mittelstand

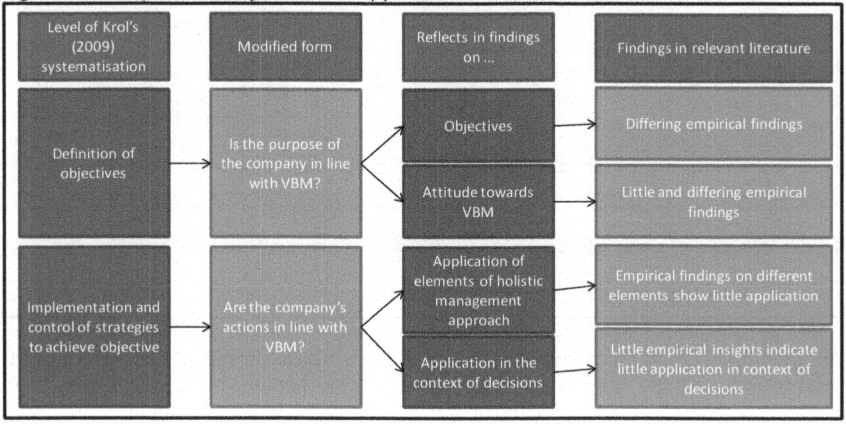

Overall, the review of the relevant literature shows a **gap in the body of knowledge** that is regarded as crucial to the development of the field. This crucial gap and the related gaps in the empirical findings will be pictured in the following and summarised in Figure 9.

It is puzzling that there is a gap between the consensus on VBM being valuable for mittelständische companies existing in the relevant literature and the low level of application of VBM tools that becomes evident from the empirical findings. A higher level of application was expected given that the consensus in the literature is based on a persuasive reasoning regarding drivers and hurdles of VBM and that VBM concepts adapted to the characteristics of Mittelstand exist. Authors in the field also mention this gap.[28] The existing findings on influencing and success factors do not fully explain this gap. Thus, further research in the field seems to be valuable.
Based on the outline of the empirical findings on the application of VBM in Mittelstand along two dimensions, gaps have been identified in the empirical insights. It is regarded as beneficial to address these to gain further understanding in relation to

[28] It is expressed that there is a gap between VBM being regarded as appropriate/valuable/important management approach for Mittelstand and the low application found in empirical studies (Becker et al. (2010b); Gonschorek (2015b), Günther (2014a, 2015b), Krol (2009c); Lehmann (2012)).

the gap found between the literature's consensus on the applicability of VBM and the application in Mittelstand's management practice.

The researcher agrees with some authors in the field that a prerequisite for the application of VBM is that a company is willing to apply VBM. This is influenced by the overlap of a company's objectives to VBM's focus on increasing the company value. In this respect there are differing findings and further research is regarded as valuable. Another factor that affects the willingness to apply VBM is the attitude towards VBM. There is a research gap in this respect as there are little empirical findings and these point in different directions. However, empirical studies indicate that the owner-manager's and/or top management's attitude towards VBM and their behaviour are an important factor for the application of VBM in Mittelstand. Thus, it is beneficial to further analyse this aspect. Therefore, a potential contribution to the body of knowledge is

- to empirically analyse the objectives of mittelständische companies and whether these are in line with VBM's focus on the objective to increase the company value and
- to empirically analyse owner-managers' attitudes towards VBM.

It is regarded as valuable to address these aspects together with an analysis of the application of VBM. In this respect the overview of empirical findings in the relevant literature shows that there is a gap in relation to the application in context of decisions. Decision-making is an important element of the understanding of VBM. However, while several empirical studies address different elements of a holistic value-based management there are only few insights on decisions. In light of the gap between the literature's view and the application in practice it is therefore regarded as valuable

- to gain empirical insights into the application of VBM in the context of decision-making.

In this respect the focus shall be on the application of management tools in strategic decision-making (SDM).

Consequently, the **aim of research** is to understand the relevance of VBM in these specifically identified areas of management in Mittelstand. The **overall research question** is:

> In what way is VBM relevant for specifically identified areas of management in Mittelstand (strategic decision-making, objectives, attitudes)?

This adresses part of the identified gaps in empirical research and shall also generate further understanding regarding the overall research gap.

Beyond the gaps that are addressed by this research project additional gaps have been identified. However, an empirical analysis of the economic benefit of an application of VBM is beyond the scope of this work. Further research might also address the gap in relation to influencing and success factors. The empirical analysis of the three identified areas of management partly addresses this but does not focus on a holistic analysis.

Figure 9: Summary of the relevant literature on VBM in Mittelstand and related gaps

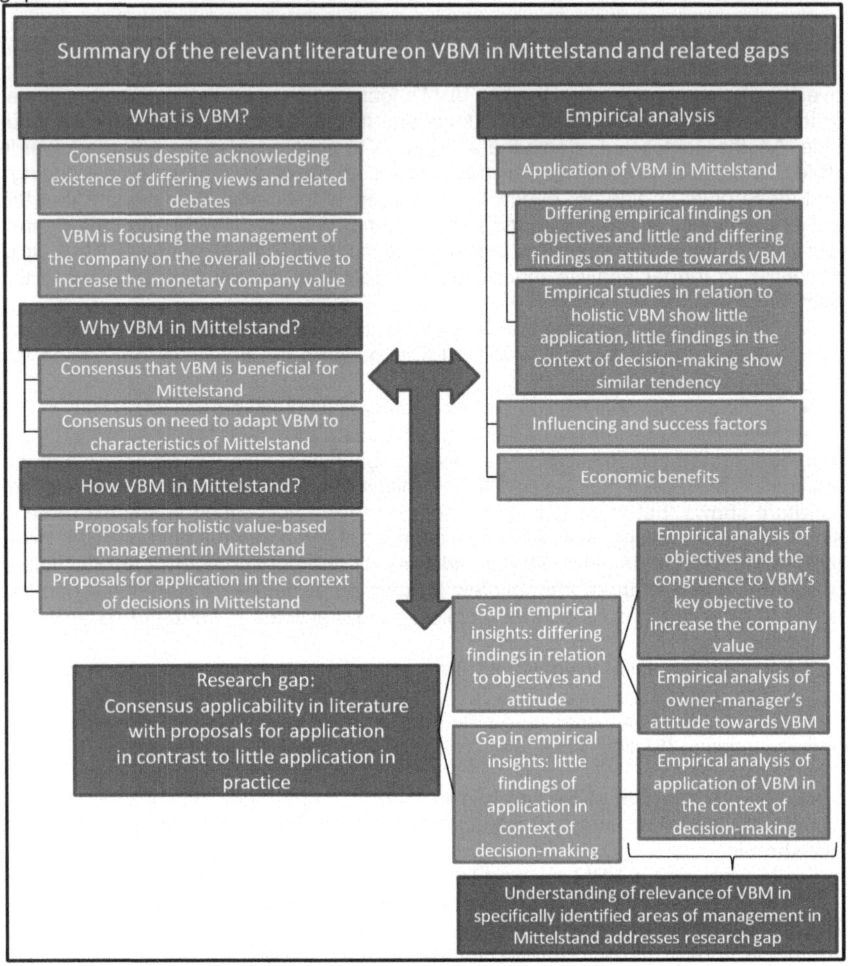

2.4 Framework for the evaluation of the role of VBM in Mittelstand

2.4.1 Aim and approach of the subsections

This research aims at gaining an understanding of the application of VBM in three specifically identified areas of management. As background and point of reference for the empirical study, this section will provide insights into the existing body of knowledge regarding the relevance of VBM in strategic decision-making, objectives and attitudes. On this basis, supplementary research questions that guide the empirical investigation will be formulated.

For each of these three selected areas of management this section will cover two aspects. Firstly, a background for researching VBM in the context of this area of management will be provided (subsections 2.4.2.1, 2.4.3.1 and 2.4.4.1). This includes views existing among VBM in Mittelstand researchers in relation to the application of VBM in the respective area of management. To gain a broader understanding, this perspective of VBM in Mittelstand researchers is expanded by a brief outline of important aspects addressed in the body of knowledge on objectives and strategic decision-making in Mittelstand that does not focus on VBM.[29] Secondly, there will be a review and synthesis of empirical studies that provide insights into the application of VBM in the selected areas of management (subsections 2.4.2.2, 2.4.3.2 and 2.4.4.2). Following a similar reasoning this includes insights from empirical studies on VBM in Mittelstand as well as relevant insights from more general empirical studies on objectives and strategic decision-making in Mittelstand.

These two aspects will firstly be addressed for strategic decision-making (subsection 2.4.2). Then, they will be outlined for objectives (subsection 2.4.3). Finally, the attitude towards VBM will be looked at (subsection 2.4.4). Each of the three subsections will be summarised at the end of the subsection. A summary of the section as a whole is therefore redundant.

2.4.2 Value-based management in strategic decision-making in Mittelstand

2.4.2.1 Background for researching VBM in strategic decision-making in Mittelstand

As a background for researching VBM in decision-making in Mittelstand, it is regarded valuable to be aware of **possibilities how VBM can be considered in decision-making**. On the basis of the proposals for the adaptation of VBM to mittelständische characteristics in literature (for an overview see subsection 2.3.4), these possibilities shall be broadly grouped into two categories – the use of specific VBM tools or KPIs and the use of tools that reflect VBM's basic economic view.

Firstly, VBM can reflect in decision-making in the **use of specific VBM tools or key performance indicators proposed in literature**. This can be based on the adoption of one of the approaches for a holistic value-based management proposed by Achleitner and Bassen (2000), Arbeitskreis "Wertorientierte Führung in mittelständischen Unternehmen" der Schmalenbach-Gesellschaft für Betriebswirtschaft e.V. (2003a; 2004b; 2006) and Khadjavi (2005). These approaches focus on the management of the overall company in line with VBM and do not specifically address how this reflects in decision-making. However, when a company implements such an approach of a holistic VBM this should also reflect in decision-making.

[29] The body of knowledge on objectives and SDM might provide insights that are valuable for researching the application of VBM in this context. In relation to attitudes towards VBM it is assumed that it is difficult to identify a body of knowledge beyond the literature on VBM in Mittelstand that might similarly provide a valuable background for researching owner-managers' attitude towards VBM in the understanding underlying this thesis. Thus, the respective subsection is exclusively based on views and empirical insights from literature on VBM in Mittelstand.

Given the aspects addressed in relation to a holistic VBM approach this might especially be the case when considering the effects of a decision on the VBM KPI chosen by the company. In this respect, the proposed approaches refer to different VBM KPIs which include EVA, CVA, Economic Profit, the discounted cash flow (DCF) method or Total Business Return. Beyond this, VBM can reflect in decision-making in the use of one of the tools that are in line with VBM's basic economic view according to Günther (2015b) e.g. a break-even analysis on the basis of discounted cash flow. Günther (2015b) emphasises that the tools mentioned are only examples and that the basic economic view of VBM can also reflect in different tools.

Secondly, in line with Günther's (2015b) view VBM can thus be considered in decision-making in Mittelstand in that **the tools used in decision-making reflect VBM's basic economic view.**[30] In the following, the key elements of this basic economic view shall be displayed on the basis of the understanding of VBM derived in subsection 2.3.2.[31] In this understanding, management focuses on an increase of the monetary company value, i.e. the net present value of future cash flow in the long run. An increase of the company value is only achieved when the rate of return exceeds the costs of capital. Thus, one key element of evaluating the economic feasibility from a VBM perspective is the consideration of costs of capital. This includes the expected interest on equity capital. This is related to a second key element, the consideration of risks (Günther, 2015b; Krol, 2009c). VBM considers risk-adequate costs of capital as investors expect a higher return the higher the risk is (Günther, 2015b; Krol, 2009c). A third key element is the orientation towards the future. This includes considering the future economic consequences. This reflects in the focus on the future cash flow and in being focused on an increase of the company value in the long run. A fourth key element of VBM is that it is oriented towards cash flow. Thus, management tools need to reflect the following aspects to evaluate the economic feasibility from a VBM perspective:[32]

- Consideration of costs of capital including cost of equity capital
- Consideration of risks
- Orientation towards the future
- Orientation towards cash flow

It must be mentioned that the consideration of all these aspects is a prerequisite for evaluating the economic feasibility from a VBM perspective but not necessarily sufficient. It is necessary that the aspects are considered together in a way that allows evaluating a decisions' effect on the company value.

---

[30] A similar view is expressed by Krol (2009c) who expresses that in addition to explicitly using VBM management tools and KPIs, VBM can also be implemented in a Mittelstand company by considering its basic economic principles.

[31] In favour of readability the relevant aspects of this understanding are briefly addressed to emphasise the key elements of VBM's basic economic view. It is refrained from addressing the detailed derivation of this understanding from literature as well as from adding the respective sources used to derive this understanding in subsection 2.3.2. These are only included where aspects are looked at in more depth.

[32] It can be noted that the key characteristics and principles of VBM addressed by Günther (2015b) and Krol (2009c) are formulated in a slightly different way. However, they result in a similar overall orientation. The details will be considered if necessary in the outline of the findings of the empirical study.

Beyond being aware of possibilities how VBM can be considered in decision-making, it is regarded as valuable to be **aware of specifics of decision-making in Mittelstand**. In this respect, the following aspects are addressed by researchers looking at VBM in the context of decision-making in Mittelstand. On the basis of outlining mittelständische characteristics from a process-related perspective, Krol (2009c) concludes that decision-making in Mittelstand is influenced by intuition and that there are a multitude of potential shortcomings to rationality. For Krol (2009c), one driver for an implementation of VBM is that it enhances decision-making and thus contributes to an improvement of the management of the company.[33] This view is shared by Piontkowski (2009), for whom the lack of rational decision-making is a threat to the existence of the company. Tappe (2009) outlines how VBM ideally reflects in phases of the decision-making process. However, in a similar manner to Krol (2009c) he assumes that decision-making in Mittelstand is less formalised and rather based on intuitive decision-making by the owner-manager. In relation to decision-making, Wenzel (2014) addresses that it is important that strategic as well as operative decisions are consistently focused on the increase of the company value.

Overall, it can be noted that **VBM in Mittelstand literature briefly addresses different aspects of the consideration of VBM in decision-making**. This mainly focuses on how VBM should be considered in decision-making in Mittelstand. The specifics of decision-making in Mittelstand are addressed only briefly and without a review of respective empirical insights. While a holistic review of empirical insights into decision-making in Mittelstand is not possible given the scope of this work, a familiarisation with key topics in this context is regarded as valuable. The respective insights will be summarised in the following. In line with the focus on strategic decision-making (for details see subsection 2.4.2.3), this is mainly based on literature on strategic decision-making.

In the following **core topics of the body of knowledge on strategic decision-making in the context of Mittelstand**, which includes small firms, SMEs and family businesses shall be outlined. Firstly, it has to be mentioned that several authors address that there is little empirical research in this context (Brouthers, Andriessen, & Nicolaes, 1998; Gibcus & van Hoesel, 2008; Gibcus, Vermeulen, & de Jong, 2009; Gibcus, Vermeulen, & Radulova, 2008; Jocumsen, 2004). The „disparate, fragmented, large organisation focussed and multidisciplinary literature“ (Jocumsen, 2004, p. 665) provides little insights into decision-making processes in small businesses.

A second relevant aspect is that decision-making in Mittelstand is assumed to be different than in large companies. Several authors address that it is acknowledged that differences exist and/or that decision-making in Mittelstand is a distinct phenomenon (Curseu & Vermeulen, 2008; Gibcus & van Hoesel, 2008; Gibcus et al., 2009; Gibcus et al., 2008; Jocumsen, 2004; Lucas, Vermeulen, & Curşeu, 2008). One aspect repeatedly addressed in this context is the decision-maker. The owner-manager plays a key role and his/her characteristics and decision-making style

[33] The improvement of the management has been addressed as key driver of VBM in Mittelstand by others as well (see subsection 2.3.3.1).

have a considerable impact on decision-making in Mittelstand (Brouthers et al., 1998; Curseu & Vermeulen, 2008; Gibcus et al., 2008; Lucas et al., 2008).

Thirdly, another key topic in research on SDM in the context of Mittelstand is the decision-making process and its phases. These are touched upon in literature reviews and empirical studies (Brouthers et al., 1998; Gibcus et al., 2008). In addition, models of the decision-making process in Mittelstand are developed on the basis of empirical insights (e.g. Gibcus & van Hoesel, 2004; Gibcus & van Hoesel, 2008; Jocumsen, 2004).
Fourthly, it is interesting that the topics of rationality and intuitive decision-making are also addressed in literature focusing on SDM in the context of Mittelstand. This includes authors mentioning these as key topics in the area of research (Curseu & Vermeulen, 2008; Gibcus et al., 2008). Furthermore the empirical study of Brouthers et al. (1998) focuses on the rationality of decision-making. The use of intuition is also touched upon in empirical studies (e.g. Jocumsen, 2004; Posch & Speckbacher, 2012).

Overall, the familiarisation with the body of knowledge on strategic decision-making in the context of Mittelstand leads to the following inferences in relation to the role of VBM in decision-making. Firstly, one observation is that VBM in Mittelstand authors only briefly mention the specifics of decision-making in Mittelstand. One possible reason for this could be that there is only limited empirical knowledge of this phenomenon. Secondly, as SDM in Mittelstand is regarded as distinct, it is valuable to be aware of and consider the existing knowledge. This includes the crucial role of the owner-manager as a decision-maker. In doing this, the research at hand goes beyond previous empirical studies on VBM in Mittelstand. Thirdly, it is interesting that rationality and intuitive decision-making are briefly addressed in VBM in Mittelstand literature and are also a key topic in research on SDM in the context of Mittelstand. Fourthly, while Tappe (2009) does not use existing, Mittelstand-specific models of the decision-making process, he nevertheless looks at different phases of decision-making which is also an important aspect in the body of literature on SDM in the context of Mittelstand. After outlining views that are relevant in the context of research on VBM in the context of decision-making in Mittelstand, specific empirical insights will be addressed in the following.

2.4.2.2 Review of empirical studies in the context of VBM in strategic decision-making in Mittelstand

In the following, the approach taken, aspects looked at and conclusions of existing empirical studies in relation to VBM in decision-making in Mittelstand are outlined. The empirical studies will be addressed consecutively with remarks on differences and similarities and a subsequent synthesis.
Piontkowski (2009) gains insights into decision-making on the basis of a questionnaire and additionally analyses five other areas of management. Decision-making is addressed with a few questions on the basis of investment decisions, methods for reviewing investment decisions and about the basis of management decisions. In relation to investment decisions, it is looked at how often the respondents use experience and the net present value/return. Piontkowski (2009) concludes that intuitive decision-making still plays a strong role in investment decision-making. How-

ever, the majority of the respondents states that management decisions are made on the basis of facts rather than on intuition. Additionally, Piontkowski's (2009) empirical insights indicate that VBM, in the form of the net present value method, is less important for investment decisions than experience. However, this is based on only a few questions with a limited number of options given. Thus, the findings provide initial, but superficial insights into the role of VBM in decision-making in Mittelstand.

Just as Piontkowski (2009), **Krol (2009c)** analyses VBM in decision-making on the basis of a questionnaire and looks at investment decisions. Similarly, decision-making is only one of several aspects looked at.[34] However, it includes more questions and investment appraisal is analysed in more depth.[35] Furthermore, the formalisation of decision-making in mittelständische companies is looked at as an influencing factor for the application of VBM. For evaluating the relevance of VBM in decisions, Krol (2009c) analyses how often a selection of different management methods as well as experience is used as a basis for investment decisions. Beyond the net present value method, Krol (2009c) considers the use of the internal rate of return as a method of investment appraisal that is in line with VBM. Similar to Piontkowski (2009) he concludes that experience is used most often and that there is a lack of consideration of VBM methods. In relation to costs of capital, Krol (2009c) finds both, a strong role of practices that are not in line with VBM but also a certain use of methods in line with VBM.

Additionally, Krol (2009c) briefly mentions potential reasons for the low relevance of VBM. He assumes that one limiting factor can be that Mittelstand does not see a need for using modern methods of investment appraisal due to the infrequency of large investments. Furthermore, he assumes that owner-managers have a high confidence in their decision-making competence and regard respective tools as unnecessary. In contrast, Krol (2009c) finds that the formalisation of decision-making has a positive influence on some dimensions of the application of VBM in Mittelstand. It can be concluded that while Krol (2009c) also uses a questionnaire, he looks at VBM in decision-making in Mittelstand with more breadth and depth than Piontkowski (2009). The resulting findings similarly indicate that VBM is of lower relevance for decision-making in Mittelstand than experience and other methods of investment appraisal.

In contrast to the empirical studies already addressed, **Tappe (2009)** looks at VBM in decision-making in Mittelstand on the basis of interviews. Again, decision-making is only a partial aspect, as it is part of one of seven areas of management looked at. Under consideration of literature on planning and decision-making he derives requirements of how VBM has to be considered in different phases of decision-making. Based on this, he empirically addresses the different phases, analyses their formalisation and comments on management tools as well as decision-making criteria used in the different phases. In contrast to his expectations, Tappe (2009) finds the decision-making process to be, to some extent, formalised. However, he con-

[34] Decision-making is part of one of five areas of management looked at.

[35] Beyond looking at the basis for investment appraisal, Krol (2009c) looks at the use of costs of capital in this context.

cludes that decision-making is not value-oriented. Similar to Krol (2009c) he mentions a potential reason for this: the lack of defining objectives in line with VBM. Despite that Tappe (2009) looks at decision-making in Mittelstand from a different perspective and on the basis of a different approach, the conclusion that VBM is of little relevance points in a similar direction as Krol (2009c) and Piontkowski (2009).

Wenzel (2014) also approaches VBM in decision-making in Mittelstand on the basis of interviews that look at the implementation of VBM in five areas of management and the respective influencing factors. One of the areas of management addressed is management decisions. This includes questions regarding the relevance of the increase of the company value for several strategic decisions such as acquisitions, growth and disinvestments. Furthermore he looks at investment decisions like Piontkowski (2009) and Krol (2009c). In the analysis of the strategic decisions he refers to the motives that are the basis for the decisions. This goes in a similar direction as the decision criteria referred to by Tappe (2009). Wenzel (2014) concludes that strategic as well as operative decisions are rarely oriented towards the increase of the company value. The only exception is the allocation of capital to areas of business, where VBM is "taken very seriously" (translated from Wenzel, 2014, p. 165).

In relation to investment decisions, Wenzel (2014) addresses the formalisation and the methods used. It is found that the majority of family businesses formally analyses investments mainly on the basis of the net present value. This is however relativised by the finding that in relation to strategic investment decisions partly other non-financial objectives or strategic considerations are more important. In this context Wenzel (2014) finds that in only a few cases the decision is taken solely and strictly on the basis of the net present value. Overall, Wenzel's (2014) findings look closer at VBM in the context of decisions than the other empirical studies with focus on VBM in Mittelstand. While noting differences in the findings, these tend to paint a similar picture as Krol (2009c), Piontkowski (2009) and Tappe (2009) and indicate that VBM is of little relevance for decision-making in Mittelstand.

In relation to **empirical insights into decision-making in VBM in Mittelstand literature** it can be concluded that different aspects are looked at with different approaches in different contexts. This will be summarised in the following. An overview is shown in Figure 10. Firstly, Krol (2009c) and Piontkowski (2009) use questionnaires while Tappe (2009) and Wenzel (2014) conduct interviews. The empirical studies also vary in that the insights are generated in the context of different decisions. In this respect, investment decisions are repeatedly looked at (Krol, 2009c; Piontkowski, 2009; Wenzel, 2014). Furthermore, different aspects are considered to evaluate the relevance of VBM. Partly, the focus is on evaluating whether investment decisions are taken on the basis of the net present value method, other tools of investment appraisal or experience (Krol, 2009c; Piontkowski, 2009; Wenzel, 2014). In addition, criteria and motives relevant in decision-making are looked at (Tappe, 2009; Wenzel, 2014).

However, the studies all have in common that decision-making is only a subcomponent of the empirical investigation. Moreover, the specifics of decision-making in

Mittelstand are mostly not considered.[36] Despite the different perspectives taken, it has become evident that the existing findings tend to indicate that VBM only plays a minor role in decision-making in Mittelstand. Wenzel (2014) additionally finds differences between investment appraisal and different kinds of strategic decisions. Potential reasons for the low level of application of VBM in decision-making are briefly touched upon by a few authors (Krol, 2009c; Tappe, 2009).

Figure 10: Empirical studies into VBM in Mittelstand addressing decision-making

Aspect of the comparison (column), empirical study (line)	**Approach**	**Kind of decision analysed**	**Evaluation of the relevance of VBM**
Krol (2009c)	Quantitative, questionnaire	Investment decisions	Net present value method and internal rate of return less relevant than experience and other management tools
Piontkowski (2009)	Quantitative, questionnaire	Investment decisions, management decisions in general	Net present value method/return less relevant than experience
Tappe (2009)	Qualitative, interviews	decision-making in general	Decision-making process does not meet requirements of how VBM has to be considered (among others decision-making criteria)
Wenzel (2014)	Qualitative, interviews	Different strategic decisions, operative decisions, investment decisions	Motives in decision-making do not reflect orientation towards the increase of the company value, differences between investment decisions (analysis of methods of investment appraisal and its formalisation) and different kinds of strategic decisions.

Additional empirical studies have been searched to complement the insights into VBM in decision-making in Mittelstand gained in the empirical studies with focus on VBM in Mittelstand. This has included searching for relevant insights in empirical studies on decision-making in the context of Mittelstand, SMEs, small firms and family businesses. Given the emphasis on management tools in the empirical findings in VBM in Mittelstand literature, relevant insights have additionally been looked for in empirical studies related to management accounting in the context of Mittel-

[36] An exception is Tappe (2009) who considers the existing body of knowledge on decisions in deriving the requirements how VBM shall reflect in different phases of decision-making. However, the empirical analysis is primarily conducted from a VBM perspectve and only touches briefly upon the characteristics of decision-making in Mittelstand.

stand. In the following overview of empirical studies with relevant insights those with a similar focus will be outlined together.

Schlegel, Frank, and Britzelmaier (2016) use a questionnaire to empirically analyse methods and techniques that German manufacturing companies use in making investment decisions. Among others this includes analysing company size differences in the use of different methods of investment appraisal. In a similar way Britzelmaier, Pöpplow, and Andraschko (2018) analyse the status quo of capital budgeting in SMEs in Baden-Württemberg. This includes the investment decision-making process and the instrumental, functional and institutional design of capital budgeting. Overall, the approach of Schlegel et al. (2016) and Britzelmaier et al. (2018) is comparable to that of Krol (2009c) and Piontkowski (2009) in empirically analysing the use of (VBM) management tools in investment decision-making on the basis of questionnaires. In addition to analysing the use of NPV this includes an analysis of the use of other DCF methods of investment appraisal in contrast to non-DCF methods which are not conform to VBM principles. Thus, Schlegel et al. (2016) and Britzelmaier et al. (2018) provide recent empirical insights into the relevance of VBM in investment decision-making.

Furthermore, empirical studies have been identified that look at the use of financial statements in small firms. Halabi, Barrett, and Dyt (2010) conduct an exploratory study into financial and management accounting practice in small firms in Australia. One of four aspects looked at is how financial information is used to make business decisions. Carraher and van Auken (2013) examine the use of financial statements in small businesses. On the basis of questionnaires they analyse factors influencing the use of financial statements in decision-making on the one hand and owner's comfort in using financial statements on the other. Similarly, van Auken and Yang (2014) analyse factors affecting the use of financial statements for decision-making in the context of Chinese SMEs. While these empirical studies touch upon the use of management tools in decision-making their findings do not provide insights into the respective relevance of VBM management tools as they focus on elements of the financial statements. Overall, Carraher and van Auken (2013), Halabi et al. (2010) and van Auken and Yang (2014) provide insights that are related to decision-making as one key aspect of this research. However, they do not provide directly relevant insights into the relevance of VBM in decision-making.

Beyond this, there are several empirical studies looking at different aspects of strategic decision-making in SMEs (e.g. Gibcus & van Hoesel, 2008; Gibcus et al., 2009; Jocumsen, 2004). However, only Brouthers et al. (1998), Jocumsen (2004) and Posch and Speckbacher (2012) touch upon aspects addressed in the context of VBM in decision-making in Mittelstand. Brouthers et al. (1998) empirically analyse SDM in small firms which includes exploring its rationality, examining the influence of power and politics as well as the type of strategy pursued. They touch upon the use of management tools by looking at the use of information and quantitative analysis. However, they do not specify this further and thus do not provide insights into which management tools are used and whether these include VBM management tools. On the basis of empirical insights Jocumsen (2004) proposes "a model of strategic marketing decision-making process in small business" (Jocumsen, 2004, p. 659). In the context of addressing that learned as well as inherent competencies are used in strategic decision-making, Jocumsen (2004) addresses the use of analytic tools. However, he does not specify the specific tools. Thus, insights into the relevance of VBM management tools in decision-making cannot be gained. This is also given for Posch and Speckbacher (2012) whose empirical study looks at specifics of family business management in comparison to non-family businesses. On the basis of data from questionnaires they compare family businesses' use of management tools for facilitating management decisions and for influencing employee behaviour. While they provide insights into the use of data and figures in decision-making they also do not distinguish between different tools. Thus, Brouthers et al. (1998), Jocumsen (2004) and Posch and Speckbacher (2012) provide insights that are relevant in the wider context of looking at the use of management tools in decision-making in Mittelstand but do not directly address VBM in this context.

It can be concluded that beyond the empirical studies which focus on VBM in Mittelstand there are little empirical insights into VBM in decision-making in Mittelstand. This is also summarised in Figure 11. There are empirical studies which look at financial statements in small businesses which include their relevance in decision-making (Carraher & van Auken, 2013; Halabi et al., 2010; van Auken & Yang, 2014). In addition, there are empirical studies which look at aspects of decision-making in the context of Mittelstand and that touch upon the use of data, quantitative analysis and tools in decision-making (Brouthers et al., 1998; Jocumsen, 2004; Posch & Speckbacher, 2012). However, beyond the empirical studies focusing on VBM in Mittelstand only Britzelmaier et al. (2018) and Schlegel et al. (2016) look at the use of different methods of investment appraisal which gives insights into the relevance of VBM management tools in investment decision-making. Thus, further research into which management tools are used in decision-making and whether these reflect VBM seems to be beneficial.

Figure 11: Empirical studies with relevant insights in the context of using management tools in decision-making

Aspect of comparison (column), empirical studies (line)	**Approach**	**Relevance in the context of this research**
Britzelmaier et al. (2018), Schlegel et al. (2016)	Quantitative, questionnaires	Empirical analysis of the use of (VBM) management tools in investment appraisal, comparable to Krol (2009c) and Piontkowski (2009) → directly relevant insights
Carraher and van Auken (2013), Halabi et al. (2010), van Auken and Yang (2014)	Quantitative, questionnaires (exception: Halabi et al. (2010) semi-structured interviews)	Analysis of the use of financial statements in decision-making without insights into VBM management tools → indirectly relevant insights
Brouthers et al. (1998), Jocumsen (2004), Posch and Speckbacher (2012)	Quantitative, questionnaires (exception Jocumsen (2004) in-depth interviews and case studies)	Analysis touches upon use of management tools in the context of decision-making but without insights into specific tools → indirectly relevant insights

2.4.2.3 Summary of the subsection

Previous paragraphs have outlined aspects that provide a background for empirically analysing the application of VBM in the context of decision-making. This included relevant views addressed by literature which focuses on VBM in Mittelstand (see subsection 2.4.2.1). These have been amended by respective insights gained from a familiarisation with the body of knowledge on SDM in the context of Mittelstand. Furthermore, existing empirical studies have been outlined (see subsection 2.4.2.2). The insights gained will be summarised in the following and in Figure 12.

One important aspect is **how VBM can be reflected in decision-making in Mittelstand**. From the different proposals for the adaptation of VBM to Mittelstand characteristics in the literature there are several possibilities. These have been broadly classified into two groups:

- Use of VBM management tools and KPIs
- Use of other management tools that consider the basic economic view of VBM

The first group includes the use of VBM KPIs resulting from the application of a holistic VBM approach. Additionally, it includes the examples of VBM tools given by Günther (2015b). When considering the different approaches taken in the empirical studies these groups can be complemented in other ways. Krol (2009c), Piontkowski (2009) and Wenzel (2014) empirically investigate the use of methods of investment appraisal. This can be regarded as a possibility to use (VBM) management tools and KPIs in the context of investment decision-making and thus complements the first group. Furthermore, Tappe (2009) and Wenzel (2014) look at whether motives and criteria in decision-making are in line with VBM, which is regarded as an additional way of considering VBM in decision-making.

Additionally there has been a familiarisation with aspects addressed in relation to decision-making in VBM in Mittelstand literature and the more general literature on SDM in Mittelstand. This has shown that there is little empirical evidence on the specifics of decision-making in Mittelstand. However, the crucial role of the owner-manager as a decision-maker is addressed. Additionally, rationality and intuitive decision-making are a topic in VBM in Mittelstand literature as well as in research on SDM in the context of Mittelstand. These aspects are partly reflected in the empirical studies that touch upon VBM in decision-making in Mittelstand.

The **few empirical studies looking at VBM in decision-making in Mittelstand** differ in their approach. However, they are similar in that decision-making is only one of several aspects of VBM looked at. Thus, there are little empirical insights on VBM in decision-making in Mittelstand. Despite the differences in the approach these indicate that VBM is of minor relevance for decision-making in the context of Mittelstand. It can be noted that the empirical studies also partly touch upon the use of intuition, experience or qualitative assessment as alternatives to the use of management tools in decision-making in Mittelstand. Together with the rationality of decision-making this is a topic that is also looked at in literature on SDM in Mittelstand. Further empirical studies have been searched to complement the relevant empirical insights from VBM in Mittelstand literature. This yielded two more empirical studies that give insights into the relevance of VBM in the context of investment appraisal (Britzelmaier et al., 2018; Schlegel et al., 2016). In addition, there are some empirical studies providing insights into the context of the use of management tools in decision-making on a more general level. These include empirical studies looking at the use of financial statements in decision-making (Carraher & van Auken, 2013; Halabi et al., 2010; van Auken & Yang, 2014). Beyond this, the empirical studies of Brouthers et al. (1998), Jocumsen (2004) and Posch and Speckbacher (2012) touch upon the use of management tools in decision-making in Mittelstand. However, it can be noted that there are not only little insights into the use of VBM management tools and KPIs in decision-making in Mittelstand but also little insights into what management tools are at all used in decision-making in Mittelstand. The empirical studies either focus on financial statements as specific kinds of tools or address the use of tools on a general level without specifying the kind of tools. This is only different with regard to investment appraisal, where the use of management tools has been empirically investigated on the basis of questionnaires.

Based on the insights gained from the literature review it is regarded as valuable to **further research the use of management tools in strategic decision-making in Mittelstand and whether these reflect VBM**. The focus on strategic decision-making is regarded as valuable for several reasons. Firstly, strategic decisions are important for the success of Mittelstand (Curșeu & Vermeulen, 2008; Gibcus & van Hoesel, 2008; Gibcus et al., 2009; Lucas et al., 2008). Secondly, VBM is a holistic management approach which means that all management activities shall be focused on the company value (Golsner, 2012; Günther, 2015b; Krol, 2009c; Lehmann, 2012). This encompasses all decisions in the company. Due to VBM's strategic focus on increasing the company value in the long run it is regarded as particularly important to apply VBM in strategic decision-making. However, only Wenzel (2014) looks at strategic decisions in empirically analysing VBM in the context of decision-making. A third reason for empirically analysing management tools in SDM is that that there are not only little empirical insights into the respective relevance of VBM management tools but also few insights on what management tools are relevant in SDM in Mittelstand in general. Beyond focusing on management tools in strategic decision-making, the research approach shall consider that the review of literature on SDM in Mittelstand has shown the crucial role of the owner-manager (Brouthers et al., 1998; Curseu & Vermeulen, 2008; Gibcus et al., 2008; Lucas et al., 2008).

In further researching VBM in strategic decision-making the relevance of VBM shall be evaluated mainly on the basis of the use of VBM management tools. This is similar to the approach of previous empirical studies looking at VBM in the context of investment decisions (Britzelmaier et al., 2018; Krol, 2009c; Piontkowski, 2009; Schlegel et al., 2016). However, while focusing on management tools there are aspects that demand the research approach being open for new aspects. Due to the lack of empirical insights it is unclear whether, how and what management tools play a role in strategic decision-making. Thus insights into the relevance of VBM in strategic decision-making in Mittelstand shall be gained on the basis of the following **supplementary research questions**:

- Research question 1 (RQ1):
  What management tools are used in strategic decision-making in Mittelstand, and in which ways are these tools relevant for strategic decision-making?

- Research question 2 (RQ2):
  How is VBM reflected in the use of management tools in strategic decision-making in Mittelstand?

In addition, it shall be considered that VBM might reflect differently in strategic decision-making than the possibilities derived from literature. This might be the case given that literature suggests that decision-making in Mittelstand is different to that of large companies which might include a decision-making style relying more on intuition than on rationality. In this respect, gaining an understanding of the approach to strategic decision-making is regarded as a valuable context for the analysis of the use of management tools in SDM and whether this reflects VBM.

Figure 12: Summary of views and empirical insights in relation to VBM in decision-making in Mittelstand

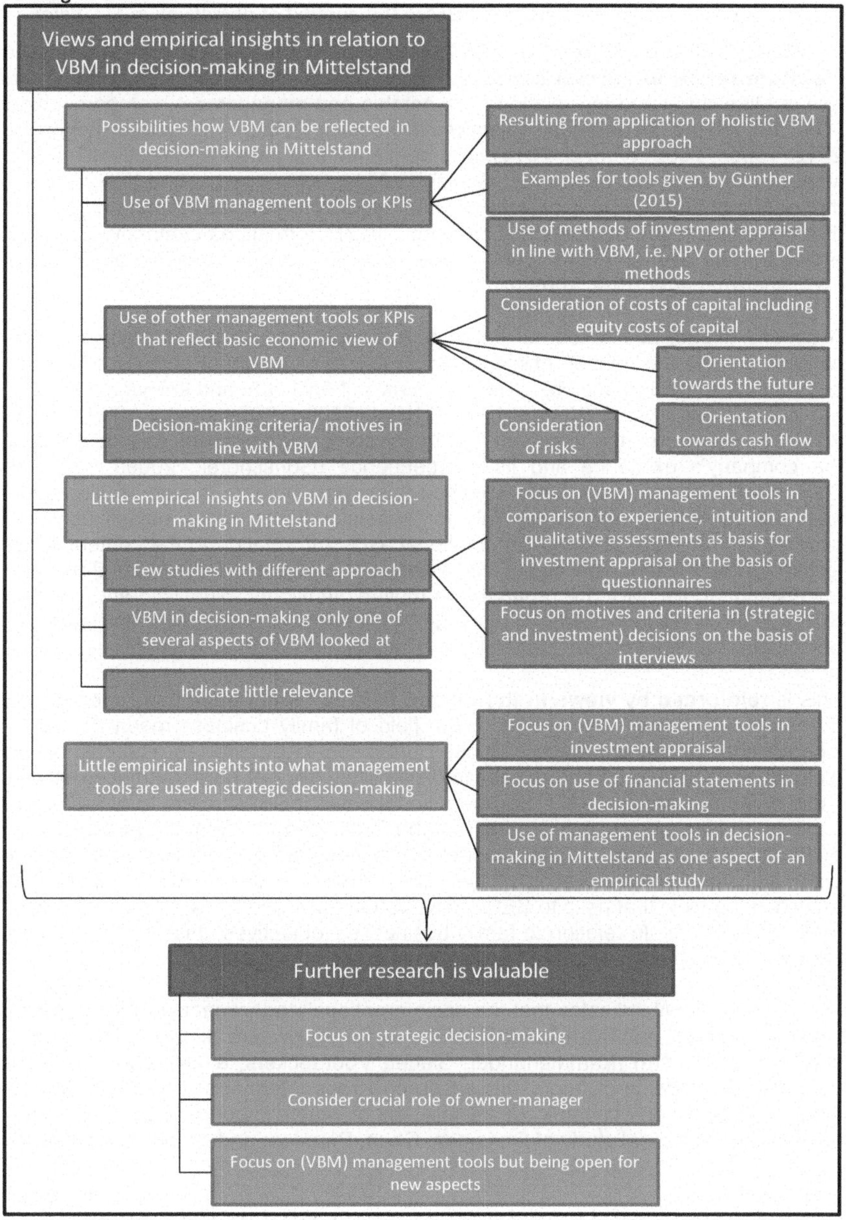

2.4.3 *Value-based management in objectives in Mittelstand*

2.4.3.1 Background for researching VBM in the context of objectives in Mittelstand

In relation to the objectives[37] of mittelständische companies **VBM in Mittelstand literature refers to several aspects**. Firstly, due to the owner-managers' central role in Mittelstand and the relation of ownership and management, company objectives are related to personal objectives (Khadjavi, 2005; Krol, 2009c; Lehmann, 2012; Tappe, 2009; Wenzel, 2014). It is mentioned that personal objectives have an influence on company objectives (Wenzel, 2014). Others go beyond this and state that personal and company objectives often fuse into each other (Tappe, 2009) and that there is a high congruence (Lehmann, 2012). Sometimes company objectives are even regarded as a means to achieve the higher-ranking personal objectives of the owner-manager (Krol, 2009c).

A second aspect addressed, is that Mittelstand's objectives are distinctive in their content. Due to the relation of company objectives to personal objectives, it is assumed that non-economic objectives, such as self-fulfilment and enjoyment of work, are of high importance (Khadjavi, 2005; Krol, 2009c; Piontkowski, 2009; Tappe, 2009). Furthermore, it is assumed that major company objectives include securing the company's existence and its independence (Gonschorek, 2009a; Khadjavi, 2005; Krol, 2009c; Tappe, 2009). Beyond this, some authors mention that employees and customers play a key role for Mittelstand's company objectives (Gonschorek, 2009a; Krol, 2009c). An additional aspect in relation to the content of objectives in Mittelstand are ecological and societal objectives (Krol, 2009c). Thus, Mittelstand's objectives are regarded as multi-dimensional, pluralistic and complex (Krol, 2009c; Lehmann, 2012; Wenzel, 2014). Overall, it is assumed that company objectives in Mittelstand are pluralistic and include non-economic objectives.

This is **reinforced by views in the related field of family business research** (for the interrelation see section 2.1). In the field of family business research the socioemotional wealth approach has been proposed to be used to assist when explaining why family businesses behave distinctively (for this paragraph see Berrone, Cruz, & Gomez-Mejia, 2012). Socioemotional wealth (SEW) refers to non-financial aspects and the affect-related value that the family firm has from the perspective of the family. According to the SEW model "family firms are typically motivated by, and committed to, the preservation of their SEW" (Berrone et al., 2012, p. 259). This results in the view that risks to SEW preservation have priority over financial risks in family businesses. In relation to family businesses' objectives, this implies that non-economic objectives are more important than economic objectives.

Research on SEW indicates that the socio-emotional endowments of family owners result in specific, non-financial goals such as family owners aiming at maintaining control over the firm (Kammerlander, Sieger, Voordeckers, & Zellweger, 2015). In their literature review of family firm research Kraus, Harms, and Fink (2011) also expresses that non-economic goals may be of major importance in family businesses. The empirical study of Chrisman, Chua, Pearson, and Barnett (2012) points

[37] An objective represents normative views on an organisation's future condition that shall be realised by actions (Heinen (1966, p. 45); Welge, Al-Laham, and Eulerich (2017, p. 207)).

in a similar direction. Under consideration of socioemotional wealth and other theoretical views they suggest that family-centred non-economic (FCNE) goals exist in family firms and that these may have an influence on firm behaviour. Based on an empirical investigation they conclude that "as the literature suggests, the pursuit of FCNE goals that create socioemotional wealth for family members, is an important factor that drives family firm behaviours" (Chrisman et al., 2012, p. 288; Kammerlander et al., 2015 also point towards similar findings). Achleitner et al.'s (2010) empirical study is also based on the view that the owners of a family business have socio-emotional goals which cannot be expressed in a monetary way. Overall, these views addressed in family business research and some related empirical findings reinforce that it is important to consider non-economic objectives in empirically studying company objectives in Mittelstand.

Given that views in literature suggest that objectives in Mittelstand are pluralistic and include non-economic objectives it is **interesting to empirically analyse the relevance of VBM's objective to increase the monetary company value for the owners of the company in the long run**. This is interesting for several reasons. Firstly, VBM's key objective clearly has an economic focus, which will be interesting to look at given the assumed role of non-economic objectives in Mittelstand. Secondly, VBM authors clearly argue for defining the increase of the company value as a monoistic overall objective. Thus, it will be interesting to empirically analyse this given the pluralistic character assumed for objectives in Mittelstand.

In taking a closer look at existing findings it shall be kept in mind that several authors in VBM in Mittelstand literature argue for VBM being advantageous in the context of Mittelstand objectives (see subsection 2.3.3.1). This includes different arguments. Some authors argue that VBM's focus on a long-term and sustainable economic development is in accordance with mittelständische company objectives (Gonschorek, 2015b, 2016c; Krol, 2009c; Lehmann, 2012). Other authors address a potential conflict of VBM's objective to increase the company value with non-economic objectives in Mittelstand (Gonschorek, 2015b; Lehmann, 2012). However, it is argued that VBM is nevertheless beneficial in such a situation (Krol, 2009c; Lehmann, 2012). It is outlined that the influence of the owner-manager can lead to an increasing emphasis on non-economic objectives (Krol, 2009c; Piontkowski, 2009). In extreme cases this can be a threat to the long-term existence of the company. Thus, Krol (2009c) and Piontkowski (2009) regard an orientation towards the objective to increase the company value in the long run as a valuable opposite pole to non-economic objectives.

2.4.3.2 Review of recent empirical studies in the context of VBM in objectives in Mittelstand

Based on the existing views on objectives in Mittelstand it is interesting to look at recent empirical findings. Before outlining these results there is an overview on how objectives are addressed in the empirical studies. Together with the existing findings this will be considered in indentifying suitable ways for further research on the relevance of VBM in the context of objectives.

2.4.3.2.1 Level of analysis

An important aspect of the dissertation of **Khadjavi (2005)** is to empirically assess the objectives of Mittelstand in relation to VBM. This is done by analysing three cases inductively. The approach includes eight problem-centered interviews with owners, managers and controlling staff as well as a document analysis. On this basis Khadjavi (2005) provides an overview of the company objectives and analyses them from a VBM perspective.

Wenzel (2014) looks at objectives as one aspect of the application of VBM in large family businesses. These are empirically analysed on the basis of qualitative, semi-structured interviews with chief financial officers (CFOs). The interview guide with leading questions for ten topics includes an open question regarding the key objectives of the company as well as another topic and follow-up questions related to objectives (Wenzel, 2014, p. 264). Wenzel (2014) gives an overview of the objectives addressed and looks more closely at aspects mentioned in relation to the key objectives, especially in relation to the objective to increase the company value.

While there are differences in the approach taken Khadjavi (2005) and Wenzel (2014) both contribute to the body of knowledge by gaining an understanding of the importance of the increase of the company value in relation to other company objectives with an approach that allows the interviewees to address objectives openly.

Gonschorek (2009a), Krol (2009c) and Piontkowski (2009) address objectives in a way that is different to that of Khadjavi (2005) and Wenzel (2014). In all three studies objectives are only one of many different aspects that are addressed in relation to VBM in Mittelstand and the insights are based on questionnaires with closed questions regarding objectives.[38] While respondents can still choose from a selection of different company objectives, there is no possibility to openly add company objectives. The selection of the objectives that can be chosen varies in terms of number of options and their content (for details see Appendices-Figure 6). Piontkowski (2009) addresses only four different company objectives, of which one is the maximisation of the company value.[39] In Krol's (2009c, p. 408) and Gonschorek's (2009a, p. 258) questionnaire, the respondents can specify the importance of the increase of the company value and nine or fifteen other objectives for their company on a five-tier scale. In addition they can express the importance of six or seven different stakeholder groups for setting company objectives. Gonschorek (2009a), Krol (2009c) and Piontkowski (2009) contribute to the body of knowledge by giving an overview of the importance of the increase of the company value and other objectives on the basis of large samples. However, there is no possibility for the respondents to openly address company objectives.

[38] Piontkowski (2009) derives insights into VBM in six areas of management in Mittelstand from an empirical study with 120 questions. On the basis of his outline only one question is related to company objectives. The questionnaire of Gonschorek (2016c) includes questions in eleven different areas of which one is the company objectives (Gonschorek (2016c, pp. 256–264)). Krol (2009c) groups the questions in the questionnaire into eight groups, of which one refers to the company's objectives and strategy (Krol (2009c, pp. 405–413)).

[39] It has to be noted that this judgement is only based on the outline of the results. Piontkowski (2009) does not address the questions posed and the answers that could be selected.

Additionally, **Tappe (2009)** empirically addresses objectives in Mittelstand from a VBM perspective. In his semi-structured interview guide, this is one of seven areas of management that is covered (Tappe, 2009, pp. 293–294). Tappe (2009) formulates requirements on how VBM shall reflect in the system of objectives and hypotheses regarding the role of the increase of the company value in the system of objectives. Then, he yields empirical insights into the relevance of the objective to increase the company value. Apart from the objective to increase the company value other objectives are not analysed. Thus, Tappe (2009) contributes to the body of knowledge by narrowly focusing on the objective to increase the company value and analysing this in depth.

Apart from the empirical studies focusing on VBM in Mittelstand **other recent empirical studies** provide insights related to objectives in Mittelstand. Similar to Gonschorek (2009a), Krol (2009c) and Piontkowski (2009) the empirical studies of Achleitner et al. (2010), Deloitte & Touche GmbH Wirtschaftsprüfungsgesellschaft (2015), Schlepphorst and Schlömer-Laufen (2016) and PricewaterhouseCoopers AG Wirtschaftsprüfungsgesellschaft (2014) give an overview of the importance of different objectives in Mittelstand on the basis of questionnaires. This is usually done in the context of an empirical study also covering other topics. Thus, similar to the empirical studies addressed in previous subsections, objectives are only one of several aspects analysed. An exception is Achleitner et al. (2010) who focus on the analysis of the relationship between firm and family goals in family businesses. [40]

Previous paragraphs showed that several recent empirical studies provide insights into company objectives in Mittelstand. Company objectives are mostly only one part of a broader empirical study. The empirical studies take different approaches in analysing company objectives and look at the topic with different levels of breadth and depth. This is summarised in Figure 13. On the one hand, there are several empirical studies on the basis of questionnaires that give an overview of company objectives (Achleitner et al., 2010; Deloitte & Touche GmbH Wirtschaftsprüfungsgesellschaft, 2015; Gonschorek, 2009a; Krol, 2009c; Piontkowski, 2009; PricewaterhouseCoopers AG Wirtschaftsprüfungsgesellschaft, 2014; Schlepphorst & Schlömer-Laufen, 2016). On the other hand interview-based studies analyse company objectives and particularly the objective to increase the company value more in-depth (Khadjavi, 2005; Tappe, 2009; Wenzel, 2014). These can be distinguished additionally in terms of whether they exclusively focus on the objective to increase the company value (Tappe, 2009) or cover other objectives as well (Khadjavi, 2005; Wenzel, 2014).

[40] Following the reasoning of Reinemann and Ludwig (2015) insights from related areas of research are also considered (see section 2.1, especially subsection 2.1.2.4 for family businesses). Apart from Achleitner, Bock, Braun, Schraml, and Welter (2010) this applies to Schlepphorst and Schlömer-Laufen (2016) who focus on quickly growing companies. Based on the quantitative definition of the Institut für Mittelstandsforschung Bonn (2018b) the companies in the sample of Schlepphorst and Schlömer-Laufen (2016) are small- and medium-sized companies (for details on the sample see Schlepphorst and Schlömer-Laufen (2016, p. 7)), which are also closely related to Mittelstand (see section 2.1, especially subsection 2.1.2.2).

Figure 13: Approaches of empirical analysis of objectives in Mittelstand in recent empirical studies

Aspect of the comparison (column), empirical study (line)	**Approach**	**Depth to that objectives are analysed**	**Breadth of objectives adressed**
Achleitner et al. (2010), Deloitte & Touche GmbH Wirtschaftsprüfungsgesellschaft (2015), Gonschorek (2009a), Krol (2009c), Piontkowski (2009), PricewaterhouseCoopers AG Wirtschaftsprüfungsgesellschaft (2014), Schlepphorst and Schlömer-Laufen (2016)	Quantitative, questionnaire	Overview	Selection of different company objectives
Khadjavi (2005), Wenzel (2014)	Qualitative, interviews	Overview and in-depth analysis	Company objectives openly expressed, increase company value
Tappe (2009)	Qualitative, interviews	In-depth analysis	Increase company value

2.4.3.2.2 Existing findings

This subsection presents and synthesises empirical insights into objectives in Mittelstand particularly regarding VBM's objective of increasing the company value. The synthesis is important for being able to discuss the findings that will be gained in the empirical study at hand in relation to existing findings. However, it must be noted that the synthesis of existing empirical studies has the shortcoming that these are only comparable to a limited extent for a few reasons. Mainly, it has to be considered that the findings are based on different approaches and levels of analysis. Firstly, a direct comparison of findings from questionnaire studies and interview-based studies is regarded as difficult. Thus, these are looked at separately and then compared on an overall level. Secondly, the differences in the presentation of the data in the questionnaire studies impede a synthesis of existing findings.[41] The following paragraphs will outline how the questionnaire studies are compared under consideration of these constraints. Then, the synthesis of the findings of the questionnaire studies will be presented before addressing findings from the interview-based studies.

As shown in subsection 2.4.3.2.1 several empirical studies give an **overview of objectives on the basis of questionnaires**. Many of the questionnaire studies are

[41] Furthermore, the empirical studies differ in their definition of the population looked at. This is regarded as consequence of the lack of a generally accepted definition of Mittelstand (for details see subsection 2.1.2) and thus needs to be accepted.

based on the respondents' rating of the importance of a selection of company objectives on a scale. Gonschorek (2009a, p. 258) for example uses a scale reaching from 1 (not at all important) to 5 (very important). On this basis the authors usually calculate the arithmetic mean for each of the objectives. This allows comparing the objectives with regard to their importance. This is done with an approach that is oriented towards the aim to evaluate which objectives have been found to be more or less important in recent empirical studies and analyse similarities and differences across the different empirical studies. The focus is on the overall picture and not on slight differences e.g. of the arithmetic mean. To achieve this aim, the results of each questionnaire study have been analysed before comparing the findings. For each empirical study objectives with roughly similar results in relation to importance have been grouped together. Based on this, objectives of first, second and third level importance as well as those with lower importance have been identified. This has been done for each of the questionnaire studies. The findings of the questionnaire studies, prepared for the comparison, are displayed in Appendices-Figure 6. On this basis, the importance of specific objectives has been compared across the different questionnaire studies. This is displayed in Figure 14. The related inferences will be presented in the following. While all inferences in the following paragraphs are based on the data in Appendices-Figure 6 and Figure 14 the outline is in favour of readability written without repeated reference to these figures.

The synthesis of findings from recent questionnaire studies shows that **securing existence** seems to be the most important company objective. This becomes especially evident as it is found to be the most important objective by Krol (2009c), Piontkowski (2009) and PricewaterhouseCoopers AG Wirtschaftsprüfungsgesellschaft (2014). This is directly supported by the results of Gonschorek (2009a) and indirectly by Achleitner et al. (2010). Furthermore, the importance of this objective reflects in the arithmetic mean being more than 4,4 in all studies using a five-point scale (Gonschorek, 2009a; Krol, 2009c; PricewaterhouseCoopers AG Wirtschaftsprüfungsgesellschaft, 2014).

Given the focus of this research, the findings regarding the importance of the **objective to increase the company value** are particularly relevant. The questionnaire studies find the increase of the company value to be rather important in comparison to other objectives but not as important as securing the existence of the company. The arithmetic mean of this objective in the questionnaire studies with a five-point scale is between 3,88 (PricewaterhouseCoopers AG Wirtschaftsprüfungsgesellschaft, 2014) and 4,03 (Gonschorek, 2009a). Additionally, the increase of the company value belongs to the group of objectives of second or third level importance. Gonschorek (2009a) and Krol (2009c) also look at other financial objectives and find the increase of the company value to be the most important financial objective. It is more important than the financial objectives of profit maximisation, increase of the Return on Equity and the increase of turnover. Beyond the findings it has to be noted, that the item to be selected is formulated slightly different in the different questionnaire studies. The most significant difference is that Piontkowski (2009) looks at a maximum company value as an objective while the other questionnaire studies look at an increase of the company value.[42] An influence of the different formulation on the findings is not evident. Thus it can be concluded that the synthesis of empirical findings from recent questionnaire studies consistently shows that the increase of the company value is

- the most important financial objective,
- and one of several important objectives on the overall level
- but not the most important overall objective.

The following paragraphs will address which objectives are found to be important beyond securing existence and the increase of the company value.

Customer satisfaction and securing/increasing customer satisfaction is found to be of major importance. The questionnaire studies that address it find it to be of first or second level importance. Based on the arithmetic mean it is nearly as important as securing the existence of the company.[43]

While **employee satisfaction and securing/increasing employee satisfaction** and **securing the entrepreneurial independence** are also found to be important objectives, they are both slightly less important than securing existence and customer satisfaction. Both objectives are found to be of second or third level importance. Indirectly Achleitner et al. (2010) support this as they find objectives that are related to independence and employees as being of first and third level importance.

Beyond the objectives found to be of major importance by the questionnaire studies it is interesting to look at **personal, societal and ecological objectives** as there is the notion that these play a role in Mittelstand (see subsection 2.4.3.1). The findings of objectives that are related to society are not consistent. Krol (2009c) and Gonschorek (2009a) find the reputation in society to be one of the least important objectives. In contrast, PricewaterhouseCoopers AG Wirtschaftsprüfungsgesellschaft (2014) and Schlepphorst and Schlömer-Laufen (2016) find the comparable objective of improving the company's image and reputation to be one of the more important objectives but not one of those with major importance. While there are differences with regard to how important the reputation in society is in comparison to other objectives, the arithmetic mean of above 3 shows that it still tends to be important. This is similar for social responsibility and other objectives related to society. Ecological and personal objectives are only addressed in a few questionnaire studies. Ecological objectives are always found to be one of the least important objectives in comparison to the other objectives addressed. Nevertheless, it has to be noted that the mean value of at least 3 in the questionnaire studies with a 5-point scale shows that ecological objectives are not unimportant but of medium importance. PricewaterhouseCoopers AG Wirtschaftsprüfungsgesellschaft (2014) is the only empirical study addressing personal objectives and finds them to be of medium

[42] Beyond this and slight differences in the wording Piontkowski (2009), Schlepphorst and Schlömer-Laufen (2016) and PricewaterhouseCoopers AG Wirtschaftsprüfungsgesellschaft (2014) are different by the supplement of „long-term".

[43] The (reversed) arithmetic mean is between 4,34 (PricewaterhouseCoopers AG Wirtschaftsprüfungsgesellschaft (2014)) and 4,72 (Krol (2009c)). The maximum difference to the arithmetic mean for the objective to secure the company's existence is 0,08 (PricewaterhouseCoopers AG Wirtschaftsprüfungsgesellschaft (2014)).

importance in comparison to other objectives. Overall, society-related objectives, ecological and personal objectives tend to be less important than other objectives.

Figure 14: Importance of objectives found in questionnaire studies

Questionnaire studies included in the analysis
1) Achleitner et al. (2010)
2) Deloitte & Touche GmbH Wirtschaftsprüfungsgesellschaft (2015)
3) Gonschorek (2009a)
4) Krol (2009c)
5) Piontkowski (2009)
6) PricewaterhouseCoopers AG Wirtschaftsprüfungsgesellschaft (2014)
7) Schlepphorst and Schlömer-Laufen (2016)

Objective	**Level of importance of the objective found in the questionnaire studies (arithmetic mean for the studies using a five-point scale)**	**Overall evaluation**
Securing existence	1) Indirect indications: prevention of loss of ownership/independence of 1st level importance, firm transfer to next family generation of 3rd level importance 2) No equivalent objective included 3) 1st level importance (4,6) 4) Most important objective (4,77) 5) Most important objective 6) Most important objective (4,42) 7) No equivalent objective included	1st level importance
Increase company value	1) 2nd level importance 2) No equivalent objective included 3) 2nd level importance, most important financial objective (4,03) 4) 3rd level importance, most important financial objective (3,92) 5) 2nd level importance 6) 3rd level importance (3,88) 7) 2nd level importance	2nd/3rd level importance
Customer satisfaction and securing/ increasing customer satisfaction	1) No equivalent objective included 2) No equivalent objective included 3) 1st level importance (4,58) 4) 1st level importance (4,72) 5) No equivalent objective included 6) 2nd level importance (4,34) 7) No equivalent objective included	1st level importance

(figure continued on next page)

Objective	Level of importance of the objective found in the questionnaire studies (arithmetic mean for the studies using a five-point scale)	Overall evaluation
(retention and/or increase of) employee satisfaction	1) Indirect indications: preservation and creation of jobs of 3rd level importance 2) No equivalent objective included 3) 2nd level importance (4,01) 4) 2nd level importance (4,12) 5) 3rd level importance 6) No equivalent objective included 7) No equivalent objective included	2nd level importance
(securing) entrepreneurial independence	1) Indirect indications: prevention from loss of ownership/independence of 1st level importance 2) No equivalent objective included 3) 2nd level importance (4,02) 4) 2nd level importance (4,33) 5) No equivalent objective included 6) No equivalent objective included 7) 3rd level importance	2nd level importance
Objectives related to society – reputation in society	1) No equivalent objective included 2) No equivalent objective included 3) Reputation in society second-least important objectives (3,52) 4) Reputation in society: least important objectives (3,56) 5) No equivalent objective included 6) Improving corporate image: fourth-most important company objective (3,78) 7) Increase of the company's reputation: 3rd level importance	Inconsistent findings, in a tendency still important
Other objectives related to society	1) No equivalent objective included 2) Social objectives: 2nd level importance (3,96) 3) Societal objectives: all three items belong to the least important objectives (3,19 to 3,66) 4) Social/societal responsibility: 3rd level importance (4) 5) No equivalent objective included 6) Societal objectives: one of the least important objectives (3,41) 7) High social engagement: least important objective	Inconsistent findings, in a tendency still important

(figure continued on next page)

Objective	Level of importance of the objective found in the questionnaire studies (arithmetic mean for the studies using a five-point scale)	Overall evaluation
Ecological and personal objectives	1) No equivalent objectives included 2) Ecological objectives: Least important objective (3,3) 3) No equivalent objectives included 4) No equivalent objectives included 5) No equivalent objectives included 6) Ecological objectives: second least important objective (3) 6) Personal objectives: medium importance (3,61) 7) Ecological objectives: second least important objective	Less important than other objectives
Additional objectives found to be of 1st or 2nd level importance by single studies	1) No additional objectives of 1st or 2nd level importance 2) Turnover objectives and cost objecties: 1st and 2nd level importance, not addressed in an equivalent way by the other studies 3) – 6) No additional objectives of 1st or 2nd level importance 7) continuity of company policy: 2nd level importance, not addressed by the other studies	Inconsistent findings

It is also interesting to acknowledge that in all questionnaire studies the majority of objectives tend to be rated **as rather important rather than rather unimportant**. In Deloitte & Touche GmbH Wirtschaftsprüfungsgesellschaft (2015), Gonschorek (2009a) and Krol (2009c) all objectives have an arithmetic mean of more than 3 with 1 being “absolutely not important”/“not important” and 5 being “very important”. In Achleitner et al. (2010) and PricewaterhouseCoopers AG Wirtschaftsprüfungsgesellschaft (2014) a clear majority of the objectives tends to be important. Schlepphorst and Schlömer-Laufen (2016) also find 5 out of 9 objectives to be (very) important for more than two thirds of the respondents.

The synthesis of findings on company objectives in Mittelstand of recent questionnaire studies will be complemented by findings in empirical studies based on qualitative data (for details on the level of analysis see subsection 2.4.3.2.1). The findings of Khadjavi (2005), Wenzel (2014) and Tappe (2009) will be outlined consecutively.

Khadjavi (2005) analyses Mittelstand’s objectives on the basis of interviews for three cases. Firstly, he gives an overview of the company objectives and then analyses them in relation to the application of value-based management. Khadjavi (2005, p. 252) concludes that all companies are primarily focused on the interests of the owners, which are mostly financial interests. The emphasis on the owners is in line with VBM. However, this consensus cannot be fully confirmed by the content of the strategic goal. While one company is primarily oriented towards a maximum shareholder value, another company aims at a maximum Return on Equity and the third focuses on "handing over a well operating company" (Khadjavi, 2005, p. 252). Thus, the strategic objective of one company is in line with the VBM approach (for details see Khadjavi, 2005, pp. 127-129, 135). The second company's aim, to achieve a maximum return, also leads to an increase of the company value and is thus in line with the VBM approach (Khadjavi, 2005, pp. 104-107, 112).[44] From a VBM perspective the third company's objective of "handing over a well operating company" can at its best be interpreted as aiming at securing the company value (Khadjavi, 2005, pp. 115-119, 124). However, it is obvious that the company has not clearly formulated an objective related to the increase of the company value. This shows that a definition of the company objectives in line with VBM can only be partly found in Khadjavi's (2005) results. Khadjavi (2005) contributes to the body of knowledge as he proposes different possibilities how VBM can reflect in objectives of Mittelstand on the basis of the empirical findings.

In interviewing 20 CFO's of family businesses **Wenzel (2014)** has asked after the key company objective.[45] He finds retention of financial independence (9 out of 20 interviewees) and securing existence or preservation of the company for the next generation (7/20) to be the key company objectives addressed most often (for the results addressed in this paragraph see Wenzel, 2014, pp. 124–126). It has to be noted that the formulation of these two objectives is specific. While the questionnaire studies address "entrepreneurial independency", Wenzel's (2014) findings relate to the narrower understanding of financial independence. In contrast, the understanding of the objective to secure the company's existence is broadened by including the preservation of the company for the next generation. Additionally, Wenzel (2014) finds the increase of the company value to be a key company objective for only 2 out of 20 companies. Thus, the increase of the company value seems to be much less important than according to the questionnaire studies.[46] This is still valid when taking into account that Wenzel (2014) finds that the increase of the company value is implicitly pursued by additional interviewees.[47]

Overall, Wenzel (2014) supports the findings from the questionnaire surveys in relation to the high importance of securing existence and independence as objectives. However, Wenzel's (2014) findings are different in that these are formulated in a slightly different way and in that the increase of the company value is found to be

[44] However, Khadjavi (2005) notes that this objective is not achieved.

[45] Beyond looking at key company objectives Wenzel (2014) comments on the relation of financial and non-financial objectives and other aspects related to objectives Wenzel (2014, pp. 123–142). While the focus of the comparison is on the key company objectives, these additional insights are considered when they are relevant in interpretation of the key company objectives.

[46] This can be illustrated by a comparison to the findings of Krol (2009c). Krol (2009c) finds that the increase of the company value is a (very) important objective for 73 % of the respondents (arithmetic mean 3,92). On this basis one would expect more than 2 out of 20 interviewees to formulate the increase of the company value as a key objective.

[47] This includes for example interviewees that state that the company's financial objectives have an effect on the company value, even without the increase of the company value being explicitly formulated as an objective. In addition, this includes interviewees that mention the increase of the company value to be an objective that helps to achieve the overall objective of securing the companies' independence.

less important than in the questionnaire surveys. An interesting detail in Wenzel's (2014) findings is that some interviewees refer to the relation of the increase of the company value to other company objectives.

Further insights into the relevance of VBM for Mittelstand's objectives are gained by **Tappe (2009)**. He focuses more narrowly on the objective to increase the company value than Khadjavi (2005) and Wenzel (2014). Tappe (2009) analyses the insights into objectives from interviews with 10 managers of mittelständische companies in relation to whether these are in line with three VBM aspects. He concludes that similar to VBM, Mittelstand's objectives have a long-term focus (for details on the results addressed in this paragraph see Tappe, 2009, pp. 204–212). However, the companies do not aim at the objective to increase the company value in line with VBM as cash flow orientation and consideration of costs of capital are not given. Furthermore, Tappe (2009) briefly states that while the companies want to increase the company value, they understand the increase of the company value in a way that is different to that of VBM. However, he does not elaborate this in more detail. Beyond this, Tappe (2009) mentions that the interviewees confirm that "primarily profitable growth and securing existence" (translated from Tappe, 2009, p. 208) are at the heart of mittelständische objectives. This supports the findings of the questionnaire studies in relation to the importance of securing existence. Beyond briefly mentioning this, an overview of the objectives is not given.

It can therefore be concluded that Tappe's (2009) findings are similar to those of Wenzel (2014) in that VBM is found to be of little importance for Mittelstand's objectives. There are slight indications that support the questionnaire studies' findings in relation to the importance of securing existence as company objective. A summary of the findings on an overall level is included in the following subsection.

2.4.3.3 Summary of the subsection

This subsection has outlined several aspects that provide a background for empirically analysing the objectives of mittelständische companies and whether these are in line with VBM's focus on the objective to increase the company value. This has included gaining insights into existing views related to objectives in Mittelstand in literature as well as a synthesis of recent empirical insights.

In relation to **mittelständische company objectives several aspects are addressed in literature** (see subsection 2.4.3.1). This includes that objectives are pluralistic and include non-economic objectives due to the relation to personal objectives of the owner-manager. This notion is reinforced by similar views addressed in family business research. It is noted that in Mittelstand securing the companies' existence and its independence are important as well as ecological and societal objectives. Furthermore, customers and employees are assumed to play a role in Mittelstand objectives. Against this background it is interesting to analyse empirical insights into the role of VBM's objective to increase the monetary company value for the owners of the company in the long run. According to the VBM approach, this economic objective shall be the overall company objective.

To synthesise **existing empirical insights in relation to mittelständische objectives,** empirical studies on VBM in Mittelstand as well as other recent studies in the context of Mittelstand have been analysed (see subsection 2.4.3.2). The overview of how Mittelstand's objectives are addressed in these empirical studies has shown that there is a dominance of questionnaire studies. However, there are also empirical studies that analyse Mittelstand's objectives more in depth and on the basis of interviews.

The findings in relation to the content of objectives in Mittelstand are synthesised in the following and in Figure 15. In relation to the content of mittelständische objectives recent empirical studies reinforce the existing view in literature and find securing existence to be of the topmost importance. Furthermore, in line with the expected importance of customers for Mittelstand's objectives, securing and/or increasing customer satisfaction is a key objective. This also is the case for securing entrepreneurial independence and retention and/or increase of employee satisfaction. However, these seem to be slightly less important. The empirical evidence is ambiguous in relation to other aspects of the literature's notion. While the empirical studies show that objectives related to society tend to be important, the findings are inconsistent with regard to their importance in comparison to other objectives. Furthermore, personal and ecological objectives are less important than other objectives. The findings also differ in relation to the increase of the company value. Recent questionnaire studies suggest that the increase of the company value is

- the most important financial objective,
- and one of several important objectives on the overall level
- but not the most important overall objective.

Empirical studies analysing Mittelstand's objectives on the basis of qualitative data and more in-depth, paint a slightly different picture and either find differences among the companies in the sample (Khadjavi, 2005) or the increase of company value being not very relevant for the objectives in Mittelstand (Tappe, 2009; Wenzel, 2014). Furthermore, the questionnaire studies support the notion of pluralistic objectives in Mittelstand by finding the majority of objectives tending to be important.

Figure 15: Summary of findings of recent empirical studies on the content of objectives in Mittelstand

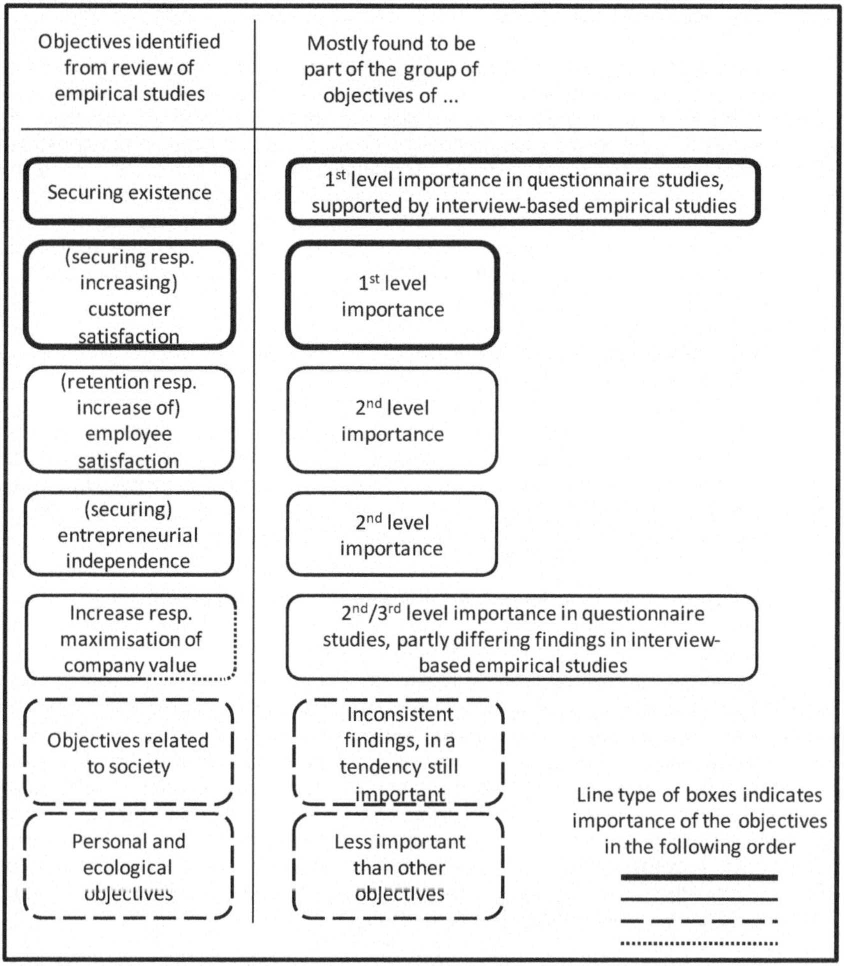

Further empirical insights into Mittelstand's objectives and the role of the increase of the company value as an objective are interesting especially for the following logic. On the one side, the empirical studies support the notion of pluralistic objectives in Mittelstand and the role of non-economic objectives. On the other side, there has also been some support for the increase of the company value being an important objective in Mittelstand. This is puzzling as one argument in VBM in Mittelstand literature is that the increase of the company value shall be defined as a monoistic overall objective. However, there is also the argument that the increase of the economic value is a valuable opposite pole to non-economic objectives. Given this and the differences in the empirical studies with regard to the importance of the objective to increase the company value it seems to be valuable to gain further understanding of the relevance of VBM in the context of objectives in Mittelstand.

In this respect, it is valuable to openly gain an overview of company objectives in Mittelstand. An overview of the company objectives is crucial to evaluate the relevance of the increase of the company value in comparison to other objectives in Mittelstand. Doing this in an open manner is regarded as beneficial to not constrain the potential insights by a selection and formulation of objectives done by the researcher. Beyond this, it is regarded as valuable to look at the objectives in depth. In this respect, especially the relation of the economic objective to increase the company value to other company objectives is interesting. Thus, the **following supplementing research questions** shall guide the empirical analysis of VBM in the context of objectives in Mittelstand:

- Research question 3 (RQ3):
  What are the objectives of Mittelstand?
- Research question 4 (RQ4):
  How is VBM reflected in the objectives of Mittelstand?

In comparison to the approaches taken in existing empirical studies (see subsection 2.4.3.2.1), the topical focus of this research is, in a broader sense, comparable to that of Khadjavi (2005) and Wenzel (2014) as it shall include an overview of company objectives openly expressed (RQ3) as well as a more in-depth analysis especially with regard to the increase of the company value (RQ4).

2.4.4 Attitudes towards value-based management in Mittelstand

2.4.4.1 Background for researching the attitudes towards VBM

Empirically analysing the attitudes of owner-managers in Mittelstand towards VBM is regarded as beneficial on the basis of some views addressed in the literature. These refer to **requirements for an application of VBM in Mittelstand related to the owner-manager**. This includes, that for an implementation of VBM it is necessary that VBM is known. Krol (2009c) relates this to the commercial knowledge of the management board and assumes this to be positively related to the application of VBM. A similar reasoning in the reverse way can be found in Gonschorek (2009a) who regards a lack of knowledge as a potential barrier to the application of VBM. Beyond this Gonschorek (2009a) addresses a second aspect. This is that there needs to be a willingness to implement VBM.

In this respect the **owner-manager's attitude is regarded as especially relevant**. Based on findings in relation to VBM and other management tools Wenzel (2014) identifies the managers of a company as a crucial driver of an implementation of VBM. In his view, their support and power is decisive for the implementation of VBM. Wenzel (2014) as well as Krol (2009c) refer to the cost-benefit-ratio expected by the managers in this context. Given that the implementation of new management tools includes costs, it is necessary that the owner-manager recognises the benefit of these new management tools. Otherwise the owner-manager will not strive for its application. In this respect, some authors assume that there might be reservations towards VBM resulting from a different understanding of VBM and a negative attitude towards VBM (Becker et al., 2010b; Krol, 2009c; Wenzel, 2014). This could be related to a general criticism of the orientation of VBM towards the owners of the company in society (see subsection 2.3.2.2). It is therfore interesting to see whether this assumption is supported by empirical findings.

2.4.4.2 Review of empirical studies touching upon attitudes towards VBM

The empirical studies focusing on VBM in Mittelstand have been analysed with regard to whether they yield insights into attitudes of owner-managers towards VBM. The analysis of the approach taken and the insights gained shows four aspects.

Firstly, as already mentioned in subsection 2.3.5.2 there are **little empirical insights** into attitudes towards VBM. Only three of the relevant studies gain empirical insights into attitudes towards VBM (Gonschorek, 2009a; Krol, 2009c; Wenzel, 2014). Furthermore, these studies do not address attitudes towards VBM in their research questions but only touch upon this topic briefly.[48] Thus, it can already be noted that the study at hand is the first empirical study in the relevant literature specifically focusing on an empirical analysis of attitudes towards VBM.

Secondly, the **conclusions drawn in relation to attitudes towards VBM are different**. Gonschorek's (2009a) conclusion, that in particular smaller companies have not yet dealt much with VBM and have reservations towards its application, points towards a lack of knowledge and a negative attitude as reasons for the minimal application of VBM. However Krol's (2009c) conclusion, that the minimal application is less related to a refusal of the concept but more towards a lack of knowledge and tools, indicates that there is no such negative attitude. This is supported by his conclusion that the majority of the respondents is open towards defining the company success in a value-oriented manner and that they ascribe potential benefits to VBM. This indicates a rather positive attitude. On the basis of interviews Wenzel (2014) finds evidence for positive and negative attitudes.[49] Thus, there are not only few but also differing findings in relation to owner-managers' attitudes towards VBM.

Thirdly, a closer look at the findings shows that the **conclusions regarding attitudes are not based on posing direct questions but derived indirectly**. This will be illustrated with a closer look at the findings in the following. Wenzel's (2014) indications, in relation to owner-managers' attitudes towards VBM, have been gained indirectly by asking for influencing factors of an implementation of VBM in interviews. Wenzel (2014) finds that owner-managers exerted influence on the implementation of VBM in ten companies.[50] This influence is hindering in four cases and beneficial in six cases, which indicates that the owners have a negative attitude towards VBM in four cases and a positive one in six cases. Additionally, he finds an

[48] This will become more evident from the outline of the insights gained later in this subsection.

[49] On the one hand, in all cases where a family business implemented VBM the driver of the implementation was the owner-manager (for this paragraph see Wenzel (2014, pp. 230–231)). This points towards a positive attitude as it is assumed that an owner-manager acts in this way only when he has a positive attitude towards VBM. On the other hand, Wenzel (2014) also finds owners refusing the implementation of VBM. This will become more evident from the outline of the insights gained later in this subsection.

[50] In total Wenzel (2014) has conducted 20 interviews with CFOs of German family businesses.

explicit or implicit rejection of VBM in some cases. Beyond finding a positive as well as a negative attitude, Wenzel (2014) also gains insights into the origins of these attitudes. In case of an implementation of VBM, which is supposedly related to a positive attitude, this includes among other things an upcoming or completed change of generation and a fundamental revision of the management tools. In case of a refusal of VBM, this among other things includes doubts on the cost-benefit-ratio and the owner having been involved in implementing other KPIs and not wanting to change them. Beyond the indirect questioning approach, Wenzel's (2014) findings only provide indirect insights into owner-manager's attitudes towards VBM because the majority of the interviewees have been external managers and not owner-managers.

Gonschorek's (2009a) conclusion regarding reservations towards an application of VBM, especially in smaller companies, is also derived indirectly in the context of analysing the respondents' assessment of VBM as influencing factor of an application of VBM. This includes the respondents' agreement to several statements on the content and understanding of VBM, as well as on potential barriers of implementation.[51] Similarly Krol's (2009c) conclusion that the minimal application of VBM is less related to a refusal of the concept but more towards a lack of knowledge and tools is obtained indirectly in the context of analysing influencing factors. However, he considers more aspects than Gonschorek (2009a). While also being based on statements that mainly refer to the understanding of VBM Krol (2009c) puts more emphasis on analysing the attitude. In addition to asking after barriers of implementation like Gonschorek (2009a), Krol (2009c) considers the agreement to statements referring to potential benefits of VBM to approach the respondents' assessment of the cost-benefit-ratio of an application of VBM. From the analysis of the respondent's assessment of different statements related to potential benefits of VBM, Krol (2009c) finds that the agreement is unexpectedly high given the minimal application of VBM. This can be illustrated with the finding that nearly three fourths of the respondents do not only agree to the statement that VBM leads to an increase of the company value but also to the statement that VBM improves the company's performance.[52] Thus the respondents in Krol's (2009c) empirical study associate an economic benefit with VBM.

Fourthly, in this context **the understanding of VBM seems to be relevant**. In this respect, a number of the statements in Krol's (2009c) and Gonschorek's (2009a) questionnaires to analyse influencing factors on VBM focuses on elements of the definition of VBM (for the definition see subsection 2.3.2.1). Thus, they gain initial insights into the respondents' understanding of VBM and use this to evaluate the respondents' attitudes towards VBM. These shall be presented in the following.

Both ask their respondents to assess the statement that an increase of the company value means that in the long run a return that is above the expected Return on Equity is achieved on a 5-point-Likert-scale. Around two thirds of the respondents

---

[51] The detailed findings will be addressed later in this subsection.

[52] The sum of respondents that regard this statement as „rather correct" or „fully correct" is 73 % for the statement that VBM is beneficial for increasing the company value and 72 % for the statement that VBM improves the company's performance (Krol (2009c, pp. 216–217)).

agree to this core aspect of the definition of VBM.[53] This indicates that the respondents understand an increase of value in a similar monetary understanding than in the understanding derived from literature which includes that the rate of return does not only exceed costs of capital but also the expected interest on equity capital. An indicator for an agreement to VBM's key element to consider the costs of debt and equity capital in measuring value creation, can also be found in the assessment of another statement in a different part of Krol's (2009c) questionnaire. Nearly two thirds of the respondents agree to the statement that economic success is achieved only when the success indicator exceeds the costs of the total capital employed.[54] While this statement does not include a reference to VBM, it points in a similar direction as the findings just addressed. Together this indicates that the respondents' understanding of VBM is parallel with the understanding in literature that there is a focus on increasing the monetary value in the long run by generating a return that exceeds costs of debt and equity capital.

A similar indication results from the answers to another statement, which expresses that the focus of VBM is (mainly) on the short-term maximisation of the Return on Equity. By referring to the Return on Equity this statement is indirectly in line with VBM's focus on the monetary company value for owners. However, the statement is in contrast to the understanding of VBM, as it includes that this shall be maximised in the short run. Indeed, VBM aims at an increase in the long run. As around 60 % of the respondents disagree with the statement there is another indication for an understanding of VBM similar to that derived from literature.[55] However, there is no agreement on whether the findings are to be interpreted in relation to the understanding of VBM or the attitude towards VBM. In contrast to the interpretation just addressed, Krol (2009c, p. 203) uses the respondents' assessment to find a rather positive attitude towards VBM. Gonschorek (2009a) interprets the responses as a predominant agreement to the content and understanding of VBM. Similar to Gonschorek (2009a) the researcher would rather interpret the answers, especially for the statement referring to the expected rate of return included in both studies, in relation to the understanding of VBM. Thus it is ambiguous whether the findings refer to the understanding and/or attitude towards VBM. This limits the significance of the existing findings in relation to attitudes towards VBM. This is also limited as the conclusions are derived only on the basis of the assessment of a few statements. It must also be noted that the statements address most of the key elements of the understanding of VBM underlying this thesis but not all aspects.[56]

[53] This results from adding up the percentages of interviewees who selected the two items expressing agreement which results in a total of 69,1 % for Gonschorek (2009a, p. 273) and 62 % for Krol (2009c, p. 201).

[54] This results from adding up the percentages of interviewees that selected the two items expressing agreement which results in a total of 62,7 % (Krol (2009c, p. 204)).

[55] This results from adding up the percentages of interviewees that selected the two items expressing disagreement which results in a total of 58,9 % for Gonschorek (2009a, p. 273) and 64 % for Krol (2009c, p. 201).

[56] The statements do not address whether VBM is understood as a holistic management approach that includes decisions taken in the company. Furthermore the consideration of the interests of other stakeholders and that VBM is supposed to help to secure the existence of a company are not included.

In relation to the understanding of VBM, there is some indication that the respondents' understanding at least partly overlaps the understanding derived from literature. This includes the focus on the monetary company value, the long-term focus and the key element that costs of debt and equity capital are considered in measuring the creation of value. Given the existence of other understandings of value and the related debates (see subsection 2.3.2.2) this is not self-evident. In this respect it must be noted that Krol's (2009c) questionnaire includes a short statement on the understanding of VBM directly before the statements the respondents shall assess in relation to VBM.[57] This can be a sign that Krol (2009c) also does not regard it as self-evident that the respondents understand VBM similar than in literature.

2.4.4.3 Summary of the subsection

The **insights gained from the analysis of existing empirical studies as well as the respective views in literature** addressing attitudes towards VBM are displayed in Figure 16. This includes that beyond knowledge of VBM a positive attitude of the owner-manager towards VBM is regarded as a requirement for the application of VBM. Furthermore, there are little empirical insights as well as different conclusions on attitudes towards VBM. Additionally, the conclusions are only derived indirectly and are partly also or even more related to the understanding of VBM than to attitudes towards VBM.

Given the relevance of the owner-manager's attitude for the application of VBM and the little and differing existing empirical insights it is regarded as valuable to gain empirical insights into owner-managers' attitudes towards VBM. This shall be addressed empirically on the basis of the following **supplementary research question**:

- Research question 5 (RQ5):
  What are Mittelstands' attitudes towards VBM?

In conducting the empirical study, attention shall be paid to whether and how the understanding towards VBM needs to be considered.

[57] This German statement can be translated as following: "VBM is understood as focusing all management activities on the long-term and sustainable increase of the company value." (Krol (2009c, p. 411)).

Figure 16: Summary of views and empirical insights related to attitudes towards VBM

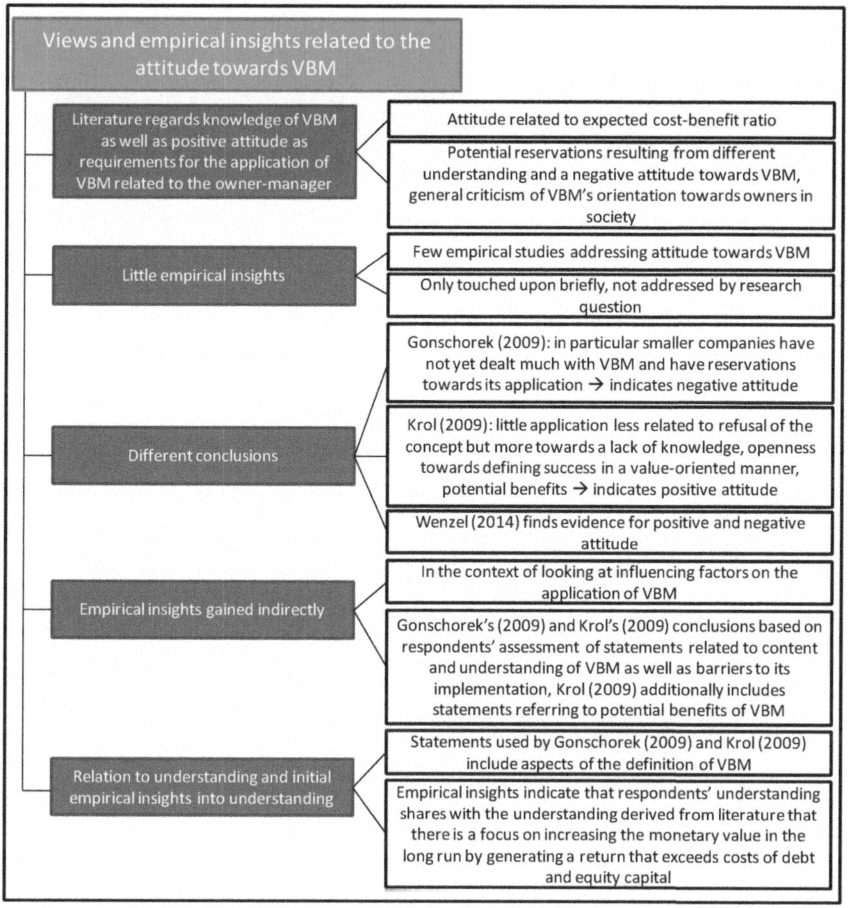

3 Research approach

3.1 Aim and approach of the chapter

In this chapter the methodological approach chosen to achieve the aim of research and to address the research questions is outlined. The terms “research approach” and “methodological approach” will be used as synonyms in the following to describe the purpose of the research and the approach that will be used to achieve this purpose. The research approach includes reflections and decisions on different levels. These are often interconnected. To give a comprehensive overview of these reflections and decisions, a construction of the elements of the research approach shall be used. This construction has been developed by combining the outlines of “four ... basic elements of any research process” by Crotty (1998, pp. 2–9) and the “five major elements of investigative theory” of the “mental model” by Hallebone and Priest (2009, pp. 23–30). The key elements of the research approach that will be outlined in this section and the respective definitions used are shown in Figure 17.

Figure 17: Elements of the research approach

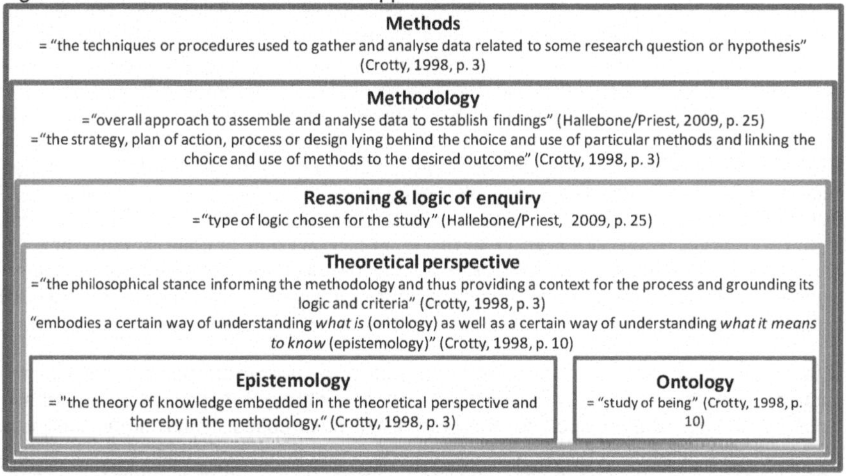

Before outlining the key elements of the research approach, section 3.2 will present the insights gained from a familiarisation with Mittelstand as a field of research. Against this background, the reasoning and logic of enquiry will be outlined (section 3.3). This involves the nature of the phenomenon to be researched and the aim of research. Based on this, the research methodology is described (section 3.4). Then, it is addressed how underlying assumptions influence the perception of the field of research, the definition of the aim of research and the methodological approach (section 3.5). This outline of the theoretical perspective involves making the assumptions with regard to epistemology and ontology explicit. Then, the choice and use of methods is explained in light of the methodological approach chosen and the

© Springer Fachmedien Wiesbaden GmbH, part of Springer Nature 2020
C. Normann-Tschampel, *Value-Based Management in Mittelstand*,
Familienunternehmen und KMU, https://doi.org/10.1007/978-3-658-29228-7_3

underlying assumptions (section 3.6). The order of these sections gives the most comprehensible, yet not too extensive outline of the different elements of the research approach.

3.2 Key characteristics of the field of research

The familiarisation with the field of research has been a valuable background for the review of the body of knowledge on VBM in Mittelstand and identifying ways in which further research might contribute to the development of the body of knowledge. However, there is the difficulty that little literature focuses on Mittelstand as a field of research. Comments on the field of SME research are more common. As shown there is a large overlap of SMEs and Mittelstand (see subsection 2.1.2). In line with Reinemann and Ludwig's (2015) reasoning, this subsection will thus also consider literature on SME research.

One aspect to be considered is that Mittelstand seems to be a **complex but rich issue to research**. The complexity has already become evident from the difficulties to define and demarcate Mittelstand as a phenomenon from related phenomena. Furthermore, several authors emphasise the complexity of small businesses as a phenomenon (Blackburn & Curran, 2001; Landström, 2010). Blackburn and Curran (2001) argue that the distinctive features of small businesses actually make them more difficult to research than large enterprises (for this paragraph see Blackburn & Curran, 2001). SMEs cannot be seen as "a scaled-down version of a large business" (Blackburn & Curran, 2001, p. 5). Different people are involved and their diverse and complex motivations can result in very complex and subtle interactions in SMEs. Furthermore, activities are not clearly structured and recorded which makes measurements difficult. There are also a lot of connections with the environment and SMEs have less ability to influence their wider environment. Beside this, there is an enormous range of different forms of SMEs. All this results in difficulties researching SMEs, especially with regard to generalisation. However, due to their complexity SMEs also "offer an immense range of topics to investigate" (Blackburn & Curran, 2001, p. 7).

It is emphasised that small business research is a **multi-disciplinary field of research**. Blackburn and Curran (2001) remark that different disciplines in social science have been drawn upon to research small businesses. Thus, small business research has "disparate roots, which span the social sciences" (Blackburn & Smallbone, 2008, p. 279). The multi-disciplinary character of small business research also becomes evident from Landström's (2010) detailed outline of the historical-doctrinal development of the field, where he points towards aspects of small businesses that have been addressed from different scientific disciplines (for this paragraph see Landström, 2010). This includes research in the behavioural sciences, especially in psychology that was aimed at understanding the entrepreneur as an individual in the 1950s. Furthermore, there was already an interest in researching the importance of small businesses for societal dynamics and development in the late 1970s and early 1980s. In the 1990s several dynamics led to a multitude of opportunities for researchers and the field developed in many different directions. While the research community grew in this period it is „to a very great extent .. fragmented“ (Landstöm, 2010, p. 66) with many researchers from different disciplines addressing this field of research temporarily and few researchers continually researching this phenomenon.

A lack of a stable research community is criticised by some authors in the field as they regard this as an obstacle to achieving an understanding of the phenomenon (Low, 2001 according to Landström, 2010). This refers to the **theoretical development** of the field which seems to be at the heart of a major debate. According to Blackburn and Kovalainen (2009), small business research is in a pre-paradigmatic state. Landström (2010) addresses difficulties in achieving a convergence in the theoretical development of small business research in the 1990s. While much knowledge has been generated, Landström (2010, p. 82) concludes that „the field is still young and of an eclectic nature“ and asserts that its „cognitive development ... has been rather slow“. Blackburn and Smallbone (2008, p. 279) also conclude that limited progress has been achieved „in developing an integrated theoretical approach“ and mention the complexity of the phenomenon as well as the broad paradigmatic lenses as reasons. Blackburn and Kovalainen (2009, p. 131) express that „poor conceptual and theory development“ can result from researchers struggling with different demands of different stakeholders. However, it can be noted that there are authors who do not seem to regard the lack of a common theoretical basis as too problematic. Welter and Lasch (2008) express the opinion that the often-expressed call for convergence within the field can be questioned and that it is necessary to cross disciplinary boundaries. Blackburn and Smallbone (2008, p. 281) emphasise that it is open to debate whether the “pre-paradigmatic state” of the field of research means that it is less developed than other fields of research. Furthermore, it is mentioned that different views on whether it is possible to develop a coherent theory exist (Blackburn & Smallbone, 2008). There also seem to be different views with regard to whether the field has gained academic legitimacy. On the one hand, Landström (2010) concludes that the field of research has had difficulties in obtaining legitimacy and states that it is too early to assess that the field of research is “irreversibly anchored within academia” (Landström, 2010, p. 69). On the other hand, Blackburn and Smallbone (2008, p. 281) say that it has become a “mainstream activity” and has gained legitimacy through a range of activities. Furthermore, there is the view that the field needs “to retain linkages to mainstream disciplines rather than seek to define its boundaries and develop its own theory” (Blackburn & Kovalainen, 2009, p. 141).

Against the background of characteristics of the field of research there also are **demands and proposals on how research shall be conducted**. For discussing the focus of small business research, Landström (2010) harks back to a distinction made by March (1991) (for this paragraph see Landström, 2010). According to March (1991), a field of research can be explored or exploited. While exploration includes novelty, innovation and discovery, exploitation is more concerned with refining existing knowledge and the implementation of knowledge. Regarding small business research, the 1980s and 1990s showed a high level of experimentation and variety. Thus exploration prevailed. A possible trap of exploration is that new ideas and a lot of experimentation do not have an impact in the long run. Landström (2010) therefore demands for a balance between exploration and exploitation instead of an emphasis on one of them. The explorative focus that dominated for a long time has been beneficial for the development of the field. However, it included a lack of conceptual standardisation and a fragmentation of research. Thus, Landström (2010) demands for a stronger focus on exploitation. In his view, this will help to achieve a better balance between exploitation and exploration and be beneficial to achieve scientific maturation.

Blackburn and Kovalainen (2009) see a need to raise the quality in the field of research and make several suggestions (for this paragraph see Blackburn & Kovalainen, 2009). These include prioritising the research agenda, using appropriate methodologies and being aware of ideological nuances and assumptions. Based on the position that all empirical studies involve theoretical assumptions, they criticise that a lot of researchers in the field of small firm research take assumptions for granted and fail to question them. A shortcoming in this respect is that a positive ideological stance exists towards small businesses and often remains unquestioned. Another aspect Blackburn and Kovalainen (2009) regard as critical, are the methods used. In their opinion there is "some reticence by researchers to go beyond both functionalist paradigms and quantitative approaches" (Blackburn & Kovalainen, 2009, p. 129). They demand that "more attention should be given to explanatory mechanisms underlying social and economic phenomena" (Blackburn & Kovalainen, 2009, p. 130).

Similarly to the demands of Landström (2010) and Blackburn and Kovalainen (2009) in relation to researching SMEs, Becker and Ulrich's (2009a) criticism can be regarded as a **demand for researching Mittelstand in a more in-depth and reflective way**. Becker and Ulrich (2009a) criticise that Mittelstand's heterogeneity is neglected in favour of a simplified and flat description. This results in the drawback of a lack of appropriate knowledge. Among other things they demand to develop an understanding of specific challenges in Mittelstand. This must be based on theoretical considerations and empirical insights in order to provide adequate solutions. They emphasise that it is not possible to transfer typical challenges and their solutions from large business to Mittelstand (for this paragraph see Becker & Ulrich, 2009a).

Building upon the insights gained from the familiarisation with the field of research, there will be careful reflection on the focus of research and its methodological approach. This includes questioning assumptions. In this respect it needs to be acknowledged that choosing the topic of this research has not only been influenced by Mittelstand's importance but also by the researcher's interest for Mittelstand. Beyond this, the demands in relation to how research shall be carried out can be summarised as demanding for research that gains an in-depth understanding of the phenomenon. This also informs the reasoning and logic of enquiry.

3.3 Reasoning and logic of enquiry

Hallebone and Priest (2009, p. 25) define the reasoning and logic of enquiry as "type of logic chosen for the study". This definition leaves room for interpretation. The explanation of the issues that shall be outlined with regard to a study's reasoning and logic gives a more specific insight but is partly overlapping with the understanding of methodology.[58] In this chapter the focus is on outlining the rationale underlying the definition of the research aim and the research questions. In line with Crotty's (1998) definition of methodology, the focus of the illustration of the methodology in the next subsection shall then be on the strategy chosen to achieve the research aim.

In the literature review it has been concluded that a **research gap** exists with regard to VBM in Mittelstand (for details see section 2.3, especially subsection 2.3.6). In the literature there is a consensus regarding VBM being applicable and valuable for Mittelstand. Furthermore, there are proposals for VBM concepts adapted to the characteristics of Mittelstand. Given this, it is puzzling that empirical studies find a low level of application of VBM across different areas of management in Mittelstand. This gap is regarded as crucial to the development of the field of research. Furthermore, gaps in empirical insights for some areas of management have been identified. Thus, further research into VBM in Mittelstand is regarded as beneficial.

On this basis the **aim of research** is to understand the relevance of VBM in specifically identified areas of management in Mittelstand. The empirical study shall address areas in management in which gaps in empirical insights have been identified through the literature review – strategic decision-making, objectives and attitudes towards VBM. This provides **potential for a contribution to the body of knowledge**. Furthermore, the focus on these specifically identified areas of management shall yield insights with regard to the overall research gap in the field. This might be the case on the basis of the following reasoning. The selected areas of management can be assigned to different levels of a framework modified from the levels Krol (2009c) uses to systemise VBM management tools (for details see subsection 2.3.5.2). In this framework objectives and attitude are referred to the purpose of a company. Strategic decision-making is related to the actions of a company. Gaining insights into the relevance of VBM on these different levels might provide valuable insight regarding the research gap. When previous findings are confirmed in relation to the low level of application of VBM on the level of actions in a company, this research allows the evaluation of whether it is also evident on the level of Mittelstand's purpose. In this respect previous empirical studies are differing (for details see subsection 2.3.5.2).

On this basis the **research question** that maps the overall aim of research best is:

> **In what way is VBM relevant for specifically identified areas of management in Mittelstand (strategic decision-making, objectives, attitudes)?**

Based on the more in-depth review in section 2.4 this shall be evaluated by gaining empirical insights into the following research questions:

---

[58] According to Hallebone and Priest (2009, p. 27) the outline of a study's reasoning and logic of enquiry "argues for, and explains the major form of reasoning to be used in answering the research question with the use of empirical data, and the particular logic(s) on which such reasoning is based". This cannot be separated clearly from methodology which is defined as "overall approach to assemble and analyse data to establish findings" (Hallebone and Priest (2009, p. 25)). This shows the interconnected nature of the different reflections involved in the research approach.

1. What management tools are used in strategic decision-making in Mittelstand, and in which ways are these tools relevant for strategic decision-making?
2. How is VBM reflected in the use of management tools in strategic decision-making in Mittelstand?
3. What are the objectives of Mittelstand?
4. How is VBM reflected in the objectives of Mittelstand?
5. What are Mittelstands' attitudes towards VBM?

In relation to strategic decision-making and objectives it has been decided to use two research questions. The reason for this is that it is regarded as difficult to immediately evaluate the relevance of VBM for these two areas of management. The existing empirical insights do not provide a good understanding of the use of management tools in SDM and objectives in Mittelstand.[59] However, a thorough understanding is regarded as necessary to be able to evaluate the relevance of VBM adequately. This also meets the demand for a careful reflection on the focus of research and for gaining an understanding of the phenomenon that are raised with regard to conducting research on Mittelstand and SMEs (see subsection 3.2). In line with these demands the following subsections will include considerations regarding appropriate methodologies and theoretical assumptions. The reasoning and logic of enquiry is summarised in Figure 18.

Figure 18: Reasoning and logic of enquiry

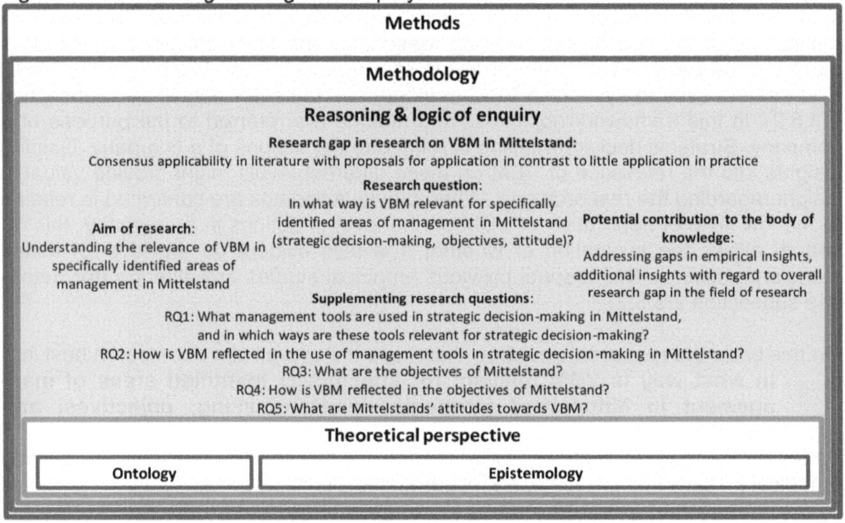

[59] There is very little empirical evidence on the use of management tools (for details see subsection 2.4.2.2) for SDM. In relation to objectives, the findings differ in relation to the role of VBM and it is regarded as necessary to gain an understanding of the objectives before being able to evaluate the respective relevance of the increase of the company value (for details see subsection 2.4.3.2 and 2.4.3.3).

3.4 Methodology

Hallebone and Priest (2009, p. 25) state that the methodology is the "overall approach to assemble and analyse data and to establish findings". Crotty's (1998, p. 3) view of methodology as "the strategy, plan of action, process or design lying behind the choice and use of particular methods and linking the choice and use of methods to the desired outcome" puts an additional emphasis on the influence of the research aim on the decisions regarding methods. Based on these views the focus of this subsection will be on deriving aspects that need to be considered in the choice and use of methods to collect and analyse data from the reasoning and logic of enquiry. It will then be outlined, how these aspects have influenced the choice and use of methods (subsection 3.6).

Firstly, to achieve the aim of research, **in-depth insights** shall be gained. Previous research into VBM in Mittelstand addressed different aspects of VBM in Mittelstand. On this basis the research gap has been identified. However, existing research does not give insights that allow for an understanding of the research gap. An in-depth understanding of the relevance of VBM in the specifically identified areas of management may give the opportunity to understand the overall research gap and might point towards ways to overcome the research gap.

Secondly, some of the existing empirical studies focus on influencing factors on the application of VBM in Mittelstand. The existing insights do not allow explaining the research gap. Thus, additional influencing factors may exist and research shall be carried out in a way that is **open to new aspects and multiple perspectives** to the topic. The openness is also valuable given that there are little previous empirical insights with regard to the use of management tools in SDM and atitudes of owner-managers towards VBM.

Thirdly, the empirical study shall **focus on owner-manager's practical experience**. Given the consensus on VBM's applicability in literature, the minimal application in practice is puzzling. Due to this overall research gap, it is essential to gain insights into the practical experience in Mittelstand to reflect the application in practice. As the owner-managers are crucial for mittelständische companies in general and more specifically for strategic decision-making (see subsections 2.1.2.3, 2.1.3 and 2.4.2.1), it is a necessity to build on their practical experience.

Fourthly, additional insights with regard to the research gap are regarded as valuable to further develop the field of research. To contribute to the body of knowledge it is regarded as beneficial to be able to link the findings to the existing body of knowledge. Thus, the openness that is sought shall be limited to some extent to allow for points of reference to the existing body of knowledge. The research shall thus be **semi-structured**.

Figure 19: Methodology

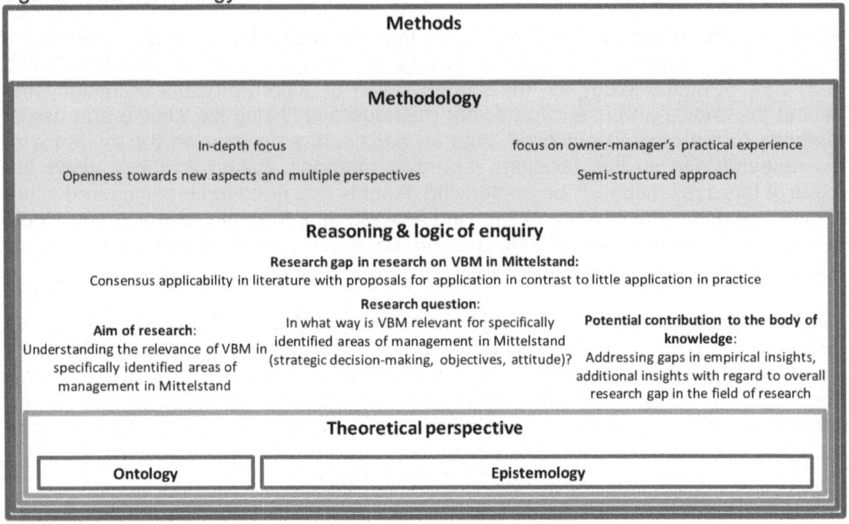

3.5 Theoretical perspective

Some authors emphasise that a researcher always has a number of **assumptions which influence the methodology** chosen. For Guba and Lincoln (1994, p. 105) the worldview or basic belief system of the researcher is more important than the research methods as it guides the researcher "not only in choice of method but in ontologically and epistemologically fundamental ways". The underlying assumptions of the researcher are important for other authors as well (see for example Blackburn & Kovalainen, 2009; Crotty, 1998; Saunders, Lewis, & Thornhill, 2009). Apart from the assumptions of the researcher, it has to be acknowledged that research methods and research methodologies also bring about different philosophical assumptions (Eriksson & Kovalainen, 2008). Several authors regard it as beneficial to reflect upon and state the underlying assumptions as best as possible (Blackburn & Kovalainen, 2009; Crotty, 1998; Eriksson & Kovalainen, 2008; Saunders et al., 2009). Crotty (1998, p. 17) even goes as far as to state that without explication and explanation of the theoretical perspective and epistemological assumptions "research is not research".

The view that underlying assumptions are of importance and that they need to be explicated is shared. Following Crotty's (1998) structure, the term "theoretical perspective" shall be used as an umbrella term. According to Crotty (1998, p. 7) the theoretical perspective is the "view of the human world and social life within that world" wherein the assumptions the researcher brings to the methodology chosen are grounded. It has to be noted that many different theoretical perspectives are discussed in literature under a multitude of different headings by different authors.[60] However, to give a comprehensive overview of this discussion goes beyond the scope of this research project. Rather, the aim of this subsection is to explicate the assumptions that are inherent in the reasoning and logic of enquiry and the way in that they inform the methodology and choice of methods.

The research approach of this research project can be classified as taking a broadly **interpretive stance**. Interpretivism has several specific assumptions which result in a specific way of addressing research. In interpretivism an emphasis is put on describing, understanding and explaining human behaviour (Bryman & Bell, 2011; Crotty, 1998; Hallebone & Priest, 2009). This involves taking an empathetic stance and trying to understand how individuals or groups interpret the world around them (Eriksson & Kovalainen, 2008; Saunders et al., 2009). However, it has to be noted that taking an interpretive stance is not only about eliciting and outlining the subject's view of the world but researchers usually also aim at placing the interpretations into a social scientific frame (Bryman & Bell, 2011). Thus, the methodological approach of this research project, with its aim to develop an understanding of the relevance of VBM in specifically identified areas of management in Mittelstand and relating this to the existing body of knowledge to gain additional insights concerning the research gap, can be regarded as taking an interpretive stance. An interpretive theoretical perspective involves underlying assumptions.

One aspect regarding the **assumptions about the nature of reality** is that it is acknowledged that "there is no single reality that can somehow be discovered, but many perspectives on the issue" (Easterby-Smith, Thorpe, & Jackson, 2012, p. 20). As understanding is regarded as subjective and being influenced by the lenses through which people or groups see and interpret reality, multiple versions of reality are possible (Rubin & Rubin, 2012). Reality is thus regarded as being **subjective and relative**. Another assumption about the nature of reality is that social phenomena are regarded as being "created from the perceptions and consequent actions of social actors" (Saunders et al., 2009, p. 111). Reality is thus regarded as **socially constructed** (Bryman & Bell, 2011; Easterby-Smith et al., 2012). Social phenomena are changing constantly as they result from a continual process of social interaction (Saunders et al., 2009).

In line with the view that people are influenced by their lenses, it has to be noted that researchers are also affected by their specific lens and that their lens influences how research is conducted (Rubin & Rubin, 2012). Thus the "researchers own accounts of the social world are constructions" (Bryman & Bell, 2011, p. 22) as well. Consequently, it is assumed that knowledge is created interactively by the researcher and the researched while the investigation proceeds (Guba & Lincoln, 1994). This involves "the conventional distinction between ontology and epistemology disappears" (Guba & Lincoln, 1994, p. 111). Based on this view, it is regarded as important for the researcher to be self-aware, explore his/her own assumptions

[60] This results from reading respective parts in a range of literature on research methods (e.g. Bryman and Bell (2011); Crotty (1998); Creswell (2013); Easterby-Smith, Thorpe, and Jackson (2012); Guba and Lincoln (1994); Hallebone and Priest (2009); King and Horrocks (2010); Lincoln, Lynham, and Guba (2011); Rubin and Rubin (2012); Saunders, Lewis, and Thornhill (2009); Stokes (2011); Stokes and Wall (2014)).

and make them apparent to the readers of the researcher's work (Rubin & Rubin, 2012). In the research project at hand this view already becomes evident in the belief that assumptions shape the research and need to be explored which has been expressed at the beginning of this subsection. This view has further implications for the assumptions about the nature of knowledge.

The assumption that reality is relative and subjective and social phenomena are socially constructed has implications for the **view of what constitutes knowledge**. One consequence is that "reality ... can be known only indirectly, through the interpretations of people" (Rubin & Rubin, 2012, p. 14). To be able to understand actions of social actors, "subjective meanings motivating the actions of social actors" (Saunders et al., 2009, p. 111) need to be studied. Thus, the focus of research is on understanding and explaining what is going on (Rubin & Rubin, 2012; Saunders et al., 2009). The "core of understanding is learning what people make of the world around them, how people interpret what they encounter, and how they assign meanings and values to events or objects" (Rubin & Rubin, 2012, p. 19). Thus the "goal is to describe particular events, processes, or culture from the perspective of the participants" (Rubin & Rubin, 2012, p. 22) and "understand their world from their point of view" (Saunders et al., 2009, p. 116). In line with this the researcher needs to adopt an empathetic stance (Saunders et al., 2009). Accordingly, a key element of the methodological approach of this empirical study is that an **empathetic stance** is taken to **describe, understand and explain social phenomena**. To achieve this, it is important to gain rich insights and to allow for gathering multiple perspectives (Easterby-Smith et al., 2012; Saunders et al., 2009).

However, it has to be noted that the interpretive stance taken, is not only about eliciting and describing individual views. Rather, also "groups of people create and then share understandings with each other" (Rubin & Rubin, 2012, p. 19). Thus "contending and overlapping versions of reality" exist (Rubin & Rubin, 2012, p. 22). It is regarded as valuable to focus on these "contending and overlapping versions of reality" because they represent the basis for the social construction of phenomena. The interest is not only on the individual views but on how these views inform action. Consequently, the focus shall not be exclusively on the individual views but on contending and overlapping versions of reality. It is believed that "the 'truth' of a particular idea is reached through discussion and agreement between the main protagonists" (Easterby-Smith et al., 2012, p. 19). Based on these assumptions, findings "may be relevant to theory or may be the basis of proposed action" (Rubin & Rubin, 2012, p. 23). With regard to the epistemological assumptions this involves that the nature of knowledge can be described as "individual reconstructions coalescing around consensus" (Guba & Lincoln, 1994, p. 112) and that knowledge can be accumulated in the form of "more informed and sophisticated reconstructions" (Guba & Lincoln, 1994, p. 112).

The underlying assumptions embodied in the theoretical perspective **inform the methodology, provide a context for the research and represent a basis for its logic and criteria** (Crotty, 1998). The key elements of the theoretical perspective, the reasoning and logic of enquiry and the methodology are shown in Figure 20. The emphasis on describing, understanding and explaining human behaviour influences the way in which the research gap shall be addressed. Using the in-depth focus on specifically selected areas of management, insights shall be gained that describe the behaviour of mittelständische companies, which shall help to understand the relevance of VBM accordingly. Openness towards new aspects and multiple perspectives is regarded as crucial to develop an understanding of the phenomenon and identify potential tenative explanations. Evolving from the theoretical perspective, interpretations shall be placed into a social scientific framework which involves the relation of the findings to the existing body of knowledge and gaining insights with regard to the overall research gap. Thus, a semi-structured approach shall be taken. The empathetic stance is reflected by focusing on owner-manager's practical experience. These aspects are also considered in the choice and use of methods, which will be described in the next subsection.

Figure 20: Theoretical perspective of the research approach

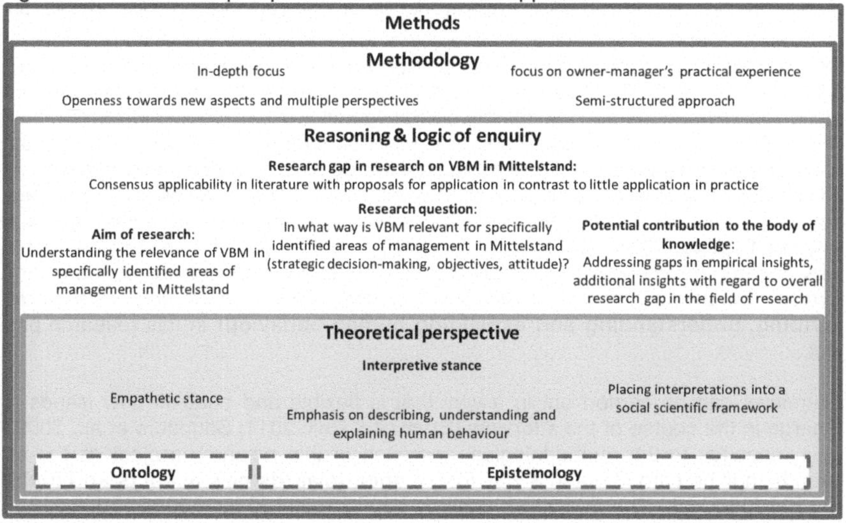

3.6 Methods

In this section the choice and use of methods, i.e. "the techniques and procedures used to gather and analyse data related to some research question or hypothesis" (Crotty, 1998, p. 3) will be outlined. This encompasses the choice of interviews as a method of data collection (see subsection 3.6.1), outlining decisions regarding the sample, sampling techniques (see subsection 3.6.2) and getting access (see subsection 3.6.3) as well as the way in which the interviews shall be conducted (see subsection 3.6.4) and data shall be analysed (see subsection 3.6.6). Furthermore, it is described how the fieldwork in form of a pilot and a main study are conducted (see subsection 3.6.5).

3.6.1 Interviews as a method of data collection

Within an interpretive stance, several methods of data collection can be used. Interviews are a method of data collection that is suitable to interpretive research approaches (Saunders et al., 2009; Stokes & Wall, 2014). It has been decided to carry out **semi-structured, in-depth interviews**. This decision is grounded within the methodological approach. As will be shown in the following, interviews as a method of data collection can be conducted in a way that enables gaining in-depth insights into owner-manager's practical experience. At the same time interviews can be open and semi-structured. Thus, interviews can reflect the four key aspects of the methodological approach.

Interviews can be used to gain rich, detailed answers (Bryman & Bell, 2011; Stokes & Wall, 2014). This suits the **in-depth focus** of this research project. Interviews provide an "opportunity to discuss and reveal experience, as much as possible, in their own terms and through their own perspectives in an in-depth manner" (Stokes & Wall, 2014, p. 149). Thus, the meaning and interpretation the interviewee attaches to a phenomenon based on his/her worldview can be captured (Bryman & Bell, 2011, Kvale, 1996 according to Easterby-Smith et al., 2012). This suits the **focus on owner-manager's practical experience** and the **empathetic stance** that shall be taken in this research project. In doing so, an understanding can be gained, not only of the viewpoint of the participants but also "why they have this particular viewpoint" (King, 1996, according to Easterby-Smith et al., 2012, p. 132) and what they regard "as important in explaining and understanding events, patterns, and forms of behaviour" (Bryman & Bell, 2011, p. 467). This suits the emphasis on **describing, understanding and explaining human behaviour** in this research project.

Interviews can be carried out in a way that is flexible and enables new issues to emerge in the course of the interview (Bryman & Bell, 2011; Saunders et al., 2009). This responds to the methodological approach of this research project as the research shall be carried out in a way that is **open towards new aspects and multiple perspectives**. The interviews shall be semi-structured as a semi-structured interview allows not only for flexibility but also for gaining specific and systematic data (Stokes & Wall, 2014). This fits the methodological approach of this research project as the interpretations shall be **placed in a social scientific framework**. Easterby-Smith et al. (2012, p. 132) note that interviews are regarded as appropriate "when the step-by-step-logic of a situation is not clear". Thus, interviews are regarded as suitable to **gain insights given the research gap and the differing existing results regarding the importance of the increase of the company value as objective** (for details see section 3.3 and subsection 2.4.3.2).

It has to be noted that the way in which interviews are conducted may vary considerably (Bryman & Bell, 2011). Thus details on how the interviews shall be conducted and how these reflect the aspects of the methodological approach will be given in subsection 3.6.4. The aspects outlined are also considered in the choices regarding sampling which will be outlined in the next subsection.

3.6.2 Sampling technique

For an empirical investigation a sample is drawn from a population. Sampling is done by applying techniques to select cases for investigation from the overall population (Stokes, 2011). A form of sampling that is often used in qualitative research is **purposive sampling** (Bryman & Bell, 2011). This suits the methodological approach of this research project and will be applied in accordance with the following considerations. In purposive sampling subjects are selected in a strategic way so that they are relevant for the research question (Bryman & Bell, 2011). Often a variety in the sample shall be ensured and subjects are selected as they are regarded as relevant to understanding a social phenomenon (Bryman & Bell, 2011).

According to Saunders et al. (2009) it is important that there is a logical relationship between the sampling technique, the size of the sample and the purpose of the research. In qualitative research, data is usually collected until **data saturation** is achieved, i.e. additional new data provides no or only a few new insights (Saunders et al., 2009). When the sample is drawn from a heterogeneous population, as in the study at hand (see sections 2.1 and 3.2), Saunders et al. (2009) would follow the recommendation of Creswell (2007) and would expect 25 to 30 interviews.

Several strategies may be applied within purposive sampling (for an outline of common purposive sampling techniques see e.g. Saunders et al., 2009, pp. 237–240). In consideration of the research approach and the characteristics of the population, heterogeneous and homogeneous sampling are suitable purposive sampling strategies.[61] However, a **conflict of aims of the methodological approach** becomes evident in relation to selecting one of these strategies. Heterogeneous sampling is beneficial to allow for openness towards new aspects and multiple perspectives. Homogeneous sampling, in contrast, might allow for more possibilities for comparison, which is advantageous for gaining in-depth insights. This is also influenced by the breadth and depth of the insights gained in the interviews. In this respect, it is expected that owner-managers in Mittelstand will only be available for an interview of at most an hour, which might limit the potential for in-depth insights.[62] Without having conducted interviews, it is difficult to evaluate whether heterogeneous or homogeneous sampling is more suitable in this context. Thus, the pilot study shall yield insights with regard to these aspects. Based on this rationale, a sample of rather heterogeneous companies is selected for the pilot study to have some point of reference to judge whether it is still possible to gain in-depth insights. The sample of the pilot study is heterogeneous in terms of size and industry, as well as ownership and management structure (for details see subsection 3.6.5.1). The insights from the pilot study suggest that it is beneficial to apply **heterogeneous sampling** with a stronger industrial and regional focus as well as based on a nar-

[61] Extreme case sampling, typical case sampling and critical case sampling are regarded as difficult in the context of Mittelstand. As Mittelstand is a heterogeneous population, it would be difficult to identify extreme, typical or critical cases. Furthermore, they are less suitable in light of two crucial aspects of the research approach. Heterogeneous and homogeneous sampling provide more potential to gain in-depth insights and being open towards new aspects and multiple perspectives at the same time.

[62] Owner-managers are expected to be very busy given their crucial role in Mittelstand and Mittelstand's general characteristics (for details see subsection 2.1.3).

rower definition of Mittelstand. Firstly, the focus shall be on manufacturing companies in Baden-Württemberg. This is valuable given that Mittelstand is not only important for the German economy but also crucial for the economy in Baden-Württemberg. Furthermore, the manufacturing industry seems to be even more important for Baden-Württemberg than for Germany as a whole (for details see subsection 2.1.4 and Appendices-Figure 7).

Secondly, the diversity of the insights gained in the pilot study suggests to use quantitative criteria to supplement the qualitative criteria of the Mittelstand definition. The reasoning of Becker, Staffel, and Ulrich (2008) is followed in two ways. Firstly, they express the view that externally-managed Mittelstand loses the specific character of Mittelstand with an increasing size (Becker, Staffel et al., 2008). Based on a growth threshold identified by Simon (1992) they thus argue that in addition to fulfilling qualitative criteria rough quantitative criteria should be used to supplement the definition of Mittelstand for externally-managed companies. Following the definition of Becker, and Fischer et al. (2008) for the main study, externally-managed companies are only regarded as Mittelstand up to a number of employees of roughly 3.000 and/or a turnover of roughly 600 Mio. Euro. Secondly, it is decided to exclude micro enterprises. Following the remark of Becker, and Staffel et al. (2008) companies with less than 30 employees are therefore excluded. In this respect the study at hand is in line with the reasoning of part of previous empirical studies on VBM in Mittelstand. While using different thresholds Khadjavi (2005), Krol (2009c) and Tappe (2009) all exclude micro or small enterprises as they argue that it can be assumed that these are not suitable users of VBM management concepts.[63] This is due to the limited resources, the comparably lower complexity and the clearer radius of action.

It needs to be emphasised that despite using quantitative supplementary criteria, the definition of Mittelstand underlying this work builds upon qualitative criteria (for details see subsection 2.1.2.3). Consequently, each company needs to be evaluated separately with regard to fulfilment of the definition of Mittelstand. Wolter and Hauser (2001) regard this as unrealistic, especially for statistical survey. However, qualitative characteristics are regarded as fundamental for Mittelstand and the methodological approach with an expected sample size of 25 to 30 interviews allows for a separate evaluation of each company. Thus, the related effort is accepted. The definition of "Mittelstand" and the sampling strategy used for the main study are summarised in Figure 21.

Given the expected difficulties in getting access, the overall purposive sampling strategy is supplemented by snowball sampling and convenience sampling. This involves that interviewees are asked whether they can recommend further potential

[63] Krol (2009c, pp. 18–20) follows the definition of IfM Bonn and excludes micro enterprises with less than 10 employees. Khadjavi (2005, pp. 52–55) makes use of the definition of the EU commission and excludes micro entreprises and small companies with less than 50 employees and a turnover of less than 10 Mio. Euro. Tappe (2009, pp. 20, 22, 196) mentions different employee thresholds (50, 100, 150) and finally aims at companies with 150 to 1,000 companies. This shows that the threshold is a difficult decision. As the upper limit for externally managed companies is defined on the basis of Becker, Staffel, and Ulrich (2008), it is regarded as consistent to similarly define the lower limit.

interviewees. Furthermore, the researcher makes use of her contacts to recruit participants for the sample. This includes considering companies the researcher already has contact with for participation. Additionally, two professors and a former employee of the German job centre are asked whether they can recommend potential participants. Using snowball sampling and convenience sampling is susceptible to influences that are beyond the control of the researcher (Saunders et al., 2009). Thus, in line with Saunders et al.'s (2009) respective comments, these sampling techniques are used with caution and mainly to recruit participants for the pilot study. Furthermore, a considerable part of the sample is recruited without making use of snowball sampling and recommendations.[64]

Figure 21: Definition of Mittelstand and sampling strategy underlying the research project

Mittelständische companies are companies

- where single natural persons or family members hold at least 50 % of the shares (directly or indirectly) and
- have a significant influence on the management of the company (directly or indirectly) and
- that are legally and economically independent from corporate groups.

Sampling strategy: heterogeneous sampling within modified, narrower definition of "Mittelstand"

- Heterogeneity esp. with regard to size and ownership and management structure
- Manufacturing industry
- Baden-Württemberg
- Externally-managed companies are only regarded as "Mittelstand" up to a number of employees of roughly 3.000 and/or a turnover of roughly 600 Mio. Euro
- Exclusion of companies with less than 30 employees and/or a turnover of roughly 6 Mio. Euro

3.6.3 Approach to getting access

Access is a critical aspect for the success of a research project (Saunders et al., 2009). It is necessary to identify companies and intended interviewees before being able to approach the intended interviewees with the aim of getting access. Thus, the **approach to getting access in this research project involves the following four steps**:

1) Identifying companies
   At first, companies are identified from different sources.[65] This is beneficial in terms of the heterogeneous sampling strategy.

[64] For the main study only one third of the contacts made is based on a recommendation or on snowball sampling. For details on the contacts made for the main study and the respective outcome see Appendices-Figure 12.

[65] The sources for identifying companies are named in Appendices-Figure 8. Appendices-Figure 8 includes details of the first three steps of the approach to getting access.

2) Checking companies consecutively
   The identified companies are checked consecutively with regard to whether they fulfil the definition of Mittelstand underlying this research project.[66] The main source for this is the company website. Due to the specifics of the definition underlying this research project this is a rather time-consuming process as the homepage must be browsed in search of information to judge whether the qualitative criteria are fulfilled or not. In addition, not all information necessary might be available. Especially in relation to the significant influence of the owners on management, this can probably only be completely assessed through certain questions during the interview.
3) Identifying intended interviewee
   The identification of the internded interviewee is a clear decision in case of only one owner-manager. If the company is led by several owner-managers, one of them needs to be selected. To do this in a consistent way, guiding principles are formulated.[67] Still, the selection is a rather time-consuming process and it might be impossible to identify the intended interviewee if the respective information is not given.
4) Making contact
   After a Mittelstand company and the respective intended interviewee are identified, the intended interviewee can be contacted with the aim of getting access.

An overview of the steps involved in getting access is shown in Figure 22. Of the companies identified only a small share will pass all steps and agree to participate in the research project. A considerable number of companies will either be excluded or will refuse to grant access. This can, in both cases, either be a final decision or a decision only for this point in time.

[66] Notes on details of checking companies are shown in Appendices-Figure 8.
[67] The principles applied are named in Appendices-Figure 8.

Figure 22: Steps involved in getting access

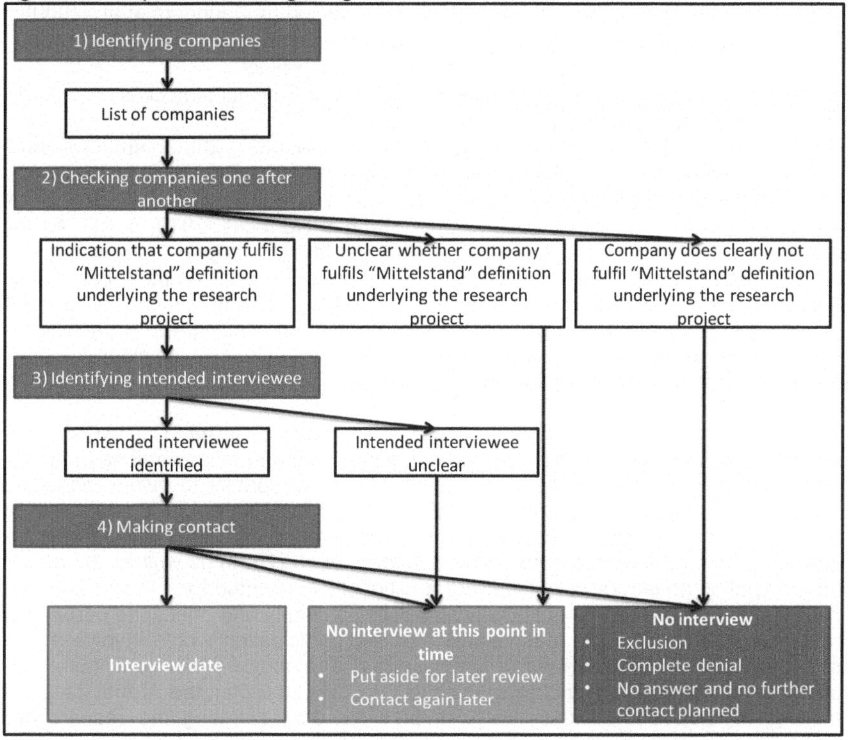

Given that a lot of time and effort is already devoted to each intended interviewee to be contacted in step 4, a well-thought-out approach to making contact and a careful preparation before each contact shall yield a high success rate in making contact.[68] In line with this decision the details of the approach to making contact will be outlined in the following.

The **approach to making contact** is developed in paying attention to the aspects that need to be considered in getting access according to Saunders et al. (2009) and the proposed strategies to gain access. Firstly, potential difficulties in getting physical access are accounted for. In this respect, it is considered that owner-managers as intended interviewees are part of the top management level and expected to be busy. Additionally, cognitive access is crucial for semi-structured interviews. Cognitive access means that the intended participants are willing to share information with the researcher which enables the researcher to address his/her

[68] A well-thought-out approach is regarded as being more efficient than spending less time on making contact, which is expected to lead to a lower success rate. This seems to be less efficient as it would be necessary to carry out all steps of getting access for more companies to achieve a comparable number of interview appointments.

research question and objectives. As the researcher is an external researcher, specific attention is paid to the following aspects addressed by Saunders et al. (2009):

- Demonstration of research competence and integrity
- Clear and concise explanation of the research project
- Sensitivity to goodwill and fostering it at each level level of access
- Potentially important role of a gatekeeper

A gatekeeper is defined in a narrow sense as “the person ... who controls research access” (Saunders et al., 2009, p. 592) and in a slightly broader sense as “someone who has the authority to grant or deny permission to access potential participants and/or the ability to facilitate such access” (King & Horrocks, 2010, p. 31). As the intended participants are at the top management level it is upon them to grant or deny access. However, a secretary or other persons in the company can act as gatekeeper as they might facilitate or impede getting in contact with the intended interviewee. Based on these general considerations the resulting approach includes **four key elements**. These are displayed in Figure 23. The key considerations will be briefly addressed in the following.

At first, contact to the intended interviewee will be made by **letter**. This way of making initial contact acknowledges the role of secretaries and other persons in the organisation as potential gatekeepers. Given that direct contact to owner-managers via e-mail or telephone is probably difficult it is more likely that a letter will be passed on to the intended interviewee for consideration. However, this is also not guaranteed and the issues outlined by Saunders et al. (2009) as well as the advice on formulating an introductory letter are additionally accounted for.[69] In line with this, the letter is formulated in a polite way and outlines clearly and briefly the purpose of research. Additionally, the letter states that the participation would involve a personal and confidential interview of approximately one hour. Furthermore, numerous small decisions shall contribute to creating a good basis for the further steps of making contact. Some illustrative examples for demonstrating the researcher's competence and credibility are shown in Figure 24.

Secondly, the letter is followed-up by a **telephone call** approximately 1,5 weeks after sending the letter. In this telephone call the relevant information is repeated to the intended interviewee, further details are given and questions from the intended interviewee are answered. This aims at convincing the intended interviewee to grant access and agreeing an interview date. It is considered that the call might be answered by a receptionist, a secretary or another employee of the company and that several calls might be needed to talk to the intended interviewee directly. Again, the general aspects addressed by Saunders et al. (2009) have been accounted for in deciding on details (for illustrative examples see Figure 24).

When the telephone call is successful and access is granted it is still important to pay attention to the aspects addressed. This involves further establishing the credibility of the researcher by sending a **project description via e-mail** after agreeing the interview appointment. This gives a brief summary of the research project adapted to owner-managers as interviewees. In this e-mail the researcher thanks

[69] The template used for the letter is displayed in Appendices-Figure 9. A translation of the text into English is shown in Appendices-Figure 10.

the interviewee for the willingness to give insights into his/her knowledge and experience on the date agreed. In addition, particular attention is paid to the information given before starting the **interview** and also to the interviewer's appearance at the interview.

Figure 23: Key elements of making contact with the intended interviewees

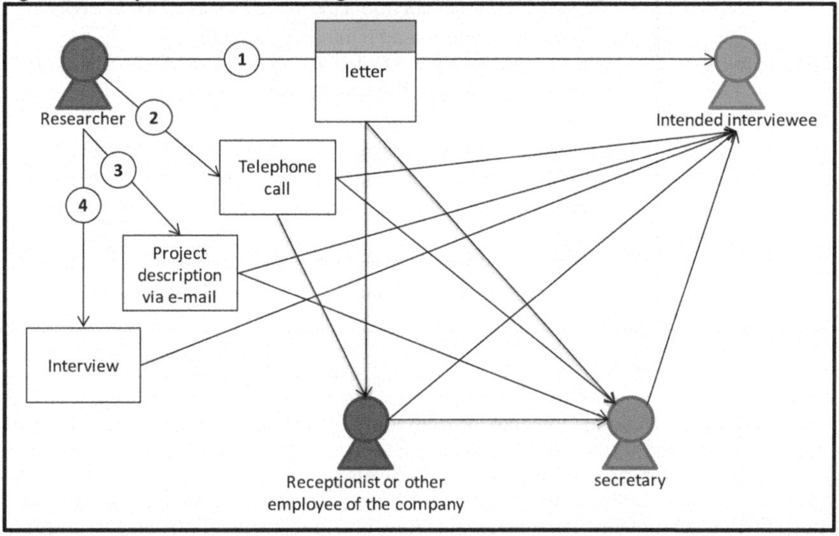

All elements of making contact address the need to communicate the research project clearly and concisely and demonstrate the researcher's competence. This is not only considered in relation to the intended interviewee but also in relation to potential gatekeepers. This is also accounted for in the implementation of the elements. Some illustrative examples are shown in Figure 24.

Figure 24: Examples for consideration of the need to demonstrate researcher's competence in the approach to making contact

Element of making contact	**Aspects that shall contribute to a favourable perception of the researcher's competence and credibility**
Letter	• Use of letter paper of Pforzheim University, where the researcher works at the time of the fieldwork and which is an established and well-known university in Baden-Württemberg
	(figure continued on next page)

Element of making contact	Aspects that shall contribute to a favourable perception of the researcher's competence and credibility
Letter & telephone call	• If the intended interviewee has been recommended by another person (e.g. a professor or another interviewee) this person is mentioned (only when this person has agreed) • Researcher finds out about the specific role of the intended interviewee and addresses him/her in this role
Telephone call	• Preparation of notes of what to say to persons with different roles who might answer the telephone (i.e. receptionist, secretary, intended interviewee) • Familiarisation with notes on characteristics of the company made when checking the company, mentioning one or two aspects if suitable to show that researcher has informed herself about the company • Take notes on date, time, dialogue partner and content of each telephone conversation, these are considered in subsequent telephone calls

The research approach is **specific in another aspect of getting access**. In negotiating access, the key topics of the interview are presented to the interviewees as strategic decision-making, the use of management tools, objectives and management in Mittelstand. Value-based management is not mentioned but couched in more general terms as management in Mittelstand for the following reasons. The literature review mentioned the existence of understandings of value that are alternative to that underlying VBM and that there is a debate on VBM and its implications (see subsection 2.3.2.2). Differences in the understanding of value as well as a positive or negative attitude towards VBM might influence the perceived value of the research project and thus the decision to participate. However, it is not possible to consider upfront how this might influence the decision to participate. One reason for this is that there are only few and ambiguous results in relation to the attitude towards VBM in Mittelstand (for details see subsection 2.4.4.2). As this research shall give insights into multiple perspectives it is preferred to refer to the more general term management. In doing this, insights can be gained without the sample being influenced by the attitude of the interviewees towards VBM. Only on this basis, insights into the relevance of VBM in the selected areas of management in 'ordinary' Mittelstand can be gained.

The approach to getting access is applied and monitored in several rounds. This includes analysing the characteristics of the companies in the sample after each round of interviews in light of the heterogeneous sampling strategy. This finally results in a sample with adequate heterogeneity (for details on the sample see section 4.1). The reflection after each round of interviews also shows that the strategy to get access has paid off (for details on the main study see subsection 3.6.5.2).

3.6.4 *Conducting semi-structured, in-depth interviews*

The key aspects of the methodological approach are considered in the interview guide. The **four parts of the interview guide** reflect the supplementary research questions. This relation is shown in Figure 25. Part 1 on strategic decision-making shall provide the background for and initial insights into the first and second supplementary research questions. This includes asking about the strategic decisions taken in the company in the last years and the follow-up request of a description how a decision is taken for one of these. In part 2 these research questions are then addressed by more direct questions on the use of management tools in SDM. Insights regarding the third and fourth research question shall be gained in the third part on objectives of the company. Part 4 on value-based management provides the basis for the fifth supplementary research question. The key research question will then be reflected upon on the basis of the insights gained with regard to the supplementary questions.

Figure 25: Relation of the parts of the interview guide to the research questions

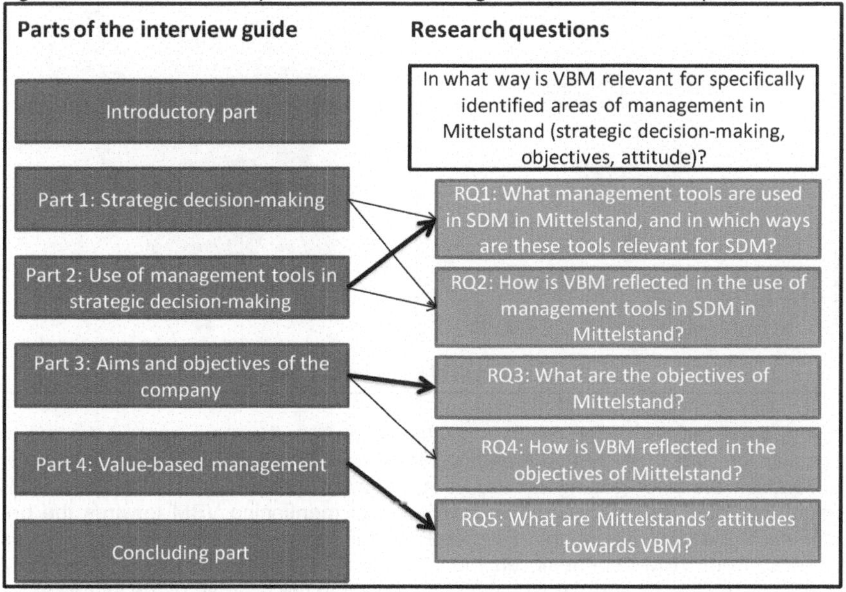

The **detailed interview guide** has been developed based on Helfferich (2011). Each part starts with a relatively open question which shall spur a detailed and in-depth narrative. This enables gaining in-depth insights and being open towards new aspects and multiple perspectives. To be able to identify conformities and differences to previous research, aspects are noted to recognise particularly relevant aspects. These and respective formulations of questions can then be used during the interview to follow these up.

The **order of the parts of the interview guide** follows a specific rationale that is visualised in Figure 26. In the first part, strategic decision-making is addressed on a general level before narrowing down to the role of management tools in SDM in the second part. In the third part there is a shift to the objectives of the company, which is followed by the part addressing the attitude towards VBM. This can be regarded as a shift back from the specific level to a more general level. The alternative to move from general themes to more specific issues is obviously neglected in favour of the order chosen.

Figure 26: Comparison of two ways of ordering the parts of the interview guide

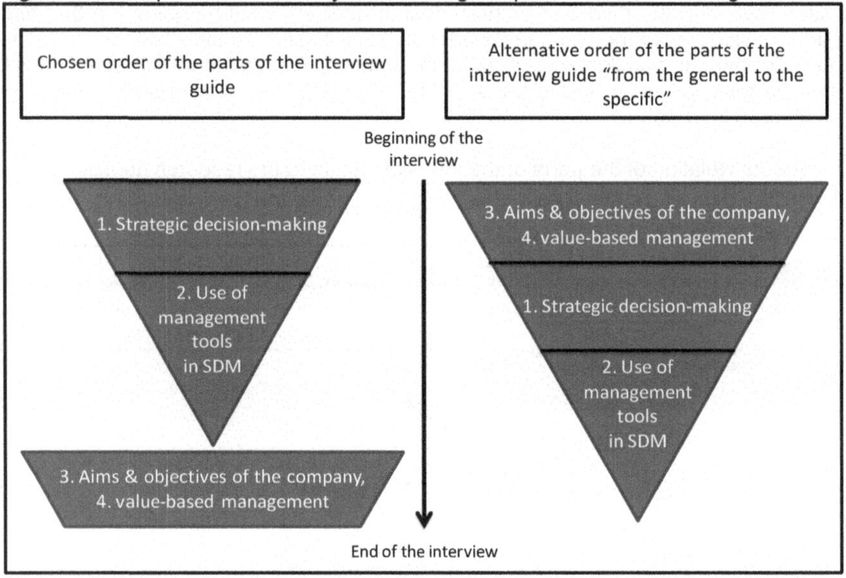

It was deliberately decided not to follow the order from the more general themes to specific topics for mainly two reasons. Firstly, in line with the rationale outlined in subsection 3.6.3 for getting access, it is assumed that the attitude towards VBM might influence the interview. This involves that mentioning VBM towards the beginning of the interview might influence the outlines in the first three parts towards or away from VBM depending on the attitude of the owner-manager. Thus, VBM shall only be directly addressed by the interviewer in the last part of the interview.

Secondly, the alternative order of going from the general to the specific might involve details of the decision-making process that are not in line with the overall objectives being omitted. However, these might be especially interesting given the differing findings in relation to the relevance of the increase of the company value as an objective. When interpreting the results of part of the existing empirical studies in light of the selected areas of management addressed in this thesis, there might be a gap between the relevance of VBM for Mittelstand's objectives and its relevance for strategic decision-making. Addressing the different aspects of the topic in the order mentioned above provides more potential for evaluating whether this is the case for the sample at hand or not. This is because the approach provides potential to capture details of SDM that might be in contradiction to the company objectives. This involves the underlying assumption that while a person might omit details not fitting into the "overall picture" there are fewer tendencies to paint the "overall picture" differently so that it suits the details already given.

The aspects of the methodological approach also have a significant influence on the **questions posed** in the specific parts of the interview guide. An illustrative example is that the focus of the questions in part 1 is on generating a detailed narrative of at least one specific strategic decision. In comparison to other alternatives this provides most potential for thick descriptions.[70] These are necessary to gain in-depth insights into the role of management tools in strategic decision-making practices in Mittelstand. Only then can it be evaluated whether and how this reflects VBM.

The **interview guide is tried out and revised in the pilot study** (for details on the pilot study and the implications for the research approach see subsection 3.6.5.1). The resulting changes involve including an open question regarding the understanding of VBM in part 4 of the interview guide as the findings of the pilot study show that the attitude towards VBM is influenced by the understanding of VBM. Part 2 is changed in that it starts with a question regarding the evaluation of the profitability in strategic decision-making. In addition, a question regarding the use of the net present value method is included.

3.6.5 Conducting the fieldwork

In the following, insights into the considerations involved in conducting the pilot and the main study are summarised.

3.6.5.1 Pilot study

The **pilot study** serves three purposes:

- Gaining interview experience
- Refining the approach to sampling
- Refining the interview guide

For **refining the approach to sampling** in line with the rationale outlined in subsection 3.6.2, a sample of 5 rather heterogeneous companies is selected for the pilot study. This shall provide a point of reference to evaluate whether the aim to gain in-depth insights can still be achieved. The companies selected for the pilot study differ in three aspects, i.e. in terms of:

- size
- industry
- ownership and management structure

The characteristics of the companies in the pilot study are displayed in Appendices-Figure 11. All companies fulfil the qualitative criteria of the definition of Mittelstand

[70] Other alternatives included asking about how strategic decisions are taken on a more general level.

underlying this work. In terms of **size** the sample ranges from a company with 12 employees (I-1) to a company with several thousand employees (I-3). Two other companies (I-2 and I-7) have around 400 employees. The fifth company has approximately 160 employees. This heterogeneity in terms of size is also evident when applying common definitions of SMEs (see Appendices-Figure 11). The companies are also heterogeneous in terms of **industry**. Three companies are manufacturing companies (I-2, I-3, I-4). One company (I-1) is a trading firm in the business-to-business segment. The fifth company (I-7) is a public transport company. The companies are also different in terms of the **ownership and management structure**. I-1 has a single owner-manager. I-4 has three owners with leadership positions in the company. In I-7 there is a key owner-manager and additional owner-managers. There is also I-2 with one owner-manager and another owner who is not involved in managing the company. In I-3 there are several owners who are descendants of the founder. The company is managed by an external chief executive officer (CEO) and the owners influence the management indirectly.

Insights are gained on the basis of a pragmatic data analysis.[71] The insights indicate that the companies **differ in terms of internal aspects as well as in terms of the business environment**. As this limits the possibilities of gaining an in-depth understanding of the phenomenon the sample in the main study shall be more homogeneous than in the pilot study. Considerable differences have been found in internal processes, which makes it difficult to compare the companies.[72] Consequently, it is decided to exclude small companies as well as using a modified definition of Mittelstand which excludes large companies when there is only an indirect influence of the owners on the management. Resulting from the differences in the business environment it is beneficial to focus on one industry i.e. manufacturing companies (for the resulting sampling strategy see subsection 3.5.2).

The pilot study also leads to changes of the **interview guide**. A major insight is that there are different understandings of VBM. Despite the fact that the understanding derived from literature has been explicated to the interviewees and that they have been asked to state to what extent this is relevant for them, they comment on the relevance of VBM from the perspective of their own understanding. This understanding of VBM differs in most cases, to a considerable extent, to the understanding derived from literature. In addition, there seem to be remarkable differences in the understanding of VBM among the interviewees. Thus, the approach is changed to first asking the interviewees for their understanding of VBM. Then the understanding derived from literature on VBM in Mittelstand is introduced to the interviewees and they are asked for their views on it. Consequently, research question 5 is modified in the following way:

What are Mittelstands' understanding of and attitudes towards VBM?

[71] This includes listening to the record of each interview and taking notes, reading the transcript several times and writing a summary for each interview. After analysing all interviews in this way a comparative analysis is done.

[72] This includes for example that according to I-3 a lot more different people with differing interests are involved in strategic decision-making and in determining the company objectives than for I-1 where the single owner-manager plays a crucial role. It is thus difficult to gain in-depth insights by comparing these companies with each other and with the other companies.

Changes are also made to the second part of the interview guide on the use of management tools in strategic decision-making. It is recognised that many interviewees switch to the company level when they are asked about the role of management tools in SDM. Then, there is repeated use of the term "management tool". When talking about aspects related to the use of management tools in the first part on SDM the interviewees referred to profitability ("Wirtschaftlichkeit"). As the research question focuses on such use of management tools in SDM, the wording of the introductory question to the second part of the interview guide is changed accordingly. The interviewer now asks about the evaluation of profitability in SDM instead of asking about the respective use of management tools. In fact the question still aims at the use of management tools but the language has been changed to be more near to that of the interviewees used in the context of SDM. Thus there is a more gentle transition from the first to the second part of the interview guide.

In the second part another change is introduced. In the analysis of the pilot study it is difficult to establish the link with VBM. While some of the interviewees indirectly address aspects that suit VBM's basic economic view, none of the interviewees directly refers to a management tool that is in line with VBM. This leaves the researcher with the difficulty of not knowing whether these tools are not used or just not mentioned because no respective question is asked. While still keeping to the principle, not to mention VBM directly in the first three parts, it is decided to introduce a direct question focusing on the use of VBM management tools at the end of this part. Thus, the interviewees are asked whether the net present value method is used. The reference to the net present value method provides the possibility to compare the findings to several previous empirical studies (for details see subsection 2.4.2.2).
Overall, the pilot study has allowed gaining interview experience and refining the approach to sampling as well as the interview guide. This is a sound basis for the main study.

3.6.5.2 Main study

The **main study** was conducted from July 2015 to June 2016. In this period the main study was conducted in three rounds with breaks of several weeks in between. An overview is shown in Figure 27.

The main study confirms the expectation that getting access is a challenging and time-consuming process. The approach is successful in that making contact to 45 intended interviewees resulted in 30 interviews.[73] However, slightly more than 100 companies have been checked to identify potential interviewees to be contacted and several telephone calls to follow up the letter were usually needed. The approach to getting access requires carefully managing the process of following up the letters. This is one factor in the decision to carry out the main study in several rounds. As the researcher contacts a manageable number of potential interviewees in each round she is able to comply with the preferred date of the potential interviewees. Furthermore, breaks between the rounds of interviews are valuable for reflection on the fieldwork. During the second break for example initial insights into

[73] For an overview of the contacts made see Appendices-Figure 12.

the findings are gained, which are valuable to later evaluate the level of data saturation.

Figure 27: Overview three rounds of interviews of the main study

Round no.	Number of interviews	Period of time
1)	4	July & August 2015
2)	12	October to December 2015
3)	14	April to June 2016
Total	30	July 2015 to June 2016

As it is not only necessary to gain physical access but also important to gain cognitive access (Saunders et al., 2009) each interview is prepared carefully in advance. An overview of the information gathered is shown in Appendices-Figure 13. Despite this careful preparation it is not always possible to clearly assess in advance whether a company is in line with the Mittelstand definition and sampling strategy of this research project. Thus, the relevant aspects are addressed at the end of the interview. On this basis, two interviews are not included in the sample.[74] Thus, a final sample of 28 interviews is analysed in the main study.

3.6.6 Data analysis

The method of data analysis is also chosen and applied in a way that reflects the key aspects of the research approach. The decision for template analysis has been made after considering two possibilities to distinguish methods for analysing qualitative data. This will be outlined in the following. Then, an overview of elements of template analysis and how these are implemented in the research at hand is given.

Firstly, qualitative data can be analysed using a **deductive or inductive approach** (Saunders et al., 2009). In adopting a deductive approach, theoretical propositions or practical commitments are used to guide data analysis. This is also referred to as “top down” approach to data analysis (King, 2012). In contrast, data is explored without a descriptive or theoretical framework determined in advance in inductive or “bottom up” approaches (King, 2012; Yin, 2003 according to Saunders et al., 2009). Saunders et al. (2009) emphasise that in research practice, data analysis may begin by adopting one of these approaches but will probably combine elements of both. Such a combination is in line with the research approach. Deductive elements suit the semi-structured approach that shall be taken. Inductive elements reflect the in-depth focus of this research and its openness towards new aspects and multiple perspectives.

Secondly, forms of data analysis are commonly distinguished with regard to whether they **focus on language or content** (for this paragraph see King

[74] In one case (I-22) the interview shows that the company purchases the manufacturing products it sells and does not produce them itself, which was not clear in advance. In the case of I-23 the number of employees was not clear in advance. The interview shows that the company has less than 30 employees.

& Horrocks, 2010). In the former it is analysed how language is used in social interaction. Empirical studies adopting the latter are "principally concerned with understanding their participants' lived experience from their own position" (King & Horrocks, 2010, p. 143). This is in line with the interpretive stance taken in this research and the focus on understanding owner-manager's experience.

On this basis, **template analysis as a specific type of thematic analysis** is chosen. Template analysis is a style of thematic analysis that provides a "clear, structured and systematic approach" (King & Horrocks, 2010, pp. 447–448) but is also flexible and can be adapted to the needs of a specific research project. As will become evident, template analysis focuses on interpreting the meaning of what is expressed by the interviewees and its key characteristics reflect a combination of deductive and inductive elements. Template analysis includes

- the identification of themes,
- the formulation of a priori themes,
- coding and
- the use of a template, which involves the development of an initial template and its modification into a final template.

These elements will be described in the following. In line with King and Horrocks's (2010) advice, the specifics of the research project are considered and the elements of the analytic process are modified accordingly.

In thematic analysis patterns in the data, so-called **themes**, shall be identified, analysed and reported (Braun & Clarke, 2006). In a common-sense way, it can be stated that a theme "captures something important about the data in relation to the research question, and represents some level of patterned response or meaning within the data set" (Braun & Clarke, 2006, p. 82). In relation to themes Braun and Clarke (2006) and King and Horrocks (2010) emphasise three aspects. Firstly, it includes some repetition within the data set. Secondly, the identification of themes and their prevalence involves the judgement of the researcher. Thirdly, themes should be distinctive. However, King and Horrocks (2010) also acknowledge that it is impossible to identify themes without overlap. In line with this, the definition of a theme given by King and Horrocks (2010, p. 15) shall be used in this research:

> "Themes are recurrent and distinctive features of participants' accounts, characterising particular perceptions and/or experiences, which the researcher sees as relevant to the research question."

One key element of template analysis is that the researcher can formulate some themes before starting data analysis (King, 2012; King & Horrocks, 2010). The **a priori themes** used in this research include themes resulting from the research questions such as "strategic decision-making", "objectives" and "value-based management". King (2012, p. 430) describes template analysis as being "in the middle ground between top down and bottom up styles of analysis". In this sense, additional a priori themes are used that have evolved from an initial familiarisation with the data. This includes for example "planning", which is repeatedly addressed by the interviewees and might be relevant in SDM.

Themes are identified based on **coding**. Coding is defined as "the process of attaching a label (code) to a section of text to index it relating to a theme" (King, 2012, p. 431). To prepare the interview material for coding it is transcribed. In this respect the advice of King and Horrocks (2010) is considered in several ways e.g. by using a transcription system to ensure that the transcription follows a consistent style. The system described by Dresing and Pehl (2013, pp. 20–25) is used. Beyond this the reseacher provided the transcriber with a glossary of terms, for example. As recommended, each transcript is proofread before coding (King, 2012). In line with King's (2012) and Braun and Clarke's (2006) advice there is a familiarisation before coding each transcript. Given the amount of data to be analysed it is decided to use software for coding and handling data.[75] Following King's (2012) advice, a sheet displaying the a priori themes is put next to the screen during coding. Then manageable chunks of data are read, key points highlighted, notes are taken on what is said and the data is initially coded. To grasp the meaning of what an interviewee says on the level of the complete interview, the sub-themes and codes are read after coding the complete interview. On this basis notes to summarise the insights gained in relation to each of the themes are taken. This is beneficial as the particular experience shall be analysed within the context of the full account of the participant (King & Horrocks, 2010). Furthermore, this contributes to balancing within-case and cross-case analysis, which is a key principle of thematic analysis (King & Horrocks, 2010).

The themes are organized in a **template** (Saunders et al., 2009). The construction of this template is another key element of template analysis (King & Horrocks, 2010). In template analysis the template is organised on the basis of the scope of the themes. Furthermore, the template is distinct as the number of hierarchical coding levels is not fixed. The depth of coding of individual aspects rather depends on how rich the insights are with regard to the research question (King & Horrocks, 2010). This is considered in relation to the a priori themes. The rather wide formulation of the a priori themes might make it difficult to gain as in-depth insights as intended. Thus, sub-themes are used from the beginning of data analysis. In relation to the application of VBM in strategic decision-making this, among others, includes a sub-theme for the use of VBM management tools and a sub-theme for the use of other management tools. As the literature review has outlined that VBM might potentially reflect in a different way (for details see subsection 2.4.2), sub-themes are also formulated to capture the consideration of VBM's basic economic view in SDM beyond the use of management tools.

Template analysis is also specific in that not all steps of the analysis are carried out on all transcripts (for details on the stages of thematic analysis see Braun & Clarke, 2006; King & Horrocks, 2010). Instead an **initial template** is developed on the basis of a sub-set of data (for the rest of this paragraph see King, 2012). This initial template is then applied, modified and re-applied to the whole data set. Thus, if carried out properly the data analysis is more efficient without a serious risk to the depth of the data analysis. This makes template analysis especially valuable for research projects which include 10 to 25 interviews with a duration of about an hour. This suits the estimate of the sample size in this research project. One quality criterion in carrying out thematic analysis is that the researcher records the major stages in the development of the template. These will be briefly outlined in the following.

[75] Saunders et al. (2009) additionally mention that the use of computer aided qualitative data analysis software usually makes the modification of the template more straightforward.

In relation to the number of interviews that shall be coded before developing the initial template there is no fixed rule (King, 2012). King and Horrocks (2010) mention six out of 20 interviews as an example. In King's (2012) outline of exemplary steps, one out of three focus groups is used to create the initial template. King (2012) mentions that the diversity of the accounts shall be considered. In the study at hand the initial template is created on the basis of 7 out of 28 interviews. In this decision the diversity of the accounts, which is particularly given for strategic decision-making, is balanced towards King's (2012) demand to use a priori themes tentatively. This includes always considering redefining or discarding a priori themes (King, 2012). While systematically coding the initial interviews the researcher has repeatedly found that a number of the sub-themes formulated in advance, on the basis of the research questions, does not adequately reflect the views expressed by the interviewees.[76] Thus, the researcher has decided to interrupt coding and has taken time for reflection on the codes, sub-themes and themes. On this basis it is decided to use different sub-themes that are broader and provide a more meaningful grouping of the codes that evolved from coding.[77] As the research is conducted by only one researcher it is not possible to develop the initial template in close cooperation with other researchers involved in the research project as in King's (2012) example. However, the researcher discusses the changes with the supervisory team and other doctoral students.

As described by King (2012), inadequacies of the initial template are revealed when systematically coding the full data set. These require different changes. **Modifications,** such as insertion of new sub-themes and giving a higher or lower order to a sub-theme, are not done immediately when the idea emerges. Instead, such ideas are noted during coding and then reflected on under consideration of a larger subset of the data. Thus, coding is interrupted for modification of the template again after coding 23 out of 28 transcripts. The process of modifying the template results in the **final template**. This still includes the broad themes defined a priori to cover the focus on strategic decision-making and objectives. However, in the process of analysing data these have been amended and added to in line with the general approach of template analysis (Saunders et al., 2009). This mainly includes changes on the level of sub-themes. Beyond this the scope of the theme on value-based management is defined more narrowly to cover the attitude of and understanding towards VBM. The continuous modification of the template ends when the researcher regards the template as "clear and thorough enough to serve as a basis for building an account of the findings" (King & Horrocks, 2010, p. 166). The resulting final template provides a structure for the outline of the findings.

3.7 Ethical considerations, transparency and reflexivity

Increasing attention is paid to **ethical considerations** in the context of doing research (Stokes, 2011). Broadly speaking, these shall protect the researcher and the

[76] This is the case for the sub-themes formulated to capture the potential additional aspect of whether elements of VBM's basic economic view reflect not only in the use of management tools but also in considerations involved in SDM. While there is reference to different aspects considered in SDM, it is difficult to relate them to these elements.

[77] In relation to the reflection of VBM's basic economic view it is decided to use the broader themes of "economic considerations" and "other considerations", for example.

respondents from harm during, but also before and after, the research project (Stokes, 2011). In addition to this general aim, the research governance handbook of the University of Chester names informed consent and confidentiality/anonymity as fundamental principles that shall be considered (University of Chester, 2016). Informed consent means that the participants express they are willing to participate in the research project (Stokes, 2011). The researcher needs to communicate sufficient information in an appropriate way to ensure that the participants are well informed before they decide to participate (University of Chester, 2016).

To ensure **informed consent**, the researcher provides the potential interviewees with key information when making contact via letter and in follow-up telephone call(s). When an interviewee agrees verbally to participate in the study, he/she receives a participant information sheet via e-mail before the interview. Furthermore, the project description is again handed over to the interviewee before starting the interview. In addition, the researcher repeats key information and explicitly points out that the interviewee always has the possibility not to answer questions, to end the interview or withdraw from the study. The interviewees are also asked for their agreement to record the interview and whether they have questions before beginning the interview. The interviewees are made aware that the researcher might use the data for later publications. During the fieldwork one interviewee indicates that he prefers the researcher to take notes instead of an audio record. Another interviewee explicitly asks to receive the transcript for approval. Both requests are met and the interviewees have not raised any further concerns. Informed consent is recorded, with the interviewee and the researcher signing an interview agreement.

Beyond this, attention is paid to ensure **confidentiality and anonymity**. This includes that the information given in the description of the sample (see section 4.1) does not always include specific numbers e.g. on the size of the company, but states the range to that the company and/or interviewee belongs. Furthermore, a confidentiality undertaking is agreed with the transcriber of the interviews. This includes an encrypted transfer of the interview records and the transcripts. In a few cases third persons are involved in getting access. This includes persons working for an interviewee such as his/her secretary. In addition, a number of interviewees have been recommended by a third person. In this case the potential interviewee is made aware of the recommendation in the introductory letter.[78] The researcher does not tell the person who has recommended the interviewee whether the interviewee agrees to participate or not. On this basis, each interviewee is aware of the people that are potentially aware of his/her participation and is able to decide on this basis whether he/she participates in the study or not. Overall, it must be considered that the intended interviewees are owner-managers of Mittelstand companies. Thus, it is assumed that they are experienced businesspeople and that no additional ethical precautions are necessary. Ethical approval has been sought and granted by the University of Chester.

In addition to ethical considerations a researcher should consider procedures related to the **quality of research**. In this respect reflexivity plays a key role in interpretivist approaches (Stokes & Wall, 2014). One understanding of reflexivity is that

[78] This is of course only done after previous approval of the person giving the recommendation.

it "involves the way in which the researcher and the research participants interact with each other during the course of a given project" (Stokes, 2011, p. 108). During the research there is a reciprocal influence of the researcher and the participants, which also has an effect on the data generated and the findings derived (Stokes, 2011). In this respect there is the demand to recognise ones "own role, values, beliefs and perspectives in generating the data and writing the research" (Stokes & Wall, 2014, p. 99). This includes how these affect the research approach and what implications the methods used and decisions taken have on the knowledge generated (Bryman & Bell, 2011). This shall not only happen after the interaction but also during the interaction (Bryman & Bell, 2011). Furthermore, the researcher shall provide the reader with information on how the data and findings evolved (Stokes, 2011). Overall, considering reflexivity and transparency suits the overall interpretive stance of this research.

Consequently, the researcher tries to achieve **transparency** by providing adequate information on the approach of this research project and its findings within the predefined boundaries of the thesis. In the sense of **reflexivity** the researcher's background is regarded as an influencing factor. Prior to the doctoral studies the academic education of the researcher had a strong emphasis on applied management. This included work experience during undergraduate studies. Furthermore, the researcher worked in a manufacturing company at the beginning of her doctoral studies. The researcher is thus not only interested in theoretical concepts of business and management research, but also in its effects on management in Mittelstand. This has an influence on the interpretive stance taken in this research in general and on several aspects of how the research is conducted. Examples are the approach to getting access as well as the way the interviews have been conducted. Furthermore, the researcher's interest in management of mittelständische companies as well as her interest in managerial accounting have influenced the research projects' focus on VBM in Mittelstand.

Based on the reflection on the interaction of the researcher and the interviewees it has been found crucial to demonstrate the researcher's competence and gain the interviewees' confidence. In this respect it is acknowledged that during the interviews there is an interaction of a female around the age of 30 and interviewees who will probably be mainly male and have considerable practical experience. Thus, many of the potential issues related to demonstrating credibility and obtaining confidence by Saunders et al. (2009) are considered. This includes looking for information on the company and the interviewee already before trying to get access and more extensively before the interview. Being able to draw upon such information helps to demonstrate competence and might encourage the interviewee to give a more detailed account (Saunders et al., 2009). Another example is acknowledging the impact of the first few minutes of the conversation and putting effort into being credible and friendly to establish confidence. Thus, not only the participant information sheet and the consent form were prepared in advance but also the verbal information given on the research project and the researcher.

Beyond this, attention is paid to ensure reflexivity throughout the research project. This includes recurrent breaks for reflection, e.g. breaks of a few days between interviews and breaks of a few weeks during data collection and analysis. During the breaks for reflection and throughout the research, notes are constantly taken. Beyond this, occurring thoughts are regularly shared and discussed with supervisors and other doctoral students.

3.8 Summary of the chapter

Firstly, background knowledge on specifics of the field of research has been developed (see section 3.2). The field of small business research seems to be a complex but rich field to carry out research. On the one hand, the phenomenon itself is often described as being complex and heterogeneous. On the other hand, the topic is addressed from a research community that is said to be heterogeneous. Beside this, there does not seem to be a dominating research paradigm and there are ongoing debates on the theoretical development of the field. Nevertheless, the proposals on how to conduct research in this context have been considered in developing the research approach.

Based on the overall research gap identified in the literature review, the aim of research is to gain an understanding of the relevance of value-based management in specifically identified areas of management in Mittelstand. This contributes to the body of knowledge as gaps in empirical insights are addressed. In addition, insights with regard to the overall research gap might be gained (for details see section 3.3).

In the research project an interpretive stance is taken which involves an empathetic stance and an emphasis on describing, understanding and explaining human behaviour. The insights are placed into a social scientific framework. Based on this theoretical perspective the methodological approach shall be semi-structured and involves an in-depth focus, a focus on owner-managers' practical experience as well as openness towards new aspects and multiple perspectives (see sections 3.4 and 3.5).

On the basis of this methodological approach semi-structured and in-depth interviews have been selected as the method of data collection. This choice reflects the four aspects of the methodological approach (for details see subsection 3.6.1). These aspects have also been considered in making decisions regarding sampling and getting access, designing the interview guide and in relation to the method of data analysis.

Regarding sampling, the in-depth focus and the openness towards new aspects and multiple perspectives are partly conflicting. Furthermore, due to a qualitative definition of Mittelstand, each company needs to be evaluated separately. On this basis the insights gained in the pilot study led to the decision to use a slightly more narrow definition of "Mittelstand" and focus on manufacturing companies in Baden-Württemberg. Together with a heterogeneous sampling strategy, this is a way which allows achieving both methodological aspects (for details see subsection 3.6.2).

As it is expected to be difficult to get access to owner-managers of Mittelstand the approach to getting access has been carefully reflected. This covers all steps of getting access and especially the different aspects involved in making contact (for details see subsection 3.6.3).

With regard to the interview guide, an important aspect is to use a specific rationale for the order of the parts. Additionally, the interviewer avoids using the term VBM in the first three parts of the interview. The approach to conducting interviews shall allow for gainging in-depth insights with a focus on owner-managers' practical experience and being open towards multiple perspectives and new aspects (for details see subsection 3.6.4).

The pilot study is conducted to gain interview experience and refine the sampling strategy as well as the interview guide before conducting the main study (for details see subsection 3.6.5).

Template analysis has been chosen as the method of data analysis. This allows relating the findings to the existing body of knowledge and to be open for new insights and multiple perspectives. This also reflects in how the elements of template analysis such as a priori themes are applied in the study at hand (for details see subsection 3.6.6).

The details of the research approach are designed under consideration of ethical aspects. Furthermore, reflexivity and transparency as quality criteria suitable to the interpretive stance of this research project have influenced the research approach (for details see subsection 3.7).

An overview of the research approach is shown in Figure 28.

Figure 28: Research approach

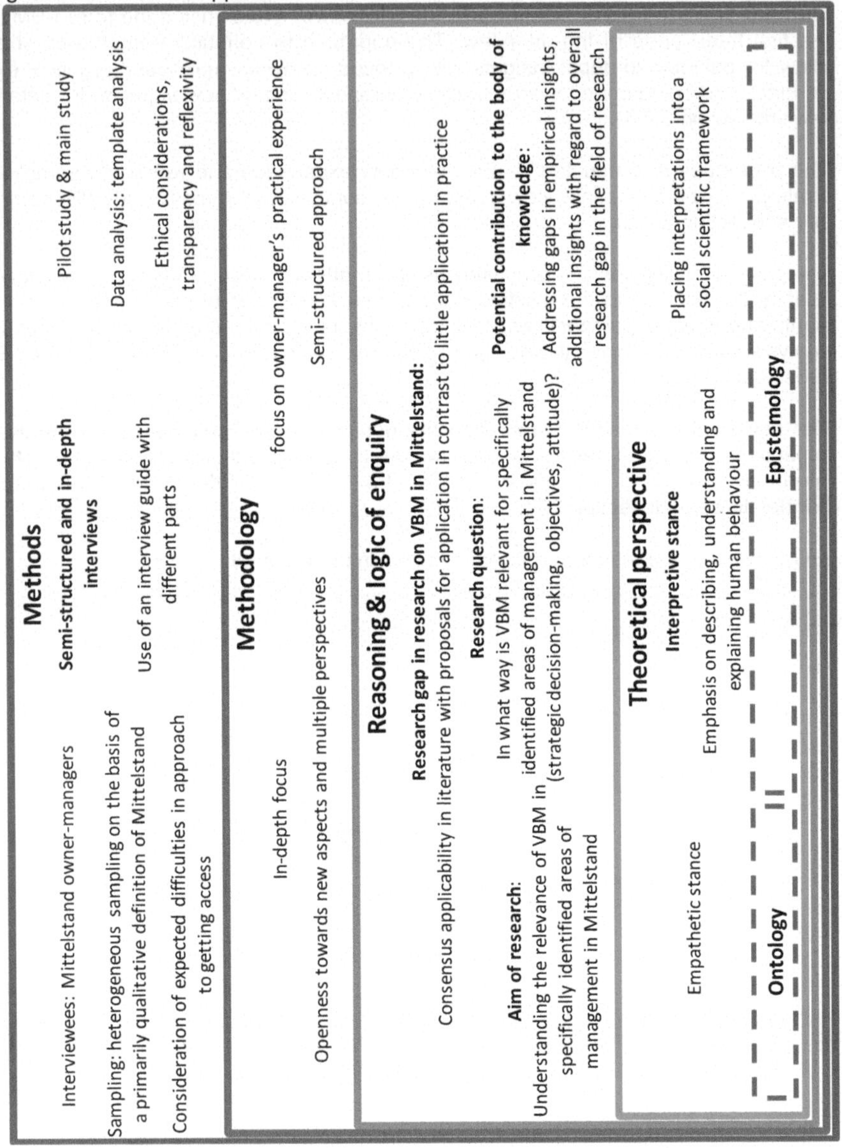

4 Findings and discussion

Firstly, this chapter describes the sample of the empirical study (section 4.1). Then, the findings gained in the relevance of VBM in specifically identified areas of management will be outlined and discussed. This starts with the findings in relation to strategic decision-making (section 4.2). Then, the analysis of objectives is presented (section 4.3). Finally, the understanding of and attitudes towards VBM are addressed (section 4.4).

In line with the research approach the focus is on developing an understanding of the relevance of VBM in each of these areas of management. This will be illustrated with views expressed by the interviewees. The reader shall have the possibility to evaluate the significance of such views. In addition to the content of the views, the outline provides information on how common the views are in the sample. In doing this, the format y/28 is used with y being the number of interviewees that refers to the views addressed. In a few instances, this format is modified to x/y/28. Then x states the number of interviewees of a subset of the interviewees y that expresses a certain view. This can be illustrated with an example from subsection 4.2.2.2. This states that a majority of 23 out of the 28 interviewees refers to strategic decisions in relation to market positioning, which is made evident with the amendment 23/28 in brackets at the end of the sentence. The following sentence then states that two thirds of these interviewees address this kind of decision extensively, which is clarified with the amendment 16/23/28 in brackets at the end of the sentence.[79]

All quotes from the interviews used to illustrate the findings are translated from German by the researcher. The translation tries to reflect, as best as possible, what the interviewee has said. Sometimes it is difficult to find equivalent terms in English. In the sense of transparency such terms or phrases are indicated by a respective remark.

4.1 Description of sample

As background for the presentation of the findings in the following sections, this section will present a brief description of the characteristics of the sample. This includes an overview of the company characteristics and the characteristics of the interviewees.

4.1.1 Company characteristics

The 28 companies in the sample can be described using several characteristics. The detailed information for each company is shown in Appendices-Figure 14. In line with the sampling approach, all companies in the main study are **manufactur-**

[79] To avoid misunderstandings the format x/y/28 is only used when the relating number y has been addressed in the respective subsection previously.≙ In addition, each subsection including the format x/y/28 only uses this format in relation to a steady number of interviewees addressing a view y. Exceptions are subsections that provide a summary. In these subsections the number of interviewees addressing a view y is constant for each paragraph.

© Springer Fachmedien Wiesbaden GmbH, part of Springer Nature 2020
C. Normann-Tschampel, *Value-Based Management in Mittelstand*,
Familienunternehmen und KMU, https://doi.org/10.1007/978-3-658-29228-7_4

ing companies from **Baden-Württemberg** that fulfill the definition of **Mittelstand** underlying this work (see subsection 3.6.2).

Beyond this the companies can be described in terms of **size**. On the basis of the definition of the European Commission (20.5.2003) two companies are small (7 %), 14 companies are of medium size (50 %) and 12 companies (43 %) exceed the thresholds for SMEs and are thus large companies. In line with the sampling strategy the sample is rather heterogeneous in terms of size. However, the share of small companies is comparatively low which results from the sampling approach.[80] The heterogeneity in terms of size can be further illustrated by looking at the number of employees. The number of companies that can be assigned to different size ranges on this basis is displayed in Figure 29. This shows that the sample includes companies of all size ranges with two to eight companies from each of the ranges. With an approximate share of one quarter of the companies each, there is a slightly stronger presence of three of the six size ranges.

Figure 29: Size of the companies in the sample based on the number of employees

Number of employees	**30-49**	**50-99**	**100-249**	**250-499**	**500-999**	**>1.000**	**Total**
Number of companies	2	7	8	2	7	2	28
Percentage	7%	25%	29%	7%	25%	7%	

Secondly, the companies can be described by their **age**. To protect anonymity of the companies the age is not specified as an exact value but in terms of the age range that a company belongs to. The number of companies for each range is shown in Figure 30. The sample comprises companies of various ages. The youngest company is ten years old and the oldest company was founded before 1850. A considerable number (39 %) of the companies is between 40 and 59 years old, which means that they have been founded in the boom years between around 1950 and 1970.

Figure 30: Age of the companies in the sample

Age	**0-19**	**20-39**	**40-59**	**60-79**	**80-99**	**>100**	**Total**
Number of companies	2	5	11	3	4	3	28
Percentage	7%	18%	39%	11%	14%	11%	

Thirdly and most importantly, the companies can be characterised by their **structure in terms of ownership and management**. In this respect the approach proposed by Litz (1995) is used under consideration of the refinements of Hausch (2004). For each of the two dimensions Litz (1995) distinguishes three basic states i.e. ownership and/or management being exerted by

[80] Based on the insights from the pilot study it has been decided to use a lower limit of 30 employees (for details see subsection 3.6.2). The European Commission (20.5.2003) regards companies only as small companies when they have up to 49 employees. Consequently, the sample can only include small companies with 30 to 49 employees. This is the case for two companies. These also meet the turnover threshold for small companies of the European Commission (20.5.2003).

- an individual,
- a family and
- a diverse group of individuals.

The resulting nine different types are described in more detail and merged into 6 more general types by Hausch (2004) In line with the definition of Mittelstand underlying this work three of these more general types of Mittelstand are represented in the sample.[81] These will be described in the following and are displayed in Figure 31.

The sample includes ten owner-managed companies. Following Hausch's (2004) approach this includes companies that are owned and managed by a single person. In line with Hausch (2004) this also comprises of five businesses that are owned and managed by a single family member. Following the reasoning used in defining Mittelstand in this empirical study, this also includes companies that are owned and managed by a few individual persons and not only those managed by a single individual.[82]

In addition, there are ten mittelständische family businesses. In the sample at hand they are owned by several family members and managed either by one or several family members.

Finally, Mittelstand with the influence of external managers is identified as a separate type of company (eight companies). This type consists of companies that are managed by owner(s) and external manager(s). These are not immediately covered by the types identified by Hausch (2004) and Litz (1995). Both of them do not account for a potential combination of owners and externals as managers.[83] It is nevertheless valuable to differentiate this type of companies for two reasons. Firstly, the involvement of an external manager gives rise to a principal-agent-situation. Based on the reasoning in the literature this might make the use of VBM more probable (Gonschorek, 2015b; Krol, 2009c; Wenzel, 2014). Secondly, an external manager extends management capacity and capability which might influence the use of VBM. This is relevant, as limited management capacity and capability in Mittelstand are regarded as a hurdle for the application of VBM (Becker et al., 2010b; Krol, 2009c). For each of the three types of Mittelstand identified in the sample there are eight to ten companies. Within the boundaries of the Mittelstand definition ap-

[81] The three types of companies that include ownership by a diverse group of individuals are in contrast to the Mittelstand definiton of this work. In line with Hausch (2004) this is interpreted as companies where the shares are owned by diverse shareholders. This is not compatible with the definitional element of ownership by single natural persons or family members. Consequently, only the three types of traditional Mittelstand identified by Hausch (2004) can be represented in the sample.

[82] As Litz (1995, p. 23) notes the three basic states of ownership and management cannot “represent the complex range of ownership and management forms found in real life”. Assigning these companies to the state “individual” and thus the type of owner-managed Mittelstand according to Hausch (2004) is regarded as more suitable than assigning them to “a diverse group of individuals”.

[83] Litz (1995) distinguishes management by an individual, a family or a diverse group of individuals. Hausch (2004) modifies this by replacing management by a diverse group of individuals with management by externals.

plied, the sample is rather heterogeneous in terms of the ownership and management structure.

Figure 31: Type of companies in the sample on the basis of the ownership and management structure

Type of company	Owner-managed Mittelstand	Mittelständisches family business	Mittelstand with influence of external management	Total
Number of companies	10	10	8	28
Percentage	36%	36%	29%	

4.1.2 Background information on the interviewees

The sample can also be described in terms of characteristics of the 30 interviewees.[84] The details are shown in Appendices-Figure 15.

Firstly, in terms of **gender,** the vast majority of interviewees is male with only one interviewee being female. I-19 is a descendant of a male founder similar to one female owner-manager in the pilot study.

Secondly, the interviewees can be characterised in terms of **age**. The average age is 51. A characterisation of the sample in terms of the age of the interviewees is shown in Figure 32. The age is shown in different ranges to protect anonymity. It is interesting that three interviewees are already 65 or older. Thus, they are beyond the age that has been the legal age of retirement in Germany for decades.[85] Two of these interviewees are only slightly beyond this age, a third interviewee is around 80 years old. It can be expected that these interviewees need to deal with succession in the next few years. Furthermore, this might also be a topic for the seven interviewees that are 55 to 64 years old. This is interesting as the situation of succession is addressed as one driver of the use of VBM in Mittelstand (Gonschorek, 2015b; Krol, 2009c; Lehmann, 2012). Additionally, it can be noted that half of the interviewees is 45 to 54 years old. Thus, the age of the interviewees covers a broad range but there is an accumulation around the age of 50. On the basis of their age, the majority of the interviewees seems to be experienced businesspeople.

Figure 32: Age of the interviewees

Age of the interviewee	25-34	35-44	45-54	55-64	>=65	Total
Number of interviewees	3	2	15	7	3	30
Percentage	10%	7%	50%	23%	10%	

[84] In two cases the owner-manager brought a second person to the interview.

[85] From 2012 to 2029 the legal retirement age in Germany is increased step by step from 65 to 67.

Thirdly, it is important to consider the interviewees' **position in the company**. There has been the intention to interview owner-managers in Mittelstand. Consequently, the vast majority of the interviewees are owner-managers (83 %). However, it must be noted that not all interviewees are owner-managers (as displayed in Figure 33). In two interviews the owner-manager was accompanied by an external manager or authorised representative. As the owner-manager decided to bring a second person to the interview, on the basis of the information given on the research project in advance, it is assumed that they can also give valuable insights. In three other cases it was only possible to agree a date with an external manager or authorised representative and not with the owner-manager.[86] The views addressed by these interviewees do not necessarily represent the viewpoint of the owner-manager in the company. However, all these interviewees have important positions in the company.[87] Thus, they can provide insights into objectives and strategic decision-making in Mittelstand. To allow the reader to consider the position of the interviewee when individual views are outlined in the following, the respective abbreviations are amended by "EM" for those interviewees that are not owner-managers. For the sake of readability the outline of the findings of the study on a general level will nevertheless only refer to owner-managers or interviewees.

Figure 33: Position of the interviewees

Position	**Owner-manager**	**External manager**	**Authorised representative**	**Total**
Number of interviewees	25	3	2	30
Percentage	83%	10%	7%	

Fourthly, the interviewees can be described in terms of their **educational background.** This is shown in Figure 34. It is interesting that the vast majority of the interviewees has university education (21 interviewees, 72 %). Three of these interviewees even have a doctorate. The number of interviewees that has a technical or business background is nearly the same and amounts to about a third of the sample for each of them. Furthermore, a third of the interviewees has both, a business and a technical background. This includes five interviewees that have graduated from a programme of studies that combines industrial engineering and management. Furthermore, several interviewees have successfully completed two educational programmes with different focuses.[88] Overall, the sample does not seem to reflect the

[86] In all three cases it was asked whether an interview date with the owner-manager would be possible but this was denied. As such difficulties in getting access had been expected it was decided to nevertheless conduct the interview.

[87] Two interviewees are part of the management board. The third interviewee is the only authorised representative of the company which is owned and managed by the founder of the company. According to the interviewee he is "in principle part of the management board" and is hierarchically directly subordinate to the owner-manager.

[88] This includes a variety of combinations. For example an interviewee is trained as industrial management assistant and as electroplater. Another interviewee expanded his university education as engineer by completing a Master of Business Administration.

notion in literature that Mittelstand is often led by owner-managers with a technical background that have little management expertise.[89]

Figure 34: Educational background of the interviewees[90]

Type of education (column), area of education (line)	University education	Vocational training	Total
Technical/ engineering	5	4	9
Business	8	2	10
Business and technical/ engineering	8	2	10
Total	21	8	29

The characteristics of the sample are summarised in Figure 35. In line with the sampling strategy the sample is heterogeneous in several aspects.

Figure 35: Summary description of the sample in the main study

Sample of the main study includes	
• **28 mittelständische companies,** • that belong to the manufacturing industry • in Baden-Württemberg and are heterogeneous in terms of • size, • age and • type of company on the basis of the ownership and management structure.	• **30 interviewees,** • who are mainly male, • who cover a broad range of age with an accumulation around the age of 50, • are mainly owner-managers and • have a high level of education that has a technical and/or business background.

4.2 Strategic decision-making

4.2.1 Aim and approach of the section

Two research questions have been formulated to gain insights in relation to strategic decision-making. The first research question shall allow for open insights into the role of management tools for SDM:

> What management tools are used in strategic decision-making in Mittelstand, and in which ways are these tools relevant for strategic decision-making?

The insights into this research question are based on openly asking the interviewees about how strategic decisions are taken and will be outlined in subsection 4.2.3.

---

[89] Most importantly, the course of education of two thirds of the interviewees includes business knowledge. Additionally, the majority of the interviewees that have a solely technical educational background has a respective university degree. Based on the experience of the researcher the study program of engineers from Universities of Applied Sciences includes some basic modules on business and management.

[90] In the German educational system vocational training usually involves three years of combined training in a professional field in a company and at a vocational school. When interviewees have both, vocational training and a university degree they have been assigned to „university education" as this is the higher degree in terms of academic background. The total in this table does not add up to 30 as one interviewee did not provide information on his educational background.

Relevant aspects are partly addressed after the prior introductory question asking about the strategic decisions taken in the company in the last few years.

The second research question reflects the focus on VBM:

How is VBM reflected in the use of management tools in strategic decision-making in Mittelstand?

To gain insights, the management tools addressed in subsection 4.2.3. will be analysed accordingly. This is complemented by analysing the interviewees' view towards the net present value (NPV) method, which is a method of investment appraisal in line with the VBM approach. This will be presented in subsection 4.2.4. It has been found that the insights that can be gained are strongly influenced by how the interviewees address strategic decisions. Thus, this will firstly be addressed in subsection 4.2.2.

4.2.2 How strategic decisions are addressed in the interviews as context

4.2.2.1 Aim and approach of the subsection

The interviewees refer to different kinds of decision and talk about those decisions on different levels. It is important to understand and outline this context in that the findings are derived.

4.2.2.2 Different kinds of decision

Different kinds of decision are referred to by the interviewees. The majority of the interviewees refers to strategic decisions related to the **market positioning** of the company. This includes decisions such as offering a new or different kind of product and/or service. An example for this is the decision to expand the product portfolio of a tool manufacturer through offering serial production of these tools (I-6). Another example is the decision of a machine construction company to develop a new kind of machine (I-9). The decisions related to the market positioning also include focusing on customers of a specific industry e.g. the automotive industry as well as changes in this focus and not wanting customers from a specific industry. It can be noted that this kind of decision seems to be important from the viewpoint of the interviewees. This reflects in two ways. On the one hand, more than three quarters of the interviewees refer to decisions in relation to market positioning (23/28). On the other hand, two thirds of these interviewees address this kind of decision extensively (16/23/28).

There is also repeated reference to a **foundation of subsidiaries** as a kind of decision (9/28). This includes a foundation of subsidiaries in Germany as well as abroad. Partly this has a dimension of market positioning e.g. when a subsidiary is founded to enter a new market. However, market positioning can also be achieved in different ways. In addition, the interviewees put emphasis on the aspect of founding a subsidiary. Thus, a foundation of subsidiaries is regarded as a specific kind of strategic decision.

In addition, some interviewees talk about **acquisition of companies** as a strategic decision (6/28). This can also be related to market positioning. However, in line with the reasoning for a foundation of subsidiaries, acquisition of companies is also identified as a separate kind of decision.

Another kind of strategic decision addressed by some interviewees is the **investment in new buildings or enlargement of buildings** (9/28). It is interesting that five of these interviewees address this decision extensively. The construction of a new building or the enlargement of a building, in these cases, is either ongoing or has been finished in the two years before the interview. **Machine investments** are also a common topic (14/28). However, it must be noted that eight of these interviewees do not address machine investments at the beginning of talking about strategic decisions but talk about other decisions and address machine investments later on. In these cases, it is often unclear whether they regard the machine investment as a strategic decision or not.

In a similar way the interviewees talk about **orders** from customers. These are addressed by some interviewees when talking about strategic decisions (7/28). However, in roughly half the cases the decision is addressed more towards the end of outlining strategic decisions and is not clearly identified as a strategic decision. A few interviewees also address **succession or change of generation** as a strategic decision (5/28).[91] Furthermore, some interviewees talk about strategic decisions on a more **general level** (10/28).

The majority of the interviewees (17/28) additionally addresses a range of other strategic decisions, that cannot be related to one of the kinds of decisions identified. However, similar decisions can only be identified for a few interviewees (less than 5). These decisions are mostly only briefly addressed.[92] When taking a very broad view, some of these decisions could be grouped together as being related to the organisational structure. However, it has been decided not to create a separate theme for these decisions.[93] In addition to identifying different kinds of decisions there are differences in how the interviewees address the decisions.

4.2.2.3 Different levels of talking about strategic decision-making

The interviewees talk about strategic decisions on different levels. In this respect different groups of interviewees have been identified in the way displayed in Figure 36. Firstly, the different decisions each interviewee talks about have been distinguished. It is then evaluated whether each of these decisions is addressed briefly, superficially or extensively. After this has been completed for all interviews a holistic

[91] In one case the interviewee does not use the term “strategic decision” and addresses the decision towards the end of the interview on a superficial level. As the interviewee emphasises the importance for the future the decision is nevertheless considered.

[92] There are a few exceptions. The decision to found the company (I-13), the decision to restructure the company (I-34) and the decision to develop the organisational structure of the company (I-30) are addressed extensively.

[93] The decisions are only addressed briefly or superficially apart from the decisions mentioned in the previous footnote. Thus, it is difficult to gain an understanding of the decision-making approach. Additionally, the decisions seem to be quite diverse and range from implementing a new IT system, via securing financing to the implementation of lean management. Overall, these diverse decisions are still only addressed by some interviewees (6/23).

view of each interview has been taken and patterns to identify the different groups have been looked for. The resulting four different groups will be illustrated briefly.

Figure 36: Approach to identification of groups of interviewees in relation to different levels of talking about strategic decisions

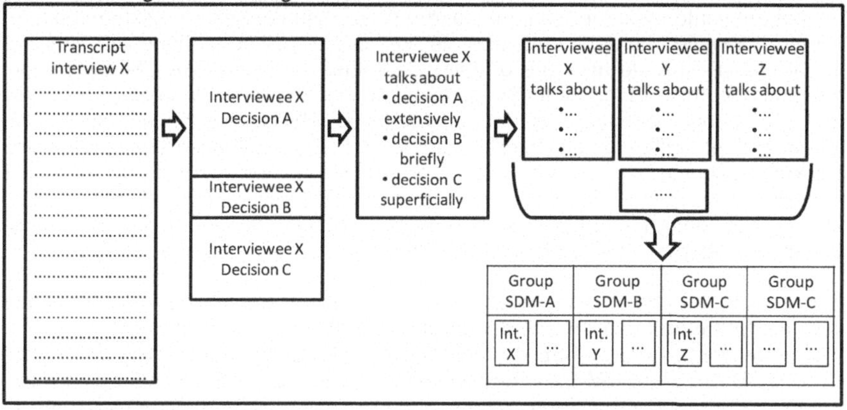

It has been recognised that a few interviewees **talk about strategic decisions on a superficial, more general level** (Group SDM-A). These interviewees address specific strategic decisions taken in the company only briefly or superficially. An extensive outline of a specific strategic decision is not given. Thus, it is difficult to gain an understanding of how a specific strategic decision is taken in the company. An example for this group is I-5. After the question regarding strategic decisions taken in the last few years, he refers to the orientation of the company and states that it has been essential to develop from a supplier to a system provider. This is a decision related to the market positioning of the company. The interviewer poses some questions to encourage a more extensive narrative but the interviewee switches to market positioning on a more general level and the foundation of a subsidiary after only five minutes. He then talks about the foundation of a subsidiary for another five minutes and then about the market positioning in general terms for another four minutes. Subsequently, he talks about investments in the company on a more general level. When being asked about the net present value method he introduces another decision by briefly referring to a machine investment. Thus, he touches upon three different kinds of decisions, i.e. market positioning, foundation of a subsidiary and machine investments. In addition, he talks about decisions in general terms more extensively but he does not elaborate on one of the specific decisions in-depth.

Additionally, **interviewees talk about several strategic decisions on a superficial level and give several examples** (Group SDM-B). Both, Group SDM-B and Group SDM-A, share that decisions are addressed superficially. Though, the interviewees of Group SDM-B address several specific decisions for different kinds of decisions. This includes several examples of specific decisions for at least one kind of decision. This can be illustrated when looking at I-15. I-15 refers to three kinds of decisions – market positioning, foundation of subsidiaries abroad and new buildings. He puts emphasis on outlining the decisions regarding the entry into new markets right from the beginning. He starts by outlining the approach towards identifying and entering new countries on a general level. When asked about specific decisions he refers briefly to the market entry in China some time ago. Then he mentions the market entry into two other countries and a production facility that existed in a third country. However, he does not elaborate on these decisions at this point. After being asked to explicate how one of these decisions has been taken he talks about the market entry in China for four minutes but then switches again to other countries and more general comments about market entries. Throughout the interview he refers to market entries in six different countries.[94] Thus, while extensively addressing market positioning, he does not outline one specific decision extensively. While the more extensive outline allows a more in-depth understanding of one kind of decision (market positioning) than for the interviewees of group SDM-A, it is yet not possible to gain an in-depth understanding of the decision-making of one specific decision.

Furthermore, a number of the interviewees **talks about some strategic decisions with a slight emphasis on one decision** (Group SDM-C). Similar to Group SDM-B the interviewees of Group SDM-C talk about multiple decisions. They differ from Groups SDM-A and SDM-B as they emphasise one or two specific decisions which are then addressed extensively. In comparison to Group SDM-B this allows more in-depth insights of this decision. However, two to four other decisions are addressed briefly or superficially. This limits the potential to gain a holistic understanding of one decision. An example for this group is I-10. After being asked about the strategic decisions taken in the last years, I-10 briefly mentions the training of employees. He then moves on to superficially address the positioning in the market in general and the specific decision to develop the original business model of trading semi-finished products to producing these semi-finished products. In total he addresses market positioning for ten minutes and then talks about a new building that will be built in the near future. The interviewer then asks how this decision was taken and the interviewee talks about this decision for a quarter of an hour with some questions by the interviewer to encourage a more detailed description. He then switches to more general comments about the company which include some reference to machine investments. Together with later references, he refers to the building decision in roughly a quarter of the transcript of the 1,5 hour interview. In addition, he refers superficially to positioning in the market and machine investments and briefly mentions the training of employees and a change in the organisational structure of the company. Thus, a rough understanding of the positioning in the market and machine investment decisions as well as a good understanding of the building decision can be gained. However, a stronger focus on the building decision would have allowed a more in-depth and holistic understanding.

Finally, the interviewees of Group SDM-D **talk about a few strategic decisions with a strong emphasis on one decision**. As the interviewees of Group SDM-C, the interviewees of Group SDM-D also address different decisions and put emphasis on one decision. However, they address fewer decisions and put a stronger emphasis on one decision. Each of them talks about one decision for at least a third of

[94] This partly includes the foundation of subsidiaries abroad.

the interview. This can be illustrated by I-16. After the question regarding strategic decisions in the last years, I-16 outlines some aspects in relation to building a new logistics centre. He also mentions the building of another building and the annual investments into machinery. On further request, and with some questions by the interviewer, he then outlines how the decision to build the logistics centre was taken for more than 20 minutes. Only after being asked about the use of the net present value method does he refer to machine investments again on a superficial basis. The extensive outline of the decision to build the logistics centre allows a good understanding of decision-making. In the context of the different levels of talking about strategic decisions and the different kinds of decisions addressed insights into the use of management tools and Key Performance Indicators are gained.

4.2.3 Use of (VBM) management tools and Key Performance Indicators

4.2.3.1 Aim and approach of the subsection

The first two research questions focus on the use of management tools and performance indicators in strategic decision-making. An open question regarding the approach to strategic decision-making and a question regarding the role of profitability shall spur accounts that provide insights into the first research question:

> What management tools are used in strategic decision-making in Mittelstand, and in which ways are these tools relevant for strategic decision-making?

Beyond this, insights into RQ2 shall be gained:

> How is VBM reflected in the use of management tools in strategic decision-making in Mittelstand?

In relation to RQ2 the management tools applied in SDM are analysed with regard to two aspects.

At first, the focus is on whether VBM management tools and KPIs are applied. Based on the possibilities of how VBM can be reflected in decision-making in Mittelstand identified in the literature review, this includes references to management tools or KPIs that are in line with the VBM approach (for details see subsection 2.4.2). Examples are Economic Value Added, Return on Capital Employed, Cash Flow Return on Investment and a Value Driver Tree. This also comprises the examples of tools that consider VBM's basic economic view given by Günther (2015b) like a DCF-based break even analysis or real options valuation. Additionally, this covers references to methods of investment appraisal that are in line with VBM such as the internal rate of return method and the net present value method.

In line with the openness of the research approach, additionally it is analysed whether VBM's basic economic view reflects in the use of management tools in SDM (for details on the elements of VBM's basic economic view see subsection 2.4.2.1). This second aspect complements the outline of the management tools. It will be addressed where possible on the basis of the insights given by the interviewees.

Several different management tools referred to by the interviewees will be presented in the following. It must be noted that a number of the interviewees refers to a combination of different tools.[95] As the focus is on gaining a holistic understanding of the use of management tools in SDM, the outline can accordingly include references to several tools. Thus, each interview might be mentioned repeatedly and the examples might include references to management tools addressed in another subsection.[96]

4.2.3.2 Business plan and/or planning profit and loss statement

Half of the interviewees refer to business plans as well as setting up plans in the context of strategic decision-making (14/28).[97] This does not consider references where the interviewees refer to planning as an element of using another tool for SDM e.g. investment appraisal. These are only addressed in the respective subsection.

The views regarding business plans and/or profit and loss statements are quite different and range from mentioning that planning is not relevant, via a relevance of pragmatic business plans to elaborated business planning for strategic decision-making.

A few interviewees briefly express that **(business) plans are not relevant for strategic decision-making in the company**. An example for this is I-25. When outlining two decisions regarding market positioning he states that these decisions have not been based on a business plan but on gut feeling. Later on, he says that there have been intuitive considerations regarding acquisition costs, follow-up costs and when there is the first piece "that we can produce for 50 Euros and sell for 80 for example". However, he immediately adds that this can only be estimated very roughly and emphasises his view with the following example. A group of companies that is a customer of the company approached a market positioning decision in an analytic manner. He told them that based on his experience and gut feeling they will never accomplish their plan. According to his view it is not possible to forecast this with an analytic model. Thus, while there seem to be some economic considerations on the basis of gut feeling, the interviewee makes clear that business plans are not relevant for him. The view that business plans are not relevant for SDM is expressed briefly by two other interviewees.

Additionally, there are two other interviewees who say business plans exist in their companies but they do not seem to be relevant for SDM. I-20 mentions that for the building decision, different scenarios for the development of the company in the following three to four years existed. However, this is only mentioned briefly towards the end of the interview. Furthermore, I-20 immediately adds that the scenarios are

95 When an interviewee refers to a combination of management tools this is considered in the subsections for each of the tools mentioned.

96 An example is I-16 who uses a combination of a business plan and methods of investment appraisal and is thus accounted for in both subsections. In the outline of I-16's approach as an example for methods of investment appraisal the business plan is also mentioned.

97 It must be noted that planning as well as other management tools are also addressed for the companies as a whole. The focus of this research is on the role of management tools e.g. planning in SDM. Thus, references that only refer to planning for the company without relation to SDM are not considered. This is also applicable to the management tools addressed in the following subsections.

not correct anyway as it is difficult to forecast future development. Thus, while plans exist they have not been crucial in SDM. The scenarios only seem to exist as management accounting is a key aspect of the academic studies of the owner-manager's son, who has developed the scenarios. The situation is similar for I-13. A business plan was set up when it was decided to found the company. However, from the account of the interviewee it is clear that this business plan was not relevant for him in taking the decision, but was relevant to get financing from banks. This, for example, is reflected in the following quote:

> "With the business plan or that thing, I did not worry very much[98], because I basically knew that it must work."

I-13 justifies this having worked as a managing director for a company with a similar business model and working in the industry for several years. In addition to three interviewees briefly expressing that plans are not relevant in strategic decision-making, there are two interviewees where the existing plans are not relevant for the strategic decision. Thus, a few interviewees express that business plans are not relevant for SDM (5/14/28).

There are also two companies where **planning has some relevance for strategic decision-making**. In I-8 and I-30 investment plans are set up for the company. These are relevant for machine investments. I-30-EM adds on a general level that business plans are beneficial for strategic decisions. While acknowledging that the numbers might not be correct in the end, these can at least provide a point of reference after the decision has been taken. For I-30-EM this is the difference of an entrepreneurial decision towards a decision based on gut feeling.

Additional interviewees talk extensively about business plans. For these interviewees different approaches to business planning in the context of SDM can be distinguished. While some put some effort into planning, others plan in a more pragmatic manner.

I-15, I-26 and I-31 describe a **pragmatic planning approach**. I-26 states that detailed and extensive feasibility studies are not relevant. Nevertheless, economic advantageousness is an "absolute prerequisite" for the acquisition of companies. While neglecting formal business plans, there are still respective considerations. This includes whether one can trust the business plan presented by the seller of the company with some limitations when "removing the fantasy". It is also reflected when break-even is in the worst case. In addition, it is evaluated how the company can recover the costs of acquisition afterwards. This can happen via know-how transfer, new products and additional sales. The respective risk is also considered. This involves whether the company can afford to lose the investment without threatening the existence of the company. In this respect, it is important for I-26 to consider whether the risk is to lose the cost of acquisitions or what "comes after" the acquisition e.g. when acquiring a company from bankruptcy. On further request I-26 states that it would be necessary from a theoretical point of view to consider costs of capital. However this is not done as these costs have been very favourable for the company in the last years and the company is trying to stay independent from

[98] As a translation of „keine großen Gedanken machen“, a modificaction of the German saying „sich Gedanken machen“.

banks. It can be concluded that the pragmatic planning approach for strategic decisions regarding acquisitions includes elements of VBM's basic economic view i.e. an orientation towards the future and consideration of risks. However, as costs of capital are not considered the economic advantageousness of the decision cannot be evaluated from a VBM perspective.

I-31 is similar to I-26 in that there are pragmatic considerations regarding the economic development in the future. For a decision regarding the foundation of a subsidiary abroad "a bit of a business plan" has been set up. This included estimating the number of people needed, the respective costs and additional costs. A local partner has been consulted in estimating costs. The company added a reserve of 20, 25 % to have a buffer for unforeseen circumstances. Furthermore, turnover targets have been set. In doing this it has been important to consider increases of turnover on a realistic level. For the estimation, the focus was on the next five years and the aim was to break-even after roughly three years. In taking the decision costs of capital were not considered as the company had enough money available. The risk was accepted as it was regarded as manageable given that the company is healthy and has enough resources. It can be concluded that there was some awareness of risks and that these were considered with a buffer in the rough calculations. The approach also includes the VBM element of orientation towards the future but does not consider costs of capital. Thus, I-31 is similar to I-26 in that there are some elements of VBM inherent in the pragmatic planning approach but the strategic decision is not taken on the basis of a VBM management tool.

I-16, I-33, I-34-EM and I-35 have in common with I-26 and I-31 that the planning approach involves some elements of VBM.[99] However, they are different in that the **business plan is elaborated in more detail**. I-33 outlines that for the foundation of a subsidiary abroad a student developed a business plan for the company. This included different scenarios, as well as how the capital is provided, a forecast of costs and figures such as break-even. The company already knew the market. While it was not possible to say which products are actually sold, there have been worst case and best case figures for the product groups. While being aware that the development will not be as planned, I-33 regards the business plan as valuable. In case of deviations one can then reflect on what needs to be changed to "stay on track somewhat". When there is no plan "that can become a never-ending story". I-33 states that costs of capital are included but adds that the subsidiary usually does not need to pay these in the first two years. This might be prolonged if necessary. He emphasises that there is the risk that this cannot work and that he would recommend others not to go to the limit. This shows that there is some awareness of costs of capital and risks. However, it remains unclear whether this also includes costs of equity capital. While the business plan for the foundation of subsidiaries abroad includes some elements of VBM it is still unclear whether the evaluation fully reflects VBM's basic economic view.

Another example is I-34-EM. In this case business plans are used in a specific context, i.e. for changing the company positioning after a succession and for the re-

[99] I-16 and I-35 set up business plans in the context of other management tools (see subsections 4.2.3.4 and 4.2.3.7).

structuring of the company. I-34-EM emphasises that there has been a change from a "hands-on" planning to a "truly well-grounded planning". This has involved preparing a profit and loss statement for the next two years. In addition specific actions have been defined with specific numbers for their effect on costs and income, clear dates and responsibilities. This resulted from the involvement of consulting companies and is regarded as beneficial by the interviewee:

> "The longer I am engaged in this topic, the more I think that this is the more enduring variant."

After being asked about the reasons, he relates to the possibility to reflect whether one is still on one's way. In addition to an orientation towards the future, risks as well as costs of capital are important. There is a strong focus on bank liabilities but it remains unclear whether costs of equity capital are also relevant. Similar to I-33 there is an elaborate planning that involves some aspects of VBM. However, as before there does not seem to be an evaluation of the economic advantageousness that fully reflects VBM's basic economic view.

Overall, the multiple references to planning reflect different views (14/28). Some interviewees briefly address planning and neglect it, partly referring to the difficulty to forecast the future (5/14/28). Others deal with this situation differently and prefer to formulate a plan (9/14/28). This is done partly through rough considerations (3/14/28) and partly on a more sophisticated level (4/14/28). For those interviewees where planning is addressed more extensively in relation to strategic decision-making it has been found that these approaches partly involve considerations that are favourable from a VBM perspective. There is an orientation towards the future and some awareness of risks. With regard to costs of capital there are differences. These are partly not relevant, and partly relevant. In all cases there is no clear reference to costs of equity capital. Thus, while (business) plans are used, they are not formulated in a way that fully reflects VBM's basic economic view.

4.2.3.3 Cost accounting

It is surprising that many interviewees refer to cost accounting in the context of strategic decision-making (17/28). This includes references to different terms and concepts that are related to cost accounting such as (post) calculation, contribution margin, machine hour assessment costs, margin, profit and/or cost centre and cost distribution sheets.

The analysis of these references shows that cost accounting seems to be relevant for all interviewees. However, in a few cases the shortness of the reference does not give an understanding of the role of cost accounting for SDM (7/17/28). This includes cost accounting being mentioned in the context of the application of another management tool. In the case of I-15 the contribution margin is part of the business plan. Another example is I-12, where the calculation is part of the investment appraisal. The more extensive references include three dominant aspects.

One way that cost accounting is relevant for SDM is that **strategic considerations result from insights gained in regular analysis of cost accounting information** (4/17/28). I-18 for example outlines that there is a need to reflect on machine investments when the cost calculation repeatedly shows that the price expectations of customers cannot be met. Cost accounting also influenced strategic decisions regarding market positioning addressed by I-6, I-19 and I-29. They express that they gained the insight that one area of business is more advantageous for the company through cost accounting. This resulted in the decision to focus more on this area of business. This can be illustrated by I-19, where it has been decided to focus on larger orders. This decision resulted from the experience made by some large orders. A post calculation was done for these orders. The result of which was that money can be earned easier with larger orders than with smaller orders. Other aspects were also relevant. While all companies want large orders, not all can fulfill them. I-19 has been good in handling large orders and thus had the ability to develop a unique selling proposition. As there are consequently fewer competitors than for smaller orders I-19 can sell for higher prices. It was decided that "under the current circumstances this is the better way for us rather than further handling those smaller orders" and the company "swung to this side". Based on the literature on SDM, this can be interpreted in the way that the insights gained from cost accounting have been the trigger for the decision.[100] Later on, I-19 states that a similar approach is still applied. I-19 emphasises that on a company level the annual balance sheet is analysed together with the tax accountant. This can be the basis for deriving strategies and decisions. However, the analysis on product basis is much more important in order to recognise where there is a need for action. This shows that I-19 is using regular analysis of cost accounting information as a basis for identifying the need for a decision. This supports the notion of cost accounting serving as a trigger for the evaluation of the economic advantageousness of different areas of business. However, it mostly remains unclear as to what extent cost accounting is used in evaluating and implementing a strategic decision. Furthermore, cost accounting is not a VBM management tool and elements of VBM's basic economic view are not evident from the respective accounts of I-6, I-18, I-19 and I-29.

In addition, cost accounting plays a **role in the evaluation or implementation of strategic decisions** (3/17/28). I-18 also uses cost accounting as part of the evaluation of new machine investments, which is triggered when customers' price expectations for a product cannot repeatedly be met. On the basis of the calculation and the underlying process sheet, it is identified for which processes a machine investment might be beneficial in order to reduce costs. In the case of I-17 cost accounting was crucial for the strategic decision regarding market positioning. It was decided to develop a new model range that meets the expectations of customers of a new market segment. This involved market analysis which included analysing the market position of competitors, prices on the market and an estimation of the number of items that can be sold in different countries on the basis of data for the last few years. From this a target price and a target for the manufacturing costs were derived. Then a feasibility study analysed whether the sales and cost target can be achieved. This involved a constructional sketch with respective calculation.[101] The resulting cost estimation has then been compared to the respective target. This has been re-

[100]The trigger is an element of the process of SDM in Mittelstand empirically identified by Gibcus and van Hoesel (2008). It is the "direct stimulus for the entrepreneurs to take action and elaborate on their idea" (Gibcus and van Hoesel (2008, p. 93)).

[101]In the calculation the parts that are most relevant for the costs were calculated as precisely as possible. The costs for parts that have less influence on total costs were estimated on the basis of experience. Where possible, data from existing products was used as a point of reference for the calculation.

peated at different stages throughout the evaluation and implementation of the decision. The development of the new product would have been stopped if the cost target had seemed unachievable at one of these stages. This approach was possible and valuable as the company had empirical data for a similar market, a similar product and for the production of similar products. This example illustrates that cost accounting information has been used throughout the evaluation and implementation of the strategic decision.

A third way in which cost accounting is addressed by the interviewees, is to express the **importance of doing cost accounting for orders** (8/17/28). This is done by I-6, I-18, I-19 and I-29, where cost accounting for orders also triggered strategic decisions. In addition, three others address cost accounting in relation to orders. An example is I-9, a machine construction company that has decided to introduce a new kind of machine to the product portfolio. During the interview I-9 extensively addresses this strategic decision regarding market positioning that resulted from single machine construction projects.[102] In describing considerations regarding market positioning, I-9 states that a double digit EBIT to turnover is regarded as adequate for machine projects under consideration of the size of the company and the risks. After some further comments I-9 is then asked for the role of profitability in decision-making. I-9 then outlines that preliminary costing and post calculation are done for each project. For the company economic feasibility means that the costs calculated prior to the projects are achieved. As the strategic decisions described also relate to projects, it is assumed that cost accounting also plays a role in the strategic decisions. However, there is no direct reference to cost accounting in relation to those projects that the interviewee clearly relates to the strategic decisions on market positioning. Thus, it was not possible to unambiguously gain an understanding of how cost accounting influences strategic decisions.

Similarly, I-14 puts a slight emphasis on strategic decisions regarding market positioning and initially outlines the role of cost accounting for orders without making it clear whether these are regarded as strategic decisions or not. As I-14 signalled that it is possible to conduct the interview for longer than an hour, there was the possibility to ask an additional question to turn the outline more towards strategic decisions regarding market positioning again. I-14 then expresses that there is a relation to an order and it is then tried to invoice the costs as much as possible to the customer. Thus, there is the possibility for a market entry "without spending giant amounts of money". Thus, in contrast to I-9 the interviewee points at the relation of orders where cost accounting plays a role to strategic decisions. Such an indirect relation of cost accounting to strategic decisions is also given for I-24 and I-13. While there are only indications for the role of cost accounting for strategic decisions in these cases it becomes clear that cost accounting is of major importance for decisions on orders and that it is important enough for the interviewee to talk about during the interview.

At first, it is surprising that cost accounting is referred to in relation to strategic decision-making because it is regarded as a management tool commonly used in operative business. However, the analysis of the more extensive references shows that

[102] I-9 gives several examples of such machine construction projects.

for several interviewees cost accounting influences strategic decisions (10/17/28). This includes interviewees where cost accounting plays a role in SDM in three different ways.[103] Firstly, cost accounting serves as a trigger for strategic decisions for a few interviewees (4/17/28). Secondly, cost accounting is used by a few interviewees in evaluating and implementing strategic decisions (3/17/28). Thirdly, cost accounting is important for decisions regarding orders and projects for some interviewees (8/17/28). Cost accounting does not allow evaluating the economic feasibility from a VBM perspective. While single interviewees consider the future development in the cost calculation, there is no clear reference to cash flow and often also not to risks and costs of capital.

4.2.3.4 Methods of investment appraisal

Methods of investment appraisal are addressed by several interviewees (13/28). This includes references where the interviewees use terms related to investment appraisal. In addition, this includes interviewees that describe an approach that is similar to a method of investment appraisal.

A few interviewees refer to amortisation of investments or investment appraisal briefly and on a general level (4/13/28). In these cases it is not possible to gain an understanding of its relevance in strategic decision-making.

An approach that is similar to **the profit comparison method** is described by a few interviewees (4/13/28). In the context of the decision to build a new building I-10 describes the "calculation on a beer coaster" that was done. I-10 roughly estimated the additional revenues and costs as well as the change of the profit of the company resulting from the new building. While this calculation is very rough there is yet a comparison of the profit of two different decision-making alternatives – building and not building. While I-10 does not use the respective term, the approach described is similar to the profit comparison method. Similar to I-10 the considerations of I-8 resemble the profit comparison method. In relation to a strategic decision regarding market positioning I-8 decided not to make an investment demanded by two customers. This was done because the investment was not regarded as advantageous given three aspects:

- the costs (estimated initial investment and follow-up costs)
- the margins that can be achieved with customers from this industry
- the portion these two customers have of the total turnover

A broadly comparable approach can also be found in the case of I-12. However, profit comparison is not a DCF method and does not show whether a decision is beneficial for the company from a VBM perspective.

In a more sophisticated manner I-16 also applies an approach that resembles the profit comparison method. The strategic decision for a new building resulted from the dissatisfaction that costs incurred for I-16 because of the need to rent external space. It was then reflected whether it is economically beneficial to build a new

[103] As some of the interviewees make use of two of these ways the numbers mentioned in relation to the three ways do not add up to the overall number of interviewees where cost accounting has an influence on SDM.

building. In doing this, three different scenarios for the new building were developed and the respective costs were compared to the costs of the initial situation. This was done under consideration of the planning of the company as a whole for the next five and ten years and the need for space resulting from different potential developments. This involved analysing the effect on the debt ratio, the equity ratio and the EBITDA. The aim was that the company is still able to afford the debt service in difficult times. The company was supported by external advisors in doing this. While this approach to decision-making does not make use of a DCF method it still includes several elements that are beneficial from a VBM perspective. On the one hand, risks are considered in planning different scenarios on the level of the strategic decision as well as on the level of the company. On the other hand, it is strongly oriented towards future development. However, EBITDA is used as a measure for decision-making. This does not consider costs of capital. On further request the interviewee also expresses that costs of capital were only considered for the debt capital and not for equity capital, which was also used for financing the investment. In addition, EBITDA is a measure based on the profit and loss statement and not based on cash flow. It can be concluded that for the building decision, a thorough calculation was used which involves some elements that are beneficial from a VBM perspective but is not completely in line with VBM's basic economic view.

Such an element of the VBM approach can also be found in another method of investment appraisal that has been referred to by some interviewees – **Return on Investment** (RoI) (6/28).[104] In relation to RoI different positions can be identified.

Two interviewees address that RoI is relevant. I-21 briefly addresses that RoI is used in the context of machine investments. For I-30-EM RoI is the "key criterion for investments" in the company. RoI has also been used for one of the strategic decisions described i.e. the implementation of a new IT system.[105] However, it must be noted that I-30-EM does not talk about RoI in relation to other strategic decisions addressed. On further request he explicitly states that RoI is not used for all strategic decisions. When bringing a "completely new product" onto the market "then yes I have no RoI". Then one needs to be aware of the risk and take an entrepreneurial decision. This is not only based on gut feeling, as there is a business plan with "at least some figures ... which can at least be subsequently controlled"[106]. He expresses that in the case of investment "then I am more near to the actual figures". This gives the impression that the certainty in forecasting figures in relation to a strategic decision seems to influence whether RoI is used for the decision or not.

For I-18 and I-33 RoI is partly relevant. I-33 refers to the foundation of subsidiaries. He emphasises that subsidiaries need "to be in the black" after roughly five years. However, he emphasises that RoI is only of subordinate importance. From the context there are indicators that he seems to relate RoI to short-term returns:

> "I cannot recommend anyone to invest, for example, in the U.S. and say that after two years the U.S. pays off my debts here, the capital invested. That is

[104] I-25 only refers to RoI to emphasise that it is not relevant. As this is an individual case it is not addressed in detail.

[105] However, it becomes clear that in this case the RoI did not turn out as planned in the end.

[106] The interviewee uses the English term "controlled" in a Germanized way ("controllen").

> too dangerous. It may be the case but I know more where this did not work than where it worked. Yes. Back then, people also told me that, "Oh, it is dangerous. U.S. is a truly difficult market." Yes, of course. But .. when I look at the Return on Investment, yes. But when I look at what happens, that we generate much more turnover here than before, yes, I need to consider that as well."

This indicates, that I-33 aims at a long-term economic benefit but not at a Return on Investment during a specific time. In addition, I-33 adds that it is important that the investment does not "break the neck"[107] in case that "it does not work at all". I-18's view that he has the freedom to make an investment even if it is not possible to say that he has a Return on Investment after two or three years is similar to I-33's view. I-18 expresses that it is often difficult to calculate the RoI. Nevertheless, he calculates roughly. But he states that he does not use a "tally sheet and say "OK, another month where I saved 50,000" or something like that". This shows that RoI has some relevance for investment decisions in the company but is only applied as a rough indicator.

In relation to VBM's basic economic view it is beneficial that RoI allows evaluating the return on the capital invested. Additionally, I-30-EM and I-33 seem to be aware of the risks taking strategic decisions. I-33 is additionally oriented towards the future. While RoI does not allow an evaluation of the economic advantageousness from a VBM perspective, the way in that the interviewees use it includes some of its elements. This is explicitly evident for I-14. He says that RoI is used alongside planning the cash flow for projects. I-14 also mentions that imputed interests are considered. Thus, this includes several elements of VBM's basic economic view i.e. consideration of costs of capital including equity costs of capital and an orientation towards the future and cash flow. Apart from discounting cash flow to determine the net present value, this is very close to the net present value method.[108]

Overall, the analysis of the more extensive references to methods of investment appraisal has shown that such methods are applied in some cases (8/28). This encompasses approaches that are similar to the profit comparison method as well as using RoI. However, there are differences in that these are used in a pragmatic or more sophisticated manner. This partly involves elements of VBM but to a varying extent. The approach of I-14 includes several elements of VBM. The pragmatic analysis of economic feasibility applied by I-8 and I-10 only reflects future orientation and partly an awareness of risks. Thus, these only reflect VBM's basic economic view to a minimal extent. The approaches of I-12, I-16, I-18, I30-EM and I-33 are in between.

4.2.3.5 Cash flow

An element of VBM can also be identified where cash flow are addressed (4/28). It has already been mentioned that cash flow is relevant for I-14 in the context of projects. I-9 also briefly mentions that cash flow is planned for each machine construc-

[107] German saying for becoming bankrupt.

[108] It is interesting to note that despite this, I-14 states that he does not apply the NPV method and is unsure what is meant by that (in his answer regarding the respective question which will be addressed in chapter 4.2.4).

tion project. Thus, it involves the VBM element of future orientation as well as the focus on cash flow. However, I-9 expresses that costs of capital are not considered. I-30-EM also refers to cash flow. He states that there is an investment plan for the company which includes cash flow on a monthly basis and that each investment is checked and approved. Thus, there are indications that cash flow is regularly relevant in investment decisions. As cash flow is only addressed briefly, an understanding of its role in strategic decision-making cannot be gained.

This is different for I-32, where it becomes evident that cash flow is an aspect considered in the strategic decision regarding a new building. It was considered which new orders are needed to be able to pay off the building on the basis of cost accounting information. As the building also needs to be paid off when there are no new orders it was also looked at the possibilities to pay off the building from the company's cash flow. It is emphasised that "one ... also needs to build in security precautions" and that the risk shall not be so large that it poses a threat to the existence of the company. The risk should be manageable as the company, as a family business, has a responsibility towards its employees. This shows that the strategic decision involved some risk considerations as well as an orientation towards cash flow and the future. However, I-32 also makes it clear that all this has been estimated roughly and that there has not been a "perfectly elaborated plan, how what is paid down to the exact cent and euro".". These considerations were based rather on gut feeling and experience. In addition, costs of capital have only been of minor importance. I-32 justifies this with the remark that the company does not have difficulties getting money as the figures of the company have been quite good in the last few years. When the bank signalled that there should be no problem getting money "one does not agonise anymore"[109]. Thus, while the mixture of rough calculations and intuition applied in the strategic decision-making by I-32 involves some elements of VBM, it is not holistically oriented towards the company value.

Overall, cash flow has been considered in a few cases (4/28). The consideration of cash flow is the basis for the application of discounted cash flow methods. DCF methods for investment appraisal are preferred over non-DCF methods from a VBM perspective (Britzelmaier et al., 2018; Schlegel et al., 2016). However, there is still a considerable gap to the application of DCF methods. The initial considerations do not allow evaluating the economic feasibility from a VBM perspective. Nevertheless, this could be the basis, although small, for a more sophisticated investment appraisal.

4.2.3.6 Balanced Scorecard

A Balanced Scorecard (BSC) is addressed in the context of strategic decision-making by two interviewees. I-6-EM outlines that the BSC of the company had some relevance for the company's strategic decision regarding market positioning. He states that on the basis of the BSC the growth strategy of the company resulted in a certain turnover growth rate that needs to be achieved on average in the next 10, 15 years. To achieve this, it has been analysed which processes and activities

[109]As a translation of the interviewee using the German saying "sich einen Kopf machen" in the reverse sense.

the turnover of the company result from. From this analysis it has been concluded that it is necessary to gain new customers. Then, there has been the decision to change the products and services offered by the company. Thus, the BSC of the company has been used to some extent in the analysis that was the basis for the strategic decision. In this, the focus has been on an increase of the turnover which can result in an increase of the company value if the gain in profit exceeds the costs of capital. However, costs of capital and other key elements of VBM's economic view are not addressed. Thus, it is unclear whether the BSC is used in line with VBM.

According to I-30-EM the BSC was one of the results of the strategic decisions related to remodelling the management structures of the company. Nowadays it includes turnover figures, contribution margins and also storage costs as this is important with regard to capital lockup. In addition, there is a strategic BSC with Return on Investment as KPI. The awareness to capital lockup and using RoI as a key figure are beneficial from a VBM perspective as these might be further developed to evaluate whether the return on capital exceeds the cost of capital. However, costs of capital are not mentioned in this context and it is unclear whether the BSC is used in line with VBM.

This shows that for a few of the companies using BSC to manage the company, there is a relation to strategic decision-making (2/28). However, the findings do not provide sufficient insights to evaluate whether the BSC is used in SDM to evaluate the economic feasibility from a VBM perspective.

4.2.3.7 VBM management tools and Key Performance Indicators

It has been found that only one interviewee refers to a VBM KPI. I-35 refers to the use of Economic Value Added in strategic decision-making. Additionally, it will be illustrated that the significance of this reference is limited for three reasons. Firstly, the reference is only a short one. Secondly, EVA is not mentioned at the beginning but on further request of the researcher. Thirdly, the interviewee expresses that EVA is only partly relevant for decisions.

I-35 refers to strategic decisions of market positioning and acquisitions on a superficial level. Furthermore, I-35 mentions briefly securing financing and a change in the management of one of the company's divisions as strategic decisions. When outlining these decisions there is no reference to EVA. Towards the end of the interview the interviewer mentions that she has seen in the financial report of the company that EVA is used as KPI. The interviewee then confirms this and comments on the advantages of EVA as KPI. In his answer he does not refer to strategic decisions. The interviewer therefore asks about the role in taking strategic decisions. This is followed by the following quote:

> "(5 seconds break, interviewee breathing deeply) Yes. (3 seconds break). Of course, when I then want to make a business plan,[110] ..., the EVA is an essential standard of evaluation. But when I am now completely honest, on a

[110]In an earlier part of the interview I-35 briefly mentioned setting up a business plan as part of making decisions.

strategic level these decisions are taken rather emotionally and on the basis of a holistic understanding. ... when we make acquisitions ... of course it is important to us, when we make acquisitions, does that cost 20 million or 100 million? Of course that is the holistic view. Can we afford them at the moment? Does it meet the risk bearing ability of the whole company? I preach again and again, does it meet our risk bearing ability, yes? But real strategic decisions are in many cases taken on a gut level. That is how it is."

This shows that while EVA seems to be relevant at some point in time, "real strategic decisions" are based more on gut feeling and a "holistic view of the company". Unfortunately, due to the short time the interviewee had for the interview it was not possible to gain further insights into when EVA is relevant in strategic decisions. This gives the impression that while EVA is considered, it is not the core aspect of strategic decision-making.

4.2.3.8 Other management tools

Several interviewees use other management tools in strategic decision-making (12/28). This includes tools that are only mentioned by single interviewees and that do not have an obvious relation to VBM. These tools can partly be regarded as strategic tools. This includes the model used by I-16 for market positioning[111], the strategy paper[112] addressed by I30-EM and the "strategy days" done by I-11[113]. In addition, there seem to be different views regarding the value of market analysis.[114]

4.2.4 Views on the net present value method

4.2.4.1 Aim and approach of the subsection

To further evaluate the relevance of VBM management tools in strategic decision-making, the interviewer has posed a question regarding the relevance of the net present value method (NPV) at the end of the part of the interview on management tools in strategic decision-making (Part 2). This has been done by mentioning the NPV method as a method to evaluate investments, then briefly outlining how this is done and asking how far such an approach plays a role in decision-making. This questioning approach allows to relate the findings to existing results on the use of the NPV in investment appraisal (for details see subsections 2.4.2.2). Thus, insights are gained with regard to the application and awareness of the NPV method (subsections 4.2.4.2 and 4.2.4.3). Additionally, the questioning approach makes use of

[111]While I-26 does not use the term, it becomes evident that this is the Ansoff matrix, a strategic planning tool that can be used as a framework for developing product-market strategies.

[112]This was one of the results of a strategic decision related to the internal development of the company. The strategy paper is used to communicate the key company objectives, the vision, the strategy, the values and the objectives for different parts of the company to the employees.

[113]When being asked about the strategic decisions in the last years, I-11 outlines that it is important to involve key employees in the decisions and states "the tool for that is, that we do strategy days since two years". They are done once a year and involve a review of the last year on the basis of performance indicators as well as an exchange of different views. The direction of the company is then decided on. This tool can thus be the origin of strategic decisions.

[114]While a few interviewees have conducted a market analysis together with business planning or other management tools (e.g. I-17, I-33), there are also interviewees for whom market analysis is not relevant (I-11, I-15, I-25).

the research approach's potential to gain more in-depth and open insights by encouraging an answer that goes beyond a yes/no-answer. Thus, insights into views related to the application of the NPV in specific and management tools in general are gained (subsection 4.2.4.4). At the end of each subsection the findings will be discussed in relation to previous empirical studies on VBM in Mittelstand. Furthermore, existing research in the context of decision-making and/or the use of management tools in Mittelstand will be considered.

4.2.4.2 Application of the net present value method

Different positions are identified with regard to the application of the net present value method. These will be outlined in the following.

The majority of the interviewees clearly states that the net present value method is **not applied** (16/28). Some other interviewees do not express this directly but their answer clearly indicates that the NPV method tends not to be applied (8/28). This becomes evident from answering the question in an evasive way or naming aspects which can be interpreted as reasons for not applying management tools in general or the net present value method in specific (for details on such views see subsection 4.2.4.4). This also includes I-25 who interrupts the interviewer after the term NPV method is mentioned and states that he does not know the method. The interviewer then goes on giving a short outline of the method. The interviewee then states that the "mathematically correct" approach does not play a role but this is exactly what one does intuitively. He then outlines his intuitive considerations. The following quote gives a good summary of this approach:

> "What is my investment of personnel and money? When do I have the first items, that we produce for 50 Euros and can sell for 80, for example. These considerations are there, but you can only estimate them very, very roughly."

This shows that the net present value method is not applied in the way that it is understood in literature. However, respective considerations are done on a very rough level and after having understood the approach I-25 says that he applies the method intuitively. He can thus not be classified as clearly not applying the NPV method but likely does not apply the method as in the understanding of the literature.

In addition, a few interviews are **unclear whether the method is applied or not** (2/28). An example is I-28, who states that the NPV method is of course applied but then refers to difficulties in the use of management tools. Thus, there is doubt, whether the NPV is a decisive element in SDM.

There are also a few interviewees for whom the NPV method is **relevant in specific situations** (2/28). I-17 states that the NPV method has not been applied for strategic decisions regarding market positioning but that he would use it for machine investments. I-35 states that the NPV method is applied for decisions relating to the acquisition of companies. However, he also adds the following comment that shows that there are also decisions where NPV is not considered:

> "When it is[115] about the strategic position or about basic development or basic research or even research, then this does not play a role at all. No role at all."

Thus, even for the interviewees that state that the NPV method is applied, it is not applied for every strategic decision. The sample does not include an interviewee where the NPV method is clearly and strictly applied in SDM.

The different positions identified are summarised in Figure 37. Overall, it has been found that only a few interviewees apply the NPV method and then only in specific situations. A clear majority of the interviewees likely or clearly does not apply the NPV method (24/28).

Figure 37: Findings of the application of the net present value method

Clearly no application	Likely no application	Application unclear	Application in specific situations	Clear application in strategic decision-making
16	8	2	2	0

Previous empirical studies mostly evaluate the use of the NPV on the basis of a questionnaire with a five-point scale and then look at the percentage of respondents that use the NPV "very often" or "often" (see Figure 38). The corresponding percentage for the data at hand would at best be 7 %. This is even less than in recent empirical studies. The lowest percentage for the application of the NPV which has been found by Britzelmaier et al. (2018) is 15 % and thus twice as high. The difference is quite clear in comparison to Krol (2009c) and Schlegel et al. (2016) where a good third of the relevant respondents uses the NPV. An even clearer difference can be found in relation to Piontkowski (2009) and Wenzel (2014), who find the NPV being relevant for more than half of the respondents. However, it must be noted that the comparability is limited, as this high level of usage is found in combination with other methods of investment appraisal.

[115] The interviewee uses the personal verb I in the formulation, which is difficult to translate into English, thus the less personal formulation is used that reflects best what he says.

Figure 38: Existing empirical insights into the application of the net present value method

Aspect of comparison (column), empirical study (line)	**Approach to evaluate application of the net present value method**	**Findings application net present value method**
Britzelmaier et al. (2009), p. 10	Questionnaire on application of methods of investment appraisal, five-point scale	15 % of the respondents "(strongly) agree" to NPV
Krol (2009), p. 192		35 % of the respondents use NPV "(very) often", 4 % "unkown"
Piontkowski (2009), p. 360		56 % of the respondents use NPV/return "(very) often", 12 % "never applied/unkown"
Schlegel et al. (2016), pp. 72-73, 75		NPV relevant for 40 % of small companies in the sample
Wenzel (2014), pp. 146-147	Interviews among others looking at methods of investment appraisal	7 out of 18 interviewees addressing methods of investment appraisal use the net present value method (i.e. 39 % of the interviewees using methods of investment appraisal and 35 % of all interviewees). Additionally 6 interviewees combine NPV with other methods of investment appraisal. Thus a total of 13 interviewees applies the net present value method (i.e. 72 % and 65 %)

Due to the differences in the research approach a direct comparison is difficult and shall be considered with caution. Nevertheless, the comparison illustrates that finding a minimal application of NPV supports existing empirical studies that find a low level of application. The study at hand finds this in a specific context and with a specific approach. This includes looking at strategic decisions instead of investment decisions as previous empirical studies have done. In addition, asking about the relevance of the net present value method in a semi-structured interview enables more open insights than the questionnaires mostly used in previous empirical studies.[116] This has the limitation that it has, in some cases, not been possible to evaluate unambiguously whether the NPV is applied or not due to evasive answers. However, the approach also provides the potential to gain insights that go beyond the application of the NPV method.

[116] In this respect the empirical study is similar to Wenzel (2014), who also conducts semi-structured interviews but is different to the study at hand as he does not directly ask after the net present value method.

4.2.4.3 *Awareness of the net present value method*

The questioning approach also enables looking at the awareness of the NPV method. A respective analysis is valuable as a reason for not applying the NPV method could be that the interviewees do not know the method.

Some of the interviewees explicitly state not knowing the NPV method. In other cases the awareness needs to be judged by the researcher. Where a tendency is found, but there is no definite evidence, this is made transparent by using the categories “likely not known” or “likely known”. The findings are shown in Figure 39.

Several interviewees do not or likely do not know the net present value method (13/28). However, some interviewees also likely know or clearly know the net present value method (10/28). This becomes evident from remarks the interviewees make, e.g. I-6-EM’s reference to the NPV method as a method of dynamic capital budgeting. Another example is I-26 who refers to the discounting of cash flow. This needs to be done to determine the NPV. As this has not been mentioned by the interviewer the remark shows that the interviewee is aware of the NPV method.

Figure 39: Findings of the awareness of the net present value method

Clearly not known	Likely not known	unclear	Likely known	Clearly known
10	3	5	3	7

In comparison to previous empirical studies, a lower level of awareness of the NPV is found in the specific context of strategic decision-making. In the surveys of Krol (2009c) and Piontkowski (2009) the NPV is unknown to only 4 % and 12 % of the respondents.[117] In the study at hand 10 interviewees clearly express not knowing the NPV method, this corresponds to 36 % of the interviewees. The lower level of awareness is even more evident when taking into account that only 7 out of 28 interviewees are clearly familiar with the NPV method. The findings are also distinct in that they have been derived from interviews with owner-managers.

The low level of awareness of the NPV in the sample is regarded as a factor that limits the application of the NPV. The assumption that the NPV method can only be applied when it is known is in line with Scheiber, Wruk, Huppertz, Oberg, and Woywode’s (2012) reasoning that the knowledge of innovative management concepts puts a ceiling on their application. On that basis, training of owner-managers or other measures to raise the awareness of NPV are necessary for increasing the level of application. Britzelmaier et al. (2018) express a likewise view as they conclude that there is a need for measures to raise awareness of DCF methods on the basis of their finding that the NPV and other DCF methods are not adopted in practice.

Furthermore, this view is in line with similar implications from empirical studies on the use of other management tools in decision-making. According to van Auken and

[117] The results of Piontkowski (2009) refer to „net present value/return“ being „never applied/unknown“.

Yang (2014), different elements of financial statements are used more often in making decisions by owners who have the ability to interpret and use financial statements. In a similar way, Carraher and van Auken (2013) find owners more often using financial statements in decision-making when they are more confident in their use. They conclude that training can determine the use of financial statements in decision-making. Halabi et al. (2010) also conclude that there is a need to enhance financial literacy skills among small firm owners. This is also in line with Lavia López and Hiebl (2015), who identify a lack of training of the owner/manager as a factor decreasing the usage of management accounting systems in SMEs. Thus, the demand that measures are needed to raise awareness of the NPV method to allow for a higher level of usage in decision-making is in line with similar views in the broader context of the use of management tools in decision-making in Mittelstand.

The low level of awareness of the NPV in the sample is regarded as a factor that limits the application of the NPV. However, it must be noted that more interviewees seem to be aware of NPV than those who apply the method. Thus, not being aware of the method cannot be the only reason for the minimal application. In this respect, the questioning approach allows to gain further insights.

4.2.4.4 Views relating to the application of the net present value method and management tools

The answers, regarding the relevance of the net present value method, also give insights into the interviewees' views on the NPV method and management tools on a more general level. This includes several different aspects that are related to the relevance in strategic decision-making. The aspects are also addressed when talking about the use of management tools. The respective comments are included in the following outline.

Several interviewees refer to the **uncertainty of future development as an aspect that limits the benefit of calculations** (13/28). I-8 for example states that forecasting is very difficult and not possible as the market is of a very short-term nature. I-5 questions the benefits of plan calculations, independent of their form, if they are not achieved afterwards. In relation to the strategic decision to enter a new market, I-25 expresses that this cannot be forecasted with analytical models for example in this quote:

> "A look in a crystal ball, how will it look in the future? That will not be accomplished scientifically. The formula behind it is clear, but one will not be able to make it work."

I-25 also punctuates this view with a reference to benchmarking that is done in the industry. This includes benchmarking the turnover of approximately a dozen companies in the industry. In the view of I-25 based on these numbers, some of the companies should already have been bankrupt for a long time but they still exist and others must have "walls of gold". He thus concludes that even for this benchmarking there is insecurity and that he therefore does not rely on such methods. Likewise, I-16 expresses that one will never invest, if one wants to calculate everything because of the imponderability. As there is often not enough degree of capacity utilisation, an expected return is not achieved in the first years. This is achieved when the degree of capacity utilisation increases but "no one can tell you" when this point in time is. Even I-35, who applies the NPV method, does not apply it in all decisions because of the difficulty of forecasting. In the case of strategic positioning and fundamental research and development, the NPV method is not used, as the cash flow forecasts can only be guessed. However, calculations are used when a specific calculation and evaluation are possible, for example when the market and product are defined and numbers of items can be estimated. He emphasises this with reference to the forecast period in planning. In his view, the forecast for years four, five and following are "a highly theoretical forecast, which actually has no particular value" as these include so many insecurities, risks and chances. These examples illustrate that the uncertainty to forecast future developments limits the value of calculations for several interviewees.

I-26, I-27, I-28 and I-30-EM also refer to a limited benefit of calculations but in a slightly different sense. This can be illustrated with a quote by I-28:

> "... one can effectively calculate each investment to death or even beautifully, because one effectively makes assumptions when doing these calculations..."

For these interviewees the uncertainty of the future does not only limit the benefit of calculations as these are based on uncertain estimations but it also opens up opportunities to influence the result.

A second aspect addressed in relation to the NPV method and management tools, is that a majority of the interviewees expresses that they **use a different decision-making style** (18/28). Some of those interviewees refer to the use of gut feeling (10/18/28). Others say that the decision is taken according to the will of the owner (5/18/28) or as an "entrepreneurial decision" (3/18/28). Additionally, this includes reference to intuitive decision-making or decisions on the basis of experience. An example for an interviewee using gut feeling instead of management tools is I-27. Immediately after being asked about the approach to the strategic decision to acquire a company he responds in the following way:

> "I-27: Gut feeling.
>
> R: Gut feeling.
>
> I-27: So, I do not need anything, for such a decision, I do not need a 30 page PowerPoint presentation. I listen a lot to my feeling and you need that as an entrepreneur. Only using projections and calculations, because anyway all statistics are manipulated or can be influenced one way or another. ... One should just listen to the gut feeling."

I-15 also expresses gut feeling being more important than management tools in the context of strategic decisions to enter new markets:

> "Well, we have never done market analyses or such things before. That's gut feeling, the knowledge we have here about the markets."

For a current decision to enter a new market he mentions that projections exist, but they are difficult and he ends up making the following statement:

> "One then needs certain imaginativeness and a good gut feeling to say "Yes, if I find the right people in Finland[118] ... then we will at the end of the day generate earnings no matter what it costs.[119]"."

[118]Name of a different country used to protect anonymity of the company.

[119]The word order is slightly changed in translation.

This shows that similar to I-27, gut feeling is important in strategic decision-making for I-15. While gut feeling seems to be a major basis for decision-making, it does not completely replace the use of management tools. This is also the case for I-16, however with a different emphasis. I-16 describes scenarios that were developed, with the help of external advisors, to get a better basis for the decision to invest in a new building. In his view this is valuable for large decisions as:

> "he [the external management expert] ... only looks at the numbers, he is less emotional. As an entrepreneur you have more emotions, because one says, "Oh man, even when I cannot calculate it, it will pay off.". That means the point of view of several people, that are different and also have different pros and cons, that then makes sense. Not for every decision but for big decisions that could endanger the company."

He thus refers to an entrepreneur's gut feel by emphasising that it is not the exclusive basis for large investment decisions. However, despite the importance of scenarios the view of the owner-manager plays a crucial role:

> "one needed to take an entrepreneurial decision"

This illustrates an interesting aspect. A number of the interviewees uses management tools and also refers to using a decision-making behaviour that is related to the decision-maker's intuition. Overall, while using different terms, many interviewees express that gut feeling or the experience of the decision-maker is of importance in decision-making.[120] However, while there are indications that **decision-making on the basis of intuition, gut feeling and experience plays an important role in Mittelstand** it cannot be evaluated if it is more important than the use of management tools.

A third aspect is that some interviewees refer to the **possibility of taking wrong decisions** (10/28). Two different views can be identified in this respect.

Firstly, the possibility of wrong decisions has implications for the decision-making, in that decisions are only taken when there is no risk for the existence of the company (6/10/28). An example is I-18 who briefly mentions that an investment is done when he is of the opinion that it is valuable for the future and that it would not "kill me" if it is a mistake. I-8 also refers to the possibility of misinvestments threatening the survival of the company and the consequences for strategic decision-making:

> "I always say swabian conservative. We prefer to wait a bit longer. ... Sometimes we also discuss with the customers when they say "Why can you not do this yet?" et cetera. Well, we let ourselves in on these discussions before we take some, let me say, quick decisions that might hurt us later. Because ... just as an example to name a company, ... Würth[121] ... if he loses his investment of 2 million it is a drop in the ocean[122], yes. If we lose an investment of 2 million that can be significant for the survival of the company. In this respect, we are simply a little bit, how shall I say it, yes, conservative, simply a bit more reluctant."

[120] It can be noted that some interviewees additionally give insights into the aspects that they consider. While this is an interesting aspect this is beyond the scope of this work and is not addressed more in-depth.

[121] Würth group is a large family business from Baden-Württemberg with a total of approx. 70,000 employees.

[122] As a translation of the interviewee using the German saying „ein Tropfen auf den heißen Stein".

Thus the "swabian conservative" decision-making behaviour results from the aim to secure the existence of the company. The examples illustrate that the decision-making behaviour shall prevent wrong decisions that might threaten the existence of the company.

Secondly, some other interviewees have a different stance towards wrong decisions. Their position can be summarised as acknowledging that mistakes happen from time to time but that decisions are predominantly right (4/10/28). Examples are I-16 and I-25, who additionally give insights into how frequently wrong decisions occur. I-16 expresses that in the evaluation of the probability to get additional orders to fully utilise the machine capacity

> "you perhaps have a strike rate of 70 %. That's just the way it is. It can be possible that the machine is sometimes 50 % empty for three, four years because there are currently no orders for THIS machine [emphasis by the interviewee]. But the mix, if you take the whole mix, it needs to fit."

This illustrates I-16's view that there are misjudgments, but they are not regarded as problematic as long as the decisions are predominantly right. Similarly, I-25 expresses that 80 percent of the intuitive decisions are correct and that "you can live with the 20 percent bad ones".

A fourth aspect found in the answer regarding the relevance of the NPV method is that some interviewees see **differences in their strategic decision-making towards that of others** (10/28). In their outlines there is reference to "affiliated groups" (I-31), "large businesses" (I-16, I-18, I-25), "large affiliated groups" (I-24, I-25), "American way" (I-26) and "companies nearer to capital market" (I-35). While not using the same term, the message is very similar – in those companies decision-making is more analytical and more oriented towards numbers.[123] A quote from I-25 illustrates this:

> "In a large business you cannot decide intuitively, there you need to submit figures in order that some managing director or senior manager somewhere decides. ... They think completely, completely different, that is a completely different story. There Return on Investment is actually included..."

Some of the interviewees also give reasons for the difference in decision-making behaviour. This position becomes evident from the view outlined by I-18. He states firstly that a typical difference in comparison to large businesses is that he knows the company very in-depth. Secondly, he has the freedom to decide whether to invest in a machine when he thinks it is promising and that he is able to afford it without endangering jobs even if he cannot say that there will be a Return on Investment in the next two or three years. He emphasises this by outlining a "good entrepreneurial decision" where his father decided to invest in a machine some years ago. At the beginning the capacity utilisation was 10 % and this decision would have never been taken in a large company. In his view there are rarely "good entrepreneurial decisions" in large companies. This is because "no one has the balls and says, I stand up for this." or the person who is convinced of something has not the position to enforce the decision because it cannot be clearly calculated that the investment will pay off within two years. The two examples illustrate the view that de-

[123] The only exception is I-8 who refers to larger companies to express that misinvestments are less relevant for those companies than for his business.

cisions are more based on numbers in large companies and more intuitive in Mittelstand, an aspect that is addressed by some interviewees (6/10/28). In addition, a few interviewees refer to examples including the view that owner-managers have more freedom in making decisions than in large companies where other people need to be convinced (4/10/28).
This aspect and the other views addressed in this subsection might influence the use of the NPV method and other (VBM) management tools in strategic decision-making. These will be discussed in relation to existing insights on VBM in Mittelstand and in the broader context of research on decision-making in Mittelstand.

There are indications that **decision-making on the basis of intuition, gut feel and experience plays an important role in Mittelstand**. This supports findings in previous empirical studies that analysed VBM in decision-making from the perspective of whether decisions are taken on the basis of experience, the NPV method or other methods of investment appraisal. Britzelmaier et al. (2018), Krol (2009c), Piontkowski (2009) and Schlegel et al. (2016) all find experience or qualitative assessments to be of major importance. Firstly, experience is a basis for investment decisions for a clear majority of the respondents (for details see Figure 40). Secondly, the importance of experience is additionally emphasised as the approval ratings are higher than for the NPV. Furthermore, Krol (2009c) and Piontkowski (2009) find it to be the most important basis for investment decisions.

Figure 40: Existing empirical insights on the relevance of experience in comparison to the net present value method

Aspect of comparison (column), empirical study (line)	Finding application experience	Finding application net present value method
Britzelmaier et al. (2009), p. 9	78 % of the respondents use experience values "(very) frequently" as basis for investment decisions	15 % of the respondents "(strongly) agree" with NPV
Krol (2009), p. 192	83 % of the respondents use experience "(very) often", most important method of investment appraisal	35 % of the respondents use NPV "(very) often", 4 % "unkown"
Piontkowski (2009), p. 360	78 % of the respondents use experience "very often" or "many at a time", most important method of investment appraisal	56 % of the respondents use NPV/return "(very) often", 12 % "never applied/ unkown"
Schlegel et al. (2016), pp. 73, 75-76	56 % of the respondents regard qualitative assessments as relevant, no significant size differences for SMEs are reported	NPV relevant for 40 % of the small companies in the sample

The finding that decision-making on the basis of intuition, gut feel and experience plays a role in strategic decision-making in Mittelstand is also in line with empirical studies on decision-making in SMEs. Posch and Speckbacher (2012) find that family businesses use a decision-making style that is characterised more by intuition than the use of data and figures. In making strategic decisions, small firm managers in the empirical study of Brouthers et al. (1998) also rely more on intuition instead of information and analysis. While finding the use of simple analytical tools Jocumsen (2004, p. 670) also finds an "extensive use of gut feel and intuition". Similarly, Curseu and Vermeulen (2008, p. 193) assume that intuition "is the dominant mechanism" in SDM in SMEs. Thus, the indications for the importance of intuitive decision-making found, are also in line with similar indications in the broader context of decision-making in SMEs. The study at hand goes beyond the existing empirical insights by finding this in the specific context of strategic decision-making in Mittelstand on the basis of interviews. However, the findings at hand do not allow evaluating whether NPV or intuitive decision-making is more important.

The findings suggest that Mittelstand owner-managers have the view that the **unpredictability of future limits the benefit of calculations**. In the empirical studies on VBM in decision-making in Mittelstand, a similar aspect has until now only been addressed by Wenzel (2014). He addresses factors impeding the use of VBM in Mittelstand. According to Wenzel (2014), a key factor that causes management decisions not solely being focused on the increase of the company value, are the specifics of the industry. Even in companies where VBM is largely implemented from a technical point of view, decisions are not fully oriented towards an increase of the company value due to the dynamics of the industry. Thus, similar to the indications in the study at hand, Wenzel (2014) finds that an aspect of the decision-making environment has an influence on the relevance of VBM in SDM. While there is some overlap, it must be noted that the environmental factor found in the study at hand is different in that the emphasis is on the uncertainty of future developments and not on developments in the industry.

The view that Mittelstand's specific environment influences decision-making is in line with views in research on SDM in SMEs. Brouthers et al. (1998) address that the unpredictability of the future makes SDM in small firms difficult. Curseu and Vermeulen (2008, p. 190) acknowledge that "SMEs often operate in very dynamic environments in which business opportunities occur in an often unpredictable way". They regard this as one factor which makes SME owner-managers' decision-making different to decision-making by managers in large corporations in that there is a need for deciding quickly and implementing decisions fast. The empirical insights add to the body of knowledge by indicating that this aspect also influences the use of (VBM) management tools in SDM in Mittelstand.

The findings add to the body of knowledge by finding that **owner-managers consider the possibility of wrong decisions** in strategic decision-making. This aspect has not yet been empirically addressed in VBM in Mittelstand literature and the literature identified in the broader context of decision-making in Mittelstand.

There has been repeated reference to **the decision-making behaviour being different to large listed companies**. In the findings at hand, this difference is not only related to management tools being generally more relevant in those companies than in Mittelstand. Furthermore, it is addressed that there are differences in the decision-making behaviour in the context of characteristics of Mittelstand e.g. more freedom in making decisions. The view expressed by the interviewees is similar to findings from previous empirical studies addressing differences of VBM in decision-making in Mittelstand towards larger companies and groups of companies (Krol, 2009c; Schlegel et al., 2016). Krol's (2009c) sample includes subsidiary companies which are used as a control group. He finds that mittelständische companies rely considerably more on experience in investment decision-making than subsidiary companies. Additionally, subsidiaries use NPV and the internal rate of return (IRR), which is also in line with VBM, more often than Mittelstand (Krol, 2009c, pp. 192–193). Similarly, Schlegel et al. (2016, pp. 74–76) find that larger corporations use NPV and IRR more often than SMEs.[124]

The findings also support empirical findings regarding the role of intuitive decision-making in Mittelstand. Similar to the view addressed by the interviewees, Posch and Speckbacher (2012) find differences relating to the use of tools in decision-making. Without differing kinds of tools such as Krol (2009c) and Schlegel et al. (2016), Posch and Speckbacher (2012) come to a similar conclusion. They find decision-making in family firms to be less based on tools to support decision-making and more based on intuition.[125] Brouthers et al. (1998, p. 135) finds that within a sample of small firms decision-making in larger firms is "significantly more rational than [in] smaller firms".

Finding indications for differences of strategic decision-making in Mittelstand to large, listed companies additionally supports a notion in literature in the context of SDM in Mittelstand. Gibcus and van Hoesel (2008) and Gibcus et al. (2009) express that many researchers argue that decision-making of owner-managers in SMEs is different to that of managers in large firms. According to Curseu and Vermeulen (2008) the difference to large companies' decision-making is one of the major issues in research on strategic decision-making in SMEs. According to them SMEs make less use of decision-making tools that allow for a rational decision-making than larger companies. Furthermore, the indications from the interviews are in line with research on management accounting systems in SMEs. On the basis of a literature review Lavia López and Hiebl (2015) conclude that empirical evidence shows management accounting systems to not only be used less but also differently than in large firms. This includes management accounting practices not being used for decision-making. However, Lavia López and Hiebl (2015) add that there is little evidence for this phenomenon and demand further research.

It can be concluded that similar to the findings at hand, empirical studies in the context of decision-making in Mittelstand find differences between Mittelstand and both large firms and other kinds of companies (Brouthers et al., 1998; Krol, 2009c; Posch & Speckbacher, 2012; Schlegel et al., 2016). The findings are also in line with a no-

[124] A significant difference in the use of qualitative assessments is not reported.

[125] However, it needs to be noted that Posch and Speckbacher (2012) relate this difference to being a family business or a non-family business and not to the size as Schlegel, Frank, and Britzelmaier (2016) and as being independent from groups of companies as Krol (2009c).

tion in literature on strategic decision-making in Mittelstand (Curseu & Vermeulen, 2008; Gibcus & van Hoesel, 2008; Gibcus et al., 2009) and research on management accounting systems in SMEs (Lavia López & Hiebl, 2015). It has to be noted that the finding that Mittelstands' decision-making behaviour is different to that of large, listed companies in being more intuitive and less based on management tools is only a secondary aspect in the findings at hand and not addressed at length by the interviewees. This is nevertheless a contribution to the body of knowledge, as there does not yet seem to be a good understanding of how decision-making is different and what specifics of Mittelstand cause these differences (see subsection 2.4.2.1). In this respect, the findings at hand provide insights from the perspective of Mittelstand owner-managers. Furthermore, the findings indicate that this might be related to the unpredictability of the future. There are also indications that the views addressed by the interviewees in this context influence the use of NPV and (VBM) management tools in strategic decision-making.

4.2.5 Summary of the section and discussion

In this section the findings in relation to management tools in strategic decision-making in Mittelstand have been outlined. This contributes to the body of knowledge by generating empirical insights on the basis of the research questions. Before summarising the insights gained with regard to the research questions it shall be outlined how the approach taken goes beyond that taken in recent empirical studies.

The **approach taken in this research is specific** in the context looked at and its methodological approach. Firstly, the research is specific as the focus is on management tools in the context of strategic decision-making in Mittelstand. This becomes evident in comparison to empirical studies that focus on VBM in Mittelstand and touch upon decision-making. Additionally, this research is different to other empirical studies in the context of decision-making (for an outline of the approach taken by these empirical studies and aspects addressed see subsection 2.4.2.2). While literature empirically analysing VBM in decision-making in Mittelstand also often focuses on the use of management tools, Wenzel (2014) is the only one that focuses on strategic decisions similar to the study at hand. Several other empirical studies analyse VBM in the context of investment decisions (Britzelmaier et al., 2018; Krol, 2009c; Piontkowski, 2009; Schlegel et al., 2016; Wenzel, 2014) or management decisions on a more general level (Tappe, 2009). Management decisions on a more general level are also empirically analysed by Carraher and van Auken (2013), Halabi et al. (2010) and van Auken and Yang (2014), who focus on the use of financial statements. Additionally, there are empirical studies similar to this research in focusing on strategic decisions, but which look at management tools on a more general level without identifying specific tools (Brouthers et al., 1998; Jocumsen, 2004; Posch & Speckbacher, 2012). Beyond this there is empirical research on strategic decision-making in SMEs looking at other aspects of the phenomenon without touching upon the use of management tools (e.g. Gibcus & van Hoesel, 2008; Gibcus et al., 2009; Lucas et al., 2008). Thus, this study contributes to the body of knowledge by generating empirical insights on management tools in the specific context of strategic decision-making that has not yet been empirically analysed with this focus.

Secondly, the methodological approach of this research is specific in conducting interviews with owner-managers. This is different to previous empirical studies looking at aspects in a broadly similar context on the basis of questionnaires (Brouthers et al., 1998; Carraher & van Auken; Krol, 2009c; Piontkowski, 2009; Posch & Speckbacher, 2012; van Auken & Yang, 2014). While some empirical studies also used interviews to gain insights, there are differences in the context looked at (Halabi et al., 2010; Jocumsen, 2004; Tappe, 2009; Wenzel, 2014). Beyond focusing on strategic decision-making as a specific context on the basis of a specific methodological approach building upon interviews, further aspects make this research specific. These will be outlined together with summarising the findings in the following.

As a context for the findings, it has been outlined **how the interviewees address strategic decisions** (for details see subsection 4.2.2). Based on the specific approach of this research the interviewees talk about several kinds of decisions and on different levels. The decisions talked about include a wide range of decisions such as decisions regarding market positioning, the foundation of subsidiaries, the acquisition of companies, investment in new buildings or the expansion of buildings, succession or change of generation, machine investments and orders. In this respect the research is specific in that the kinds of decisions talked about have been identified from the strategic decisions addressed by the interviewees and not determined in advance as previous empirical studies looking at specific kinds of strategic decisions (Gibcus et al., 2009; Wenzel, 2014).[126]

With regard to the level of talking about strategic decisions, four groups have been identified (for an overview see Figure 41). These differ in the way in which and the extent that the interviewees address strategic decisions. The interviewees of group SDM-A talk about strategic decisions on a superficial and more general level. This makes it difficult to get an in-depth understanding of how specific strategic decisions are taken. This is also the case for the interviewees of group SDM-B, who talk about several strategic decisions on a superficial level, too. However, in contrast to the interviewees of group SDM-A, the interviewees of group SDM-B give several examples for one kind of decision. This allows gaining some understanding of how this kind of decision is taken. The interviewees of group SDM-C also talk about several strategic decisions. In doing this, they put a slight emphasis on one specific decision which allows some understanding of the decision-making for this decision. The interviewees of group SDM-D put a strong emphasis on one decision. Thus, a good understanding of the decision-making for this decision can be gained. They still talk about some decisions.

[126]This empirical study is also different to empirical studies that address investment decisions on a more general level and not on the strategic level (Britzelmaier, Pöpplow, and Andraschko (2018); Krol (2009c); Piontkowski (2009); Schlegel et al. (2016)).

Figure 41: Groups of interviewees identified regarding different levels of talking about strategic decisions

Group of interviewees (column), information on the groups (line)	Group SDM-A	Group SDM-B	Group SDM-C	Group SDM-D
Characteristic	Interviewees talk about strategic decisions on a superficial, more general level	Interviewees talk about several strategic decisions on a superficial level, with several examples for one kind of decision	Interviewees talk about some strategic decisions, with a slight emphasis on one decision	Interviewees talk about a few strategic decisions, with a strong emphasis on one decision
Number of interviews assigned to this group	4	9	9	6
Interviewees assigned to this group	I-5, I-21, I-28, I-35	I-9(-EM), I-15, I-25, I-26, I-27, I-29(-EM), I-30-EM, I-33, I-34-EM	I-10, I-11, I-12, I-13, I-14, I-18, I-19, I-20, I-24	I-6-EM, I-8, I-16, I-17, I-31, I-32

The level on which the interviewees talk about strategic decisions is different to the intention of the research approach. To gain in-depth and open insights in relation to RQ1 and RQ2 the questions focused on gaining an understanding of a small number of specific strategic decisions.[127] While the interviewer tried to steer the conversation towards a detailed narrative, this was difficult. As a consequence, some aspects relating to the first two research questions could not be analysed as in-depth and holistically as intended.[128] Despite this limitation valuable insights are gained.

Based on the specific research approach and in the context of interviewees talking about several kinds of decisions on different levels empirical insights have been gained on the basis of RQ1:

[127] This included warming-up with a question about the strategic decisions taken in the last few years. Then, the researcher asked the interviewees to illustrate how strategic decisions are taken on the basis of one example.

[128] It has not been possible to gain insights into the use of (VBM) management tools for all decisions addressed. As the outlines are more superficial than intended, insights into how the management tools are used could only be gained for a number of the tools and a number of the interviewees. In addition, the potential to gain insights into new aspects beyond the focus on (VBM) management tools is more limited than intended.

What management tools are used in strategic decision-making in Mittelstand, and in which ways are these tools relevant for strategic decision-making?

The empirical insights contribute to the body of knowledge as the literature review has shown that there are little empirical insights into what management tools are used in strategic decision-making (for details see subsection 2.4.2). In this respect different management tools are referred to in different ways. The insights are summarised in the following (for details see subsection 4.2.3).

Several interviewees (14/28) address business planning and/or planning a profit and loss statement. These express different views. While some interviewees express that these are not relevant (5/14/28), others regard planning as relevant (9/14/28). However, there are still differences as this is partly done in a pragmatic manner (3/14/28) while others plan more elaborately (4/14/28).

Differences in the relevance have also been found for cost accounting (17/28). This is partly addressed rather briefly and it has not been possible to gain insights into whether and how this is relevant in strategic decision-making (7/17/28). However, from the more extensive outlines, it has been found that there are three ways in which cost accounting is relevant. Firstly, a regular analysis of cost accounting information is a trigger for strategic considerations (4/17/28). Secondly, cost accounting information plays a role in the evaluation or implementation of a strategic decision (3/17/28). Thirdly, cost accounting is addressed in the context of orders (8/17/28). It is surprising that cost accounting is a topic in the context of strategic decision-making as this managerial accounting tool is usually applied in operative business.

Additionally, methods of investment appraisal have been addressed (13/28). Based on the more extensive outlines of the interviewees, profit comparison and Return on Investment are relevant for strategic decision-making (8/13/28). There are also differences as these are partly used in a pragmatic manner and partly in a more elaborate way. Beyond this, there are additional short references to other methods of investment appraisal.

It can be concluded that the following tools have been addressed by several interviewees, which has given insight into different views related to these tools and their role in strategic decision-making:

- Business planning and/or planning profit and loss statement
- Cost accounting
- Methods of investment appraisal

Beyond this a smaller number of interviewees provided insights into:

- Cash flow
- Balanced Scorecard and
- VBM management tools and/or KPIs

These have each been addressed by a few interviewees. Due to the lower number of interviewees addressing these tools only indications for their role could be derived.

For each of the tools, it has been analysed whether it is included or touched upon in one of the previous empirical studies looking at VBM in decision-making in Mittelstand (Krol, 2009c; Piontkowski, 2009; Tappe, 2009; Wenzel, 2014) and empirical studies touching upon the use of management tools in decision-making in Mittelstand (Britzelmaier et al., 2018; Carraher & van Auken, 2013; Halabi et al., 2010; Schlegel et al., 2016; van Auken & Yang, 2014). The detailed results are shown in Figure 42. From this analysis two aspects become evident. On the one hand, it is possible to identify distinct equivalents in previous empirical studies for the methods of investment appraisal addressed by the interviewees. On the other hand, cost accounting, business planning and other tools found are not or only indirectly touched upon in previous empirical studies. Thus, empirical insights into management tools in strategic decision-making have been developed further. This will be outlined in the following.

Firstly, the findings in relation to RoI and profit comparison support but also modify the insights provided by empirical studies in the context of investment appraisal (Britzelmaier et al., 2018; Krol, 2009c; Piontkowski, 2009; Schlegel et al., 2016; Wenzel, 2014). The finding that RoI plays a role in strategic decision-making supports recent empirical studies as follows. Britzelmaier et al. (2018), Krol (2009c) and Schlegel et al. (2016) all find RoI to be used by a majority of the respondents and find it to be one of the more common methods of investment appraisal in Mittelstand (for details on the existing insights see Appendices-Figure 16).[129] Previous empirical studies have, in principle, categorised the use of RoI as a non-DCF method which is not in line with VBM (Britzelmaier et al., 2018; Krol, 2009c; Schlegel et al., 2016). The more in-depth view taken in this research supports this but adds that some elements of VBM's basic economic view reflect in the way in which RoI is used by the interviewees. However, RoI still does not allow evaluating the economic advantageousness from a perspective fully in line with VBM. Additionally, the findings modify existing empirical insights as RoI is found to be relevant in the specific context of strategic decision-making in Mittelstand and that there are different ways to use RoI. Recent empirical studies are supported in a similar way with regard to the relevance of profit comparison. Britzelmaier et al. (2018) and Schlegel et al. (2016) have found profit comparison to be a widely applied method of investment appraisal among SMEs. The findings show that profit comparison is also relevant in the specific context of strategic decision-making in Mittelstand. The findings also indicate that the way in which profit comparison is applied in SDM is not in line with VBM. This supports the categorisation on principle by Britzelmaier et al. (2018) and Schlegel et al. (2016).

Secondly, it is important that beyond the methods of investment appraisal, it is difficult to relate the findings at hand to previous empirical insights. The majority of the tools is not included in most of the previous empirical studies. Individual previous studies only provide indirect indications, either by reference to a slightly different kind of tool and/or by looking at a slightly different context.

129 Piontkowski (2009) and Wenzel (2014) also find the rate of return to play a role, partly however in combination with other methods.

Previous empirical studies provide indications for related, but slightly different, management tools playing a role in decision-making with regard to three management tools. With regard to the relevance of profit and loss statements in decision-making the exploratory study by Halabi et al. (2010) provides rare indications for accounting information and planning being used for decision-making.[130] However, there are no further details on how planning elements of accounting reports, such as the profit and loss statement, is relevant in decision-making. In a similar vein, García-Pérez-de-Lema and Duréndez (2007) express that cash budgets can be used in the decision-making process but do not specifically refer to cash flow as the interviewees in the study at hand. Likewise, previous empirical studies have found that cost comparison is a common basis for investment decisions in Mittelstand (Britzelmaier et al., 2018; Schlegel et al., 2016).[131] However, the interviewees in the study at hand refer to cost accounting. While both methods share the focus on costs, cost comparison as a method of investment appraisal is usually performed to evaluate individual investments. In contrast, cost accounting is intended as a management tool for an entire company and not as a tool for investment appraisal. While some previous empirical studies also provide evidence for the relevance of cost accounting in Mittelstand (García-Pérez-de-Lema & Duréndez, 2007; Lohr, 2012) it is new to find cost accounting being relevant in strategic decision-making.

While BSC and EVA are directly addressed in previous empirical studies, the context is different. Previous empirical studies on VBM in Mittelstand all refer to the BSC for management of the company in general and not its use in decision-making (Gonschorek, 2009a; Krol, 2009c; Piontkowski, 2009; Wenzel, 2014). Similarly, empirical studies touch upon the use of EVA in a context different to strategic decision-making (Gonschorek, 2009a; Khadjavi, 2005; Krol, 2009c; Wenzel, 2014).[132] Only Schlegel et al. (2016) refer to EVA in a similar context, i.e. investment appraisal. However, they use the broader term of "value-based methods (e.g. EVA)". Yet, similar to the study at hand Schlegel et al. (2016) find these to be of little relevance.

---

[130] In relation to how financial information is used to inform business decisions Halabi, Barrett, and Dyt (2010, pp. 171–172) mention that three out of 10 interviewees address an analysis of information in accounting reports to make decisions. One of these uses financial information for future plans.

[131] For details see Appendices-Figure 16.

[132] Krol (2009c) and Gonschorek (2009a) consider EVA in the analysis of KPIs and management tools used for managing the company as a whole. Some interviewees of Wenzel (2014) refer to EVA in different contexts e.g. performance management. According to Khadjavi (2005) one interviewee is aware of EVA.

Figure 42: Analysis of insights gained in previous empirical studies for the management tools identified from the interviews

Empirical studies included in the analysis	
1) Britzelmaier et al. (2018), esp. p. 10 2) Carraher & van Auken (2013) 3) Halabi et al. (2010), esp. pp. 171-172 4) Krol (2009c), esp. p. 192 5) Piontkowski (2009), esp. p. 360 6) Schlegel et al. (2016), esp. pp. 72-73, 75-76 7) Tappe (2009) 8) van Auken & Yang (2014) 9) Wenzel (2014), esp. pp. 119-120, 142-144, 150-151, 169-170 10) Additional empirical studies addressing single management tools	
Management tools addressed by the interviewees	**Related findings in previous empirical studies**
Business plan and/or planning profit and loss statement	1) & 2) tool not included in study 3) indirect indications: use of analysis of information in accounting reports to make decisions 4) – 9) tool not included in study
Cost accounting	1) indirect indications: cost comparison method 2) – 5) tool not included in study 6) indirect indications: cost comparison method 7) – 9) tool not included in study 10) Lohr (2012): indirect indications: cost accounting 10) García-Pérez-de-Lema & Duréndez (2007): indirect indications: management accounting systems
Methods of investment appraisal	1) among others: RoI, profit comparison method 2) & 3) tool not included in study 4) among others: RoI 5) indirect indications: net present value method/rate of return 6) among others: RoI, profit comparison method 7) & 8) tool not included in study 9) among others: RoI, partly in combination
Cash flow	1) – 9) not included 10) García-Pérez-de-Lema & Duréndez (2007): indirect indications: cash budgets

(figure continued on next page)

Management tools addressed by the interviewees	Related findings in previous empirical studies
BSC	1) – 3) tool not included in study 4) indirect indications: BSC for the management of the company, not in context of SDM 5) indirect indications: BSC for the management of the company, not in context of SDM 6) – 8) tool not included in study 9) indirect indications: BSC for the management of the company, not in context of SDM 10) Gonschorek (2009a): indirect indications: BSC for the management of the company, not in context of SDM
VBM management tools and Key Performance Indicators (EVA)	1) – 3) tool not included in study 4) indirect indications: EVA for the management of the company, not in context of SDM 5) tool not included in study 6) indirect indications: value-based methods (e.g. EVA) 7) & 8) not included 9) indirect indications: EVA for the management of the company, not in context of SDM 10) Gonschorek (2009a) & Khadjavi (2005): indirect indications: EVA for the management of the company, not in context of SDM

Overall, this shows that the research approach did not only allow for further insights in relation to tools already addressed in previous empirical studies, but also made it possible to find several other tools that are relevant in strategic decision-making. Thus, the findings broaden existing insights in relation to the use of management tools in decision-making. Additionally, insights have been gained on how some of the tools are used in SDM. From this it has become evident that there are different views on the use of some of the tools.[133] Thus, the understanding of the use of management tools in SDM is not only broadened but also enhanced on the basis of RQ1.

The insights gained in relation to management tools used in strategic decision-making provide insights into RQ2:

> **How is VBM reflected in the use of management tools in strategic decision-making in Mittelstand?**

In this respect the empirical insights contribute to the body of knowledge given that the literature review has shown that there are little empirical insights on VBM in decision-making in Mittelstand (for details see subsection 2.4.2.2). In contrast to most previous empirical studies the study at hand focuses on SDM. Furthermore, the

[133] However, due to how the interviewees addressed strategic decisions these are only part indications and further research in this respect is regarded as beneficial.

analysis from different perspectives reflects different possibilities in that VBM can reflect in decision-making identified from the literature review. Overall, the findings support previous empirical studies with regard to the little relevance of VBM in decision-making in Mittelstand (Britzelmaier et al., 2018; Krol, 2009c; Piontkowski, 2009; Schlegel et al., 2016; Tappe, 2009; Wenzel, 2014) (for an overview of the findings and approach taken in these empirical studies see subsection 2.4.2). This will be illustrated in the following.

Firstly, in line with previous empirical studies, the findings indicate a preference for non-DCF instead of DCF methods of investment appraisal which are preferred from a VBM perspective (Britzelmaier et al., 2018; Krol, 2009c; Schlegel et al., 2016). The interviewees address RoI and profit comparison, which have already been found to be non-DCF methods, that are common in investment appraisal in previous empirical studies. The DCF methods included in previous empirical studies have not been addressed when asking the interviewees about the tools used in SDM. Secondly, there is also very little reference to VBM management tools and KPIs. Thirdly, none of the tools addressed by the interviewees can be related to the examples Günther (2015b) gives for how tools that reflect VBM's basic economic view can be used in decision-making. Fourthly, the minimal relevance of VBM is supported by a perspective that goes beyond previous empirical studies (Britzelmaier et al., 2018; Krol, 2009c; Piontkowski, 2009; Schlegel et al., 2016; Tappe, 2009; Wenzel, 2014). This perspective builds upon literature's notion that it is not important which specific tool is applied but that the tools need to reflect the basic economic view of VBM. On this basis the tools applied have been analysed with regard to whether they reflect the basic economic view of VBM.[134] This analysis has shown that sometimes elements of VBM basic economic view play a role.[135] However, while elements of VBM's basic economic view can be found in some cases none of these interviewees combines them to analyse the economic advantageousness of a strategic decision from a VBM perspective. While Tappe (2009) and Wenzel (2014) also go beyond focusing on the application of VBM management tools their emphasis on whether criteria and motives in decision-making are in line with VBM is different to this perspective. Thus, it is concluded that the insights support previous empirical studies with regard to the minimal application of VBM in the specific context of the use of management tools in strategic decision-making and with a specific methodological approach that includes an open questioning approach and a more in-depth analysis from different perspectives on the basis of interviews.

These insights have been complemented by asking the interviewees about the net present value method, which is a method of investment appraisal in line with the VBM approach. These findings support the little relevance of VBM in strategic decision-making but also develop the body of knowledge further (for details see subsection 4.2.4). The level of application was actually even lower than in recent empirical studies. This might be related to the specific context and methodological approach. Beyond this, the specific approach has also allowed for further insights that provide

[134]This has been done where it was possible on the basis of how interviewees addressed SDM.

[135]In this respect, orientation towards the future has been found more often than others. There is also some consideration of risks. In contrast, costs of capital tend not to be relevant and cash flow is seldom, and then only briefly, addressed.

indications for understanding the little relevance of NPV in specific and management tools in general. This includes finding little awareness of the net present value method among owner-managers. While this is more pronounced than in previous empirical studies this supports the existing notion that a lack of knowledge is a factor impeding the use of NPV and management tools in general in SDM. However, there have been indications of other influencing factors. Firstly, despite the low awareness of the net present value method the application is even lower. While not being aware of the method is certainly a reason for not applying the method, this cannot be the only reason. Secondly, the specific research approach yielded insights into views of the owner-managers, which might influence the application as well. The views addressed include unpredictability of future limiting the benefit of calculations and intuitive decision-making playing an important role in SDM. Beyond this, the possibility of wrong decisions seems to be accepted. Furthermore, the interviewees regard a decision-making style being less based on management tools as difference to large, listed companies. This supports the body of knowledge by providing indications for the way in which decision-making in Mittelstand is different to that in large, listed companies. This helps to develop the little existing knowledge on such differences (for details see subsection 4.2.4.4). It is interesting to discuss the findings further in relation to views in the broader context of decision-making in Mittelstand.

The findings might imply that the low relevance of VBM is not only related to a lack of knowledge but also to the attitudes of owner-managers towards the use of management tools in strategic decision-making in general. A likewise assumption is also expressed by Krol (2009c). He mentions that a reason for investment decisions being based on experience instead of (VBM) management tools could be that owner-managers are highly confident in their own decision-making competence and thus regard tools for decision support as unnecessary. Krol (2009c) criticises this as a shortcoming in the rationality of decision-making that needs to be reduced. Piontkowski (2009) also argues that VBM is advantageous as a basis for taking decisions on a more rational basis. Other authors in the broader context also express that a threat can result from the lack of rationality in decision-making in Mittelstand (Brouthers et al., 1998; García-Pérez-de-Lema & Duréndez, 2007). From this perspective the owner-managers' view is problematic.

However, there are also different views in literature. Posch and Speckbacher (2012) find significantly more successful family businesses using an intuitive decision-making style than less successful family businesses. On this basis they conclude that the more intuitive decision-making should not be regarded as a lack of professionalism in management but rather as an adequate adaptation to family businesses' specific environment. Jocumsen (2004, p. 670) also demands presenting changes to improve decision-making in small businesses within the context of how decisions are taken which includes an "extensive use of gut feel and intuition". In his view, understanding and accepting strategic decision-making practice instead of ignoring and destroying it, has more potential to improve SDM. Artinger, Petersen, Gigerenzer, and Weibler (2015) also acknowledge the value of heuristics in managerial decision-making. While not being related to Mittelstand their differentiated view might be valuable in this context. This includes emphasising that heuristics should not be regarded as "all-purpose tools but strategies that can perform well in particular environments" (Artinger et al., 2015, p. 27). Their successful application depends on the match with the given environment, which is termed "ecological rationality". This can be aided by using formal managerial tools. Curseu and Vermeulen (2008) also express that the interaction of intuitive and more analytic reasoning might result in more successful decision-making and should be explored further. Artinger et al. (2015) formulate a likewise demand. They state that managerial decision-making research can be significantly developed beyond the still dominant rational choice model by a broader recognition of ecological rationality.

Against the background of these views the research at hand points at valuable avenues for further research. Similar to Artinger et al. (2015), who express that the traditional rational choice model is still dominant in managerial decision-making research, this model also seems to dominate the views in relation to VBM in decision-making in Mittelstand. Given that not only this research but also other empirical studies find indications of intuition being important it seems to be valuable to acknowledge its role in decision-making in Mittelstand. This would go beyond criticising the lack of rationality and might help to enhance strategic decision-making practice. Researchers might therefore analyse, for example, whether and how VBM plays a role in intuitive decision-making. Furthermore, it could be analysed under which circumstances decision-making is more successful on the basis of tools and when intuition leads to more successful decisions.

Overall, it can be concluded that the findings in relation to management tools

- provide a broader and enhanced understanding of the use of management tools in SDM,
- support existing findings in relation to the minimal relevance of VBM in the context of decision-making on the basis of a more in-depth analysis from different perspectives,
- and provide indications for owner-managers' views that might help to understand their decision-making behaviour further.

This has been based on an approach being specific in focusing on the use of management tools in strategic decision-making as specific context and by generating insights with a research approach that enables more open and more in-depth insights on the basis of interviews.

Based on the findings in relation to strategic decision-making it is interesting to analyse the objectives and see whether VBM reflects in these objectives. One relevant view in this respect is that the lack of defining objectives in line with VBM is partly addressed as a potential reason for the minimal application of VBM in Mittelstand (Krol, 2009c; Tappe, 2009). The following section will outline the findings in relation to objectives.

4.3 Objectives

4.3.1 Aim and approach of the section

In this chapter the findings regarding objectives will be outlined. This is related to RQ3:

> What are the objectives of Mittelstand?

Based on this research question, in-depth insights into the objectives of Mittelstand shall be gained in an open manner. In relation to this research question, all interviewees refer to several objectives. The themes identified in relation to objectives will be described in subsection 4.3.2.

In addition, the findings outlined in the following are related to RQ4:

> How is VBM reflected in the objectives of Mittelstand?

This is related to economic objectives and will thus be touched upon when outlining the themes that represent economic objectives. A further analysis shows nuances that the overall target course reflects non-economic or economic objectives. This will be addressed in subsection 4.3.3.

4.3.2 Specific objectives of Mittelstand

4.3.2.1 Aim and approach of the subsection

In this subsection the objectives addressed by the interviewees will be outlined. The emphasis is on understanding the objectives by illustrating them with quotes and examples from the interviews. The objectives identified are then discussed in relation to the body of knowledge derived from the review of recent empirical studies (for details see 2.4.3.2). This focuses on discussing similarities and differences in the understanding of the respective objectives.

4.3.2.2 Securing existence

The majority of the interviewees refers to securing the existence of the company as an objective (15/28). In this context only a number of the interviewees uses the phrase "securing the existence". Mostly this objective is expressed in more colloquial language such as "survival", "not becoming bankrupt" or "safety of the company". While securing the existence itself can be regarded as a long-term objective nearly half of the interviewees additionally emphasises the long-term focus (7/15/28). This can be illustrated with a quote from I-8:

> "... We regard the topic with a long-term view. And, .. simply saying "OK, we need to take out more profit" would be nice on the one hand, but on the other hand it does not lead anywhere in our industry. ... The whole topic is set up in the long run, we also want to be in the market in 10 or 20 years insofar it does not make sense to extract money from the company now, because in the long-term view this would be a short term solution. I take out the money, fine, but in five years I'm bankrupt and then I have not won anything ... Thus .. the focus is more on long-term survival, that one needs to say very clearly."

This interviewee makes it very clear that the focus is on securing the existence in the long run. In addition, he relates securing existence to the aspect of retaining profits in the company. This relation of securing existence to making profit is made by the majority of the interviewees that address securing existence as an objective (10/15/28). This includes the view that profits are necessary to secure the existence of the company. Additionally, the interviewees express that the existence is more important than high profits similarly to I-8.

An objective that builds upon but goes beyond securing the existence of the company is the **continuance as a family business and/or owner-managed company.**[136] This is addressed by some interviewees (7/28[137]). Two of these interviewees address this indirectly by reference to family succession as an objective. This also results in the company still being owner-managed and is thus included.

This objective is addressed in different ways. For I-15 it is the key company objective. This becomes evident from the outstanding length of the comments and their content. The following quote from I-15 illustrates this:

> "But now the overarching objective for me actually is firstly the preservation of the family business as a family business. That is the topmost objective. And thereby many other things actually formulate themselves."

The interviewee then goes on, talking at length about the implications of this objective for the company, which includes integrating the next generation into the company and that offers for participation are not accepted. He specifies that the company aim is the centenary celebration as a family business. Similarly, I-25 addresses securing succession at length. I-5, I-8, I-17 and I-30-EM also make clear that staying owner-managed is important but address the topic much more briefly. Being a family business is part of the vision for I-17 and the most important objective for I-30-EM. Being owner-managed is a "great, great objective" for I-8 and securing succession is a "fundamental topic" for I-5. In the case of I-10 it is an objective that the son takes over the management of the company in the future but this does not seem to be as crucial as for the others. The differences in the importance of securing the continuance as an owner-managed company also become evident from another observation: In addition to the companies that address this as objective there are several companies in the sample that touch upon this topic during the interview but do not address it as an objective.

It is interesting to note that all companies with this objective currently **deal with passing generations**. However, they seem to be at different stages of passing generations. I-5, I-8[138] and I-30[139] are currently owned and managed by several family members of different generations. Thus, the change of generation is already happening. The change of generation seems to be in an earlier phase in the case of I-15 and I-17. In both cases the interviewees are around 60 years old and are the only managing directors of the company. However, other younger family members are already co-owners of the company and work in the company. For I-10 and I-25 the change of generation is planned for the future. In this context it is astonishing that I-25 addresses succession at such length. Similar to I-10 the interviewee is roughly 55 years old and the next generation is not yet part of the company. How-

[136] This is a broader form of securing existence as a company cannot be continued in this way when it does not exist anymore.

[137] Three of these interviewees also refer to securing the existence of the company.

[138] It is interesting that the initially contacted commercial manager of the older generation referred the researcher to the interviewee, who is an owner-manager of the younger generation.

[139] I-30 is managed by owner-managers and external managers. I-30-EM talks about a planned change of responsibility and the respective changes in the management and ownership structure. This change of generation and the respective changes in the structure have been prepared for a while. A later review of the company's website has shown that the final steps of the planned changes have been realised in the 12 months following the interview.

ever, I-25 clearly states that his vision is to decide on the succession in five years and that steps are already being taken to prepare for this decision which will be the "most difficult management decision". Under consideration of the characteristics of the companies and interviewees continuance as an owner-managed business seems to especially be an objective for family businesses where the key owner-manager is close to 60 or older.[140]

The insights gained in relation to the objective of securing existence are summarised in Figure 43. On an overall level it can be concluded that securing the existence of the company is an objective for the majority of the interviewees (19/28).[141] This research adds to the body of knowledge in deepening the understanding of this objective in the following ways.

Firstly, securing existence also has a **financial dimension** which does not become evident from existing questionnaire studies, which only include the item "securing the company's existence" (Krol, 2009c; Piontkowski, 2009). The relation to profits that is made by the interviewees has also not been addressed by existing interview-based studies (Khadjavi, 2005; Tappe, 2009; Wenzel, 2014). An indication for securing existence also having a financial dimension can only be found in Gonschorek (2009a). Gonschorek (2009a) looks at the objective to secure the company's existence in a more differentiated way than the other empirical studies – beyond the item "securing company existence" the category "existence objectives" includes "securing liquidity". However, while this also indicates a financial dimension to the objective to secure the existence of the company, the findings at hand indicate that the relation to profit seems to be more immediately relevant for the interviewees than that to liquidity. In addition, the findings add to the body of knowledge that the long-term focus inherent in this objective is so important for some of the interviewees that they mention it additionally.

Secondly, this research also adds strength to indications that the objective of securing existence can take the **broader form of continuance as owner-managed business and/or family business** and provides more in-depth insights. Wenzel's (2014) empirical study already identified "securing existence/preservation of the company for the next generation" as a key company objective. Consequently, while not explicitly commenting on this, Wenzel (2014) also provides indications that the objective to secure the company's existence can take the broader form of continuance as owner-managed and/or family business. The study at hand goes beyond Wenzel (2014) in finding this objective to be especially relevant for family businesses where the key-owner manager is close to 60 or older. Apart from this, a similar objective can only be found in Achleitner et al. (2010) who look at a "firm transfer to next family generation". This dimension of the objective to secure the existence is omitted by the majority of recent empirical studies (Deloitte & Touche GmbH Wirtschaftsprüfungsgesellschaft, 2015; Gonschorek, 2009a; Krol, 2009c; Piontkowski, 2009; PricewaterhouseCoopers AG Wirtschaftsprüfungsgesellschaft,

[140] Exceptions in terms of age are I-10 and I-25. Additionally it can be noted, that apart from I-10 all of these companies already have been passed from one family generation to another at least once.

[141] This includes the interviewees directly referring to securing existence and those that refer to continuance as owner-managed company. Interviewees that refer to both objectives are counted only once.

2014; Schlepphorst & Schlömer-Laufen, 2016). Overall, a broader and more in-depth understanding of securing the existence as an objective has been developed.

Figure 43: Findings of securing existence as an objective

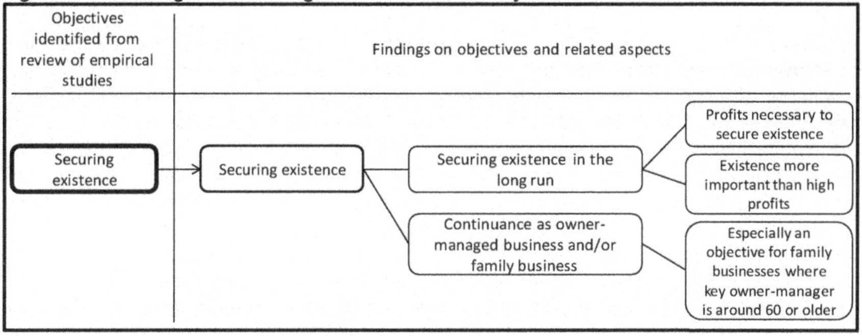

4.3.2.3 Market-oriented objectives

There are interviewees that address **customer satisfaction as an objective**. An example is I-10 who states that it is an objective to have "satisfied customers". He seems to be proud to have customers who are thankful for the cooperation which they describe as "awesome and great". Letters expressing this are hung on the noticeboard. I-24 briefly mentions the objective that all customers are satisfied. It is important to emphasise that customer satisfaction is only addressed in this way by a few interviewees (5/28). This is much less than expected from the literature review where customer satisfaction has been found to be one of the objectives of major importance (see subsection 2.4.3.2.2). However, customer satisfaction is also addressed in a second way, which will now be looked at.

An example for the second way to address customer satisfaction is I-6-EM. He outlines that the company aims at growth. I-6-EM names praise from customers and being known on the market as "parameters that somehow contribute" to this objective. This gives the impression that customer satisfaction is not the overall objective but a subordinate objective. A similar orientation is evident in the case of I-9, who emphasises that the customer needs to be satisfied because "if you do not have satisfied customers, then you cannot make deals". Another example for customer satisfaction as an objective in combination with other objectives is I-13. I-13 answers the question regarding objectives by simply stating "we want to become the best tool manufacturer in this sector. Not the largest but the best one.". On further request he mentions different aspects that are important for the customers on the market and refers to one former competitor who had an outstanding position on the market. This former competitor sold his tools on the market despite them being twice as expensive as others. He could do this because customers had confidence in the products. I-13 then states that he aims at customers having trust in the company and its products. Trust by customers is regarded as being related to customer satisfaction. This shows that for I-13 customer satisfaction is not the only objective but related to the objective of getting a certain position in the market. Overall these three cases illustrate that **customer satisfaction as an objective contributes to striving for other market-oriented objectives** (I-6: growth, I-9: "make deals", I-13: certain position on the market). A similar relation to other objectives is identified by some interviewees (7/28).

In addition, data analysis has revealed **objectives in this context that go beyond customer satisfaction**. This implies that customer satisfaction might be a too narrow view of what the interviewees aim at in the context of customers. This partly becomes evident from the examples just addressed. I-13's orientation is, for example, related to customer satisfaction, yet customer satisfaction seems to be a too narrow concept to represent the position in the market I-13 aims at. Similar to this case, other interviewees have objectives in the context of customers that go beyond customer satisfaction. This includes a range of objectives relating to customers, products and the market. Among other things, interviewees refer to objectives regarding product quality, technological advancements or being innovative. While these aspects are primarily related to a product of the company, they are often addressed together with customer expectations or positioning in the market in relation to customers. Other aspects that are addressed are a change of or strengthening of the market position, finding new market potentials or adapting to a change in the market. There is also reference to the market position in relation to competitors. Overall, these objectives are more adequately referred to by the broader view of market-oriented objectives.

The findings indicate that market-oriented objectives are important for Mittelstand, as the vast majority refers to such objectives (24/28). This includes references to customer satisfaction in two different ways as well as references to other market-related objectives. The insights are summarised in Figure 44. The findings go beyond existing empirical results in two ways.

Firstly, more in-depth insights are gained in relation to the objective of customer satisfaction. From the interviews, it has become evident that customer satisfaction as an objective can contribute to striving for other objectives. This relation is not evident from the findings of recent questionnaire studies that address this objective (Gonschorek, 2009a; Krol, 2009c; PricewaterhouseCoopers AG Wirtschaftsprüfungsgesellschaft, 2014). While Wenzel (2014) briefly addresses the relation of objectives this does not include customer satisfaction.

Secondly, the findings imply that the broader view of "market-oriented objectives" suits the interviewees' perspective better than the narrow focus on "customer satisfaction", which is dominant in recent questionnaire studies (Gonschorek, 2009a; Krol, 2009c; PricewaterhouseCoopers AG Wirtschaftsprüfungsgesellschaft, 2014). Indications that Mittelstand's objectives in relation to the market and customers are not limited to customer satisfaction can be found in few recent empirical studies. Wenzel (2014) finds not only companies aiming at customer satisfaction but also companies aiming at innovation and technology leadership and at an increase in the market. On this basis he concludes that the majority of the companies aims at a dominant market position. Hence, Wenzel (2014) combines different market-related objectives in a similar way to this empirical study. However, in the findings at hand there is no general orientation towards a dominant market position. Beyond Wenzel

(2014) a few questionnaire studies include different or additional items that indicate the relevance of a broader understanding than customer satisfaction.[142] However, previous empirical studies only refer to individual aspects included in the broader understanding and do not look at this in depth. Altogether, the findings provide a broader and more in-depth understanding of market-oriented objectives.

Figure 44: Findings of market-oriented objectives

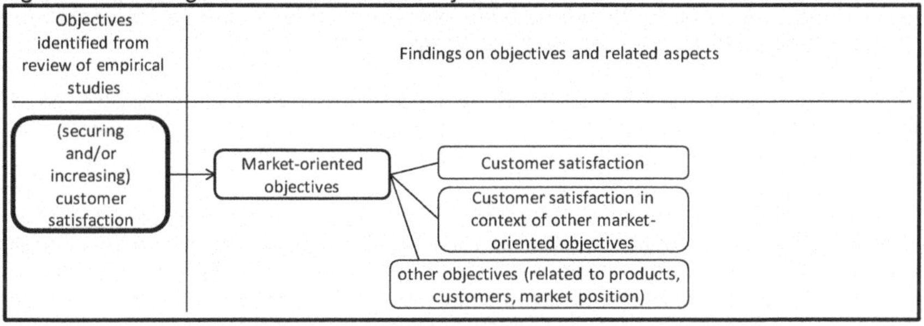

4.3.2.4 Employee-oriented objectives

Beyond the reference to employee satisfaction, the interviewees refer to other objectives relating to employees. Thus, the data suggests taking the broader view of employee-oriented objectives instead of employee satisfaction (similar to broadening the objective of customer satisfaction to market-oriented objectives in subsection 4.3.2.3).

Some interviewees refer to the objective of **employee satisfaction** (7/28). This is done by direct reference to employee satisfaction (I-20, I-21, I-26) or more indirectly by reference to "that the people come here with joy" (I-29) or "come back to work on Mondays motivated" (I-31) or that employees can work without fear as far as possible (I-35).

Beyond employee satisfaction, employee-oriented objectives referred to by the interviewees include **securing jobs** (7/28). It is interesting to note that only two interviewees refer directly to securing jobs as an objective (I-9-EM, I-26). Other interviewees address this objective indirectly by pointing towards other companies in the industry or large listed companies who dismiss staff and make clear that this should not be done. This indicates that securing jobs is not an overall objective but more an auxiliary condition in aiming at other objectives. This also becomes evident from I-26 who states that "the objective is still to keep as many jobs as possible here" and then outlines that this is only possible as the company is active in a niche sector and not a mass market, where they would not have any chance with their German production site.

[142] Deloitte & Touche GmbH Wirtschaftsprüfungsgesellschaft (2015) refer to "product-market objectives". In Gonschorek (2009a) the category "market objectives" does not only include "securing/increasing customer satisfaction" but also "preservation/expansion of international acitivities".

Additionally, the theme “employee-oriented objectives” includes a range of different objectives that can be broadly summarised as referring to the **interaction in the company** (7/28). This includes not putting too much pressure on employees as this leads to faults (I-31) or keeping employees motivated and aiming at a good interaction with each other (I-20).

A few interviewees briefly refer to **employee retention** as an objective (3/28). One interviewee directly uses this term (I-35), two others refer to this by adressing the objective of long-term employment (I-24, I-29).

The heading “**getting access to qualified employees**” can be used for what is outlined by a few interviewees (2/28). Both interviewees address the problem to find qualified personnel in the context of objectives and state that this is a “big topic”.

In addition to these different employee-oriented objectives another aspect is interesting. From the remarks some interviewees make when naming employee-oriented objectives there is the impression that these are regarded as **being valuable not only for the employees themselves but also for the company** (5/28). This is inherent in the objective to get access to qualified employees but also referred to by the interviewees. I-26 names employee satisfaction as an objective. He emphasises that the employees are needed for the company and that it is necessary to “keep them in a good mood” because they will then perform well. Thus, employee satisfaction is not only an objective in the interest of the employees but also in the interest of the company. I-12 also points at balancing the interests of the employees and the company. He outlines that most of the employees are willing to do extra hours and work on Saturdays when necessary, “thus the obligation I have towards the employees is very big”. The objectives of securing jobs and employee satisfaction result from this obligation. The examples of I-26 and I-12 illustrate that while employee-oriented objectives are at first sight beneficial for the employees they are also regarded as valuable for the company.

On an overall level, employee-oriented objectives seem to be an important objective (19/28). Employee satisfaction in a narrow sense is only an objective for some of the interviewees (7/28). The findings regarding employee-oriented objectives are summarised in Figure 45. These add to the body of knowledge in two ways. It has been seen that it is valuable to take a broader view than employee satisfaction and consider other employee-oriented objectives such as securing jobs or employee retention as well. This goes beyond questionnaire studies that only address employee satisfaction as an objective (Krol, 2009c; Piontkowski, 2009). Indications for some of the employee-oriented objectives can be partly found in previous empirical studies. Wenzel (2014) mentions, in the context of the objective of employee satisfaction, that this is related to employee retention for one interviewee. However, he does not analyse this further. Achleitner et al. (2010) and Gonschorek (2009a) also refer to objectives relating to securing jobs. However, it has to be noted that the focus of the interviewees in the study at hand is on securing jobs and not on the creation of jobs as in Achleitner et al. (2010) and Gonschorek (2009a).[143] Further-

[143]Achleitner et al. (2010) include the item “preservation and creation of jobs”. Gonschorek (2009a) refers to “preservation/creation of jobs”.

more, Gonschorek's (2009a) findings provide another indication for employee-oriented objectives. He indirectly addresses access to qualified employees as an objective by finding constant personnel development to be an objective in Mittelstand. Overall, these empirical studies touch upon single employee-oriented objectives identified from the interviews but do not provide an understanding of this kind of objective.

Furthermore, a more in-depth understanding of employee-oriented objectives is developed as it has been found that these are regarded to be of mutual benefit for employees and the company. Thus, the broader and more in-depth understanding develops the findings from previous empirical studies.

Figure 45: Findings of employee-oriented objectives

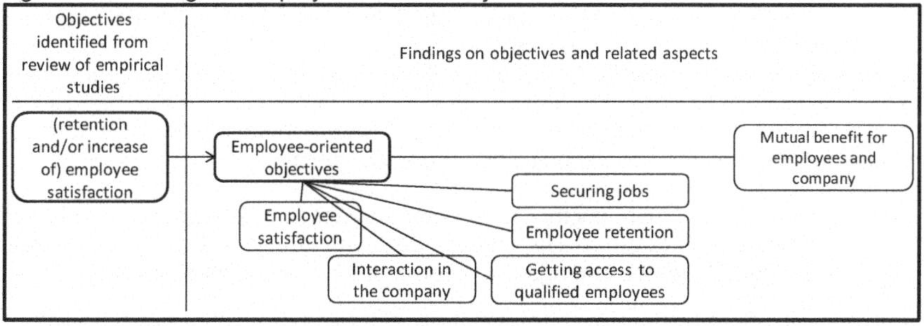

4.3.2.5 Independence

It is interesting, that the interviewees refer to independence as an objective in relation to some kind of stakeholder. In this respect, two aspects can be distinguished.

A few interviewees name **independence from banks** as an objective (4/28). The interviewees often address the topic of making a profit in the context of independency from banks. This can be illustrated with the outline of I-8. Together with the aim to stay an owner-managed company he names staying independent from banks as a "great, great objective". However he mentions that it is questionable whether it can stay like that in the future because the margins are getting smaller and the company needs to make high investments to secure its existence. I-20 also refers to this relation:

> "I want to make a profit, of course, but there is no particular figure which I am aiming at. Instead it is a healthy profit, so that we can afford our investments ourselves, without that we need a bank here."

I-20 is specific as he does not directly use the term "independent" but it is still evident that he wants to be independent from banks. These two examples show that the interviewees relate independency from banks to profit.

Apart from independency from banks some interviewees aim at **a wide spectrum of customers, products or industries to be supplied** (6/28). While the respective term is used only seldom, it is regarded as another form of independency. This is because the broad spectrum is related to being less dependant on for example individual customers. While only one interviewee directly uses the term “risk” it becomes evident that the motivation for this objective is to reduce risks. This can be illustrated with a quote from I-11:

> “.. an important point .. is that we always say, if a customer leaves[144] or an investment goes astray, this shall not bring the company into difficulties. That means always maintain a certain degree of independence. Thus we have a very broad diversification of products and customers.”

I-11 is specific in using the term independence but typical in indirectly outlining the motivation to reduce risks for the company without using the term risk. This indirect reference to independence from customers to reduce risks also becomes evident from the outline by I-10:

> “Objective for us is to have more customers in the smaller range, between 5 and 25 thousand Euros turnover per year ... If one goes, it is not that bad, you find a new one. Three or four 500 thousand Euro customers, then it would certainly hurt, if one goes.”

This shows that I-10 regards having a few larger customers as a risk for the company and aims at having many smaller customers. In doing this he is more independent from individual customers. Thus, I-10 is one of the interviewees where the relation to independency becomes evident from the context.

When considering both aspects that have been addressed independence is relevant for some interviewees (8/28[145]). The findings are summarised in Figure 46. Overall, it can be concluded that the findings are different to recent empirical studies.

In the data there is no reference to entrepreneurial independence on a general level as it is included in recent questionnaire studies (Gonschorek, 2009a; Krol, 2009c; Schlepphorst & Schlömer-Laufen, 2016). In contrast to this, the interviewees refer more specifically to independence from banks and a broad spectrum on the market. Indications for such a different understanding of the objective of independence can be found in the empirical study of Wenzel (2014) and Achleitner et al. (2010). While not addressing this in more depth, Wenzel (2014) mentions financial independence as a key company objective, which is similar to independence from banks found in this empirical study. The item “prevention from loss of ownership/independence” addressed by Achleitner et al. (2010) provides indirect indications for the interviewees’ view that independence from customers, products and industries can reduce risks. However, Achleitner et al. (2010) do not address this in more depth. Thus, the interpretation of aiming at a broad spectrum on the market as a specific form of independency goes beyond previous empirical insights.

[144] As a translation of „wenn ein Kunde abspringt“.

[145] The two interviewees that address both aspects of independence are only counted once.

Figure 46: Findings of independence as an objective

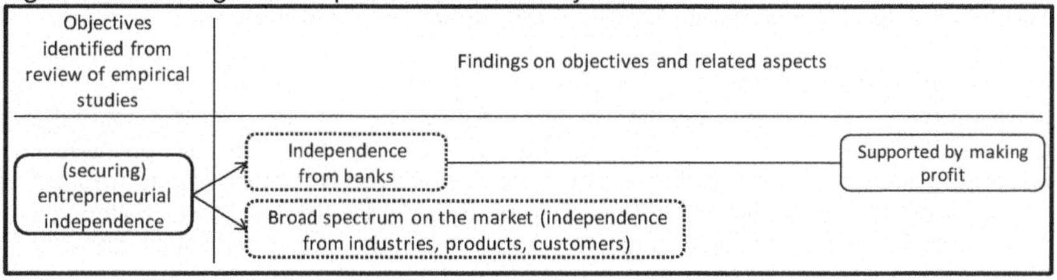

4.3.2.6 Objectives related to internal improvements

The interviewees address objectives that can be summed up as objectives related to internal improvements. This theme emerging from the data includes a **broad range of different aspects** that are regarded as primarily internal improvements by the researcher. While some of these are oriented towards the whole company, others are more specifically relevant for a specific area of the company, especially the area of production. Overarching objectives are, for example, bringing the organisation of the company "to the next level" (I-10), saving money by sharing administrative capacities (I-14), reducing energy and/or water consumption (I-16, I-19, I-24), continuous improvement (I-30-EM) and larger premises (I-31, I-32). Other objectives that are more oriented towards the specific area of production are:

- "enough utilisation of capacity" (I-12)
- Increasing efficiency and/or productivity (I-9, I-16, I-17)
- Automatisation (I-18)
- Reducing waste and/or complaints (I-19, I-29-EM)
- New machine and new technologies (I-32)

This range of different objectives related to internal improvements is addressed by half of the interviewees (14/28).

It can be recognised that many of these objectives are either directly or indirectly **related to an economic advantage for the company**. I-24 names the objective "how can one still reduce costs, save energy". I-16 states that saving energy is an objective "as the costs of energy explode". Thus in both cases saving energy is directly related to reducing costs for the company and is not only an objective for the sake of the environment. I-32 also relates the new machine and the new technologies to economic advantages for the company ("saving manpower costs", "the Return on Sales is expanded then through the new technologies"). I-20 says that a company has been engaged to give advice regarding lean management to increase productivity and reduce throughput times and "of course also the costs". These are examples where an economic advantage is directly mentioned. In addition, economic advantages for the company go along with other objectives even if they are not directly mentioned. This is the case for increasing efficiency. Another example is I-30-EM who addresses a continuous improvement process and implementing Kata in the administration as objectives. These are management methods that shall enhance the efficiency of a company.[146] These examples illustrate how objectives related to internal improvements are related to economic advantages.

The findings are summarised in Figure 47. Overall, a broad range of internal improvements is addressed by half of the interviewees (14/28). In the majority of cases this involves economic advantages for the companies, directly or indirectly. As will be shown it is difficult to relate these objectives to objectives addressed in previous empirical studies. The economic dimension inherent in these objectives is dominant in "cost objectives" and "maximum increase of the operative efficiency" found to be of major importance by Deloitte & Touche GmbH Wirtschaftsprüfungsgesellschaft (2015) and Schlepphorst and Schlömer-Laufen (2016). However, the strong focus on the economic aspect of these objectives is not regarded as suitable to reflect the objectives addressed by the interviewees. Furthermore, individual objectives addressed by the interviewees (reducing energy and/or water consumption) might be related to "ecological objectives" and "ecological sustainability" included in the studies of PricewaterhouseCoopers AG Wirtschaftsprüfungsgesellschaft (2014) and Schlepphorst and Schlömer-Laufen (2016). However, it does not seem suitable to use a similar term due to how these objectives are addressed. This gives the impression that the focus is on internal improvements like reducing costs and not just doing well for the environment. The decision to not include a theme referring to ecological objectives is a difference to the notion in literature where ecological objectives are regarded as relevant for Mittelstand.[147] Overall, none of the recent empirical studies includes an objective that adequately reflects the aspects addressed by the interviewees. Consequently, finding objectives focused on internal improvements expands the body of knowledge.

Figure 47: Findings of objectives focused on internal improvements

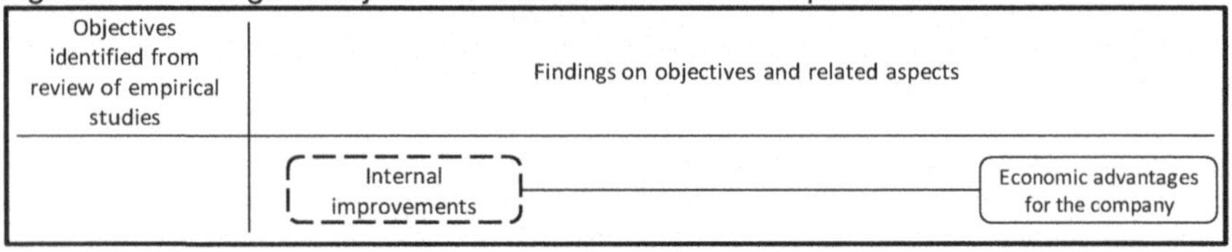

4.3.2.7 Objectives relating to the size of the company

Half of the interviewees address objectives relating to the size of the company (14/28). The analysis shows that growth seems to be an ambivalent objective for the majority of those interviewees. Only three interviewees refer to a growth objective without somehow limiting the validity of this objective.

In the other cases the **ambiguity** of this objective is reflected by two recurrent aspects. Firstly, interviewees explicitly refer to only aiming at a limited growth or to factors limiting the possibilities for growth. Secondly, growth is addressed in a fluc-

[146]Kata is a management method to enable employees to continually improve processes in the company. Continuous improvement process and Kata are terms related to lean management which include principles and methods to efficiently organise the activities of a company.

[147]For details see subsection 2.4.3 and Appendices-Figure 6. A likewise difference can be noted for objectives related to society and personal objectives.

tuating way. An example to illustrate both aspects is I-13. Right at the beginning of outlining the objectives I-13 states that the aim is to become the best tool manufacturer in this sector and adds “not the biggest but the best”. This indicates a refusal of growth as an objective. However, after outlining other objectives and being asked about further objectives he says that expansion would be done under circumstances. This shows that he does not completely refuse growth after all. He expresses that plans for expansion do exist but moans and says that “staff responsibilities is somewhat a drawback”. When being asked why, I-13 explains that the reason is firstly that it is difficult to find employees and secondly that he wants to see the employees each day and wants to know their strengths and weaknesses. Thus employees are a factor limiting the possibilities of growth. The following statement concisely gets to the heart of I-13’s, as well as other’s, attitude towards the objective to grow:

> “As an entrepreneur you have to do something. Thus we can yet grow a little, but moderately.”

This example is illustrative regarding four things. Firstly, the aim is to grow moderately. Secondly, it reflects a fluctuation in the impression one gets of I-13’s attitude towards growth. In the beginning he seems to be against growth, then his remark regarding expansion gives the impression that growth is still an objective. He then immediately refers to difficulties related to the growth as an objective and ends up expressing that he aims at growing moderately. This kind of fluctuation of the outline can be identified for nearly half of the interviewees addressing growth (7/14/28). The third aspect is that I-13 names employees as a limiting factor. Apart from employees other interviewees refer to room capacities as a limiting factor. In addition, it is emphasised that attention must be paid to customers not being dissatisfied when the company grows and might not be able to uphold quality and delivery times. Fourthly, growth is the only objective that is refused occasionally by some interviewees (I-13 not wanting to become the biggest). Overall, this illustrates that growth is an ambivalent objective.
The insights gained are shown in Figure 48. Objectives relating to the size of the company are addressed by half of the interviewees (14/28). However, this is an ambivalent topic for most of these interviewees (11/14/28). Their focus is on moderate growth or a growth under preconditions and not on growth at any price. The finding that growth is an ambivalent objective contributes to the body of knowledge by creating an enhanced understanding of this objective.

Recent questionnaire studies touch only briefly on the market-related part of firm growth by referring to the increase of turnover and/or market share (Gonschorek, 2009a; Krol, 2009c; Piontkowski, 2009; PricewaterhouseCoopers AG Wirtschaftsprüfungsgesellschaft, 2014; Schlepphorst & Schlömer-Laufen, 2016). The only questionnaire study which refers to “firm growth” is Achleitner et al. (2010). However, slight indications for firm growth being an objective which is only pursued under preconditions, can be found in Tappe (2009) and Wenzel (2014). Both briefly mention “profitable growth” as an objective but do not address this in more detail (Tappe, 2009, p. 208; Wenzel, 2014, p. 124). In a quote from an interview given by Wenzel (2014) the interviewee expresses that the turnover shall grow under the condition of an expected return and only as far as possible on the basis of the company’s financial resources (Wenzel, 2014, p. 126). The empirical findings thus provide a richer picture of objectives relating to size than previous empirical studies.

Figure 48: Findings of growth as an objective

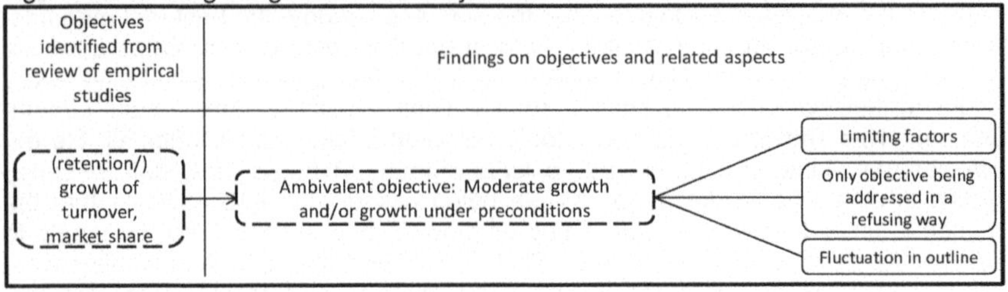

4.3.2.8 Increase of company value

The interviews have been analysed specifically with regard to the objective to increase the company value to gain insights into RQ4:

How is VBM reflected in the objectives of Mittelstand?

In relation to this research question the synthesis of findings of recent questionnaire studies (Achleitner et al., 2010; Gonschorek, 2009a; Krol, 2009c; Piontkowski, 2009; PricewaterhouseCoopers AG Wirtschaftsprüfungsgesellschaft, 2014; Schlepphorst & Schlömer-Laufen, 2016) has shown the increase of the company value to be

- the most important financial objective,
- and one of several important objectives on the overall level
- but not the most important overall objective (for details see subsection 2.4.3.2.2).

Based on this, it is surprising that only one interviewee refers to the **increase of the company value as an objective**. I-35 names the increase of the company value as an objective at the beginning of his outline of the objectives:

> "So generally there is of course the objective of our shareholders here, to sustainably create values in the company. Sustainably create values IN the company [emphasis by the interviewee]."

While the interviewee refers to creating values, this does not provide sufficient evidence to clearly identify the objective to increase the company value. The interviewee might also refer to ethical values, especially because he used the term "sustainably". The researcher thus kindly asks the interviewee to specify what he means by this after the interviewee has finished his outline of the objectives. It then becomes clear that his understanding is very close to the understanding of the increase of the company value as an objective in the literature. Among others the interviewee refers to "company value". His outline of his understanding of VBM confirms that the company value is understood in a way similar to the literature on VBM in Mittelstand:

> "Value-oriented is for me exactly, what I have just tried to explain to you. One can yet debate for a long, long time about the measures for that, maybe we touch again on this in a short while. But ultimately the company value, thus what was treated as a taboo word in companies like ours, [is] the shareholder value. This value orientation is most certainly the translation of the shareholder value to mittelständische structures. That's how I understand it, yes?"

He thus clearly relates what is done in the company to the shareholder value approach which is the origin of the VBM approach (see subsection 2.2.2). This is supported by the company's use of EVA as a key performance indicator, which measures the increase in the company value. It can thus be concluded that with the reference to the objective to sustainably creating values in the company, I-35 refers to an increase of the company value in the sense of the literature on VBM in Mittelstand.

However, when taking a closer look there is a slightly different orientation than assumed in the literature. The focus is primarily on an increase of the value in the company and only secondly on cash flow to shareholders. After being asked to specify what he means by sustainably creating values in the company I-35 states:

> "For a start this means that the company level is always before the private level of the shareholders. This means that we would never make the strategic development of the company dependant on individual desires of individual shareholders. According to the principle "We aren't investing any more, instead we are can pay a higher dividend to the shareholders". That is completely different. The company as such, with the means it has, it also does not get additional means from the shareholders but the shareholders leave the means in the company. The company has to do its best with the means it has. If there is something left, one can also distribute it to the shareholders but not the other way round. Yes. That is the thinking, creating values in the company. The company needs to grow, the company value can ultimately be calculated, should then also [grow], one then needs to look at the measures. How do I now calculate the company value? But that so is the key objective. Yes."

Shortly after this he adds that there have not been dividend payouts in the last 20 years and that "if we would have had greedy shareholders in addition [to the challenges of growth], the company would not have been able to develop in the way it has". This is interesting together with the quote because it shows that the objective to increase the company value is primarily pursued in the company. While the shareholders can benefit from an increase of the company value they currently do not receive cash flow in form of dividends and have not received any in the last 20 years. This is slightly different to the understanding in VBM in Mittelstand literature which emphasises that the value for the owners is fundamentally based on the cash flow to the owners (Gonschorek, 2009a; Günther, 2015b; Krol, 2009c; Lehmann, 2012; Wenzel, 2014). However, it has not been possible to elaborate on the shareholders' expectations.

Beyond this, there are two interviewees that refer to **securing or creating wealth as an objective** which can also be related to VBM. I-16 states that wealth can be preserved for following generations and that this is an objective. To interpret this objective in light of value-based management one can draw upon Khadjavi's (2005) conclusions. Based on his case study he expands the conceptualisation of VBM objectives by adding "satisfying value" and "preserving value" as objectives alternative to "maximising value" (Khadjavi, 2005, pp. 178–182). While not explicitly aiming at an increase of the company value I-16's aim to preserve wealth for following generations can be interpreted as aiming at preserving the company value.

In addition, it is interesting to have a look at I-11's outline. He states:

> "There is ... the effort, so I do not want maximum return from the GmbH[148], but I want a long-term, slow protection and increase of wealth. Also for the family, that is in the background with me hereafter, exactly."

A few minutes later he confirms the interpretation of this statement as objective related to the company value. After the interviewer has presented the understanding of VBM in literature with the words "monetary value of the company for the owners" I-11 states:

> "Essentially we have this currently."

It is interesting to acknowledge that all three objectives named by Khadjavi (2005) can be found in I-11's answer. From this perspective I-11's quote can be interpreted in the following way. He refuses maximisation of the company value ("I do not want maximum return"). Similar to I-16 he then says that preserving value is relevant for him ("I want a long-term, slow protection"). Contrary to I-16 he goes beyond this and states to aim at an increase of wealth which can be seen as a "satisfying value".

An overview of the findings is shown in Figure 49. Overall, beyond one interviewee aiming at a sustainable increase of value in the company, two other companies aim at a preservation (and increase) of wealth. This can be interpreted from a VBM perspective drawing upon Khadjavi's (2005) conceptualisation of different levels of VBM on the level of strategic objectives. The understanding of these objectives derived from the interviews thus provides empirical support for the different levels in Khadjavi's (2005) conceptualisation. However, the slightly different orientation of I-35's understanding of the objective to increase the company value to that in literature indicates potential for a modification of the conceptualisation in this respect.

Altogether, only three interviewees refer to objectives that relate to the company value. This is in strong contrast to recent questionnaire studies finding the company value to be one of several important objectives (Achleitner et al., 2010; Gonschorek, 2009a; Krol, 2009c; Piontkowski, 2009; PricewaterhouseCoopers AG Wirtschaftsprüfungsgesellschaft, 2014; Schlepphorst & Schlömer-Laufen, 2016). Additionally, there is a difference to a number of the recent interview-based studies (for details see subsection 2.4.3.2.2). While Khadjavi (2005) finds that a definition of company objectives in line with VBM is not given in all three cases analysed, VBM reflects in the objectives of two out of three companies. Based on this, one would expect more than one or three out of 28 companies in the sample at hand to have objectives in line with the VBM approach. A similarly low level of importance of the objective to increase the company value is however found by Wenzel (2014), where the increase of the company value is the key objective for two out of 20 companies (Wenzel, 2014, pp. 123–124). Beyond this, Wenzel (2014) finds that the increase of the company value is implicitly pursued by some interviewees. In a broadly similar way the study at hand finds that three interviewees refer to objectives that are somehow related to an increase of the company value even if the aim is not directly to increase the company value. By finding a minimal relevance of the increase of the company value as an objective in Mittelstand the study at hand does not only

[148] German equivalent of a private limited company.

support Wenzel's (2014) findings but also Tappe's (2009) findings in a different context and with a different approach.[149]

Figure 49: Findings of increase of company value as an objective

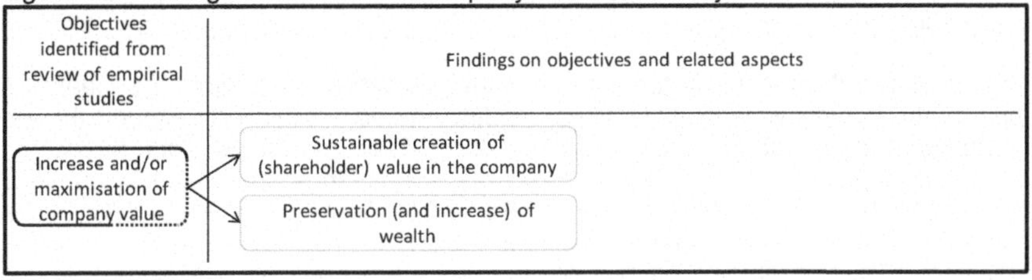

In VBM in Mittelstand literature, authors see a threat that economic objectives are neglected and suggest the increase of the company value as a valuable opposite pole to non-economic objectives (see subsection 2.3.3.1). Given this opposite pole in this form being largely absent in the data at hand, one could get the impression that economic objectives are neglected. However, it must be considered that the interviewees address profit as an economic objective.

4.3.2.9 Realisation of profit

When analysing the references in relation to profit it is evident that interviewees address this topic on different levels. Some interviewees refer to the objective to generate profit rather colloquially as “earning money” (6/28). Some express this objective with reference to profit (11/28) and/or return (12/28). Beyond this, some of the interviewees even formulate the objective to realise profit more specifically and name an expected rate of return either themselves or on further request of the interviewer (8/28). The finding that the interviewees refer to the realisation of profits with varying degrees of colloquial language and specific formulations indicates that there are also differences in how specifically this objective is formulated in the company.

It has to be noted, that in addition to specific reference to realisation of profit as an objective, the previous outline of other objectives has shown that those also partly have an economic dimension. For example, this has become evident from the majority of interviewees addressing securing existence in relation to profits (for details see 4.3.2.2) or objectives related to internal improvements being related to economic advantages for the company (for details see 4.3.2.6).

The findings are summarised in Figure 50. It is suggested to modify the understanding of this objective for the following reasoning. None of the interviewees refers to (short-term) profit maximisation, which is looked at in recent questionnaire studies (Achleitner et al., 2010; Gonschorek, 2009a; Krol, 2009c; Schlepphorst & Schlömer-Laufen, 2016). The focus is rather on realisation of profit. This is supported by the findings from the analysis of the attitude towards VBM, where some interviewees

[149] Wenzel (2014) looks at key company objectives of large German family businesses on the basis of interviews with CFOs. Tappe (2009) looks more closely at whether three aspects of VBM reflect in the objectives of Mittelstand on the basis of 10 interviews.

express that a short-term optimisation of profit is refused or not relevant (see subsection 4.4.3.1). Besides this, half of the interviewees states in this context that making a profit is relevant for them. Holistically seen, this implies that the interviewees have the objective to realise profit but do not want to achieve maximum profits in the short run.

Overall, the realisation of profit as an economic objective is relevant for a clear majority of the interviewees (20/28). Thus, the findings do not explicitly support the assumption of some authors in VBM in Mittelstand literature that there is a threat that economic objectives are neglected. However, the findings addressed in previous paragraphs do not yet provide insights that allow assessing this conclusively. It cannot yet be evaluated whether the emphasis is on non-economic or economic objectives. Thus, it remains unclear whether there is a dominance of non-economic objectives which might threaten the existence. To gain additional insights, a holistic view is taken in subsection 4.3.3. This will also include more details on realisation of profit as an objective.

Figure 50: Findings of realisation of profit as an objective

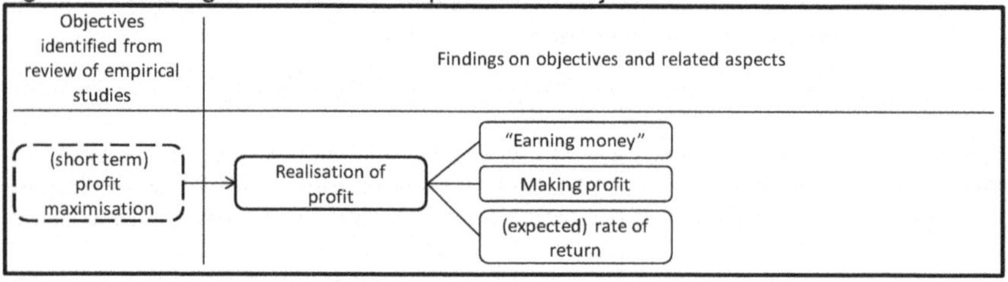

4.3.3 *Nuances in the overall target course*

4.3.3.1 Aim and approach of the subsection

This subsection outlines further insights into RQ4:

How is VBM reflected in the objectives of Mittelstand?

Based on the findings in relation to this research question gained from the specific objectives identified, a further analysis seems to be valuable (see subsections 4.3.2.8 and 4.3.2.9). In this further analysis a holistic view of the target course described by the interviewees is taken. This means that the target course of each company is analysed with a focus on whether the objectives addressed by the interviewee represent economic or non-economic objectives. When both kinds of objectives are addressed it is also considered on which kind of objectives the emphasis is placed. This is done by analysing when, at which extent and how economic and non-economic objectives are addressed. With regard to how objectives are addressed, it has particularly been looked for the specificity of the outline and for remarks that express the prevalence of one kind of objective over the other.

Based on the holistic analysis of the target course, groups of interviewees with different nuances to that the objectives are identified as non-economic or economic have been found. The groups are shown in Figure 51. In this figure the groups are shown from the interviewees with a focus on non-economic objectives on the left via interviewees where non-economic objectives are becoming more and more important in the middle to the interviewees with a focus on the increase of the company value on the right. The groups will be outlined in the following. The letters shown in Figure 51 will be used to refer to the different groups in the outline. The outline starts with group OBJ-A, being followed by group OBJ-B. For the sake of demonstrating the demarcation of groups OBJ-B, OBJ-C and OBJ-D, group OBJ-D will be outlined before turning to group OBJ-C and finishing with group OBJ-E.

Figure 51: Groups of interviews identified in the holistic analysis of nuances in the target course

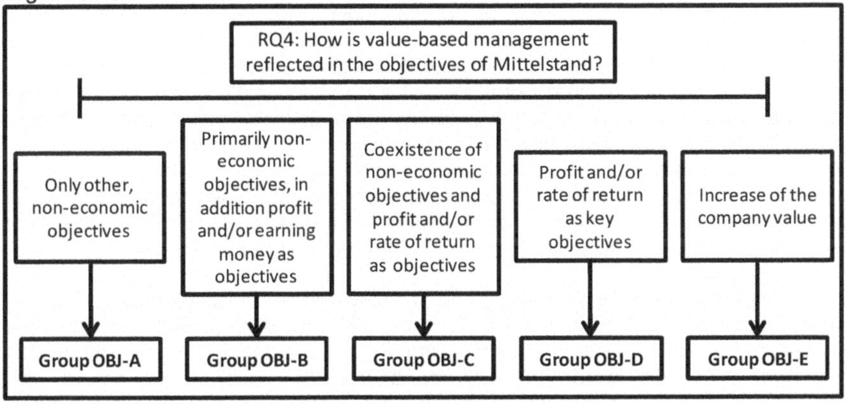

4.3.3.2 Group OBJ-A: Only other, non-economic objectives

This group of interviewees consists of the interviewees whose outline of objectives does not include the increase of the company value or the realisation of profit as economic objectives. In the following, two examples will be used to illustrate this group.

I-12's primarily non-economic objectives can be illustrated with the following statement at the beginning of his outline of the objectives:

> "I am very ambitious, sure. My objective, it has always been, from my background, I always was a sporty child, was in many sports clubs, did many sports and thus I was always someone, who enjoyed having competition. In a fair manner, I was always able to loose, that was OK. Reluctantly though if someone is better, he is better. But my internal ambition is always to be the best. Yes and to always do more than others, yes. Do more and do it better."

He then outlines that the company has become the market leader in Germany and that it is the objective to strengthen and expand the position on the market. From this quote it is very clear that this is very much influenced by the personal ambition of the owner-manager. This is emphasised in the further outline of the market-oriented objectives by remarks such as "and that is actually inspiring or encouraging then as well" in the context of winning a customer from the competitor. The additional objective to change the structures of the company has also a personal motive.

This is important as the owner-manager currently works every Saturday and nearly every Sunday and would like to work less. I-12 also confirms the link between the company objectives and the personal objectives at the request of the researcher.

I-12 names additional objectives. These include strengthening activities abroad, which is also classified as a market-oriented objective. In addition, I-12 refers to the objective to grow in the fluctuating manner outlined in subsection 4.3.2.7. This includes emphasising that the focus is keeping the current size but also expressing that "if a great customer comes around the corner[150] or something, I will not say no". Additional objectives named by I-12 are "having enough utilisation" and that the employees enjoy work, are paid and treated fairly. In relation to the employees, he emphasises that they are willing to do extra hours and work on Saturdays when necessary. Thus he has a responsibility towards the employees and needs to secure jobs ("I do not want to have to sit here and tell someone "I cannot employ you anymore", because that does not work."). This is an example of the mutual benefit that has been found in relation to employee-oriented objectives (see subsection 4.3.2.4). It has to be noted that some of the objectives have an economic dimension. A good position on the market and enough utilisation are economically beneficial for the company. However, I-12 does not refer directly to an economic objective such as making a profit, earning money or a certain rate of return and the objectives seem to be strongly influenced by personal, non-economic motives.

I-6-EM is another example of this group of interviewees. The objectives outlined by I-6-EM are similar to I-12 in that they have an economic dimension but an economic objective is not explicitly addressed and there is an influence by the owner-manager. As I-6-EM is not the owner-manager but the external commercial manager of the company he addresses the influence of the owner-manager in a different way than I-12:

> „The objectives. The objectives. The objectives, they are also something, they are, of course, typically Mittelstand. You can go to many Mittelständler and ask 20 employees somewhere in production, what the objective of the company is, then probably no one will be able to give you an answer. That is mostly the case, there are founder- or owner-managed companies, they know where they want to go, but it is never really communicated. That means, the employee at the machine ultimately does not know, where it is going. ... I just say, the primary objective is the endurance of the company. That means, what is important for a shareholder in this case is actually the continuance of the company. There of course is somewhere an emotional link, one has founded it, one has built it up, one does also not want, that it then somehow also breaks down again. I just say, important is the continuance of the company, but in principle of course also, that one grows, that one becomes bigger, that one develops further and in principle from this growth strategy all other strategies are then derived. That means, what is necessary to achieve this objective and (short incomprehensible part) Balanced Scorecard (there are?) many small subordinate targets and other factors, that need to be considered. I say, economic stability ... I say, that is somewhat a basic requirement."

[150]Direct translation of the interviewee's modified use of a German saying.

Similar to I-12 this quote shows that the company objectives are closely related to the owner-manager, who knows the company objectives and has an emotional link to the company.[151] With regard to the content of the objectives, securing the existence is the topmost objective. This is complemented by a growth strategy and subordinate objectives. In addition to the objectives referred to in the quote, I-6-EM outlines market-oriented objectives which he names as „following parameters, that then somehow still contribute, but I say primarily the continuance of the company and connected to that the growth strategy“. It is interesting to note that there is a slight reference to economic stability at the end of the quote which seems to be a subordinate objective. However, the interviewee does not outline what is meant by that and does not relate it to profit-oriented objectives. Thus, there are similarities to I-12. However, I-6-EM is different to I-12 in the emphasis of the objective to secure the existence of the company.

The two examples illustrate the common characteristic of this group of interviewees, which is that there is no specific economic objective. The focus is on other objectives such as market-oriented or employee-oriented objectives. In some cases these are related to the economic situation of the company. The interviewees partly address a personal influence of the owner-manager on the objectives. In line with VBM some of the interviewees aim at securing the existence of the company. However, it must be said that a profit-oriented objective is not explicitly addressed. As addressed in the literature on VBM in Mittelstand (see subsection 2.3.3.1) there is the threat that the economic situation of the company is neglected, which might threaten the existence of the company.

4.3.3.3 Group OBJ-B: Primarily non-economic objectives, in addition profit and/or earning money as objectives

This group of interviewees is similar to the interviewees of group OBJ-A in that non-economic objectives play a major role. These interviewees differ from those of group OBJ-A by mentioning economic objectives such as making a profit or earning money. However, these seem to play a minor role. Economic-oriented objectives are only briefly mentioned, partly after a further question regarding the interests of the owner on the objectives. Furthermore, profit is addressed in an unspecific manner. This will be illustrated by two examples.

After being asked to illustrate the company objectives, I-15 talks about a specific growth objective that has been very important in the last 20 years and the master plan that has been used to achieve this objective for some time. The researcher then asks the interviewee about the objectives for the following years. He then briefly mentions annual turnover and profit objectives. Then he states that the most important objective is preservation of the family business as a family business and outlines the effect of this key objective. This includes

- that offers for participations from other companies are neglected,
- that succession needs to be secured,

[151] In contrast to other interviewees I-6-EM addresses a potential problem of this influence – the objectives not being properly communicated to employees. While not directly relating this to the company he seems to regard this as applicable for the company even if there is a BSC.

- growth,
- new developments and
- enough financial means to finance this from equity capital.

While profit is briefly mentioned the most important objective is of a non-financial nature and profit seems to be one factor which contributes to this but not the key objective. This shows that the objectives of I-15 are primarily non-economic.

I-8 is similar to I-15 in the emphasis of the objective to stay an owner-managed company. Additionally, I-8 mentions the objectives to sustain the healthy size of the company and independence from banks. He then stresses that the company refuses to offer its customers the service to buy and resell goods from China in addition to the self-manufactured goods. This is because this would lead to a development where he would need to “send home” half of his employees and that is not his objective. He adds sustaining the flexibility of production as an objective which is important as “the last anchor” in the industry to compete. He also mentions that it is necessary to invest constantly because the company produces highly technological products. He states that the company would otherwise go bankrupt at some time. This is a first but small hint towards the necessity to earn money. The researcher then asks about the role of his interests as co-owner of the company for the company objectives to gain further insights into the objectives. I-8 then states that the objectives are identical and that it is important to reinvest money because they have a long-term focus. This is a further hint that profit plays a role. However, it is only after a further question regarding the meaning of being successful in the long run that the interviewee states that “having enough money left over at the end of the year” is important to be able to invest and secure jobs. Thus, similar to I-15, making a profit seems to be a subordinate objective to achieve other, non-economic objectives (securing jobs, staying owner-managed and independent from banks). In the case of I-8 profit as an objective is adressed in an unspecific manner and only after further enquiries by the researcher.

In contrast to the companies of group OBJ-A, the companies assigned to group OBJ-B at least address economic objectives. However, they do not seem to be of key importance and are formulated rather vaguely. Thus, there is still the danger that these are neglected in day-to-day business. This might threaten the existence of the company and thus also the achievement of a non-economic objective such as continuance as an owner-managed company and securing jobs.

4.3.3.4 Group OBJ-D: Profit and/or rate of return as key objectives

This group encompasses interviewees who make it clear that profit-oriented objectives are the most important objectives. The only objective that is sometimes more important is securing existence. It is important to emphasise that the formulation of this objective has been looked at very precisely. As addressed in subsection 4.3.2.2 there are interviewees that address securing existence in a broader sense that includes the continuance as an owner-managed business and/or family business. This formulation of the objective has a non-economic dimension. When this objective is more important than realisation of profit, there is no primacy of economic objectives. These companies are thus not part of group OBJ-B but assigned to group OBJ-C (see subsection 4.3.3.5).

Most of the interviewees assigned to this group express the primacy of economic objectives very clearly, often with the statement that this is the overall objective (I-21, I-29, I-32). I-28 makes this even clearer by stating that he only believes in one objective and that is making a profit. For him this is the originary objective of each company as one otherwise cannot further develop the company and pay wages. Apart from securing the existence of the company and "rescuing the profit margin" he does not even want to talk about company objectives.[152]

In the explanation by I-18, the priority of profit-oriented objectives becomes more indirectly evident. At first I-18 outlines the market-oriented objectives of the company, which include getting an appropriate market share ("cutting off a good slice of the cake for us") and having at least two new customers a year. In addition, it is important to have a positive development regarding automation and it is an objective to secure jobs. Apart from securing jobs all these objectives have an economic dimension. On further request about his own interests as an owner playing a role I-18 adds:

> "Of course something needs to come out of it, that is clear. Well, I have an idea of a certain Return on Sales, which we need to retain, otherwise we can work out when we cannot exist anymore. That is completely clear. Well, when nothing comes out of it, then it is generally not worth investing the money anymore. That is completely clear. But as long as this can be reasonably realised, I do not get fixed on 2 % more or less, this is a natural variation, then it is all right. But that really is the focus, what do I still have as Return on Sales? This is an important measure for me."

He refers to the Return on Sales again later. While I-18 does not want to specify an exact value for the Return on Sales he expects, he makes clear that such a measure exists and that generating return is more important than other objectives.

Similar to I-18, some other interviewees in this group also refer to a specific expected Return on Sales (I-16, I-26, I-32). It is interesting to note that the interviewees seem to share I-18's opinion and are willing, to some extent, accept lower returns on sales. One interviewee claims to aim at 8 % but that it needs to be at least 6 %. Another interviewee states a range from 5 to 7 %. A third interviewee says that the aim to achieve 5 % is ambitious. He mentions that the actual return has been between 3 and 5 % in the last years and adds that the shareholders are not greedy.

The interviewees of this group share the focus on an economic objective. This is formulated much more precisely than by the interviewees of group OBJ-B. The majority of the interviewees uses a rate of return to specify this objective. Some even have an idea of the specific return they expect. In contrast to groups OBJ-A and OBJ-B there does not seem to be the threat that economic objectives are neglected due to the importance and the specificity of the economic objective.

[152] This can indicate the importance of these objectives. However, it must be noted that during the whole interview I-28 preferred to talk on a more general level. He also was the only interviewee that did not approve to the interview being audio-recorded. Thus, this can also be related to not wanting to give too detailed insights.

However, the economic objective is not formulated as an increase of the company value. Only when taking a broader view do the objectives include an element of VBM. In line with VBM some of the interviewees do not only expect a positive return but a return that exceeds a certain hurdle rate. Indeed, the hurdle rate expressed by these interviewees is formulated as Return on Sales and not as Return on Equity which would be directly related to an increase in the company value.[153] In total, while the objectives formulated by the interviewees of group OBJ-D are not in line with VBM their target course already includes certain elements which are suitable as a basis for formulating a VBM company objective. These are the focus on an economic objective and the specific formulation of this objective and particularly a certain idea of the rate of return to be achieved that some of the interviewees express.

4.3.3.5 Group OBJ-C: Coexistence of non-economic objectives and profit and/or rate of return as objectives

This group includes interviewees who address non-economic objectives as well as economic objectives in the form of profit or the rate of return. The interviewees in this group are different to those in groups OBJ-B and OBJ-D in that a dominance of the former or the latter cannot be identified. The characteristics of this group of interviewees will be illustrated and then delineated towards those of the groups OBJ-B and OBJ-D with examples from the interviews.

I-31 is an example for the coexistence of economic and non-economic objectives with no clear dominance of one of them. He begins his answer outlining the objectives with the increase of turnover. He immediately adds that the company currently has "an extremely high number of orders" and outlines difficulties with customers, employees and space capacity arising from this situation. He summarises this with the following statement:

> "Thus the objective to do more, nice. Doable questionmark? That is a problem we have on our hands at the moment. But finally, finally what actually matters is what comes out at the bottom."

He then goes on to emphasise that the turnover shall not be increased at the cost of profit, the employees and the customers. Most of this can be illustrated with the following quote:

> "That needs to be moderate, everyone still has fun and at the end we need to earn money. What is the point of making millions and saying at the end „Damn, red figure at the bottom, that does not work at all."? Then I rather do less and have a black figure at the bottom. Very clear. Yes."

This shows that for I-31 profit is more important than increasing turnover. However, there is the impression that it is equally important to customer-oriented objectives and employee-oriented objectives. In this respect he refers to different aspects such as delivery times and that the employees shall not be exploited but should be able

[153] Under certain circumstances the Return on Equity is also positive when a certain Return on Sales is achieved. However, this cannot be taken for granted. Among other things this depends on how the Return on Sales is measured. This might be measured in a way that accounts for the cost of debt. Then, Return on Equity is positive when the Return on Sales is positive. However, Return on Sales can also be measured on the basis of the EBIT margin. Then it remains unclear whether a positive Return on Sales results in a positive Return on Equity after costs of debt capital have been deducted.

to recover and be motivated at work. Thus, apart from economic objectives there are non-economic objectives and there is no clear emphasis on the one or the other. In the following the difference of those interviewees to those of group OBJ-B are outlined.

One difference to the interviewees of group OBJ-B is evident from what has been outlined regarding I-31: Profit-oriented objectives are addressed to a larger extent. This also becomes clear from I-19's reference to making profit. I-19 addresses making a profit in her answer to the first question in the interview.[154] After giving an overview of the business model, I-19 states that the company wants to make a profit but is not focused on profit maximisation but on a "certain sustainability". I-19 emphasises that the company turns its attention to existing in 5, 10, 15 years and earning money then. While the term "objective" is not used the researcher expects profit to be referred to when being asked about the objectives because it has been addressed at the very beginning of the interview and repeated several times. The researcher then is astonished when I-19 refers to a manual of objectives including customer-oriented objectives, objectives relating to internal improvements and objectives relating to the environment but profit is not mentioned. The researcher then poses a more general question and asks whether there are other objectives. I-19 then does not add further objectives and the researcher asks more directly:

> "R: How about profit objectives or something like that?
> I-19: That is not explicitly written in the manual, yes, but that, I'd say, that is an objective that is there in the background. Because that always does not make such a good impression in front of the employees[155], because one then gives the impression, that what the company earns, "that does not belong to you, you get your wages and that then belongs to someone else", yes. Therefore one does not communicate that so loudly outwards, yes, that the objective is to make a profit."

Later on I-19, repeats that making profit is an objective and repeats the importance of "sustainable economic activities, we want to make a profit of course". This is then related to the objective to secure the existence of the company. This example illustrates that while there is the objective making a profit there are other objectives as well. The extent to which I-19 talks about profits shows that attention is paid to profits but the importance of profits in relation to the other objectives remains unclear.

These examples illustrate the demarcation towards the interviewees of group OBJ-B: While both groups address non-economic as well as economic objectives the interviewees of group OBJ-C seem to pay more attention to making a profit than those of group OBJ-B. This is reflected in the outlines being more extensive and more specific. In addition it is interesting to look at the difference between these interviewees and those of group OBJ-D. This is illustrated by a closer look at the interview with I-30-EM.

I-30-EM addresses objectives such as implementing Kata in the administration when talking about strategic decisions. According to I-30-EM, implementing Kata

[154] At the beginning the researcher asked about the business model and the interviewee's role in the company.
[155] Word order is slightly changed in translation.

offers the potential to cut down personnel by 10 %. The main focus of the implementation shall be on departments where it is known that employees will leave the company with the objective not to replace them. The outline of the company objectives then begins as follows:

> "Well, they are naturally written in the strategy document, that is clear. Well, when just taking the highest level, the greatest and most important objective, there we focus[156] on remaining an independent family business. And to successfully develop that further. We of course have economic success and gaining new market potentials, yes, continuous improvement of all processes and respectful management of our employees. Those are our main objectives, the highest company objectives, that we have."

He then talks about the consequences of these objectives. These include that the Balanced Scorecards of the company include "turnover, profit margin and accordingly profits and Return on Investment [are] also in the end on the main scorecard". From this it becomes clear that the outline of I-30-EM shares two aspects with I-31 and I-19. On the one hand, profit is addressed to some extent. On the other hand, there are non-economic objectives with similar importance. While RoI is the key performance indicator in the strategic BSC, it is nevertheless only one of the main objectives and does not seem to be of higher importance than the others. This becomes apparent from the objective to implement Kata. This is related to the main objective of continuous improvement of all processes and also influences the company objective of economic success. However, the implementation shall be done in departments where dismissal of employees can be avoided. This can be related to the objective of "respectful management of employees" and shows that the economic objectives do not precede the non-economic objectives. Thus, similar to I-31 and I-19 economic objectives are not prior to non-economic objectives. This is a difference to group OBJ-D, where the key objective is related to profit and/or the rate of return.

However, in contrast to I-19 and I-31, I-30-EM and some other interviewees of this group share two things with the interviewees of group OBJ-D. One aspect is that although economic success does not have priority over the other main objectives named by I-30-EM, there is nevertheless a hierarchy of aims. I-30-EM names staying an independent family business as the most important objective. The existence of an overarching objective is similar to the interviewees of group OBJ-D. However, the most important objective of continuance as a family business has a non-economic dimension. Consequently, I-30-EM does not share the characteristic that an economic objective is the key company objective directly situated below the overall objective of securing the existence of the company with group OBJ-D. The second aspect in that I-30-EM is similar to the interviewees with primarily economic objectives, is the more specific formulation of the profit-oriented objective. While I-19 and I-31 refer to profit, I-30-EM refers to Return on Investment.

It can be concluded that the interviewees of group OBJ-C have economic as well as non-economic objectives and there is no dominance of the former or the latter. Apart from this common characteristic this group of interviewees is slightly less ho-

---

[156] Term used to approximate the meaning of the German saying „auf die Fahnen schreiben“ which would directly be translated to „write on ones banners“.

mogeneous than the other groups. For instance I-30-EM is different to I-19 and I-31 regarding the existence of a hierarchy of aims and a more specific formulation of objectives.

When interpreting the target orientation of this group of interviewees in light of the literature on VBM in Mittelstand two aspects can be noted. VBM's normative view of defining the increase of the company value as a key company objective is not incorporated in the target course. However, the length and specificity to that these interviewees address economic objectives shows that attention is paid to the realisation of profit. Thus, the threat that economic objectives are neglected in favour of non-economic objectives is lower than for the interviewees of group OBJ-B. Portraying the difference to the group of interviewees with primarily economic objectives (group OBJ-D) shows nevertheless a potential weakness of this group. As there is no primacy of economic or non-economic objectives, it is not clear how to deal with conflicts of aims in daily business. It can thus be concluded that these interviewees are slightly closer to a value-oriented definition of the company objectives than those of group OBJ-A and group OBJ-B. However, there is still a considerable gap to defining the increase of the company value as an overall company objective.

4.3.3.6 Group OBJ-E: Increase of the company value

This group only consists of I-35, who is the only interviewee who directly refers to the creation of value as an objective (for details see 4.3.2.8). Taking a holistic view of I-35's target orientation provides additional insights. After the open question regarding objectives, I-35 immediately asks whether the strategic or the operative objectives are meant. Such an enquiry has not been posed by any other interviewee. This is an indicator for a hierarchy of aims. This also becomes evident from the remark that the creation of value shall be achieved "via a distinctive orientation on technology". Thus, market-oriented objectives seem to contribute to the overall objective to increase the company value. In addition, I-35 refers to employee-oriented objectives being part of the strategic objectives. Unfortunately, he does not further elaborate on the hierarchy of these strategic objectives towards each other and due to limited time of the interviewee a further question could not been posed. There are small indicators that value creation is more important.

The analysis of the objective to increase the company value has already shown that there are slight differences in the orientation of I-35 than that in literature (see 4.3.2.8). In addition it must be noted that from the short outline, there are only indications that the literature's demand to define the increase of value as the most important company objective is fulfilled.

4.3.4 Summary of the section and discussion

The findings in relation to Mittelstand's objectives respond to the respective research questions and contribute to the body of knowledge. The approach taken in this research to generate further empirical insights builds upon and goes beyond that taken in recent empirical studies addressing Mittelstand's objectives.

Further empirical insights have been gained on the basis of RQ3:

What are the objectives of Mittelstand?

The findings gained yield open and more in-depth insights than previous empirical studies (for an overview of the findings see Figure 52, for the review of previous empirical studies see subsection 2.4.3.2). The body of knowledge is especially developed in relation to the content of objectives. The outline of the objectives addressed by the interviewees has shown repeatedly that it is valuable to regard the objectives more broadly than in previous empirical studies. A broader understanding reflects the view expressed by the owner-managers for securing existence, market-oriented objectives and employee-oriented objectives (for details see subsections 4.3.2.2, 4.3.2.3 and 4.3.2.4). The view of the owner-managers has also been found to be different than the objectives included in recent questionnaire studies in relation to independence, growth and profit (for details see subsections 4.3.2.5, 4.3.2.7 and 4.3.2.9). Beyond this, a more in-depth understanding has been gained by insights into aspects related to the objectives. An example is that employee-oriented objectives are regarded to be of mutual benefit for employees and the company. Furthermore, it is interesting that the long-term orientation of securing existence is emphasised and that securing existence in form of continuance as owner-managed and/or family business is referred to when the key owner-manager is aroung 60 or older. Additionally, a part of the objectives such as securing existence and the independence from banks is related to profits.

It can be noted that from the review of recent empirical studies, indications for differences in the understanding of objectives have already been identified in some previous empirical studies (for details see subsection 4.3.2). Wenzel (2014) uses slightly different terms to express the content of objectives found from the interviews than those that are used in recent questionnaires (Deloitte & Touche GmbH Wirtschaftsprüfungsgesellschaft, 2015; Gonschorek, 2009a; Krol, 2009c; Piontkowski, 2009; PricewaterhouseCoopers AG Wirtschaftsprüfungsgesellschaft, 2014; Schlepphorst & Schlömer-Laufen, 2016). This also applies to a part of the objectives in Achleitner et al.'s (2010) questionnaire. Beyond this, previous empirical studies do not provide indications for the understanding of the objectives derived from the interviews or only include slight indications for individual objectives.

The study at hand has also gained new insights with identifying a range of objectives that can be summarised as "objectives focused on internal improvements" (for details see subsection 4.3.2.6). This expands the body of knowledge. Recent empirical studies only include objectives that indirectly touch upon elements of these objectives but do not adequately picture the aspects addressed by the interviewees.

Beyond contributing to the body of knowledge by gaining a broader and more in-depth understanding of the content of Mittelstand's objectives, the findings support and modify existing findings in relation to the importance of these objectives in Mittelstand. This includes that similar to recent empirical studies, securing existence, market-oriented objectives and employee-oriented objectives are of key importance.[157] However, differences have been found, for example that independence is of lower importance than in existing empirical studies. It is also interesting to note that very little or no reference has been found for objectives related to society, ecological objectives as well as personal objectives.[158] On the basis of previous empirical studies it was expected that these wouldn't be of major importance but it has still been astonishing that they are virtually completely omitted by the interviewees.

An overview of the findings in relation to objectives in Mittelstand is shown in Figure 52. This shows objectives identified in the literature review to the left. These are then related to the findings on objectives and related aspects from the interviews. Where the arrows link the objectives identified in the literature review to those empirically identified, the line type used for the boxes gives an impression of the importance of the objective (as derived in subsection 2.4.3.3 for the objectives identified from the review of empirical studies and addressed for the objectives found in this study in subsection 4.3.2).

[157] It must be noted that this is based on the broader understanding found to reflect the interviewees' understanding better than the understanding underlying recent questionnaire studies (Achleitner et al. (2010), Deloitte & Touche GmbH Wirtschaftsprüfungsgesellschaft (2015), Gonschorek (2009a), Krol (2009c), Piontkowski (2009), PricewaterhouseCoopers AG Wirtschaftsprüfungsgesellschaft (2014), Schlepphorst and Schlömer-Laufen (2016)).

[158] A small number of the objectives related to internal improvements involves ecological advantages. However, these do not seem to be the main focus (see subsection 4.3.2.6).

Figure 52: Overview of specific objectives of Mittelstand

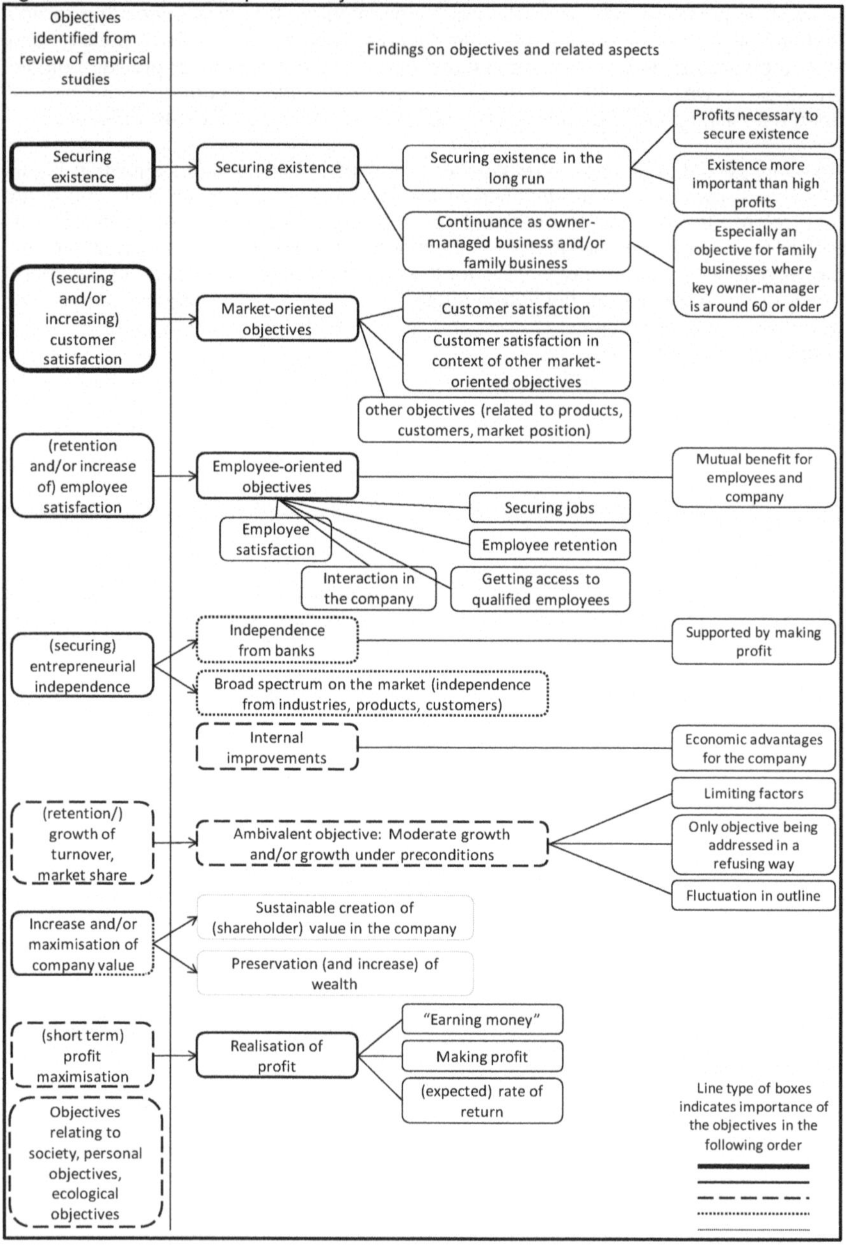

Further insights have been gained on the basis of RQ4:

How is VBM reflected in the objectives of Mittelstand?

This research question has been formulated because empirical insights from VBM in Mittelstand literature and additional recent contributions differ (for details see subsection 2.4.3). Additionally, further empirical insights might be valuable given the research gap identified from the review of VBM in Mittelstand literature (see subsection 2.3.6).

Insights have been gained from two perspectives. Firstly, the analysis of objectives addressed by the interviewees has shown that the increase of the company value is only relevant for very few interviewees. This is in strong contrast to findings from recent questionnaire studies (Achleitner et al., 2010; Gonschorek, 2009a; Krol, 2009c; Piontkowski, 2009; PricewaterhouseCoopers AG Wirtschaftsprüfungsgesellschaft, 2014; Schlepphorst & Schlömer-Laufen, 2016). The findings tend to support recent interview-based studies, which found the increase of the company value to be of lower importance (Tappe, 2009; Wenzel, 2014). Beyond this, it has been found that profit realisation is an objective for a high number of interviewees (for details see 4.3.2.9). This is interesting given that one argument for defining the increase of the company value as a company objective is that it can be a valuable opposite pole to non-economic objectives and can thus counteract a potential threat to the existence of the company resulting from a dominance of non-economic objectives. While this opposite pole is absent for the vast majority of the interviewees, the findings on specific objectives in Mittelstand do not provide clear evidence of a dominance of non-economic objectives. This gap has been addressed by applying a new perspective.

From this perspective it has been found that it is valuable to differentiate groups according to nuances in the overall target course (see Figure 53, for details see subsection 4.3.3). Groups OBJ-A and OBJ-B put emphasis on non-economic objectives. While group OBJ-A does not directly address an economic objective, the interviewees of group OBJ-B address realisation of profit but only to a limited extent. It must be noted that beyond realisation of profit there still is an economic dimension to some of the other objectives referred to by the interviewees of groups OBJ-A and OBJ-B. However, with regard to the reasoning addressed in VBM in Mittelstand literature it nevertheless needs to be concluded that there might be a threat that economic objectives are neglected in favour of non-economic objectives. The literature's normative view, that it is beneficial to focus on the increase of the company value as an objective to counteract this threat, is not incorporated in the target course of these companies.

This is different for the interviewee who has been assigned to group OBJ-E, where the focus is already on the increase of the company value. The interviewees of group OBJ-D are specific in putting an emphasis on economic objectives. While not focusing on an increase of the company value, there still does not seem to be a threat of neglecting economic objectives. It has been found that there is already partly an element of value-based management.

For group OBJ-C it was not possible to evaluate whether the emphasis is more on non-economic or economic objectives. While not having the increase of the company value as an objective, economic objectives are still obviously relevant. Thus, there does not seem to be an immediate threat that economic objectives are neglected in a way that endangers the existence of the company.

Overall, there is still a considerable gap between the normative view on the relevance of the increase of the company value and the views of the interviewees. This is particularly the case for the high number of interviewees where there is little or no emphasis on realisation of profit as an explicit economic objective (12 interviewees of groups OBJ-A and OBJ-B). However, the new perspective shows that some interviewees put an emphasis on economic objectives in a way that there is no danger of neglecting the economic objectives in a way that threatens the existence of the company, even if the increase of the company value, in a narrow sense, is not incorporated as an objective (15 interviewees of groups OBJ-C and OBJ-D).

Figure 53: Findings regarding groups of interviewees with different nuances in the target course

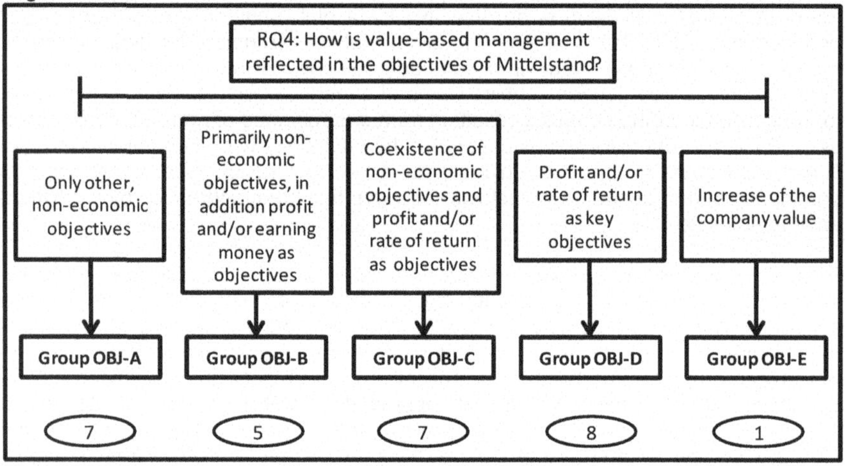

The findings have been generated based on a **specific research approach**. The review of recent empirical studies addressing Mittelstand's objectives has shown that different approaches to analysis are taken (for details see subsection 2.4.3.2.1). On a general level, the approach to research Mittelstand's objectives taken in this research is closest to that of Khadjavi (2005) and Wenzel (2014). Similar to Khadjavi (2005) and Wenzel (2014) and different to other recent empirical studies (Achleitner et al., 2010; Deloitte & Touche GmbH Wirtschaftsprüfungsgesellschaft, 2015; Gonschorek, 2009a; Krol, 2009c; Piontkowski, 2009; PricewaterhouseCoopers AG Wirtschaftsprüfungsgesellschaft, 2014; Schlepphorst & Schlömer-Laufen, 2016; Tappe, 2009) this empirical study involves an overview of objectives openly expressed by the interviewees as well as an in-depth analysis from a perspective that yields further understanding in relation to VBM's objective to increase the company value. However, there are also differences. Khadjavi's (2005) case study approach includes interviews with interviewees from three different companies. In contrast to this, the findings of Wenzel (2014) and the study at hand are based on interviews with individual people from 20 and 28 different companies. While Wenzel (2014) has interviewed CFOs from large family businesses, the focus of this empirical study is on owner-managers of mittelständische companies.

Beyond the differences in the general research approach the holistic view on Mittelstand's objectives is specific. This new perspective yields an enhanced understanding of objectives in relation to VBM. The new perspective results from the specific focus and the way in which this is looked at. While certain aspects of the perspective taken have been touched upon in the body of knowledge, they have not yet been combined. In the following, the specifics of the perspective taken will be illustrated in comparison to how certain aspects are touched upon in existing literature. This starts with the specific focus and will be followed by the outline of how this is approached.

In relation to the specific focus the new perspective analyses the target course holistically. The holistic analysis of the target course integrates two relevant aspects. Firstly, in light of the reasoning of VBM in Mittelstand literature the content of the objectives is analysed in terms of being non-economic or economic. Secondly, given that the empirical insights support the literature's notion of pluralistic objectives in Mittelstand, it is analysed on which kind of objectives the interviewees put emphasis on. How these two aspects integrated in the holistic analysis of the target course are touched upon in existing empirical studies (for the review of these empirical studies see subsection 2.4.3.2) will be outlined. This is also shown in Figure 54.

Part of the existing empirical studies does not address these aspects or only addresses them indirectly. In the analysis of Mittelstand's objectives in relation to VBM on the basis of interviews, Tappe (2009) neither addresses objectives from the perspective of being economic or non-economic, nor does he address where the emphasis is put. Most questionnaire studies touch upon economic and non-economic objectives indirectly as the questionnaires include objectives that are economic objectives, for example the increase of the company value, as well as non-economic objectives, for example personal objectives. However, apart from Krol (2009c) there is no differentiation of economic and non-economic objectives and no analysis from this perspective. Furthermore, while indications identified from the questionnaire studies support the notion of pluralistic objectives, they do not analyse what kind of objectives the emphasis in these pluralistic target systems is on (Achleitner et al., 2010; Deloitte & Touche GmbH Wirtschaftsprüfungsgesellschaft, 2015; Gonschorek, 2009a; Krol, 2009c; Piontkowski, 2009; PricewaterhouseCoopers AG Wirtschaftsprüfungsgesellschaft, 2014; Schlepphorst & Schlömer-Laufen, 2016). In a similar manner to the questionnaire studies just addressed, Khadjavi's (2005) findings from interviews include objectives that can be regarded as economic objectives and non-economic objectives. However, the overview of objectives and the analysis from a VBM perspective do not analyse the target course from this perspective and do not analyse whether the emphasis is on economic or non-economic objectives.

The previous paragraph shows that several existing contributions do not address the two aspects integrated into the perspective taken in this empirical study or only touch upon them indirectly. This is different for Krol (2009c) and Wenzel (2014), who both address certain aspects more specifically but also do not integrate them in a perspective in the same way as this research.

While Wenzel (2014) goes beyond the empirical studies already addressed in looking at both aspects, he still looks at them separately and does not integrate them in a holistic view of the target course in the way done in this research. On the one hand, he differentiates between financial and non-financial objectives. On the other hand, he distinguishes between key objectives and subsidiary objectives and thus looks at which objectives the companies' focus on. However, he only differentiates between financial and non-financial objectives on the level of subsidiary objectives and his analysis does not look at whether financial or non-financial objectives are more important.

A key element of Krol's (2009c) findings in relation to Mittelstand's objectives is the differentiation into economic and non-economic objectives. Based on comparing the findings for the objectives assigned to both groups, he finds non-economic objectives to be more important than economic objectives and reinforces the demand to use VBM as an opposite pole to non-economic objectives (Krol, 2009c, pp. 176–179). Krol (2009c) also finds that all objectives included in the questionnaire tend to be important, which supports the notion of pluralistic objectives. However, he does not go beyond this and does not address which kind of objectives the emphasis is on when Mittelstand companies aim at both, economic and non-economic objectives. This would have been especially interesting given that his findings show that non-economic objectives are more important than economic objectives. However, Krol (2009c, p. 177) also finds that the economic objective to increase the company value is "very important" or "rather important" for nearly three quarters of the interviewees (Krol, 2009c, p. 177). In this situation where Mittelstand companies pursue non-economic as well as economic objectives, including the increase of the company value, it would have been very beneficial to analyse what kind of objectives is emphasised more within the companies.

Figure 54: Analysis of the points of contact of the empirical analysis of objectives in Mittelstand in previous empirical studies to the perspective taken in the empirical study

Aspect of comparison (column), empirical studies (line)	**Level of analysis with regard to objectives**	**Relation to perspective taken in the study**
Achleitner et al. (2010), Deloitte & Touche GmbH Wirtschaftsprüfungsgesellschaft (2015), Gonschorek (2009a), Krol (2009c), Piontkowski (2009), PricewaterhouseCoopers AG Wirtschaftsprüfungsgesellschaft (2014), Schlepphorst and Schlömer-Laufen (2016)	Questionnaires giving an overview based on a selection of different company objectives	Aspects of the perspective taken are indirectly touched upon, Krol (2009c) directly adresses economic and non-economic objectives but does not analyse the target course holistically
Khadjavi (2005), Wenzel (2014)	Interviews provide an overview of company objectives openly expressed, in-depth analysis in relation to the increase of the company value	Khadjavi (2005) indirectly touches upon a number of the aspects Wenzel (2014) directly adresses economic and non-economic objectives and key objectives but does not analyse the target course holistically
Tappe (2009)	Interviews and in-depth analysis in relation to the increase of the company value	Aspects of the perspective taken are not addressed

A combined analysis of the two aspects, similar to the integrated perspective taken in this research, is only found in a recent contribution to family business research (Kammerlander et al., 2015). Beyond having a similar focus in content by looking at both aspects it is interesting to compare the approach taken.

The research approach of the study at hand involves an analysis of the target course on the level of each company in the sample and the resulting formation of groups reflecting the different nuances in the target course found. Indeed, Khadjavi (2005) also proposes a categorisation on the basis of three cases. However, he has a different focus of content and looks at different forms of how VBM can be implemented on the level of strategic objectives. Beyond this, the recent literature looking at Mittelstand's objectives empirically, does not include a systematic analysis on the level of individual cases and a resulting formation of groups[159] (Achleitner et al., 2010; Deloitte & Touche GmbH Wirtschaftsprüfungsgesellschaft, 2015; Piontkowski, 2009; PricewaterhouseCoopers AG Wirtschaftsprüfungsgesellschaft, 2014; Schlepphorst & Schlömer-Laufen, 2016; Tappe, 2009; Wenzel, 2014). It can however be noted that beyond having a similar focus in content, Kammerlander et al.'s (2015) approach is similar to the approach taken in this research in that groups are formed. However, there are also differences. Firstly, Kammerlander et al.'s (2015) focus is on owners of family businesses and not on owner-managers of Mittelstand. Secondly, the two aspects are looked at as separate dimensions and combined in a matrix (see Figure 55). This research combines both aspects in a placement on a one-dimensional continuum. Thirdly and most importantly, Kammerlander et al.'s (2015) groups are not derived from empirical findings as done in this research project. This shows that while Kammerlander et al. (2015) look at Mittelstand objectives from a perspective that has some similarities to the perspective applied in this research, there are considerable differences in the approach.

Figure 55: Groups of family owners based on goals identified by Kammerlander et al. (2015, p. 66)

	Low focus on financial goals	High focus on financial goals
High focus on non-financial goals	Dreamers	Professional owners
Low focus on non-financial goals		Traders

Overall, the insights gained with a specific research approach

- provide a broader and more in-depth understanding of objectives in Mittelstand,
- add a holistic view that enables a more differentiated understanding of objectives especially in relation to VBM and
- contribute to an enhanced understanding in relation to the research gap.

However, there are also limitations and there is a need for further research. The study has put more emphasis on analysing Mittelstand objectives than recent empirical studies. However, objectives are still only one of the subjects addressed in the interviews. Future research, with a stronger focus on objectives, might yield further relevant insights. In this respect, a broader understanding might be gained by

[159] The outline of findings of Wenzel (2014) only includes some respective comments on individual but not all cases. Furthermore, Krol (2009c) and Gonschorek (2009a) look at whether there are differences in the importance assigned to the objectives for different groups of companies. However, these groups are not formed on the basis of an analysis of differences in the objectives on company level but on the basis of different company characteristics such as the industry, size or listing on the stock exchange.

also addressing the formalisation of objectives and how different stakeholder groups influence objectives. A more in-depth understanding might also be gained by looking more closely at the relation of different company objectives especially hierarchical relationships. Looking at owner-managers' motives and objectives, it might be valuable to research the relevance of an increase of the company value in comparison to other objectives.

In relation to the research gap the findings imply that the gap found between the consensus on the applicability in literature and the minimal application in practice is evident on the level of company objectives. A potential reason for this might be that owner-managers in Mittelstand do not share literature's view on the advantageousness of VBM. In this respect it is interesting to look at the insights gained into owner-managers' attitudes towards VBM in the following section.

4.4 Understanding of and attitudes towards value-based management

4.4.1 Aim and approach of the section

Questions directly referring to value-based management have been posed towards the end of the interviews to gain further insights in relation to whether value-based management is relevant for the interviewees. This originally focused on the owner-managers' attitudes towards VBM. The pilot study has however shown that the respective answers refer to a different understanding of VBM than in the literature. Thus, the questioning approach has been modified to gain insights into RQ5:

What are Mittelstands' understanding of and attitudes towards VBM?

The insights in the main study have been gained on the basis of posing two questions. The first question asks interviewees for their understanding of the term VBM. In a second question the researcher has briefly explained the understanding in literature and asks how far this plays a role. The insights gained will be addressed in the following. This begins with the insights gained from the initial, open question (subsection 4.4.2) and is followed by the insights gained after the understanding in literature has been introduced (subsection 4.4.3).

4.4.2 Understanding and attitudes referred to after open question

It is noticeable that **the majority of the interviewees hesitates** after being asked for their understanding of the term "value-based management" (18/28). This is expressed in different ways. Often there is a break of several seconds before the interviewees start to answer the question. Additionally, interviewees say that they do not know VBM, have not dealt with VBM or have only just heard the term for the first time. Furthermore, this is reflected by interviewees posing questions. This includes questions that give the impression that the interviewee is not familiar with the term, e.g. I-27's query:

"Again, what was the term? Value?"

In addition, questions regarding which values are meant are posed by the interviewees. For a few interviewees the hesitation is expressed in a vague and evasive answer at the beginning. An example for this is I-8:

> "(2 seconds break) Yes, good, finally, er (taking a deep breath), I just say now one must nowadays simply put different topics more in the foreground that have not really been considered in the past[160]."

In this case the hesitation is expressed by the break at the beginning as well as taking a deep breath. In addition, the beginning of the answer is vague. The hesitation is astonishing because throughout the interviews the researcher did not notice much hesitation but the majority of the interviewees showed signs of hesitation at this point. A reason for the hesitation could be that the question regarding one's view of a term is felt to be rather abstract for the interviewees. However, in most cases the interviewees were willing to elaborate on their understanding after the initial hesitation. Only a few interviewees do not elaborate on their understanding beyond expressing their hesitation in one of the ways addressed above (3/28).

For the interviewees who outline their understanding of the term VBM **different views** can be identified. These views are quite diverse. Six groups of different understandings have been identified. These are illustrated and compared to the understanding of VBM derived from literature (for details see subsection 2.3.2) in the following.

Some interviewees describe an **understanding that is oriented towards non-economic value**s (Group VBM1-A, 6/28). This includes references to ethical and moral values, the responsibility towards and the interaction with different stakeholders as well as references to Corporate Social Responsibility and Codes of Conduct. These interviewees do not refer to economic values. This understanding is quite different to the understanding in literature, in that VBM is a holistic management approach focusing on the objective to increase the monetary company value for owners.

Another group of interviewees also **primarily refers to non-economic values**. Yet, these interviewees also **mention economic aspects** either in relation to the company or in relation to shareholders (Group VBM1-C, 8/28). An example for this is I-15 who initially expresses that values in a family business are personified by the owner-manager. This makes family businesses successful as they are more genuine than large, listed companies. I-15 then also outlines what these values are for him. He mentions "proper behaviour" and then adds the following:

> "Also the friendliness among each other, how I deal with a colleague and that are all so natural. Actually they are completely normal human values, that one also needs to exemplify through one's own behaviour ... there are also many other questions. Protection of the environment and compliance and many other things that one of course also deals with and tries to find a way, which on the one hand also stays economical, because that of course is the supreme requirement. I can set wonderful values as objectives and hang them at the top but on the other side I'm then not profitable anymore."

This shows that while non-economic values are important for I-15, they shall be balanced with economic aspects. I-15 emphasises this point again later. It is interesting to note, that interviewees referring to a balance of non-economic and economic values in a similar way, usually address non-economic values first and then refer to

[160]Word order is slightly changed in translation.

economic aspects later. This understanding is in line with the understanding in literature that economic as well as non-economic values are considered.[161] However, the interviewees do not refer to an increase of the company value but to economic values in more general terms and there is no clear focus on economic values.

For a few interviewees **incorporating values in the management of the company** is the core aspect of the term VBM, independent of what these values are (Group VBM1-B, 4/28). An illustrative example is I-19:

> "Good question. So, I think, I have not yet reflected upon that, I have also not dealt with that.[162] I assume, that is having certain values in the company and then finally also implementing them. Whether that [is] profit maximisation or sustainability or making a profit, continuance of the company, what it is, that remains to be seen, it needs to be any values, that I orientate myself on and that my decisions are respectively orientated to."

This shows the incorporation of values in management and decision-making is at the heart of the concept for I-19. While different values are mentioned that can be used for this, I-19 does not express a clear opinion on which of those values shall be used as a basis for the management of the company. This view shares the element of focusing on values in the company with the understanding derived from literature. However, in the literature on VBM in Mittelstand the focus is clearly on the increase of the monetary company value, which is not given for these interviewees.

In outlining their understanding of VBM some interviewees also **put emphasis on economic values** (Groups VBM1-D, VBM1-E and VBM1-F, 7/28). Two of these interviewees refer to profit (Group VBM1-D, 2/28). While this shares the emphasis on economic values with the understanding in literature, the emphasis is not on an increase of the company value in the sense of the literature. However, other interviewees address an increase of the company value (Group VBM1-E and VBM1-F, 5/28). A few interviewees vaguely mention an increase of the company value (Group VBM1-E, 3/28). In these cases it does not become clear what is meant by company value and it is thus not possible to analyse to what extent the understanding is similar to that in literature. In two other cases the reference points towards an understanding broadly similar to that underlying this thesis (Group VBM1-F, 2/28). I-35 refers to the shareholder value approach, which is at the origin of VBM. I-6-EM also addresses increase of the company value. He refers to the importance of achieving a certain increase in the market value for listed companies, which points towards a broadly similar understanding than that underlying this thesis.[163] These short answers reflect an understanding broadly similar to that underlying this thesis in its focus on the monetary company value. However, the answers do not allow evaluating whether the understanding also includes all aspects repeatedly addressed in the literature in relation to the understanding of VBM.

[161] This is the case as the consideration of interests of other stakeholders that is part of the understanding derived from literature is not limited to economic interests but can also include non-economic interests such as employees wanting to be treated fairly.

[162] This statement is an additional example for the hesitation that has been mentioned at the beginning of the subsection.

[163] While the market value on the stock exchange is not evaluated in the form of the net present value of future cash flow for the owners of a company as in the understanding derived from the literature, it nevertheless represents a monetary company value from the perspective of its owners. Thus, the understanding is not fully in line with that derived from literature but still broadly similar.

Despite the question focusing on the understanding of the interviewees, the answers also give insights into the **attitudes of the interviewees towards the view outlined**. Insight into the attitudes of the interviewees towards the understanding outlined can be gained from remarks or statements. In doing this, it has been found that several interviewees have a positive attitude towards the understanding outlined (11/28). Sometimes a positive attitude is expressed with clear statements such as I-14's statement that a system of values is currently being developed in the company. Indicators for a positive attitude are also positive remarks such as "is very important in the company". Such positive remarks are sometimes also expressed in a less specific manner like "one has to". Interviewees have only been classified as having a positive attitude when there have been several and specific positive remarks. In addition there are a few interviewees where some of these indicators for a positive attitude have been found but where this is not addressed as clearly as by the others (5/28). Only one interviewee clearly expresses his rejection of part of his understanding of VBM (codes of conduct). Some interviewees do not express their attitude on the understanding outlined (8/28). Altogether, this shows that the attitudes towards the understanding outlined tend to be rather positive.

Overall, the open question regarding the understanding of the term VBM yielded the following insights, which are shown in Figure 56. The understandings outlined by the interviewees are quite diverse. In some cases the focus is on non-economic values (Group VBM1-A, 6/28). Others emphasise non-economic values but add that these need to be balanced with economic values (Group VBM1-C, 8/28). For others, the focus is on incorporating values in the management of the company (Group VBM1-B, 4/28). Only some interviewees focus on economic values. In addition, there is partly only a vague reference to an increase of the company value (Group VBM1-E, 3/28). Others refer to economic values in form of profit and not in form of the increase of the company value (Group VBM1-D, 2/28). Only a few interviewees outline an understanding with a focus similar to that in literature (GroupVBM1-F, 2/28). While a number of the other understandings addressed also touches upon elements of the understanding of VBM there is no clear relation to a focus in line with the understanding of VBM underlying this thesis. It is also important to mention that the majority of the interviewees hesitates before outlining their understanding (18/28). A few do not even elaborate their understanding further (Group VBM1-0, 3/28). When having a look at the extent to which the interviewees address the respective understandings and at how many interviewees refer to which view, it can be concluded that there is a tendency towards understanding the term VBM in a way that puts much more emphasis on non-economic values than in the understanding in literature. As the interviewees also go beyond the question in indicating their attitude, the findings additionally show that there is a tendency that attitudes towards the understanding referred to, tend to be positive.

Figure 56: Different understandings and attitudes referred to after open question

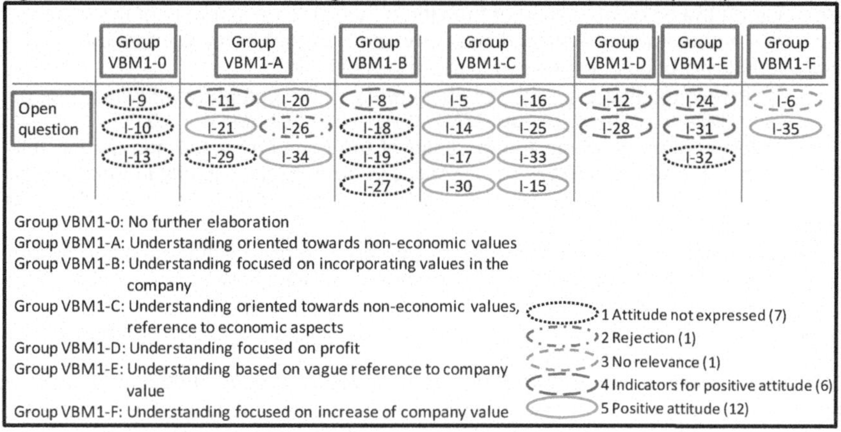

4.4.3 Understanding and attitudes referred to after the introduction of the understanding derived from the literature review

4.4.3.1 Overall view

To gain insights into the attitudes of the interviewees towards and the relevance of VBM in the understanding of the literature, the researcher has briefly outlined the understanding derived from literature after having gained insights into the interviewees' understanding. The interviewees have then been asked how far this plays a role.

In the analysis of the answers three things become evident that need to be considered. Firstly, in outlining their view on VBM the interviewees still mostly refer to an understanding that is different to that in literature. In the analysis of the attitude towards VBM it is thus important to consider what understanding the attitude is related to. Secondly, while one understanding has been dominant in the answer to the first question, the interviewees now refer to several different understandings.[164] Thirdly, it can be noted that the understandings referred to can mostly be assigned to the same categories as those identified in the answer to the first question.[165]

When taking a holistic view of the understandings addressed, it can be noted that the focus now is much more on understandings which either include or put emphasis on economic aspects. The views expressed in relation to an increase of the

[164] In contrast to subsection 4.4.2 it is thus possible that one interviewee is assigned to more than one of the groups that will be addressed in this subsection.

[165] In addition to the categories of understandings identified in the first question, an additional theme is used to include other views that cannot be related to one of the existing categories. Given the focus of this work these are not illustrated in this subsection.

company value will be presented in this subsection.[166] Different positions can be identified on the basis of looking at the attitude towards an increase of the company value and whether the understanding seems to be vaguer or more informed. On this basis four key groups of interviewees can be identified:

- Interviewees that express that an increase of the company value is not or not so relevant for them (Group VBM2-V-A, see subsection 4.4.3.2).
- Interviewees for whom the increase of the company value has certain relevance but where VBM does not seem to be applied regularly in the management of the company (Groups VBM2-V-B and VBM2-V-C see subsection 4.4.3.3).
- An interviewee who clearly states that an increase of the company value is important for the company and who briefly outlines how VBM is applied in the company (Group VBM2-V-D, see subsection 4.4.3.4).
- Two interviewees who reject the shareholder value approach (Group VBM2-V-E, see subsection 4.4.3.4).

The interviewees in the different groups additionally mention different aspects in relation to their view. To outline this comprehensively, sub-groups are formed to reflect these different stances. In addition to outlining the views these will be compared to literature where possible.

4.4.3.2 Increase of the company value not relevant (Group VBM2-V-A)

Some interviewees express that the increase of the company value is not or not so relevant for them (Group VBM2-V-A, 10/28). In the analysis it becomes evident that two subgroups can be identified on the basis of the specificity of the reference to an increase of the company value.

The interviewees assigned to Group VBM2-V-A-1 **refer to the increase of the company value vaguely and express that it is not relevant for them** (4/10/28). These interviewees seem to have different reasons for taking this stance. I-8 outlines that the increase of the company value is not relevant due to the "extremely difficult industry". In this industry the focus is more on "surviving with a reasonable financial background" than on increasing the company value to sell the company. For I-13 increasing the company value plays a "subordinate role". He expresses that he has "never before wasted a thought on that" and that he does not need to think about this as

- the company "works out and is profitable",
- he has no need to worry because he is at an advanced age and
- he does not need to give account to someone else because he founded the company.

[166] The views related to understandings that do not include an emphasis on economic aspects (similar to groups VBM1-A, VBM1-B, VBM1-C) will not be addressed in the following due to the small number of these references. Moreover, these are less relevant given the focus of the research question on the attitude towards VBM in the understanding underlying this thesis. Interesting insights are also gained in relation to an understanding focused on profit (similar to group VBM1-D). Half of the interviewees (14/28) expresses that profit and/or strengthening the equity capital has a certain relevance for them. However, some interviewees also state that a short-term optimisation of profit or the balance sheet is refused or not relevant (8/28). Given the scope of this work this will not be outlined in more depth.

Different to I-8's reference to the environmental situation of the company the reasons I-13 gives are mostly related to the owner-manager and the company. While I-13 makes clear that he has not dealt with the aspect of increasing the company value before it is not clear whether I-8 has. Despite giving different reasons, both interviewees have in common that VBM is not relevant for them and share this with the other interviewees in Group VBM2-V-A. Due to the vague reference to VBM it remains unclear whether VBM is understood in a similar way as the understanding derived from literature.

Some other interviewees also express that an **increase of the company value is not so relevant for them** (Group VBM2-V-A-2, 6/10/28). However, they are different to the interviewees in group VBM2-V-A-1 in that they refer to an increase of the company value **more specifically**. From the accounts it is clear that these interviewees have already dealt with the topic of measuring the company value. I-18 states that the value of the company needed to be determined when the company was transferred from the father to the sons. This was done in several steps and it would have thus been possible to see the development of the company value. However, this was not done as other aspects were more important for I-18. I-14 outlines that he has talked to legal experts who deal with such issues in tax matters and in the case of succession. He has been told that different approaches for company valuation lead to different results. Given the context that I-14 and his father are co-owners of the company there is the impression that the company value has been determined similar to I-18 when I-14 became co-owner of the company. I-14 refers more specifically to the company value by briefly mentioning that the company value for him is the return the company generates. This is similar for I-12, who elaborates rather specifically on the question of how the company value is determined. While he does not explicitly state that there has been a valuation of the company, he mentions that he took over the company from his father some years ago. Thus, there has probably been a valuation of the company in the situation of succession. Overall, this indicates that succession is a situation in which some interviewees have been in touch with the topic of company valuation.

However, VBM in the form of continuously focusing on an increase of the company value is not relevant for them. In this respect a potential reason for not applying VBM can be the difficulty to determine the company value. I-12 and I-14 both refer to the question of what the value of a company is and from their outline it becomes clear that they regard it as difficult to determine. The following quote from I-14 illustrates this:

> "I do not walk through the villages every second day or twice a year and ask someone what he would pay, thus I cannot tell what the company value amounts to."

I-12 additionally mentions that there is currently no intention to sell the company.

The answers by I-6-EM and I-28 make it clear that they have already dealt with the topic. However the situation seems to be different. I-28 refers to the principal agent theory and states that family businesses do not have a moral hazard problem. It has to be noted that he is a Doctor of Business Management. Thus there is the assumption that he is familiar with VBM from his academic background. This also seems to be the case for I-6-EM who has a master's degree in Business and Management and already refers to an increase of the company value in a more specific manner after the question regarding his understanding of VBM.

In both cases there are indications for potential reasons why they regard VBM as not being relevant. I-28 states that there is a moral hazard problem in externally-managed companies and that those companies need to bind the managers to the long-term increase of the company value. In contrast family businesses think more long-term. I-28 thus seems to be of the opinion that the focus on the increase of the company value is more relevant for externally-managed companies. I-6-EM also expresses the view that VBM is especially relevant for listed companies. Thus one reason for VBM not being relevant for mittelständische companies can be that interviewees do not regard it as necessary as the companies are owner-managed.

It can be noted that the understanding of the interviewees that refer to VBM in a more specific way is **broadly similar to the understanding** in literature. By refering to the principal-agent-problem I-28 refers to an argument for the use of VBM that is also addressed in literature on VBM (see subsections 2.2.2 and 2.3.3.1). This is indirectly also given by I-6-EM. However, despite being familiar with VBM these interviewees do not seem to be aware of the literature's consensus that VBM is also applicable in Mittelstand. The view expressed by I-12 and I-14 agrees with the understanding in literature that value is related to the earning power of the company. However, both do not refer to measuring this by discounting future cash flow as the DCF model that is applied to determine the monetary company value in the understanding of VBM in literature. Furthermore, the repeated reference to succession is interesting as this confirms the potential relevance of VBM in this context, where VBM is regarded as advantageous in literature (see subsection 2.3.3.1).[167] However, in contrast to the notion in literature, this situation has not led to an implementation of VBM in the company and none of these interviewees refers to a measurement of the increase of the company value on a regular basis.

The aspects referred to indicate that the difficulty to determine the company value, the absence of an intention to sell the company and the absence of the moral hazard problem are potential reasons for the interviewees not to apply VBM. In light of the key drivers and barriers of VBM identified in literature (see subsection 2.3.3) this can be interpreted in the way that there is an additional hurdle (difficulties determination) and two potential drivers of VBM are not regarded as relevant (VBM's advantageousness in case of selling the company and in case of a principal-agent-situation). Thus, the interviewees seem to come to a different conclusion regarding the applicability of VBM in Mittelstand than literature. However, it remains unclear whether this is based on a thorough consideration of potential advantages and disadvantages of VBM. On an overall level several interviewees express that the increase of the company value is not relevant for them (Group VBM2-V-A, 10/28). The insights gained are summarised in Figure 57.

[167] The advantageousness of VBM in the context of successions is one of the key drivers of the application of VBM in Mittelstand identified in literature (see subsection 2.3.3.1).

Figure 57: Views expressed by interviewees of group VBM2-V-A

View addressed by this group of interviewees	**Increase of the company value not being relevant**	
Subgroups	Group VBM2-V-A-1: increase of value addressed vaguely	Group VBM2-V-A-2: increase of the company value addressed more specifically
Details	• Partly state that they have not yet dealt with the topic, partly unclear whether VBM is known • Partly mention different potential reasons	• Understanding partly shares some elements with understanding derived from literature • Partly indicates succession as situation that is point of contact with VBM, partly indicates familiarity with VBM from academic studies • Partly refer to VBM being more relevant in externally-managed companies, partly mention difficulty to determine company value

4.4.3.3 Increase of the company value has a certain relevance (Groups VBM2-V-B and VBM2-V-C)

For several interviewees **the increase or preservation of the company value is somehow important but not the main focus** (VBM2-V-B, 14/28). An example is I-19 who emphasises that the preservation of the company value stands in the foreground and then outlines more extensively why it is important to secure the existence and financial healthiness of the company. There is only a vague reference to the company value, thus the preservation of the company value rather seems to be a purpose that goes in line with the objective of securing the existence of the company and not a specific objective that is measured. I-32 expresses a similar view more clearly after being asked about the relevance of VBM:

> "Actually rather to a lesser extent. Of course, the company value should essentially not decrease. One should rather build something than reduce it. That is clear. But it is not the case that one permanently holds the term before oneself and says "OK, that is my objective to vehemently increase the company value." That is not what we are doing. ... We are really Mittelstand, it is not a large company, where the company value is increased day by day, must be increased. ... We are simply more practical or different here[168]."

These two examples show in a different way what also seems to be the case for several other interviewees: The increase or preservation of the company value is relevant but not the main focus. The interviewees that share this view partly empha-

[168] The interviewee uses the German saying „ähnlich gestrickt sein" in a reverse way. This is shortened in translation as there does not seem to be a corresponding saying in English.

sise this with reference to different additional aspects. These will be addressed briefly in the following.

A considerable number of the interviewees for whom the increase of the company value is relevant express the opinion that the **company value increases "automatically" or "happens compulsory"** (8/14/28). Some express this directly, e.g. I-33 who states that the company value is not the main objective but increases in ensuring the long-term existence which is the main objective. In other cases this becomes evident as it is outlined what is important and then briefly stated that this also results in an increase in the company value. An example for this is I-10, who initially expresses his scepticism towards profit optimisation, then outlines what is important to him and then states "All that increases the value of the company.".

Some of the interviewees for whom the increase has certain relevance emphasise that the **specific company value is not relevant for them** (6/14/28). Aspects named in this context are, among others, that there is no intention to sell the company (I-10, I-20) and that this does not help in taking decisions (I-20).

A few interviewees emphasise that the **value of a company is more than the monetary value** (3/14/28). In the view of these interviewees other aspects need to be considered as well and they mention the notional value, the intellectual value on the basis of the employees and the know-how and the value resulting from customers.

Despite the differences in the aspects addressed by the interviewees, they agree that it becomes evident that the **increase and/or preservation of the company value is not the main focus**. While these interviewees express that an increase and/or preservation of value is relevant, none of them refers to a constant measurement of the company value and its consideration in the management of the company. Furthermore, the interviewees refer to the increase of the company value mostly in a vague way. Thus, it often remains unclear inwhowfar this vague notion is similar to the understanding underlying the thesis and whether there has been a consideration of VBM in this understanding.

Two more interviewees **address VBM being relevant** (Group VBM2-V-C). They are slightly different to the interviewees in group VBM2-V-B in that VBM seems to be **more relevant**. I-26 emphasises, on further enquiry[169], that the interests of the owners have top priority and that the company acts with a long-term focus. In doing this, the employees are needed and the task of the owner-manager is to create an environment in that the employees like to do good work. This cannot be achieved by annually trying to extract as much dividend payout as possible. I-26 also formulates an objective of 5 % Return on Sales. While I-26 does not mention that the return shall exceed the costs of debt and equity capital, he nevertheless formulates a target value. Thus, while it is unclear why this target value is defined and whether this is sufficient to fulfil the owner's expected rate of return, this understanding agrees with the understanding derived from literature that there is an economic focus and a

[169]A further question was posed after the interviewee still referred to Codes of Conduct after the interviewer introduced the understanding of VBM in literature.

focus on the interests of the shareholders. In addition, the interests of other stakeholders shall not be neglected. Thus, the outline of I-26 indicates that VBM, in the understanding derived from literature, might be more relevant than for the interviewees of group VBM2-V-B.

From what I-11 tells us it is more evident that he has a similar understanding of VBM to the literature and that this is relevant for him. He immediately answers "essentially we have this currently, don't we[170]?". He then again refers to the long-term increase of wealth that he has previously named as an objective. For I-11 this includes the refusal of a "maximum return", an emphasis of the long-term view and the diversification of products and customers. In line with the view in literature this indicates a focus on an increase of the company value in the long run. In addition, I-11 addresses that the specific company value changes constantly. He emphasises that there is no intention to sell the company and that he thus does not increase the profit for five years to increase the company value.[171] On further enquiry I-11 responds that banks have calculated the company value of the company before but that this is not done on a regular basis. Thus it can be concluded that VBM is relevant for the company in an understanding similar to that in literature with the exception that the company value is not measured and monitored constantly.

It can be concluded that the **increase of the company value has certain relevance for many interviewees** (16/28). This includes several interviewees, who have a positive attitude towards an increase of the company value but where this is not the main focus (Group VBM2-V-B, 14/28). In addition, there are a few interviewees who put more emphasis on an increase of the company value and/or the interests of the owners (Group VBM2-V-C, 2/28). This is summarised in Figure 58.

[170] To translate the use of the regional German „ne?", which is used as rhetorical question before the interview goes on.

[171] He adds that this would involve a different strategy than the current strategy. From this view it becomes evident that a long-term view for the interviewee seems to be rather decades than years. This is also evident from a statement in the outline of the objectives where I-11 neglects "maximum returns" because those include risks which could threat that the company exists another 90 years.

Figure 58: Views expressed by interviewees of group VBM2-V-B and VBM2-V-C

View addressed by this group of interviewees	**Increase of the company value has certain relevance**	
Subgroups	Group VBM2-V-B: vague notion of increase or preservation of value is relevant but not the main focus	Group VBM2-V-C: emphasis on an increase of the company value and/or interests of owners
Details	• Value increases „automatically“ • Specific company value is not relevant • Beyond monetary value other aspects need to be considered	• Economic interests of owners are important in the long run (Return on Sales/increase of wealth) • No continuous measurement of company value • Understanding partly in accordance with understanding of VBM in literature

4.4.3.4 Different attitudes towards the shareholder value approach (Groups VBM2-V-D and VBM2-V-E)

Three interviewees directly refer to the shareholder value approach.

One interviewee expresses a **positive attitude towards VBM** (VBM2-V-D). I-35 already addressed the shareholder value approach in the open question regarding the understanding of VBM. In the open question he already stated that VBM is what the company is doing and that VBM for him is the translation of the shareholder value approach to mittelständische structures. This view strongly overlaps with the understanding derived from literature. VBM originated in the development of the shareholder value approach and is regarded as applicable in Mittelstand (see subsections 2.2.2 and 2.3.3). I-35 expresses that the company applies VBM with KPIs on all levels of the company and EVA as overall KPI. Thus I-35 is the only interviewee in the sample that agrees to VBM and applies VBM in the understanding of literature.

The two other interviewees that refer to the **shareholder value approach have a quite different view** (Group VBM2-V-E). I-15 and I-16 equate the shareholder value approach to a focus on profit maximisation which for them involves either a short-term view or a hardness towards employees and is thus rejected. In this context I-16 associates a “merciless sorting out” of employees that do not completely fulfil or overfulfil their job and a management of the company with “a hard rule”[172]. This is not compatible with his ethical values and thus the shareholder value approach is not relevant in the company. I-15 also seems to associate profit maximisation with the shareholder value approach. He emphasises that the company is a family business and does not have “a shareholder way of thinking”. I-15 then adds

[172] To approximate the interviewee’s German statement „ein straffes Regiment führen“.

that the company can afford a loss in a year and that this is not dramatic when the equity capital is good. He says that he can accept that decisions involve a short-term dent in the development of the company but shall have a positive effect in the long run. In his view, decisions like the buildings built by the company wouldn't have been taken by large American companies. It can be concluded that in the view of these two interviewees the shareholder value approach is either not compatible with how the interviewees want to interact with their employees as stakeholders or not compatible with the long-term orientation of the company.

The views expressed by I-15 and I-16 go in a similar direction as the criticism of VBM's orientation that has been addressed in literature (see subsection 2.3.2.2). In the literature on VBM in Mittelstand there is explicitly an emphasis on the consideration of the interests of other stakeholders and on the long-term orientation of VBM (see subsection 2.3.2.1). However, this view in literature seems either not to be known to I-15 and I-16 or not to be shared. Thus I-15 and I-16 are empirical examples for the notion existing in literature that there are potential reservations regarding the application of VBM resulting from a different understanding and a negative attitude towards VBM (see subsections 2.3.3.2 and 2.4.4). I-35 also addresses potential reservations resulting from the problem of the short-term nature of the measurement but does not regard them as applicable in the company.[173] Overall, it can be concluded that contrasting views on the shareholder value approach exist. These are summarised in Figure 59.

Figure 59: Views towards the shareholder value approach

Views adressed towards the shareholder value approach	Group VBM2-V-D: Increase of the company value is relevant and VBM is applied	Group VBM2-V-E: rejection of the shareholder value approach
Details	• VBM as translation of the shareholder value approach to mittelständische structures • Application of EVA	• Equated with profit maximisation and a short-term view or hardness towards employees • Understanding different to that in literature

4.4.3.5 Discussion in light of the understanding of VBM derived from literature

This subsection has outlined different ways in which the interviewees refer to the increase of the company value when being asked about the relevance of VBM to gain insights into the interviewees' attitudes towards VBM. Despite the understand-

[173]In his answer to the open question he refers to VBM as "what was treated as a taboo word in companies like ours, the shareholder value". Later on he addresses that the critical stance towards the shareholder value approach mostly results from the problem of the short-term nature of the measurement and expresses that they have a more long-term view. He then emphasises that in his company the owners do not "rip our heads off" when there is a negative cash flow in a year because there has been a need to invest in new technologies. This view is very similar to the view of I-15 outlined before but instead of rejecting SHV like I-15, I-35 does not regard this as problematic in the company.

ing of VBM derived from literature being introduced by the researcher there still are differences in the interviewees' understandings. When there is reference to an increase of the company value the understandings addressed differed in whether they are expressed more vaguely or more specifically. Thus it is crucial to consider the understanding in analysing the attitude. To be able to **relate the findings at hand to the understanding of VBM underlying this thesis** the views expressed will be interpreted in light of whether the interviewees would rather express a positive or negative attitude in relation to the understanding derived from literature. This will be outlined in the following and summarised in Figure 60. In line with Wenzel (2014) and Krol (2009c) the cost-benefit-ratio expected by the owner-managers is regarded as one aspect that is related to the attitude. This shall thus be considered.

A positive attitude towards VBM in an understanding that is similar to the understanding underlying this thesis is directly expressed by only one interviewee (Group VBM2-V-D). This is the interviewee where the increase of the company is also defined as a company objective. Apart from this interviewee, there are a few interviewees who have a positive attitude and whose understanding includes some elements of the understanding of VBM underlying this thesis (Group VBM2-V-C, 2/28). These put emphasis on the increase of the company value and/or the interests of the owners. A definite statement is not possible as there is no complete accordance with VBM in the understanding underlying this thesis. Nevertheless, there is agreement to some of its elements and the interviewees might be open towards an application of VBM on the basis of a consideration of potential benefits and costs of VBM for the company. Thus, they are interpreted as likely having a positive attitude towards VBM in the understanding derived from literature. However, the findings still imply a **(likely) positive attitude towards VBM in the understanding underlying this thesis** for only a small number of interviewees (Groups VBM2-V-D and VBM2-V-C, 3/28).

It has also been found that some interviewees who seem to have been in touch with VBM regard VBM as not being relevant (Group VBM2-V-A-2, 6/28).[174] The more specific reference to VBM partly indicates an understanding that is broadly similar to the understanding derived from literature. There are also indications for potential reasons for regarding VBM as not being relevant.[175] However, the answers do not provide evidence that these interviewees have considered the potential benefits and costs of an application of VBM in the company. For these interviewees a more extensive consideration of the application of VBM in the company might either lead to an application of VBM or not. This is also the case for the interviewees that express that an increase of the company value has certain relevance for them but where this is not the main focus (Group VBM2-V-B, 14/28).[176] These interviewees address the increase of the company value in a vague manner. Consequently, the positive attitude towards VBM does not seem to refer to an understanding as in literature but

[174]The analysis of the respective answers indicates that academic studies as well as succession are situations in which there is contact with company valuation.

[175]This includes interviewees regarding the determination of the company value as difficult, the absence of an intention to sell and the absence of a moral hazard problem.

[176]Aspects referred to in the context of expressing this attitude are that the value increases automatically, that the specific company value is not relevant and that the increase of the company value needs to be regarded more broadly.

more towards a vague notion of the company value. It is unclear whether these interviewees have considered potential costs and benefits of VBM in the understanding underlying this thesis. In this respect, a clarification of the understanding of VBM seems to be necessary. Otherwise the consideration of costs and benefits of VBM might be based on a different understanding. Overall, a more extensive consideration of VBM in the understanding underlying this thesis might lead to **a positive or negative attitude** for the majority of the interviewees (Groups VBM2-V-A-2 and VBM2-V-B, 19/28[177]).

There also is a necessity to clarify the understanding of VBM before a more extensive consideration of VBM in the understanding underlying this thesis is possible for another group of interviewees. A few interviewees express that VBM is not relevant for them on the basis of a more vague reference to an increase of the company value (Group VBM2-V-A-1, 4/28). There are indications that these interviewees have not dealt much with VBM. Given the view that VBM is not relevant for them, there are doubts whether these interviewees would be willing to consider potential costs and benefits of an application of VBM. The interviews might then still tend to regard VBM as not relevant. Beyond the interviewees of group VBM2-V-A-1 who tend to have a negative attitude towards VBM in the understanding underlying this thesis other interviewees also express reservations. Two interviewees reject the shareholder value approach which the origins of VBM trace back to (Group VBM2-V-E, 2/28). The aspects mentioned in this context indicate that this rejection is based on an understanding of VBM that is different to that derived from literature.[178] A prerequisite for a consideration of VBM in these cases would be the willingness of the interviewees to exchange views about the understanding of VBM with others. Even if this would be done, it is unclear whether the interviewees would then agree with the understanding of VBM derived from the consensus existing in literature. Only then a more extensive consideration of potential benefits and costs of VBM in the understanding derived from literature would be possible. Thus it is rather **unlikely that these companies apply VBM** for a number of the interviewees (Groups VBM-V-A-1 and VBM2-V-E, 5/28[179]).

The previous paragraphs interpreted the different attitudes referred to on the basis of different understandings by the interviewees in relation to what they indicate for the interviewees' attitudes towards VBM in the understanding underlying this thesis. Overall, three interviewees can be related to a (likely) positive attitude (Groups VBM2-V-D and VBM2-V-C) and five interviewees can be related to a (likely) negative attitude (Groups VBM2-V-E and VBM2-V-A-1). For the clear majority of the interviewees it is unclear whether a thorough consideration of VBM in the understanding derived from the literature review would lead to a positive or a negative attitude

[177] The difference to the sum of the number of interviewees in groups VBM2-V-A-2 and VBM2-V-B results from I-6-EM being part of both groups because he expresses views in relation to different understandings.

[178] The negative attitude towards the shareholder value approach seems to be related to a criticism of a short-term orientation and a one-sided focus on the interests of owners at the cost of other stakeholders.

[179] There is a difference to the sum of the number of interviewees in groups VBM2-V-A-1 and VBM2-V-E as I-16 expresses attitudes in relation to different understandings and is thus included in both groups.

(Groups VBM2-V-A and VBM2-V-B, 19/28). For a number of the interviewees it seems to be necessary to clarify the understanding of VBM in literature before this can be considered (Groups VBM2-V-A-1 VBM2-V-B and VBM2-V-E, 16/28[180]).

[180]The difference to the sum of the number of interviewees of each group results from a few interviewees being part of more than one group (I-15, I-16 and I-21).

Figure 60: Summary of the views expressed in relation to an increase of the company value after introduction of the understanding derived from literature

Different views expressed by the interviewees	Increase of the company value not being relevant		Increase of the company value has certain relevance		Increase of the company value is relevant and VBM is applied	Rejection of shareholder value approach
Denomination of the group	Group VBM2-V-A		Group VBM2-V-B: vague notion of increase or preservation of value is relevant but not the main focus	Group VBM2-V-C: emphasis on increase of company value and/or interests of owners	Group VBM2-V-D	Group VBM2-V-E
Number of interviewees	10 interviewees (I-6-EM, I-8, I-11, I-12, I-13, I-14, I-		14 interviewees (I-5, I-6-EM, I-9, I-10, I-15, I-16, I-17, I-19, I-20, I-21, I-24, I-27, I-32, I-33)	2 interviewees (I-11, I-26)	1 interviewee (I-35)	2 interviewees (I-15, I-16)
Details on views expressed	• Increase of value addressed vaguely (Group VBM2-V-A-1: I-8, I-13, I-16, I-21)	• Increase of value addressed more specifically (Group VBM2-V-A-2: I-6-EM, I-11, I-12, I-14, I-18, I-28)	• value increases "automatically" • specific value not relevant • broader view of company value	• understanding partly in accordance with understanding of VBM in literature • no measurement	• under-standing similar to that in literature	• under-standing different to that in literature

(figure continued on next page)

Denomination of the group	Group VBM2-V-A		Group VBM2-V-B: vague notion of increase or preservation of value is relevant but not the main focus	Group VBM2-V-C: emphasis on increase of company value and/or interests of owners	Group VBM2-V-D	Group VBM2-V-E
Interpretation in relation to understanding of VBM derived from literature	Likely negative attitude	Consideration might result in either positive or negative attitude	Consideration might result in either positive or negative attitude	Likely positive attitude	Positive attitude expressed	Negative attitude expressed
Increase of value not addressed	5 interviewees (I-25, I-29, I-30-EM, I-31, I-34-EM)					

4.4.4 Summary of the section and discussion

The empirical insights outlined in this section contribute to the body of knowledge on the basis of RQ5:

What are Mittelstands' understanding of and attitudes towards VBM?

The findings in relation to owner-managers' understandings of VBM will be summarised and discussed before addressing the findings of their respective attitudes.

Insights into owner-managers' understandings of VBM have been gained from a respective open question (for details see subsection 4.4.2). On this basis it has been found that there are considerable differences in two ways.

Firstly, there are considerable differences in the understandings the interviewees express. In this respect six different groups have been identified. These range from interviewees with an understanding oriented towards non-economic values (Group VBM1-A) via an understanding focused on incorporating values in the company (Group VBM1-B) and an understanding oriented towards non-economic values with reference to economic aspects (Group VBM1-C) to an understanding focused on profit (Group VBM1-D). In addition there is reference to an understanding that is based on a vague reference to company value (Group VBM1-E) and an understanding that is focused on an increase of the company value (Group VBM1-F). This shows that quite a range of different understandings has been addressed. Secondly, the understandings referred to are quite different to the understanding of VBM underlying this thesis, which has been derived from the respective consensus found in the literature review (see subsection 2.3.2). This becomes evident from the comparison of the understandings of the groups identified in the empirical study with the understanding underlying the thesis (see subsection 4.4.2). Similarities can only be found for the few interviewees of group VBM1-F. The majority of the interviewees refers to understandings that are different to that underlying the thesis. Additionally, there is a tendency towards understanding the term VBM in a way that puts much more emphasis on non-economic values than the understanding in literature.

The differences found for the owner-managers' understanding of VBM are also supported by the insights gained from the question regarding the relevance of VBM (for details see subsection 4.4.3). Despite the question introducing the understanding derived from literature, the analysis of the answers shows that the interviewees still mostly refer to an understanding that is different or only vaguely related to this understanding. However, it can be noted that the focus is more on understandings that either include or put emphasis on economic aspects.

The findings on owner-managers' understanding of VBM differ to the respective initial insights from previous empirical studies. While none of the previous empirical studies focused on the analysis of the understanding of VBM, the responses to a few statements in the questionnaires of Gonschorek (2009a) and Krol (2009c) provide some indications. These statements include elements of the understanding of VBM underlying this thesis. About two thirds of the respondents have assessed two statements in a way that indicates that their understanding of VBM is similar to that in the literature in being focused on an increase of the monetary value in the long run by generating a return that is above the costs of debt and equity capital. This is supported by the assessment of additional statements (for details see subsection 2.4.4.2). In the findings at hand such accordance cannot even be identified for the interviewees whose understanding is focused on an increase of the company value (Group VBM1-F) as there is no such specific reference to return in relation to costs of capital. Beyond this, the number of interviewees referring to an understanding broadly similar to that in literature is much lower.[181] Thus, in finding considerable differences of the understanding of VBM, this study is in contrast to the existing empirical indications. This might be due to this study being the first to openly ask about the understanding of VBM and thus providing more potential to discover such differences.

Besides asking about the owner-managers' understanding of VBM, RQ5 also asks for their attitude towards VBM. The respective findings are summarised and discussed in the following. This includes the implications regarding a lack of knowledge of VBM as a barrier to the application of VBM. To gain **insights into the attitude towards VBM** in the understanding underlying the thesis the researcher briefly introduced this understanding to the interview and asked how far this plays a role in the company. The overall view on the aspects addressed by the interviewees in response to this question, shows that it is important to consider differences in the understanding referred to and the specificity of the references to the company value in analysing the attitude (for details see subsection 4.4.3). On this basis a range of different attitudes towards VBM has been found.

The attitudes expressed include that an increase of the company value is not (so) relevant (Group VBM2-V-A, 10/28), has certain relevance but is not the main focus (Groups VBM2-V-B and VBM2-V-C, 16/28) and is relevant and applied (Group VBM2-V-D, 1/28). In addition, some interviewees emphasise that the shareholder value approach is refused (VBM2-V-E, 2/28). Despite references to the increase of the company value these positions mostly do not clearly refer to the understanding of VBM underlying this thesis. To nevertheless gain indications for the attitude towards VBM in the understanding of this thesis the views expressed by the interviewees have been interpreted from this perspective.

When interpreting the insights in relation to the potential attitude towards VBM in the understanding underlying the thesis (for details see subsection 4.4.3.5) three interviewees can be related to a (likely) positive attitude (Groups VBM2-V-D and VBM2-V-C, 3/28). Five interviewees can be related to a (likely) negative attitude (Groups VBM2-V-E and VBM2-V-A-1, 5/28). For the majority of the interviewees it is unclear whether a consideration of VBM in the understanding derived from literature would lead to a positive or negative attitude (Groups VBM2-V-A2 and VBM2-V-B, 19/28).

The findings add to previous insights into the attitude towards VBM. The literature review has shown that previous empirical studies only yielded differing indications on the basis of little and indirectly gained insights (for details see subsection 2.4.4.2). While Krol (2009c), Gonschorek (2009a) and Wenzel (2014) find indications for the attitude towards VBM, none of them asks about the attitude towards

[181] Only 2 out of 28 interviewees are assigned to group VBM1-F. This is a percentage of 7 % which is much lower than the approx. two thirds of the respondents found in previous empirical studies.

VBM. Instead, the indications are gained in the context of analysing factors influencing the application of VBM. Furthermore, there is the limitation that these empirical studies do not consider differences in the understanding to which the attitudes of the respondents probably refer. This is crucial given the considerable differences found in this empirical study. In this respect Krol (2009c) and Gonschorek (2009a) only touch upon the understanding in finding indications for the attitude. Scheiber et al. (2012) explicitly address that a potentially different understanding of modern management tools might lead to distortions in analysing their level of application. However, none of the existing empirical studies analyses the attitude together with the understanding. They do not even provide the possibility that participants express their understanding of VBM openly.

Against this background, the findings primarily support and deepen the initial insights gained by Wenzel (2014), which indicate that owners of family businesses can either have a positive or a negative attitude towards VBM. While in some cases the owner has been the key driver of an implementation of VBM, for which a positive attitude can be assumed, Wenzel (2014) also finds that some owner families refuse the application of VBM. Similarly, the findings at hand show that different attitudes exist among owner-managers in Mittelstand. The empirical study at hand goes beyond that of Wenzel (2014) as this is directly found on the basis of interviews with owner-managers and not just indirectly.[182]

However, the findings also support part of the conclusion Krol (2009c) makes from indirectly touching upon the attitude towards VBM. He concludes that the little application of VBM is less related to a refusal of VBM but more towards a lack of knowledge and a lack of tools. Firstly, this is supported in that this study does not find evidence for a broad refusal of VBM. While there are a few interviewees who are assumed to have a more negative attitude towards VBM in the understanding underlying this thesis, no interviewee clearly refuses VBM in the understanding underlying this thesis.[183] Thus, the literature's notion that there might be potential reservations resulting from a different understanding and a negative attitude towards VBM (Becker et al., 2010b; Krol, 2009c; Wenzel) applies only to some interviewees in the sample at hand. The general criticism of VBM's orientation towards owners in society that is touched upon in the literature (Gonschorek, 2009a, 2015b, 2016c; Krol, 2009c; Lehmann, 2012; Tappe, 2009) seems to reflect in only two interviewees' refusal of the shareholder value approach.

Secondly, Krol's (2009c) conclusion is also supported in that the little application seems to be related to a lack of knowledge. Overall, several aspects indicate that

[182] Firstly, Wenzel (2014) addresses this indirectly in the context of analysing factors influencing VBM. Secondly, the findings of Wenzel (2014) are based on interviews with CFOs of family businesses. Only in a small number of cases are the interviewees also the owners of the company. Thus, his findings on the attitude of owner families are mostly based on the views expressed by external CFOs.

[183] The negative attitude either refers to a different or a vague understanding of VBM. Firstly, the interviewees that refuse the shareholder value approach equate this with profit maximisation and a short-term view or hardness towards employees (VBM2-V-E). Secondly, the other interviewees who express that VBM is not relevant for them only vaguely refer to an increase of the company (VBM2-V-A-1).

many interviewees have little knowledge of VBM and have not yet dealt with it. Firstly, many interviewees hesitate after being asked openly for their understanding of the term VBM. Secondly, the understanding outlined in response to this question is considerably different to that derived from literature. Thirdly, there still are recurring references to an understanding that is either different to that derived from literature or only vaguely mentioned after the introduction of this understanding to the interview. Fourthly, from the attitude outlined in relation to an increase of the company value there is the impression that there has often not yet been a consideration of costs and benefits of VBM. A similar lack of knowledge has already been found for the net present value method in the context of the use of management tools in SDM (for details see subsections 4.2.4.3). This lack of knowledge and dealing with VBM is regarded as a barrier to the application of VBM. This notion is in line with Scheiber et al.'s (2012) respective reasoning that the knowledge of modern management tools puts a ceiling to the level of their application among Mittelstand.[184] This also is in accordance with Krol's (2009c) conclusion that the lack of knowledge is a key reason why VBM is not applied. A similar view is expressed by Gonschorek (2009a) who concludes that knowledge deficits are a reason for a low application of VBM and that particularly smaller companies have not yet dealt much with VBM. Given that the owner-manager's knowledge of and attitude towards VBM seem to be of key importance for the application of VBM it is crucial to address this further.

Overall, the findings **contribute to the body of knowledge** by generating new and differentiated insights into owner-managers' understandings of VBM. The study at hand provides a new perspective as it is the first empirical study in the relevant body of literature that includes a respective research question and gains insights on the basis of openly asking owner-managers for their understanding. This new perspective allowed finding considerable differences of the understanding of VBM, which is in contrast to the existing empirical indications. Furthermore, the findings contribute to the body of knowledge by gaining unique empirical insights into owner-manager's attitudes towards VBM. Previous empirical studies provide only few indications that have been gained indirectly. The study at hand goes beyond this by addressing the attitude for the first time in the relevant body of knowledge with a direct question to owner-managers and as one of the research questions. Furthermore, the understanding referred to has been considered in the analysis of the attitudes expressed. This is crucial given the considerable differences in the understandings of VBM. Thus, limitations of previous empirical studies in this respect are overcome. On this basis the findings show that different attitudes towards VBM exist among owner-managers. The findings imply that the little application of VBM tends not to be due to a negative attitude but to a lack of knowledge. This reinforces respective conclusions in the body of knowledge.

[184] However, it must be noted that there is a contrast to their finding that nearly 70 % of the respondents to an empirical study on the level of application of modern management tools state that they know "shareholder value management" (Scheiber, Wruk, Huppertz, Oberg, and Woywode (2012, p. 45)). However, this difference might be related to the different term and to a difference in the methodology. While the finding of Scheiber et al. (2012) is based on a self-assessment of the respondents in the questionnaire, the study at hand gained much more in-depth insights and also considered differences in the understanding.

However, there are still limitations to the insights gained as the interviewees refer to different understandings in talking about the relevance of VBM. Only in a few cases, the attitudes expressed refer to an understanding similar to the understanding underlying the thesis. Mostly, the attitudes expressed are not directly related to this understanding by the interviewee. In addition, this aspect was only part of the interview and addressed at the end. Thus, there has been little opportunity to pose follow-up questions to be able to gain further insights that are more related to the understanding underlying the thesis. As a consequence, the link to the understanding underlying this thesis needed to be established via interpretation by the researcher. Consequently, while partly overcoming the limitations of previous empirical studies the study at hand still only yields indications for owner-managers' attitudes towards VBM in the understanding derived from literature for the majority of the interviewees. While the body of knowledge has been further developed, additional research into owner-managers' attitudes towards VBM is valuable. Given the differences found in relation to the understanding of VBM it is vital to consider the owner-managers' understandings in further researching their attitudes towards VBM. An interesting avenue for further research would be to explore owner-managers' attitudes towards VBM before and after a consideration of the costs and benefits of VBM.

5 Conclusion

This chapter provides a synthesis of the key findings and contributions of the research project. Furthermore, it addresses implications and limitations of the research as well as avenues for further research.

5.1 Research gaps and research questions

Based on overviews of Mittelstand and VBM as a broader thematic context, the body of knowledge on VBM in Mittelstand has been analysed. From a review of the literature on VBM in Mittelstand the understanding of VBM has been derived, and key topics in the field of research have been identified. The literature review has shown a research gap:

> On the one hand there is a **consensus on the applicability** of VBM in Mittelstand in the literature and there are **proposals for its application**. This is in contrast to the **little application in practice** that has been found in empirical studies.

Furthermore, gaps in empirical insights have been found, which include

- little empirical insights on the application of VBM in the context of decision-making,
- differing findings in relation to Mittelstand's objectives and the respective relevance of VBM and
- little findings on Mittelstand's attitude towards VBM.

To address these research gaps, the aim of the research has been to gain empirical insights to understand the relevance of VBM in selected areas of management in Mittelstand. The overall research question has been:

> In what way is VBM relevant for specifically identified areas of management in Mittelstand (strategic decision-making, objectives, attitudes)?

The following supplementary research questions have guided the empirical investigation:

1. What management tools are used in strategic decision-making in Mittelstand, and in which ways are these tools relevant for strategic decision-making?
2. How is VBM reflected in the use of management tools in strategic decision-making in Mittelstand?
3. What are the objectives of Mittelstand?
4. How is VBM reflected in the objectives of Mittelstand?
5. What are Mittelstands' understanding of and attitudes towards VBM?

The insights from the pilot study indicated differences in owner-managers' understanding of VBM. Therefore, research question 5 has been expanded accordingly.

5.2 Findings and contributions in relation to the research questions

The following subsections will summarise the findings and contributions in relation to the research questions. The verbal summary will be complemented by summary graphs at the end of each subsection (see Figure 61, Figure 62 and Figure 63).

© Springer Fachmedien Wiesbaden GmbH, part of Springer Nature 2020
C. Normann-Tschampel, *Value-Based Management in Mittelstand*,
Familienunternehmen und KMU, https://doi.org/10.1007/978-3-658-29228-7_5

5.2.1 Strategic decision-making in Mittelstand

The research approach is specific in gaining findings into RQ1 on the basis of interviews with owner-managers (for details see section 4.2):

> What management tools are used in strategic decision-making in Mittelstand, and in which ways are these tools relevant for strategic decision-making?

While previous empirical studies provide results in a broadly similar context (such as the use of methods of investment appraisal in decision-making), the literature review did not yield empirical studies with a specific focus on the use of management tools in strategic decision-making. Furthermore, the openness of the research approach allowed for valuable empirical insights on the use of management tools in SDM. Consequently, the findings do not only include management tools already addressed in former empirical investigations (such as tools of investment appraisal) but also include management tools that have not yet been empirically addressed in relation to decision-making in Mittelstand (such as business planning and cost accounting). Beyond this, the empirical findings yield indications for the role of some management tools in strategic decision-making, which expand the body of knowledge as well. For instance, an interesting new aspect is the relevance of cost accounting as a trigger for strategic decisions.

On this basis insights into RQ2 have been gained:

> How is VBM reflected in the use of management tools in strategic decision-making in Mittelstand?

This included an analysis from different perspectives that respond to different possibilities in that VBM can be reflected in decision-making. Overall, the analysis has shown that VBM is of little relevance for SDM in Mittelstand. Among others there is very little reference to VBM management tools and KPIs. Furthermore, only a few interviewees use the net present value method and if so only in specific situations. In a narrow sense, this supports existing results that show little use of the net present value method. Furthermore, it underpins empirical studies in a broadly similar context in relation to VBM's little relevance for decision-making (Krol, 2009c; Piontkowski, 2009; Tappe, 2009; Wenzel, 2014). Based on finding a low level of awareness of the NPV method, it is regarded as necessary to overcome the lack of knowledge as a limiting factor for its application. The research approach additionally allowed potentially new insights in this context. The owner-managers' views indicate that further aspects influence the application of the NPV and other management tools in decision-making, for example that intuitive decision-making plays an important role in decision-making in Mittelstand. Thus, the empirical study also goes beyond existing empirical insights in providing indications that might contribute to a better understanding of Mittelstand owner-managers' decision-making behaviour.

The insights gained in relation to RQ1 and RQ2 have the following implications: Firstly, the empirical study contributes to the body of knowledge by gaining insights into management tools and the relevance of VBM in the context of strategic decision-making, which responds to the respective gap in empirical research. This is achieved with an approach that is specific in its focus, context and methodology. Secondly, as regards to the overall research gap, the empirical insights related to the area of strategic decision-making support empirical studies that found a low level of application of VBM for several areas of management in Mittelstand. Thirdly, the findings also have implications regarding the applicability of VBM in Mittelstand and the proposals for the application of VBM in Mittelstand. The findings raise doubts regarding the applicability of existing proposals for the application of VBM in Mittelstand. While these try to account for Mittelstand specifics they are still strongly oriented towards management tools and KPIs and do not consider other decision-making styles. Building on the findings, a stronger consideration of intuitive decision-making and how VBM could reflect in this approach to decision-making is recommended as a valuable advancement. Accordingly, further research focusing on strategic decision-making practices and the potential role of VBM's basic economic view might provide a beneficial basis.

Figure 61: Overview of findings and contributions in relation to strategic decision-making in Mittelstand

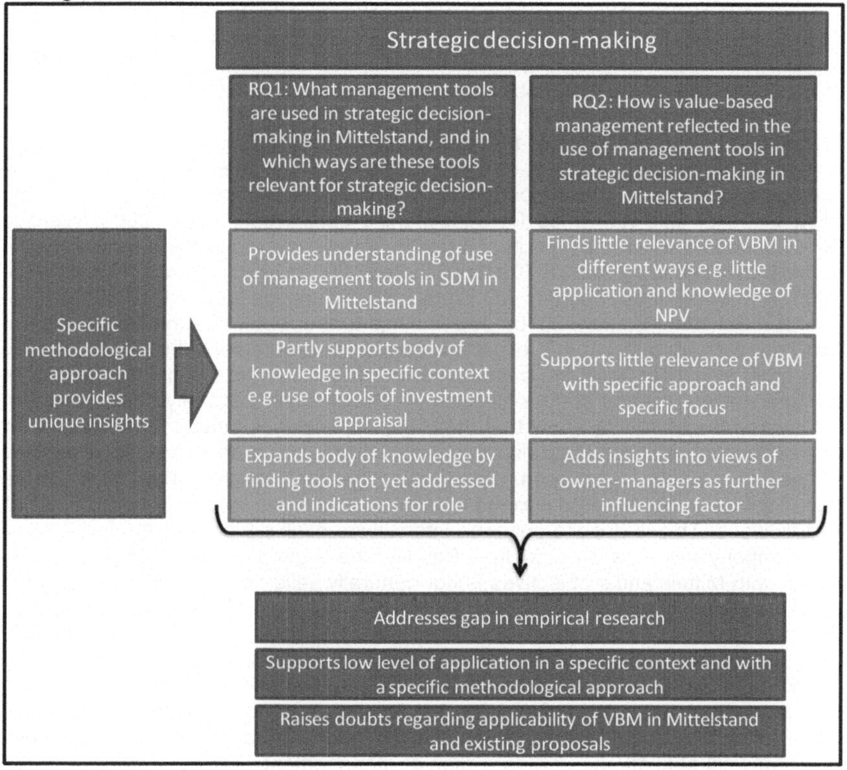

5.2.2 *Objectives in Mittelstand*

The empirical study also provides insights into RQ3 (see section 4.3):

What are the objectives of Mittelstand?

Based on a specific methodological approach, an understanding of objectives in Mittelstand from the owner-manager's perspective has been gained. The findings partly support existing evidence on the content of Mittelstand's objectives and their importance (e.g. in relation to the high importance of securing the companies' existence). However, the findings also develop the body of knowledge. This includes acquiring an enhanced understanding of Mittelstand's objectives on the basis of the owner-managers' views e.g. the broader understanding of market-oriented objectives. Furthermore, objectives not included in recent empirical investigations are relevant for the interviewees e.g. objectives focused on internal improvements. Additionally, the results are different in relation to the importance of a number of the objectives. This includes independence being of lower importance. A major contribution is that the empirical insights go beyond the existing body of knowledge by taking a holistic view of the companies' objectives (see subsection 4.3.3). This results in distinguishing groups of interviewees according to nuances, in that the overall target course reflects economic and non-economic objectives.

The insights gained regarding objectives in Mittelstand also refer to RQ4:

How is VBM reflected in the objectives of Mittelstand?

In this respect the analysis of the specific objectives pursued shows that the increase of the company value is of little importance. Given the differences in the existing empirical results this supports individual previous empirical studies that found VBM to be of little relevance for Mittelstand's objectives (Tappe, 2009; Wenzel, 2014). Indeed, the findings are in contrast to several questionnaire-based empirical studies (Achleitner et al., 2010; Gonschorek, 2009a; Krol, 2009c; Piontkowski, 2009; PricewaterhouseCoopers AG Wirtschaftsprüfungsgesellschaft, 2014; Schlepphorst & Schlömer-Laufen, 2016). The findings further show that the literature's notion, that there is a threat that economic objectives are neglected in favour of non-economic objectives is, in the sample, not dominant. Firstly, a considerable part of the interviewees named profit realisation as an objective. Secondly, the findings for the overall target course show that there are interviewees putting an emphasis on non-economic objectives but also interviewees that focus on economic objectives as well as nuances in between. This implies that the reasoning that VBM can be beneficial as an opposite pole to non-economic objectives applies to part but not all interviewees. This is despite only one interviewee explicitly naming the increase of the company value as an objective. Equally, the argument that VBM is in accordance with Mittelstand's objectives is not generally valid but must be considered in a more differentiated manner.

Overall, the results firstly relate to the differences in existing empirical findings by providing an enhanced and more differentiated understanding of objectives, which includes a new perspective. Secondly, the findings support the notion of little application of VBM in practice, empirically found in relation to objectives in some previous empirical studies and in other areas of management. Thirdly, in relation to the applicability of VBM in Mittelstand, the findings imply that the two reasonings used in literature on VBM in Mittelstand need to be looked at in a more differentiated way. The notion that Mittelstand's objectives are in line with VBM and thus a driver of the application of VBM in Mittelstand is not generally given. Furthermore, demanding the use of VBM as a valuable opposite pole to non-economic objectives in Mittelstand is also not applicable for all interviewees. Instead, the objectives partly reflect both economic objectives and non-economic objectives. Thus, a more differentiated view of objectives in the debate on the applicability of VBM in Mittelstand is recommended. Fourthly, the findings imply that it might be beneficial to consider the differences in Mittelstand's objectives in the proposals for the application of VBM in Mittelstand. An initial approach in this direction is provided by Khadjavi (2005).

Figure 62: Overview of findings and contributions in relation to objectives in Mittelstand

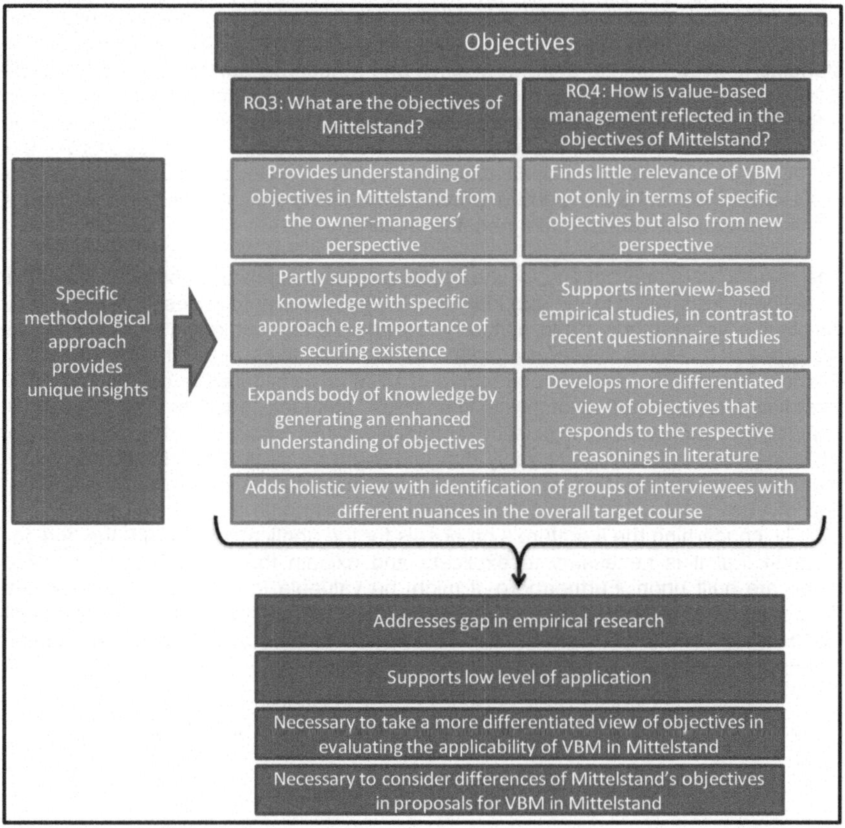

5.2.3 Understanding of and attitudes towards value-based management

Additional empirical insights have been gained in relation to RQ5 (see section 4.4):

What are Mittelstands' understanding of and attitudes towards VBM?

The specific research approach provides unique insights into owner-manager's understanding of VBM. While initially being oriented towards the attitudes towards VBM, it has been found that it is also crucial to consider the interviewees' understanding of VBM because there are persistant differences in the understandings of

VBM. These mostly deviate from the understanding derived from literature. This also indicates a non-familiarity with VBM in the understanding derived from literature. Finding that owner-managers have a different understanding of VBM is in contrast to initial empirical indications gained by Krol (2009c) and Gonschorek (2009a).

In relation to the attitudes towards VBM different views have been found. There is a tendency towards a positive attitude towards VBM, in the way the interviewees understand it. However, when the interviewees refer to an increase of the company value, after the introduction of the understanding in literature by the researcher, different views are addressed. When these are interpreted in relation to the understanding derived from literature, a positive and a negative attitude can be found for a few interviewees. However, the interviewees mostly seem to have not dealt much with VBM. These interviewees might have either a positive or a negative attitude after consideration of VBM in the understanding of literature. This supports Wenzel (2014), who already found indications for different attitudes in contrast to Krol (2009c) and Gonschorek (2009a) whose conclusions indicate on the one hand a positive and on the other hand a negative attitude.

The results have implications for the research gaps identified. Firstly, the empirical investigation responds to the gap identified in that little empirical results exist in relation to the understanding and attitudes towards VBM. New insights are gained as the approach allows owner-managers to express their understanding of VBM openly. Furthermore, the understanding of VBM is considered in developing a differentiated understanding of owner-managers' attitudes towards VBM. Secondly, against the background of existing empirical results showing little application of VBM in practice, the findings imply that this might be related to Mittelstand owner-managers' not having dealt with VBM. This is considered as a barrier to the application of VBM (Krol (2009c) and Gonschorek (2009a) come to a similar conclusion). Thirdly, concerning the literature's proposals for the application of VBM, the findings suggest that it is necessary to explicate and explain the understanding of VBM these are built upon. Furthermore, it might be valuable to consider alternative understandings of VBM. Fourthly, as a consequence of the findings it is supposed that owner-managers have different views with regard to the applicability of VBM in Mittelstand, which should be considered more in literature.

Figure 63: Overview of findings and contributions in relation to understanding of and attitudes towards VBM

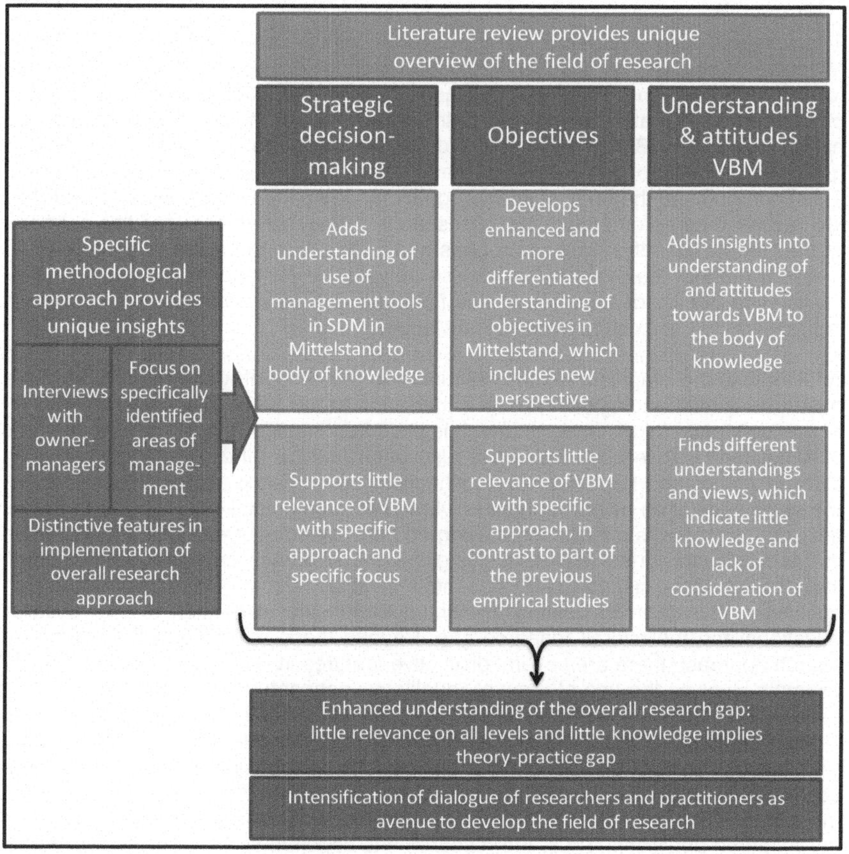

5.3 Contribution to knowledge

Firstly, the research at hand contributes to the body of knowledge by the empirical insights gained in relation to the research questions. Thus, an understanding of the relevance of VBM in selected areas of management has been obtained. Previous sections have shown that this supports, develops and adds to the body of knowledge. This responds to the overall research question and addresses the research objective as it also provides an understanding of the overall research gap. VBM has been found to be of little relevance in all areas selected for empirical investigation. Thus, the gap of the significance of VBM in literature to the little application in practice is already given on the level of the objectives pursued. Furthermore, there seems to be little knowledge of VBM in general and specifically NPV. This implies that there is a theory-practice gap. This contribution and other aspects of the contribution are summarised in Figure 64.

The research also included a literature review with a strong emphasis on VBM in Mittelstand (see section 2.3). This sounds reasonable given the focus of research for the study at hand. However, this goes beyond the existing literature in giving precedence to literature combining both topics and not mainly relying on material either looking at VBM or at Mittelstand. Furthermore, an overview of the field is given on the basis of an analysis of the topics addressed and approaches applied. This contributes to the body of knowledge by mapping the field of research, which is still regarded as an emerging field of research.[185] The researcher used this overview of the field for identifying research gaps and formulating the research questions. In a similar manner the overview might also be valuable for other researchers to identify starting points for research in this field and delineate their research project in comparison to the existing body of knowledge.

Additionally, the empirical results contribute to the body of knowledge as they are based on a methodological approach that adds to the body of knowledge. The interpretive stance taken in the research is based on interviews with owner-managers of Mittelstand. While interviews have also been used in other empirical studies on VBM in Mittelstand (Golsner, 2012; Khadjavi, 2005; Tappe, 2009; Wenzel, 2014) the study's focus on owner-managers' views provides unique insights. Furthermore, the study's stance is specific in focusing on three selected areas of management in the semi-structured interviews. In doing this the approach provided more in-depth insights into these aspects, with openness towards new aspects and multiple perspectives. This allowed gaining further understanding in relation to the research questions and the overall research gap. Beyond these specifics of the overall research approach there are several distinctive features in its implementation. This for example involves the use of a mainly qualitative conceptualisation of Mittelstand as a basis for sampling, which is regarded as more suitable to reflect Mittelstand's characteristics than mainly quantitative definitions. Furthermore, it is assumed that perceptions on VBM might influence the decision to participate as well as the aspects addressed in the interviews. As a consequence, the findings might not reflect the role of VBM in 'ordinary' Mittelstand and this is in contrast to the openness of the research approach. Thus, the research has couched its topics in general terms and the term VBM was introduced to the interviews only in the last part of the interviews. Altogether, the specific interpretive stance addressed the research gaps.

Overall, it has been shown that the empirical insights gained based on the specific methodological approach contribute to the body of knowledge, by providing an enhanced understanding based on the research questions. Finding VBM to be of little relevance in all specifically identified areas of management suggests that there is a theory-practice gap. In this context, there are further implications from the findings which add to and modify existing views in VBM in Mittelstand literature. In line with the methodological approach in-depth insights have been gained with an openness that allowed finding new aspects and different perspectives. In relation to strategic

[185]This might also be the reason for earlier contributions mainly relying on literature that either addresses VBM or Mittelstand.

decision-making an implication that demands for a modification of existing views in VBM in Mittelstand literature is that it seems to be valuable to acknowledge the role of intuitive decision-making in Mittelstand. In VBM in Mittelstand literature there commonly seems to be a focus on the use of management tools and Key Performance indicators and decision-making practice is criticised for a lack of rationality. Acknowledging the role of intuitive decision-making opens up valuable perspectives for further research which might develop the body of knowledge and help to enhance strategic decision-making practice. A valuable starting point in this respect is the notion of the consideration of VBM's basic economic view, which already had been mentioned by a few authors in VBM in Mittelstand literature and was used as one perspective in the empirical analysis in the study at hand. The findings on objectives in Mittelstand as well as owner-managers' understandings of and attitudes towards VBM showed differences among the interviewees in several facets. These might reflect the heterogeneity in Mittelstand and it is regarded as necessary to consider this more in VBM in Mittelstand literature. In the existing body of knowledge, there is a consensus on the applicability of VBM in Mittelstand in general. However, there are some weaknesses of VBM that have not yet been adequately resolved and hurdles to its application. Furthermore, it is regarded as valuable to consider the individual situation of each company and its needs. Consequently, VBM might but does not need to be applicable depending upon the differences in the individual situation of mittelständische companies. Given the heterogeneity of Mittelstand, a more differentiated view on the advantageousness of VBM for mittelständische companies might thus be valuable. In this respect, the existing empirical insights on influencing and success factors of VBM in Mittelstand provide a valuable starting point for further research. Furthermore, given the considerable differences found in this regard, it seems to be valuable to pay more attention to the understanding of VBM. While acknowledging the existence of alternative understandings of value, there is little debate on the understanding of VBM in the relevant literature. Given that in this study the consensus existing in the literature on the understanding of VBM is not reflected in the owner-managers' views, an awareness for alternative understandings of VBM is a crucial basis for further research. This is also important as differences in the understanding might lead to distortions in analysing the relevance of VBM empirically. Thus, the insights gained in relation to the research questions with a specific methodological approach that responds to the gaps identified from a unique overview of the field imply that there is a need to modify existing notions in VBM in Mittelstand literature to reflect management practice in Mittelstand more adequately.

Figure 64: Summary of contribution to knowledge

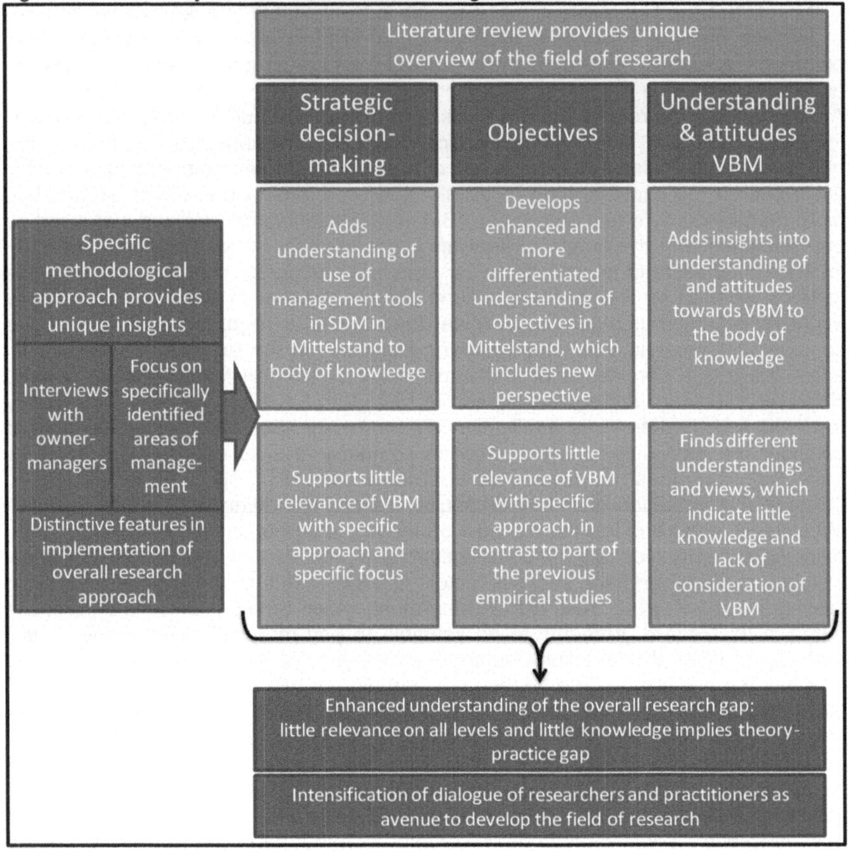

An avenue to overcome or evaluate the potential to overcome the theory-practice-gap might be an intensification of the dialogue of researchers and practitioners. Both, researchers as well as practitioners, might benefit from an exchange on the applicability of VBM in Mittelstand as well as avenues for its application. Additional insights into practitioners' views might help researchers orientate the existing proposals for the application of Mittelstand more towards the specifics of Mittelstand. In this respect, the research at hand particularly points at a consideration of intuitive decision-making and a more differentiated view of Mittelstand's objectives. Beyond this, the research emphasises the importance of explicating and explaining the understanding of VBM. Gaining insights into existing proposals for the application of VBM in Mittelstand might help owner-managers to increase their knowledge on VBM and consider the costs and benefits of an application of VBM. Researchers and practitioners might also benefit from a dialogue and a more differentiated view of drivers, barriers and the applicability of VBM in Mittelstand. In this respect, it is important to consider owner-managers' attitudes of VBM as a potential driver or barrier to an application of VBM and to take differences into account. An awareness of the differences in the understanding of VBM is a crucial basis for such a discourse of researchers and practitioners. Overall, this exchange could contribute in enhancing the impact of research on VBM in Mittelstand.

Based on the findings, a specific situation in that this general recommendation of an intensified dialogue of researchers and practitioners might be especially fruitful is the situation of succession. This is because there have been indications that in this situation owner-managers encounter the topic of company valuation. This is used as an example to illustrate the above-made recommendations. As owner-managers in Mittelstand deal with the topic of company valuation in this situation it is a good opportunity to increase the knowledge on VBM. Building on the monetary understanding of value that is involved in such a company valuation there can be an exchange on the understanding of VBM as well as the consequences of an implementation and the related costs and benefits. There could also be an exchange on existing proposals on how VBM can be applied in Mittelstand. This dialogue could help practitioners to make an informed choice on the applicability of VBM in their company in a situation where researchers assume VBM to be particularly beneficial. While this exchange might not necessarily result in an application of VBM it might nevertheless help practitioners to identify a potential for enhancing management. Based on such an exchange, researchers could gain more knowledge about owner-managers' views on drivers, barriers and the applicability of VBM. This is especially valuable given that this study has found that VBM is not relevant for the interviewees that encounter the topic of company valuation in the situation of succession. Given this contrast to literature's view, it is also valuable for researchers to understand owner-managers' views on existing proposals for the application of VBM in Mittelstand. This could help to further develop proposals of VBM in Mittelstand to meet Mittelstand's needs better. Overall, an increased consideration of VBM by practitioners and an increased consideration of owner-managers' views by researchers can thus help to reduce the theory-practice gap.

5.4 Limitations and avenues for further research

While the thematic focus and the interpretive stance underlying this research approach allowed for valuable insights there are also limitations. By looking at three specifically identified areas of management this research was more focused than previous empirical studies that look at more areas of management in evaluating the application of VBM in Mittelstand. However, the findings showed that there were still limitations regarding the depth of the understanding that could be gained. In this respect, further empirical studies using an interpretive stance with a stronger focus on one of the aspects addressed in this study, might provide a richer and more in-depth understanding. There are several facets that might be further explored. These include, for example, decision-making styles in Mittelstand and the respective role of VBM. Further research might also focus on owner-managers' motives and objectives as well as the respective relevance of an increase of the company value. Furthermore, owner-managers' attitudes towards VBM on the basis of dealing more with VBM is an interesting avenue for further research.

Additionally, the sampling method was oriented towards gaining an enhanced understanding in line with the interpretive stance. In light of this aim it was accepted that the findings cannot be regarded as representative for the whole population of Mittelstand. In this respect, it might be beneficial to empirically analyse the relevance of the views identified from this study with a focus on testing their generalisability. Furthermore, the interpretive stance strongly builds on the accounts of the interviewees and an empathetic stance is taken. While this yields valuable insights into the interviewees' views, the emphasis on understanding the phenomenon from one – albeit important – perspective, has limitations. For example, participants with a different role in a company or outside the company probably have a different view. Hence, in line with the approaches of other empirical studies on VBM in Mittelstand (Khadjavi, 2005; Tappe, 2009; Wenzel, 2014) the views of management consultants, CFOs and management accountants on the topics addressed in this research might further be explored. The researcher hopes that the contribution to the body of knowledge provides valuable insights for other researchers. Hopefully, researchers will be inspired to further explore this complex but interesting phenomenon. Some avenues for further research have been illustrated in previous paragraphs. Without doubt there are numerous opportunities for further research that might help to increase the impact of this field of research.

Appendices – List of figures

© Springer Fachmedien Wiesbaden GmbH, part of Springer Nature 2020
C. Normann-Tschampel, *Value-Based Management in Mittelstand*, Familienunternehmen und KMU, https://doi.org/10.1007/978-3-658-29228-7

Appendices

Appendices-Figure 1: Analysis of Mittelstand definitions to decide on the definition of the work

Author (year) of the publication analysed	Definition of Mittelstand	Analysis of definition with regard to common qualitative criteria identified by Hausch (2004) 1) Unity of ownership and management 2) Orientation of management towards individual person(s) 3) Economic and legal independence of the company 4) Limited size
Becker, and Fischer et al. (2008, p. 21)	"Mittelständische companies are: • owner-/family-managed companies, • externally-managed companies with up to roughly 3,000 employees and/or a turnover of roughly 600 Mio. Euro and • companies that have both defining features."	1) Broader view that includes externally managed companies 2) Apart from being owner-managed not included in definition 3) Not included in definition 4) Size limit for externally-managed companies
Institut für Mittelstandsforschung (2018b)	"IfM Bonn defines Mittelstand via unity of ownership and management. ... the definition of Mittelstand is operationalised as follows: In a mittelständische company • up to two natural persons or their family members hold at least 50 % of the shares of a company (directly or indirectly) and • these natural persons are members of the management board." • Illustration of the differences of Mittelstand and SMEs includes that SMEs that are dependent upon another company do not fulfill the Mittelstand definition	1) Broader view: significant level of unity of ownership and management 2) Apart from 1) not included in definition 3) Indirectly included 4) Not included in definition

© Springer Fachmedien Wiesbaden GmbH, part of Springer Nature 2020
C. Normann-Tschampel, *Value-Based Management in Mittelstand*, Familienunternehmen und KMU, https://doi.org/10.1007/978-3-658-29228-7

Gonschorek (2009a, pp. 44–46)	Outline results in the following definition: "Mittelständische companies are family businesses, in that the owners as natural persons significantly determine the corporate policy via the management of the company and/or the company's general meeting and/or the supervisory board." (p. 45)	1) Broader view: significant influence of owners on management (directly or indirectly) 2) Apart from 1) not included 3) Not included in definition 4) Not included in definition
Khadjavi (2005, pp. 53–58)	Outline includes the following definition: "The following three characteristics conduce to delineating the object of research: • vast unity of ownership and management • no listing on the stock exchange • legal (no branch) and economic (no dependence on parent companies or a network of companies) independence." (p. 56) • Exclusion of small companies in the style of the definition of the EU commission (companies with a turnover of less than 10 Mio. Euro and less than 50 employees)	1) Broader view: significant level of unity of ownership and management 2) Apart from 1) not included 3) Included with illustration 4) Size limit as lower limit included in definition
Krol (2009c, pp. 17–20)	Outline results in the following definition: "A mittelständische company in terms of this research thus is a company that is economically and legally independent and whose owners have a significant influence on the management of the company. In the ideal type these are companies, whose number of employees is between 10 and 499 and whose annual turnover is below 50 Mio. Euro." (p.20)	1) Broader view: significant influence of owners on management 2) Apart from 1) not included 3) Included 4) Used as supplementary criterion
Tappe (2009, pp. 19–22)	Target group of the work (p. 22): • At least 100 employees • fundamental characteristics typical for Mittelstand, among	1) Indirectly touched upon but not explicitly included in definition 2) Indirectly included

	others owner-oriented companies as well as externally-managed companies • legal and economic independence	3) Included 4) Size limit as lower limit for the target group

Appendices-Figure 2: Percentage of small- and medium-sized entities in Germany and Baden-Württemberg

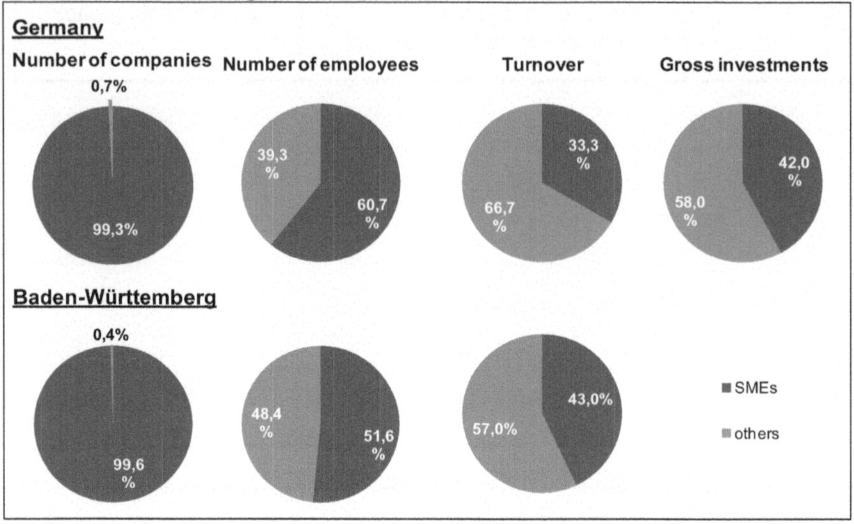

The percentages for Germany have been calculated on the basis of data from the Statistisches Bundesamt Deutschland (2018). This defines SMEs with a threshold of 250 employees and a turnover threshold of 50 million Euro based on the definition of the European Commission (20.5.2003).

The percentages for Baden-Württemberg are calculated on the basis of data from the Statistisches Landesamt Baden-Württemberg (2018a). In these statistics, only the employee threshold of 250 employees for SMEs is used. This slightly limits comparability as the data from Baden-Württemberg might include companies with less than 250 employees but a turnover of 50 million Euro or more. These companies are not included in the data for Germany.

Overall, the vast majority of companies in Germany and Baden-Württemberg are SMEs. Additionally, SMEs employ a majority of the employees and generate a considerable part of the turnover. Furthermore, a large percentage of the gross investments in Germany is done by SMEs. Data on gross investments in Baden-Württemberg is not available. Despite the differences in the exact values the data shows that SMEs are numerically significant for Germany and Baden-Württemberg.

Appendices-Figure 3: Overview of approach and key topics in literature on VBM in Mittelstand

Author (year)[186]	Approach	Key topics related to recurrent themes
Gonschorek (2016c)	Drawing conclusions from literature	Drivers, hurdles and applicability of VBM in Mittelstand Adaptation of VBM concepts to mittelständische characteristics and how Mittelstand can apply VBM Empirical insights into application of VBM[187]
Nathani et al. (2016)	Empirical analysis on the basis of quantitative data	Empirical insights into companies' value creation
Gonschorek (2015b)	Drawing conclusions from literature	Drivers, hurdles and applicability of VBM in Mittelstand Adaptation of VBM concepts to mittelständische characteristics and how Mittelstand can apply VBM Empirical insights into application of VBM
Günther (2015b)	Drawing conclusions from literature	Drivers, hurdles and applicability of VBM in Mittelstand Adaptation of VBM concepts to mittelständische characteristics and how Mittelstand can apply VBM Empirical insights into application of VBM
Mafirowanda (2015)	Empirical analysis on the basis of qualitative data	Empirical insights into application of VBM
Oliveira (2014)	Empirical analysis on the basis of quantitative data	Empirical insights into companies' value creation
Günther (2014a)	Drawing conclusions from literature	Drivers, hurdles and applicability of VBM in Mittelstand Adaptation of VBM concepts to mittelständische characteristics and how Mittelstand can apply VBM Empirical insights into application of VBM
Wenzel (2014)	Empirical analysis on the basis of qualitative data	Drivers, hurdles and applicability of VBM in Mittelstand Empirical insights into application of VBM
Golsner (2012)	Empirical analysis on the basis of qualitative data	Adaptation of VBM concepts to mittelständische characteristics (focus on organisational factors)

[186] Sorted by year in descending order

[187] When empirical insights are mentioned as topic for a contribution whose approach is „drawing conclusions from literature" this reflects that empirical insights gained by others are addressed.

	(single case study)	Empirical insights into application of VBM
Lehmann (2012)	Empirical analysis on the basis of quantitative and qualitative data	Drivers, hurdles and applicability of VBM in Mittelstand Adaptation of VBM concepts to mittelständische companies (focus on the determination of the costs of equity capital) Empirical insights into application of VBM
Bahri et al. (2011)	Empirical analysis on the basis of quantitative data	Drivers, hurdles and applicability of VBM in Mittelstand Adaptation of VBM concepts to mittelständische characteristics and how Mittelstand can apply VBM Empirical insights into companies' value creation
Dixit (2011)	Empirical analysis on the basis of quantitative data	Empirical insights into companies' value creation
Print and Reynolds (2011)	Empirical analysis on the basis of quantitative data	Empirical insights into companies' value creation
Beck and Britzelmaier (2010)	Drawing conclusions from literature	Drivers, hurdles and applicability of VBM in Mittelstand Empirical insights into application of VBM
Becker et al. (2010a; 2010b)	Drawing conclusions from literature	Drivers, hurdles and applicability of VBM in Mittelstand Adaptation of VBM concepts to mittelständische characteristics and how Mittelstand can apply VBM Empirical insights into application of VBM
Bluhm and Martens (2009)	Empirical analysis on the basis of quantitative data	Empirical insights into application of VBM
Gonschorek (2009a), initial findings presented in Günther and Gonschorek (2008), overview of findings presented in Gonschorek and Günther (2011b)	Empirical analysis on the basis of quantitative data	Drivers, hurdles and applicability of VBM in Mittelstand Empirical insights into application of VBM
Krol (2009c), presenting initial findings in Krol (2007a) and Krol	Empirical analysis on the basis of quantitative data	Drivers, hurdles and applicability of VBM in Mittelstand Empirical insights into application of VBM

(2009b), presenting an overview of findings in Krol and Wömpener (2009)		
Piontkowski (2009)	Empirical analysis on the basis of quantitative data	Empirical insights into application of VBM
Tappe (2009)	Empirical analysis on the basis of qualitative data	Drivers, hurdles and applicability of VBM in Mittelstand Empirical insights into application of VBM
Martens and Bluhm (2007)	Drawing conclusions from literature	Drivers, hurdles and applicability of VBM in Mittelstand Adaptation of VBM concepts to mittelständische characteristics and how Mittelstand can apply VBM
Breuer and Peyerl (2006)	Drawing conclusions from literature	Drivers, hurdles and applicability of VBM in Mittelstand Adaptation of VBM concepts to mittelständische characteristics and how Mittelstand can apply VBM
Khadjavi (2005), presenting an overview of findings in Khadjavi and Volery (2009)	Empirical analysis on the basis of qualitative data	Adaptation of VBM concepts to mittelständische characteristics and how Mittelstand can apply VBM Empirical insights into application of VBM
Arbeitskreis "Wertorientierte Führung in mittelständischen Unternehmen" der Schmalenbach-Gesellschaft für Betriebswirtschaft e.V. (2003a; 2004b; 2006), Schomaker and Günther (2006)	Drawing conclusions from literature	Adaptation of VBM concepts to mittelständische characteristics and how Mittelstand can apply VBM
Baxendale and Bowen (2001)	Drawing conclusions from literature	Drivers, hurdles and applicability of VBM in Mittelstand
Achleitner and Bassen (2000)	Drawing conclusions from literature	Drivers, hurdles and applicability of VBM in Mittelstand Adaptation of VBM concepts to mittelständische characteristics and how Mittelstand can apply VBM

Roztocki and Needy (1999)	Empirical analysis on the basis of qualitative data	Drivers, hurdles and applicability of VBM in Mittelstand Adaptation of VBM concepts to mittelständische characteristics and how Mittelstand can apply VBM Empirical insights into application of VBM
Bea and Thissen (1997)	Drawing conclusions from literature	Drivers, hurdles and applicability of VBM in Mittelstand Adaptation of VBM concepts to mittelständische characteristics and how Mittelstand can apply VBM

Appendices-Figure 4: Details on the aspects included in the outlines on the understanding of VBM in the relevant literature

Notes on the table:

The following table displays how the relevant literature on VBM in Mittelstand adresses the understanding of VBM and which aspects are touched upon. The column on the "Aspects included" is formulated in a way that synthesises the aspects referred to by all or a majority of the authors. These are the following aspects:

- 1) focus of management on monetary company value, holistic understanding of management, includes decisions
- 2) emphasis on interests of owners under consideration of interests of other stakeholders
- 3) value creation when costs of equity and debt capital are exceeded
- 4) value shall be increased/maximised
- 5) VBM has long-term focus, secures existence

The aspects included for each of the contributions reflect the aspects addressed by the individual author(s). Aspects that are not addressed by this author(s) are omitted. In addition, the different views in relation to whether the value shall be increased and/or maximised are expressed by amending this aspect on the basis of the terms used by the individual author(s). The column "Details" reflects the content of the text passages from which the aspects have been derived (formulation close to the text). The number in brackets at the end shows the relation to the synthesised aspects.

Source	**How adressed?**	**Aspects included**	**Details**
Becker et al. (2010b)	• Understanding underlying the paper adressed briefly • Insight into understanding from illustration of VBM for Mittelstand	1) focus of management on monetary company value, holistic understanding of management 2) emphasis on interests of owners under consideration of interests of other stakeholders 3) value creation	p. 114: besides focus on long-term increase of the company value focus on sustainability, can secure the long term viability of mittelständische companies (1, 4, 5) p. 115 - understanding underlying the contribution: "Unter wertorientierter Unternehmensführung wird im vorliegenden Beitrag ein ganzheitliches Management- und Controllingystem verstanden, welches auf nachhaltiges Wachstum des Unternehmenswertes ausgerichtet ist." → VBM in this paper understood as holistic system of management and control, which is focused on a sustainable growth of the company value (1, 5) p. 116: monetary understanding of company value becomes evident from reference to the discounted cashflow method (1)

		when costs of equity and debt capital are exceeded 4) value shall be increased 5) VBM has long-term focus, secures existence	p. 116: scepticism in Mittelstand towards basic idea of VBM, based on negative view of shareholder value concept, which is interpreted as one-sided orientation towards short-term profit maximisation, shareholder value essentially focused on sustainable realisation of profits, new understanding of VBM clearly based on sustainable increase of the company value shall be established (4, 5) p. 116: a value-driver model for Mittelstand needs to consider interests of stakeholders besides the interests of the owners, needs to emphasise the sustainable perspective and be adjusted to the individual resource situation by mathematical simplification under retention of the methodological consistence (2, 5) p. 117: orientation towards long-term increase of the company value shall be applied by Mittelstand, does not only support the overall objective of securing the long-term viability of the company but also have a positive effect on secondary objectives such as e.g. employee or customer satisfaction (2, 4, 5) pp. 117-118: monetary understanding of company value becomes evident from outline of the determination of value creation (1) p. 117: an increase of the company value is only achieved when results exceed the expected returns of all capital providers of the company (1, 3, 4)
Golsner (2012)	• Understanding of VBM underlying the thesis explicitly stated in introduction (briefly)	1) focus of management on monetary company value, holistic understanding of	p.1 - understanding underlying the contribution: „Wie aus diesem Titel hervorgeht, geht es in der vorliegenden Dissertation um Wertmanagement, verstanden als das systematische und nachhaltige Management der Wertsteigerung des Unternehmens im monetären Sinn." → VBM understood as systematic and sustainable management of the increase oft he value oft he company in a monetary sense (1, 4, 5)

	• understanding of value addressed in a respective section, with a paragraph explicitly stating the understanding underlying the thesis, reference to understanding of VBM • Further insight into understanding of VBM from illustration of fundamentals of VBM in a respective section	management 2) not addressed in context of outlining the understanding 3) value creation when costs of equity and debt capital are exceeded 4) value shall be increased 5) VBM has long-term focus → overall focus on understanding VBM in general, no reference to Mittelstand in this context	p. 12: while there is a plurality of understandings of value, it shall be understood as economic value at this point, this means that value is regarded from a financial perspective (1) p.13: the term VBM means the management of the economic value of a company, the objective of the management then is to work systematically on those factors which increase this economic value, which expresses how attractive a company is for economic agents (1) p. 15: value in this dissertation is understood in a monetary sense. Value in a financial sense is regarded as „objective" construct and the methods to determine this value are based on „objective", which means generally accepted methods (1) p. 21: reference to definition of the value of an asset which puts emphasis on cashflows, company value as net present value of future free cashflows (1) p. 23: reference to a later understanding of integrated VBM as indicator for understanding as holistic management (1) p. 22: company value equates to the net present value of free cash flow (1) p. 23: includes key element of all models of resudial profit, economic profit is only achieved when the return on the capital employed is higher than the related costs of capital, this shows that growth only generates value if the related returns exceed the costs of capital (3) p. 31 finally objective of an effective VBM is to influence the increase of the company value positively, then purposefully influencing the factors

			that have an influence on this and systematically working on an improvement of these factors is understood as VBM (1) p. 32: investments need to be profitable in the sense that they achieve returns that are higher than their costs of capital (3) p.33: value-increasing projects i.e. projects where the returns are higher than the costs of capital (3) pp. 34,36-37: repeated reference to the need for returns being higher than the costs of capital (3) pp. XI, 1, 7, 279-280, 285, 287-288: understanding as holistic management concept also becomes evident from the strong emphasis on the organisational context to be considered to implement an effective VBM concept, this is the key focus of the empirical research and is among others expressed on the pages referred to (1)
Gonschorek (2009a)	• paragraph explicitly stating the understanding underlying the thesis • Details for illustration on the next few pages	1) focus of management on monetary company value, holistic understanding of management, includes decisions 2) emphasis on interests of owners under consideration of interests of other stakeholders	p. 23 - understanding underlying the contribution: "Im Kontext dieser Arbeit wird unter wertorientierter Unternehmensführung die operative und strategische Ausrichtung des Unternehmens an der Maximierung des Unternehmenswertes verstanden. Dabei entspricht der Unternehmenswert dem Barwert derjenigen Cashflows, welche an die Eigenkapitalgeber des Unternehmens ausgeschüttet werden können. Unternehmen erzielen einen ökonomischen Mehrwert, wenn die erwirtschafteten Ertragsüberschüsse vor Fremdkapitalzinsen die Gesamtkapitalkosten bzw. Die Ertragsüberschüsse nach Fremdkapitalzinsen die Eigenkapitalkosten übersteigen." → operative and strategic orientation of the company towards the maximisation of the company value, company value is the net present value of the cashflows that can be distributed to the equity investors of the company, companies realise an economic added value when the profits gained before interests on borrowed capital exceed the total costs of capital and when the profits gained after

		3) value creation when costs of equity and debt capital are exceeded 4) value shall be **maximised**, increased 5) VBM has long-term focus	interests on borrowed capital exceed the costs of equity capital (1, 2, 3, 4) p. 24: objective to maximise company value only achievable when interests of all stakeholders are considered (2, 4) p. 25: VBM as management philosophy for the whole company, creates an integrated framework for the multiple tasks in a company, provides guiding principles for each managerial decision (1) p. 26: increase of the company value in the long run (4, 5)
Gonschorek (2015b)	• Understanding VBM addressed briefly • Insight into understanding from illustration of the origin and characteristics of VBM	1) focus of management on monetary company value, holistic understanding of management, includes decisions 2) emphasis on interests of owners under consideration of interests of other stakeholders 3) value creation when costs of equity and debt capital are exceeded 4) value shall be	p. 496: company value increasingly the objective of strategic considerations (1, 5) p. 496: long-term increase of the company value can only be achieved under consideration of all stakeholder groups, consistent orientation of decisions towards basic idea of VBM strengthens existence of the company as well as jobs, interests of stakeholders as auxiliary condition to the increase of value and to be considered by management (1, 2, 4) p. 497: VBM needs to be understood as long-term concept (5) p. 497: objective of VBM is to increase the company value as much as possible to secure future competitiveness, focus on future successes to the owners (2, 4) p. 497: all management decisions shall be oriented towards the company value (1) p. 498: long-term foucs of VBM suits Mittelstands long-term orientation (5)

		increased 5) VBM has long-term focus, secures existence	p. 500: VBM as management philosophy, which includes that all decisions of the company, strategic as well as operative ones, shall be oriented towards the company value (1, 5) p. 500: for an increase of the company value the return on capital employed needs to be higher than the costs of capital, then there is an increase of the company value and the superior objective to secure the existence of the company in the long-run is achieved (3, 4, 5) p. 503-506 monetary understanding of company value becomes evident from outline of how the increase of the company value can be measured (1)
Gonschorek (2016c)	• Understanding briefly adressed on general level • Insight into understanding from introduction and outline of VBM in Mittelstand	1) focus of management on (monetary) company value, holistic understanding of management, includes decisions 2) emphasis on interests of owners under consideration of interests of other stakeholders 3) value creation when costs of equity and debt capital are exceeded	p. 141: company value can only be secured and/or created on the basis of sustainably living company values, the management of the company needs to balance the intests of different stakeholder groups (2) p. 141: value orientation: emphasis on owners, management oriented towards the development of the economic company value (1, 2) p. 141-142: discussion whether compatible with ethical corporate principles, in the long run a harmony of interest, objective to maximise company value value can only be achieved when interests of all stakeholders are satisfied, objectives of different stakeholders as auxiliary condition to the supervior value objective (2, 4) p. 147: value orientation not an end in itself but means to the achievement of the economic objectives increase of wealth, securing existence and independency (5) p. 147: VBM is a management philosophy that involves that all decisions of the company, strategic as well as operative ones shall be oriented towards the company value, thus a company is only successfull if

		4) value shall be increased, maximised 5) VBM has long-term focus, secures existence	it increases the company value sustainably (1, 4, 5) p. 150: for an increase of the company value the return needs to be higher than the costs of capital employed, which includes equity and debt capital (3, 4) p. 151: understanding of VBM as company wide scope of action includes a respective management and communication culture (1) p. 150-151: monetary understanding of company value only indicated by reference to common framework that uses monetary KPIs for the company value (1)
Günther (2014a)	• Understanding company value very briefly adressed • Insight into understanding of VBM from illustration of VBM as measure for economic sustainability	1) focus of management on monetary company value, includes decisions 2) not addressed 3) value creation when costs of equity and debt capital are exceeded 4) value shall be created 5) VBM has long-term focus	p. 220-221: company value can be understood as monetary measure for economic sustainability, usually understood as net present value of future net returns (= discounted cashflow), thus recording all monetary measurable economic consequences in the long run (1, 5) p. 222: VBM tools provide improved support for decisions as well as corporate management (1) p. 222: for creation of company value profit alone is not sufficient as the costs of equity capital need to be earned in addition to the costs of debt capital, which are considered in annual profit (1, 3, 4) p. 224: value creation when return on capital covers at least the costs of capital (3, 4) p. 226: creation of value only possible when interests of other stakeholder gropus are considered in the decision-making (1,4)
Günther (2015b)	• Understanding underlying the paper not di-	1) focus of management on monetary com-	p. 483: long-term focus (5) p. 488: value creation for the owners only when profit covers costs of

	rectly adressed • Illustration of the origin and characteristics of VBM does not give clear insight into understanding • Some of the aspects adressed by others are briefly mentioned	pany value, holistic understanding of management, includes decisions 2) emphasis on interests of owners 3) value creation when costs of equity and debt capital are exceeded 4) value shall be created 5) VBM has long-term focus	equity capital (3, 4) p. 489-490: monetary understanding value becomes among others evident from outline of rationale underlying tools of VBM (1) p. 491: VBM adressing several management aspects, not replacing existing decision-making tools but additional perspective (1) p. 493: Mittelstand can benefit from an improved support for decisions (1)
Krol (2009b)	• Understanding adressed in a respective section	1) focus of management on monetary company value, holistic understanding of management, includes decisions 2) emphasis on interests of owners under consideration of interests of other	p. 56: approach for corporate management with the objective to increase the company value for the owners (1, 2, 4) p. 58: substantial characteristic of VBM is its long-term focus (5) p. 58: management decisions are oriented towards increase of the company value, strengthens viability of the company sustainably, beneficial for other stakeholders, necessary to consider interests of other stakeholders (1, 2, 4, 5) p. 59: understanding oriented towards economic company value, interests of stakeholders shall not be neglected (1, 2) p. 60: not necessarily focus on maximisation of the company value but

		stakeholders 3) value creation when costs of equity and debt capital are exceeded 4) value shall be <u>increased</u>, maximised 5) VBM has long-term focus, secures existence	depending on risk aversion of the owner-manager also objective to secure value or achieve a certain minimum value (4) p. 61: core intention of VBM is not primarily to determine the equity capital economically correct, it is rather about sustainably increasing the company value via entrepreneurial decisions (1, 5) p. 62: VBM serves the long-term preservation and successfull advancement of the company (5) p. 63: excess value only when profit exceeds not only costs of equity capital but also expected interest on equity capital (3)
Lehmann (2012)	• illustration in introduction • understanding addressed in a respective section, with a paragraph explicitly stating the understanding underlying the thesis • understanding summarised later	1) focus of management on monetary company value, holistic understanding of management, includes decisions 2) emphasis on interests of owners under consideration of interests of other stakeholders 3) value creation when costs of equity and debt capital are ex-	p. 3, 29, 30: all strategies and actions of the management need to be focused on an increase of the company value (1, 4) p. 4: VBM designed and implemented in a strategic manner is a management and control concept for securing the survivability of the company in the long run, is a holistic framework for the manifold tasks in a company (1, 5) p.4: guideline for each individual management decision, achieved via constructive strategic decisions and their operative implementation (1) p.4: focus on the increase of the long-term company value as core motive for management (1, 4) p.4: not exclusively focused on interests of owners, value originates from cooperation of all stakeholders (2) pp. 26-27 - understanding underlying the contribution: "Im Rahmen dieser Arbeit wird – in Anlehnung an Heger – unter dem Begriff der wert-

		ceeded 4) value shall be increased 5) VBM has long-term focus, secures existence	orientierten Unternehmungsführung ein "ganzheitliches Management- und Controllingsystem, das auf nachhaltiges Wachstum des Unternehmenswerts ausgerichtet ist" verstanden. (footnote refers to Heger (2005), p. 33). Die Wertorientierung ist damit ein langfristig orientierter, kontinuierlicher Prozess "... welcher den Erfolg und das Überleben des Unternehmens im Sinne der strategischen Führung, ausgerichtet am monetären Unternehmenswert, garantieren soll.". (footnote refers to Kunze (2008), p. 160) Die wertorientierte Unternehmensführung orientiert sich damit am Primärziel der monetären Wertschöpfung zugunsten der Eigentümer bzw. Aktionäre, und bezieht – unter expliziter Beachtung des Primärziels als notwendige Bedingung – auch die Interessen der Fremdkapitalgeber und weiterer maßgeblicher Anspruchsgruppen mit unmittelbaren Einfluss auf die Wertgenerierung ein." → in the style of Heger the term VBM is understood as holistic system of management and control that is focused on sustainable increase of the company value, value orientation is continuous process that is oriented towards the long run and shall guarantee the success and survival of the company in the sense of startegic mangement oriented towards the monetary company value, VBM is thus oriented towards the primary objetive of monetary value creation in favour of the owners/shareholders and considers – under explicit consideration of the primary objective as inevitable condition – also the interests of outside creditors and other significant shareholders with immediate influence on the value creation (1, 2, 4, 5) p. 30: in VBM the long-term and future-oriented increase of the company value is at the centre of entrepreneurial thinking and action, value creation as permanent managerial task (1, 4, 5) p.30 with focusing all strategies and actions towards the increase of the company value the long-term existence of the company is secured (1, 4, 5)

			p. 30: with focusing management on the increase of the company value the focus is put on the interests of the owners and the system of objectives is oriented towards them (1, 2, 4) p. 31-31: the value of the company only increases when the return of all investment projects of a company exceeds the minimum expected return of debt and equity investors (3, 4) p.233: in VBM long-term and future-oriented increase of the company value is prior objective of the company, all strategies and actions need to be oriented towards an increase of the company value, increase of the company value by cash flow exceeding minimum expected return of capital lenders, permanent managerial task (1, 3, 4, 5)
Tappe (2009)	• Short reference in introduction • understanding addressed in a respective section with an paragraph explicitly stating the understanding underlying the thesis	1) focus of management on monetary company value, holistic understanding of management, includes decisions 2) emphasis on interests of owners under consideration of interests of other stakeholders 3) not addressed in con-	p. 1: in its actual sense the increase/maximisation of an investment or the company value in general (1, 4) p. 63: definition of recommendations of action for people and accordingly the definition of tasks, processes and systems of those people to achieve a sustainable and long-term economic-monetary value creation and increase of value of the company, focus on monetary value (1, 4, 5) p. 66: Advocates of a focus on shareholder-value are of the opinion that owners bear the economical risk of the company and are thus entitled to the residual income (2) p. 66: focus of entrepreneurial action on the maximisation of the company value as prior financial objective (1, 4) p. 66: to sustainably increase the company value a company among others needs to consider the interests of stakeholders (2, 5)

		text of outlining the understanding 4) value shall be increased/maximised 5) VBM has long-term focus, secures existence	p. 67: interests of stakeholders are considered as well (2) p. 68: economic value as net present value of expected, future cashflow (1) p. 68: value orientation as prior financial objective that all actions and decisions need to be oriented towards (1) p. 69: VBM as holistic management concept, in that all elements and systems of management are formed and coordinated in a value-oriented manner (1) p. 71 understanding underlying the contribution: "Wertorientierte Unternehmensführung wird im Rahmen dieser Arbeit in seiner umfassendsten Form als Führungskonzept verstanden. Es stellt dabei eine der Sichtweisen des strategischen Management dar. Die strategische Unternehmensführung nach der "Value Based View" versteht die Fokussierung unternehmerischen Handelns auf die langfristige und nachhaltige Steigerung des Eigentümerwerts und ist auf grundlegende Arbeiten von Rappaport (1986) zurückzuführen. Strategische Handlungsmöglichkeiten sollen nach ihrem Wertbeitrag so gewählt werden, dass der Unternehmenswert maximiert wird." → in the context of this work VBM is understood in its most extensive form as management concept, it thus represents one of the perspectives of strategic management, strategic management according to the value based view focuses entrepreneurial action on the long-term and sustainable increase of the shareholder value and is to be traced back to the fundamantal contributions of Rappaport (1986), strategic options shall be selected according to their contribution to value in a way that maximises the company value (1, 4, 5)
Wenzel	• understanding	1) focus of man-	p. 21: no unique definition, synonm use of different terms, however con-

(2014)	addressed in a respective section, illustration in additional sections	agement on monetary company value, holistic understanding of management, includes decisions 2) emphasis on interests of owners under consideration of interests of other stakeholders 3) not addressed in context of outlining the understanding 4) value shall be increased, maximised 5) VBM has long-term focus, secures existence	sensus that focus of strategic and operative management on the financial increase in value, implementation of VBM results in changes of different management systems, VBM in a narrow sense can be regarded as including the objective to increase the company value and a respective system of value-oriented planing and control (1, 4) p. 22: value orientation includes companies adapting the increase of the company value as prior company objective and focusing management on the increase of the company value, implementation is achieved by focusing strategic and operative management decisions on the increase of the company value (1, 4) pp. 22-23: company value as value of discounted future cashflows to the owners of a company, management shall work towards a maximisation of this value on all levels of the company, supported by a value-oriented system of performance management (1, 2, 4) p. 23: maximisation of the value of future discounted cashflows is in line with the objective to secure the existence of the company (4, 5) p. 24: more attention to the interests of the owners (2) p. 27: focus of management on the objective to maximise the company value in the long run and select strategies in line with this objective, action on all levels of management shall be judged with regard to whether they contribute to the increase of the company value (1, 4, 5) pp. 27-28: in German-speaking region increase of company value as prior financial objective, enables consideration of interests of other stakeholders on an equal footing, this needs to be rejected for the level of the company objective, as optimisation of the interests of several stakeholder groups not possible and logically inconsistent (1, 2, 4)

			p. 28: owners as key stakeholder group of a company, trade-off with regard to interests of other stakeholders necessary (2) p. 29: long-term perspective with focus on long-term increase of the company value (1, 4, 5)

Appendices Figure 5: Analysis of empirical studies focusing on VBM in Mittelstand

Author (year): title[188]	Key topic empirical study	Research approach	Kind of company analysed	Details and remarks
Nathani et al. (2016): Association between EVA and CSR: A study of family owned business companies in India	Insights into companies' value creation	Quantitative, secondary data	Family owned companies	• Analysis of the impact of corporate social responsibility practices on EVA in Indian family businesses
Mafirowanda (2015): Measuring the understanding of value-based management in small businesses in Gauteng	Application of VBM in companies	Qualitative, semi-structured interviews	Small businesses	• Empirical investigation of understanding of VBM and application in small businesses in South Africa
Oliveira (2014): Economic Value Added assessment applied to portuguese SME during crisis period	Insights into companies' value creation	Quantitative, secondary data	SMEs	• Assessing the value creation of portuguese SMEs from 2008 to 2010 from a VBM perspective (EVA and Market Value Added)
Wenzel (2014): Wertmanagement in grossen Familienunternehmen	Application of VBM in companies, additional aspects: influencing factors and economic benefit	Qualitative, semi-structured interviews with Chief Financial Officers	Large family businesses	• Analysis inwhatfar VBM is implementend in large German family businesses, which factors influence the implementation and whether the implementation leads to an increase of the company value
Golsner (2012): Effektives Wertmanagement im Mittelstand – eine systemische Perspektive	Application of VBM in companies, additional aspect:	Qualitative data, single case study	Mittelstand	• Identification of organisational factors that need to be addressed by a VBM system to be effective in focusing the company on an increase of the company value

[188] Sorted by year in descending order

	organisational factors			• Based on analysing which starting points of VBM are already existing in a Hungarian mittelständische company owned by an Austrian family
Lehmann (2012): Wertoriertiertes Management mittelständischer Unternehmen: Potenziale der Ermittlung von Eigenkapitalkosten sowie Herleitung von Konzeptanforderungen im Rahmen eines Delphi-Verfahrens	Adaptation of VBM concepts to mittelständische characteristics and how Mittelstand can apply VBM	Qualitative and quantitative, Delphi survey with VBM experts from academia and Mittelstand	Mittelständische Unternehmen	• Empirical analysis of requirements related to a VBM approach for Mittelstand and evaluating inwhatfar initial VBM management approaches for VBM fulfill those requirements
Bahri et al. (2011): Economic value added: a useful tool for SME performance management	Insights into companies' value creation	Quantitative, secondary data	SMEs	• Analysis of business practices' influence on performance measured by EVA in Canadian manufacturing SMEs to propose a performance measurement and management system for SMEs
Dixit (2011): Do Indian Acquirers Create Shareholder Value? The Effect of Affiliation to a Family Business Group	Insights into companies' value creation	Quantitative, secondary data	Family business groups	• Analysis of creation of shareholder value by acquisitions, comparison of family business group acquirers and other acquirers in India
Print and Reynolds (2011): Family-controlled businesses and shareholder value	Insights into companies' value creation	Quantitative, secondary data	Family-controlled businesses	• Comparing the performance of UK family-controlled businesses from a shareholder value perspective to that of comparable non-family-controlled businesses
Bluhm and Martens (2009): Recomposed institutions: smaller firms' strategies, shareholder-value orienta-	Application of VBM in companies	Quantitative, survey	Privately owned SMEs	• Reasoning on the basis of two surveys • 1) Replication of empirical study of Gonschorek and Günther (2006a) to analyse application of shareholder-value oriented

tion and bank relationships in Germany				management tools and the respective impact of different types of owners/stockholders, this is done in the context of exploring how the institutional change in the financing sector affects privately owned SMEs in Germany • 2) focus on generational shift in German companies → excluded because of scope (insights not directly related to VBM)
Gonschorek (2009a): Einflussfaktoren der Anwendung wertorientierter Unternehmensführung im deutschen Mittelstand. Ergebnisse einer empirischen Studie	Application of VBM in companies, additional aspect: influencing factors	Quantitative data, mail survey	Mittelstand	• Analysing the status of knowledge and application of VBM in German Mittelstand in a differentiated way, identifying influencing factors that promote or constrain the use of VBM methods currently and in the future
Krol (2009c): Wertorientierte Unternehmensführung im Mittelstand: Eine empirische Analyse von Einfluss- und Wirkungsfaktoren	Application of VBM in companies, additional aspects: influencing factors and economic benefit	Quantitative, online and mail survey	Mittelstand	• Analysis on actual form of selected aspects of management in German Mittelstand, identification of possible reasons for the current state of implementation of VBM (systematic influencing factors) • Analysis whether the use of VBM management tools and KPIs as well as the consideration of VBM principles has economic effects
Piontkowski (2009): Wertorientierte Unternehmensführung in mittelständischen Unternehmen: Empirische Hinweise auf Anwendung	Application of VBM in companies	Quantitative, survey	Mittelständische Unternehmen	• Analysing insights related to the use of VBM from a survey on management accounting and financing of mittelständische companies in Germany

Tappe (2009): Wertorientierte Unternehmensführung im Mittelstand: Eine Überprüfung der Anwendbarkeit	Application of VBM in companies, additional aspect: success factors	Qualitative, semi-structured interviews with owners/ managers and external experts	Mittelstand	• Empirical analysis of application of VBM in German Mittelstand and relevant success factors identified from literature review, includes propositions regarding the applicability of VBM in Mittelstand
Khadjavi (2005): Wertmanagement im Mittelstand	Application of VBM in companies	Qualitative, three case studies with problem-centered interviews	Mittelstand	• Analysis whether and how VBM management approaches can be adapted to Mittelstand • Based on evaluating the use of VBM in German Mittelstand empirically a concept for VBM in Mittelstand is developed that shall on the one hand expand and modify existing theoretical approaches but also be applicable in Mittelstand practice
Roztocki and Needy (1999): EVA for small manufacturing companies	Application of VBM in companies	Qualitative, interviews	Small companies	• Insights into application of VBM and potential reasons for non-application in six small manufacturing companies in the United States on the basis of interviews of approximately 30 interviews → Superficial insights without adequate outline of methodology

Appendices-Figure 6: Findings of several questionnaire studies on objectives in Mittelstand

General information on the preparation of the data for comparison:

- The different questionnaire studies are presented in alphabetical order
- The data is prepared and displayed in the most suitable way for comparison:
  Where possible on the basis of the data given, the mean has been calculated in a way which is oriented towards the approach of Gonschorek (2009a). He calculates the arithmetic mean for each objective on the basis of assigning numbers to each of the items on a five-point scale (starting from 1 for "not at all important" and finishing at 5 for "very important") (Gonschorek, 2009a, p. 148). Details for the individual steps of data preparation are given below the respective figure.
- For comparison, groups of objectives have been formed for each empirical study: Objectives of first/top level importance (yellow bar, C in example below), second level importance (red bar, A and B in example), third level importance (blue bar, D in example) and those with comparatively lower importance (grey bar, E-G in example).
- When the text refers to "objectives of major importance" this encompasses objectives of first, second and third level importance.
- For each questionnaire study, the objectives included are presented in the original order and the description is unmodified with the exception of the translation from German into English.

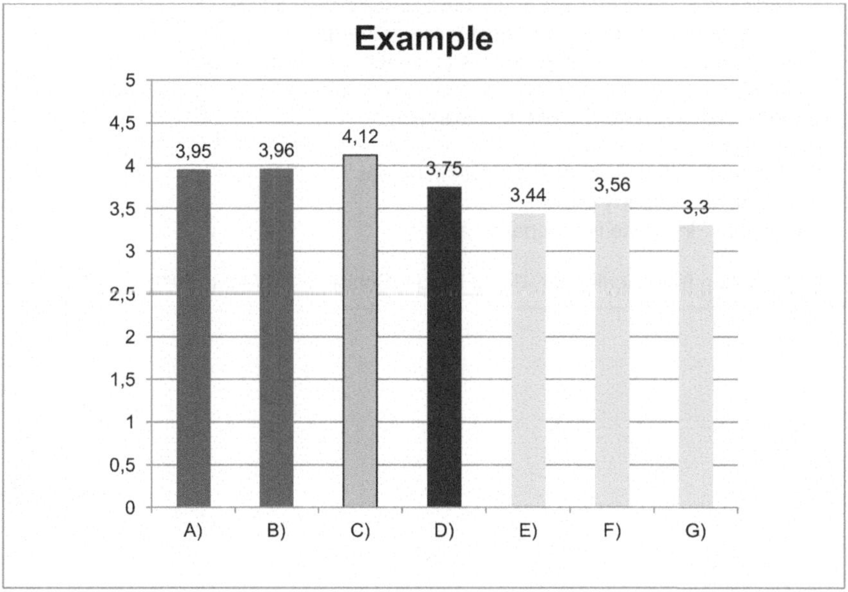

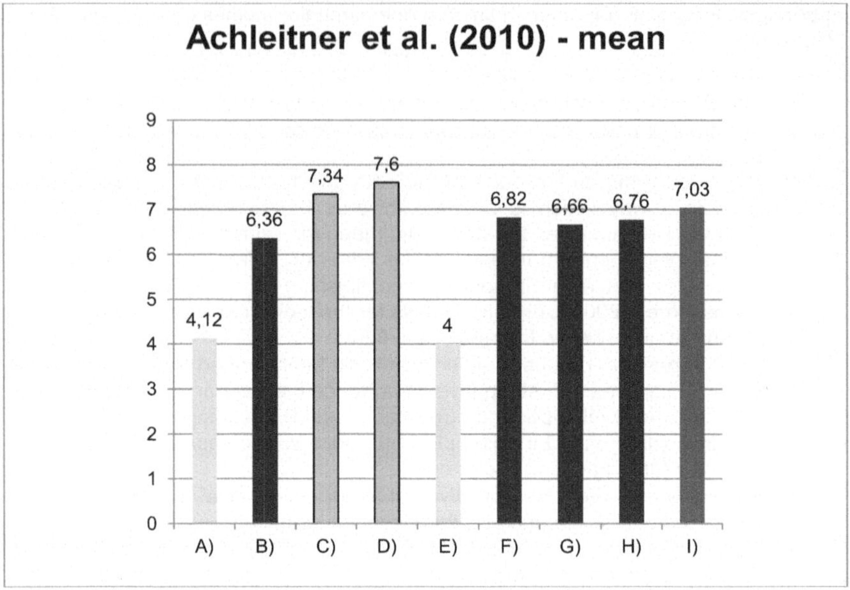

Key and information:

A) family goal - employment opportunity for family members
B) family goal - firm transfer to next family generation
C) family goal - prevention from loss of ownership/independence
D) family goal - prevention from loss of control through external debt holders
E) firm goal - short term profit maximisation
F) firm goal - firm growth
G) firm goal - preservation and creation of jobs
H) firm goal - property growth
I) firm goal - increase in company value

Means taken from Achleitner, Bock, Braun, Schraml, & Welter, 2010, p. 17

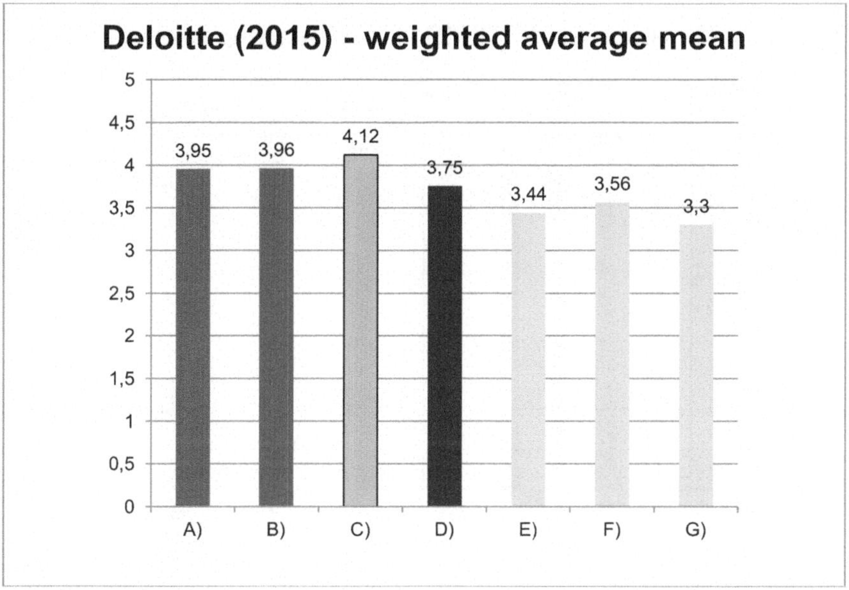

Key and information:

A) cost objectives
B) social objectives
C) turnover objectives
D) ressource objectives
E) product-market objectives
F) financial objectives
G) ecological objectives

For comparability, the weighted average mean has been calculated on the basis of the percentages of the respondents rating the objectives to be very important (5), important (4), average important (3), less important (2) and unimportant (1) given by Deloitte & Touche GmbH Wirtschaftsprüfungsgesellschaft, 2015, p. 7

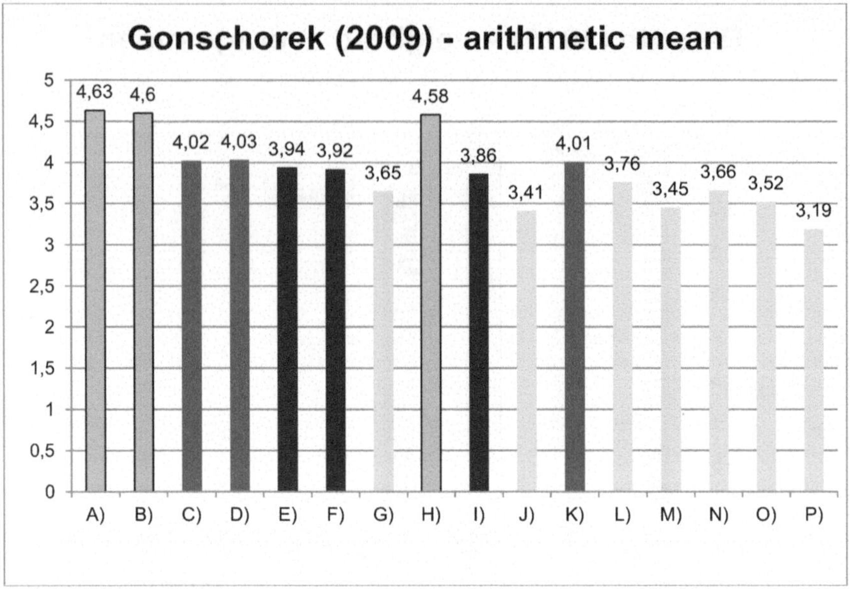

Key and information:

Existence objectives

A) securing liquidity

B) securing company existence

C) securing entrepreneurial independence

Financial objectives

D) increase of company value

E) profit maximisation

F) increasing Return on Equity

G) growth of turnover

Market objectives

H) securing/increasing customer satisfaction

I) securing/increasing market share

J) preservation/expansion of international activities

Employee objectives

K) securing/increasing employee satisfaction

L) constant personnel development

M) preservation/creation of jobs

Societal objectives

N) social responsibility towards society

O) securing/improving public reputation

P) securing/improving corporate environmental protection

Arithmetic mean taken from Gonschorek, 2009, p. 149

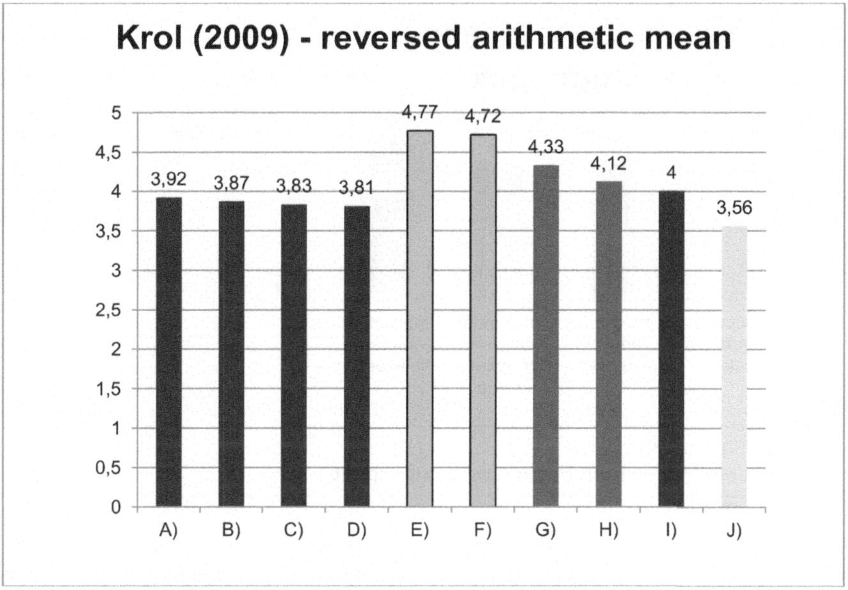

Key and information:

Financial objectives

A) increase company value

B) increase Return on Equity

C) increase turnover/market share

D) profit maximisation

Meta-economic objectives

E) non-economic objectives: securing existence

F) non-economic objectives: customer satisfaction

G) non-economic objectives: entrepreneurial independence

H) non-economic objectives: employee satisfaction

I) non-economic objectives: social/societal responsibility

J) non-economic objectives: public reputation

Arithmetic mean taken from Krol, 2009, p. 177, as these arithmetic means are based on inversed scale (reaching from 1 for „very important" to 5 for „unimportant") the values have been reversed for comparability

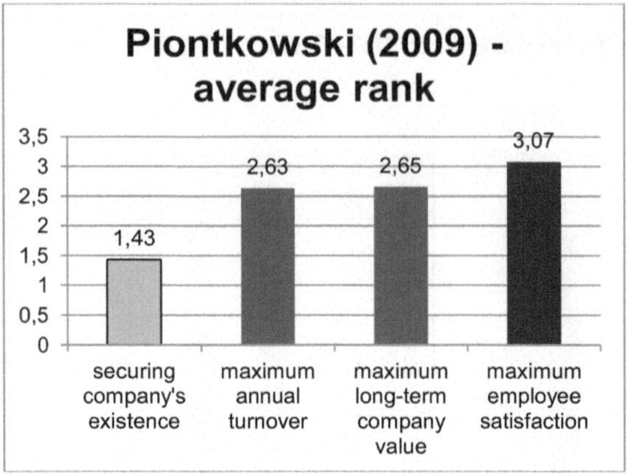

Key and information:
Average rank taken from Piontkowski, 2009, p. 361

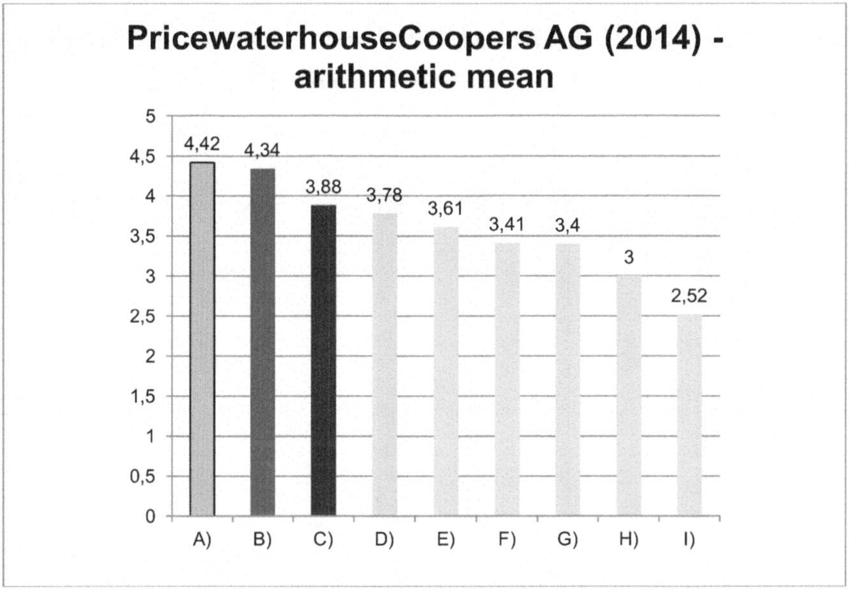

Key and information:
A) securing the company's existence
B) increasing customer satisfaction
C) long-term increase of the company value
D) improving corporate image
E) personal objectives
F) societal objectives
G) increasing market shares
H) ecological objectives
I) short-term profit maximisation

Overall arithmetic means taken from PricewaterhouseCoopers AG Wirtschaftsprüfungsgesellschaft, 2014, p. 30

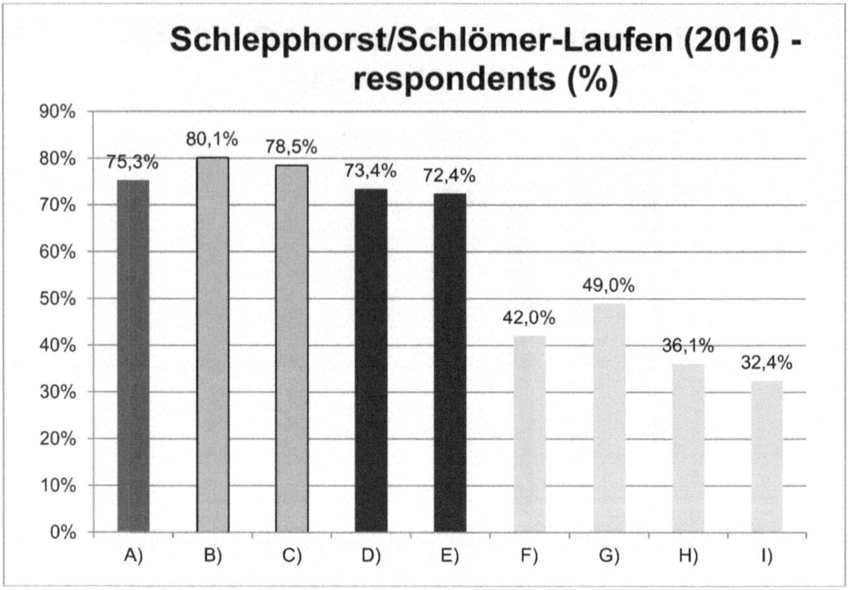

Key and information:

A) long-term increase of the company value
B) continuity of the company policy
C) maximum increase of operative efficiency
D) highest possible independence of the company
E) increase of the company's reputation
F) maximum increase of the market shares
G) maximum increase of profit
H) ecological sustainability
I) high social engagement

Schlepphorst & Schlömer-Laufen, 2016, p. 8 give the percentages of the respondents that rate the respective objective as "(very) important" for two different groups of SMEs, on this basis the weighted average mean has been calculated considering the number of SMEs in each of the two groups as stated by Schlepphorst & Schlömer-Laufen, 2016, p. 6

Appendices-Figure 7: Percentages of different economic sectors in Germany and Baden-Württemberg

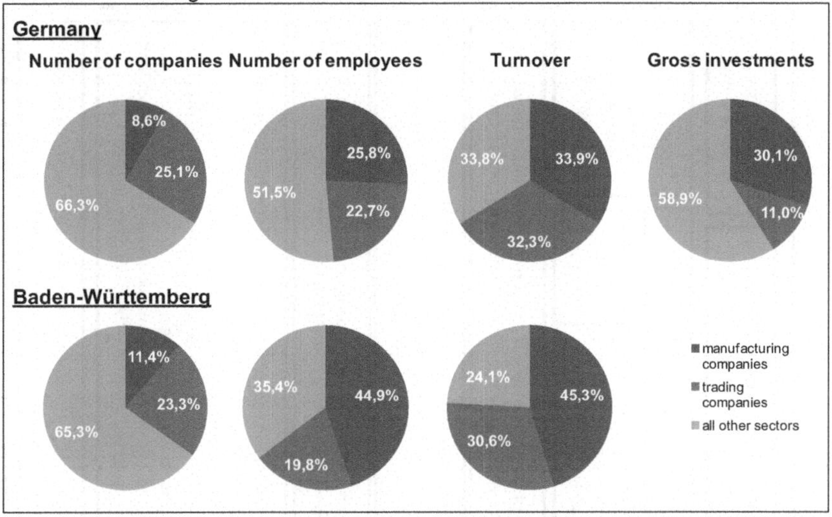

The percentages have been calculated on the basis of data from the Statistisches Bundesamt Deutschland (2018) for Germany and data from the Statistisches Landesamt Baden-Württemberg (2018b) for Baden-Württemberg. On the basis of the data available for Germany and Baden-Württemberg, the percentages are calculated using the data for the economic sectors WZ08B to WZ08N without WZ08K (for the detailed data see the Statistisches Bundesamt Deutschland (2018), which includes the denomination of the sectors and the Statistisches Landesamt Baden-Württemberg (2018b)). Thus the resulting percentages are comparable.

Of the 12 economic sectors, manufacturing companies and trading companies are the most important ones in terms of the number of employees and the turnover. Both, for Germany and for Baden-Württemberg they have the two highest number. Additionally, trading companies have the highest share of the number of companies in Germany and Baden-Württemberg. In this respect, manufacturing companies have the fifth-highest share in Germany and the fourth-highest share in Baden-Württemberg. For gross investments, data is only available for Germany and manufacturing companies have the highest share and trading companies have the fourth-highest share.

When considering both sectors together they make up a considerable part of the economy in Germany and Baden-Württemberg in all aspects that were looked at. The total values and especially the percentage of manufacturing companies are higher for Baden-Württemberg than for Germany. The importance of manufacturing companies for the economy in Baden-Württemberg is especially evident as they employ nearly half of the employees and generate nearly half of the turnover of Baden-Württemberg.

Appendices-Figure 8: Details of the first three steps in the approach of getting access

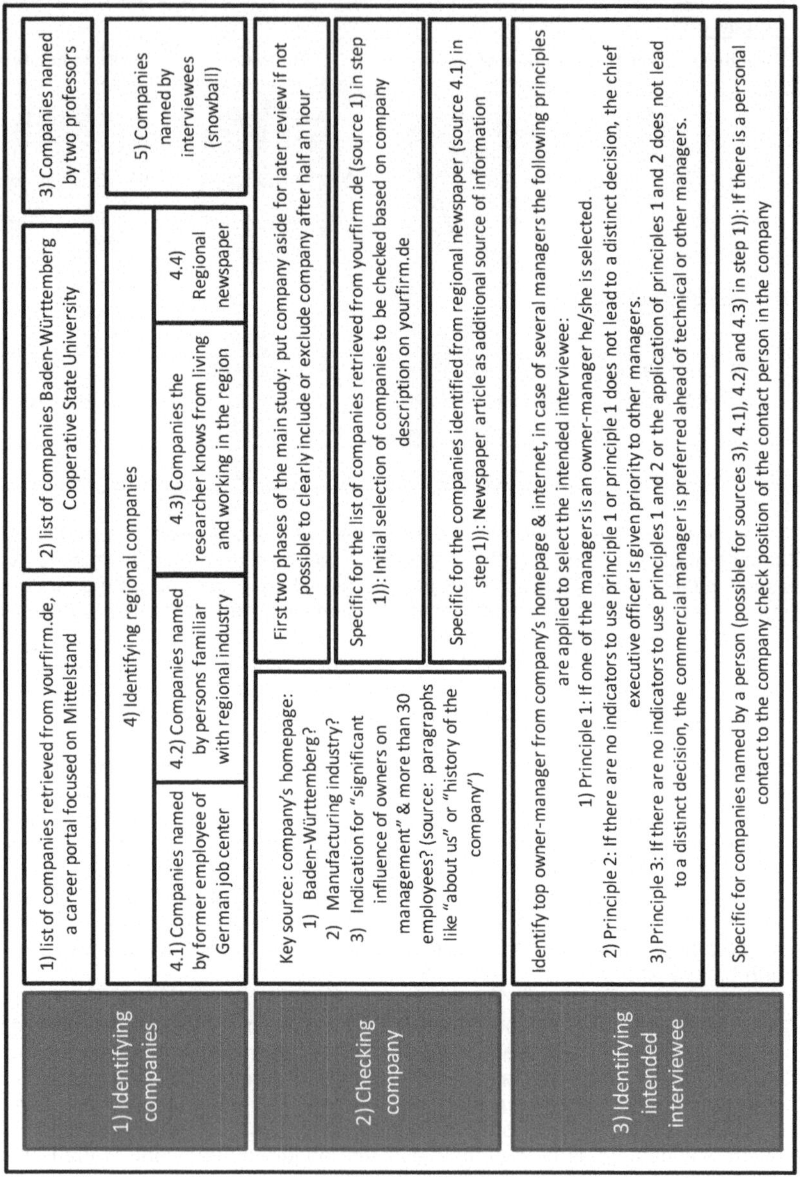

Appendices-Figure 9: Template for the introductory letter to intended interviewees

HOCHSCHULE PFORZHEIM

Fakultät Wirtschaft und Recht
Carola Normann M.A.
Wissenschaftliche Mitarbeiterin
Institut für Management-Simulation
Telefon (Büro) 07231/28-6265
Telefon (Homeoffice) 07235/9759049
Telefon (mobil) 0170/5536646
carola.normann@hs-pforzheim.de

Hochschule PF Tiefenbronner Straße 65 75175 Pforzheim
Meier GmbH
Herr Manuel Meier
Forschungsstr. 1
12345 Mittelstandshausen

Pforzheim, den 02.07.2015

Forschungsprojekt zu mittelständischen Unternehmen

Sehr geehrter Herr Maier,

ich schreibe Ihnen auf Empfehlung von Frau Martina Müller, da ich im Rahmen meiner Forschung an Ihren Erfahrungen und Ihrem Wissen als Geschäftsführer der Meier GmbH interessiert bin.

Im Rahmen meiner Doktorarbeit führe ich ein Forschungsprojekt zu strategischer Entscheidungsfindung und unternehmerischen Zielen im Mittelstand durch. Dabei sollen Einblicke in den Ablauf strategischer Entscheidungen, den Einsatz betriebswirtschaftlicher Instrumente und in die Ziele mittelständischer Unternehmen gewonnen werden. Die Studie wird u.a. von Prof. Dr. Bernd Britzelmaier, Hochschule Pforzheim, betreut.

Mittelständische Unternehmen haben einen wesentlichen Anteil an Deutschlands Wirtschaftskraft. Diese besondere Bedeutung mittelständischer Unternehmen spiegelt sich in der betriebswirtschaftlichen Forschung bisher leider nicht wider. Diese Studie soll dazu beitragen, die Besonderheiten und Bedürfnisse mittelständischer Unternehmen besser zu erforschen. Mit der Unterstützung meines Forschungsprojekts würden Sie einen wertvollen Beitrag zur Mittelstandsforschung leisten.

Ich würde mich freuen, bei einem persönlichen Gespräch Einblicke in Ihre Erfahrungen zu erhalten. Das vertrauliche Gespräch würde etwa eine Stunde in Anspruch nehmen. Die Ergebnisse der Studie werden Ihnen nach Abschluss des Forschungsprojekts selbstverständlich zur Verfügung gestellt.

Auf Ihre Gesprächsbereitschaft hoffend, werde ich mich telefonisch bei Ihnen melden, um einen Gesprächstermin zu vereinbaren. Für weitere Informationen stehe ich Ihnen gerne unter den oben genannten Kontaktwegen zur Verfügung

Mit freundlichen Grüßen

Carola Normann

Appendices-Figure 10: Translation of the letter to the intended participants

Research project on mittelständische companies

Dear Mr. Maier,

I am writing to you (on recommendation of Prof. Müller), as I'm interested in your experiences and knowledge as manager of Maier GmbH for my research.

In the context of my doctoral studies, I am conducting a research project on strategic decision-making and business objectives in Mittelstand. Insights into the process of strategic decision-making, the application of management tools and the objectives of mittelständische companies shall be gained. The study is supervised by Prof. Dr. Bernd Britzelmaier, Pforzheim University among others.

Mittelständische companies make an essential contribution to Germany's economic strength. This particular importance of mittelständische companies does not reflect in business and management research. This study shall contribute to explore the characteristics and needs of mittelständische companies. By supporting my research project you would make a valuable contribution to research on Mittelstand.

I look forward to getting an insight into your experience in a personal interview. The confidential interview would take approx. an hour. Of course, the results of the study will be made available to you after completion of the study.

Hoping for your willingness to share your experience, I will telephone you to arrange a date for an interview. For further information, please do not hesitate to contact me as listed above.

Yours sincerely,
Carola Normann

Appendices-Figure 11: Characteristics of the companies included in the pilot study

Characteristic (line) Company (column)	Interview 1 pilot study (I-1)	Interview 2 pilot study (I-2)	Interview 3 pilot study (I-3)	Interview 4 pilot study (I-4)	Interview 5 pilot study (I-7)
Number of employees	12	Approx. 400	Several thousand	Approx. 160	Approx. 400
Classification according to the IfM Bonn	Medium-sized company	Medium-sized company	No small- or medium-sized company	Medium-sized company	Medium-sized company
Classification according to the EU commission	Small company	No small- or medium-sized company	No small- or medium-sized company	Medium-sized company	No small- or medium-sized company
Industry	Trading firm supplier of manufactured products in business-to-business sector	Manufacturing company	Manufacturing company	Manufacturing company	Public transport company
Ownership and management structure	Single owner-manager	One owner-manager, one owner (relative of the owner-manager)	Several owners (descendants of the founder), several external managers	Three owners with leadership positions in the company	Key owner-manager (single owner-manager in some of the companies), in two companies additional owner-managers
Interviewee	Owner-manager	Owner-manager	External CEO	Two owners-managers	Owner-manager
Strategic decision talked about	Selection of supplier	Acquisition to grow	Acquisition to grow	Building extension to grow	Acquisition of busses

Appendices-Figure 12: Overview of contacts made for the main study and outcome

Type of contact (line), outcome (column)	Interview conducted	Date agreed but no interview conducted	Denial (time)	Complete denial	No answer	Total
Cold calling	18	0	7	3	2	30
Recommendation	8	1	1	0	0	10
Snowball	4	0	1	0	0	5
Total	30	1	9	3	2	45

Appendices-Figure 13: Information gathered in preparation of the interviews

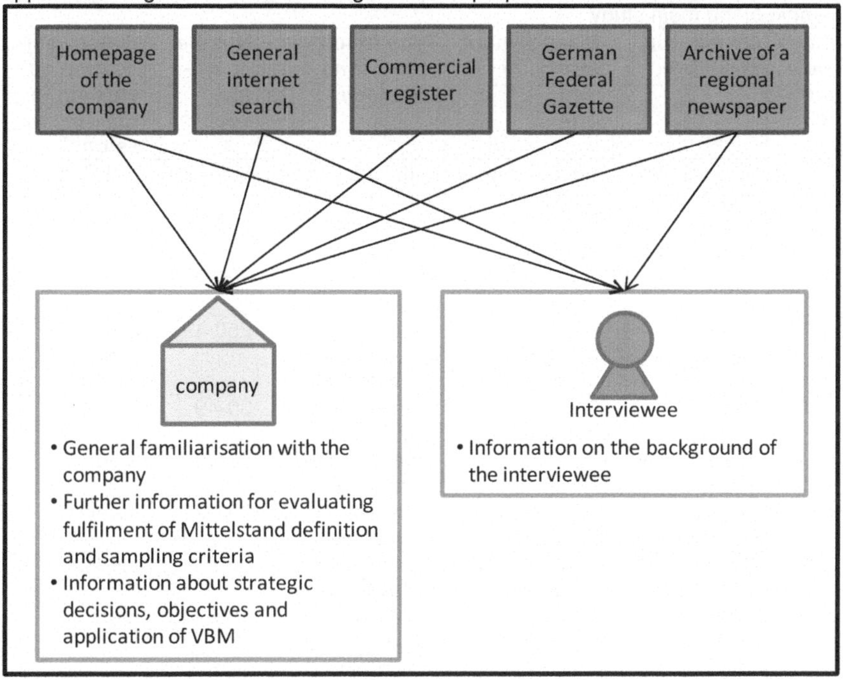

Appendices-Figure 14: Overview of the characteristics of the companies in the sample of the main study

Interview number	Ownership structure	Management structure	Type of mittelständische company	Number of employees[189]	Size classification according to EU Commission[190]
I-5	Several family members	Several family members	Mittelständisches family business	500-999	Not SME
I-6	Owner-manager(s)	Owner-manager(s)	Owner-managed Mittelstand	100-249	Medium
I-8	Several family members	Several family members	Mittelständisches family business	100-249	Medium
I-9[191]	Owner-manager(s)	OM[192] and ext. Managers	Mittelstand with influence of ext. managers	250-499	Not SME
I-10	Owner-manager(s)	Owner-manager(s)	Owner-managed Mittelstand	30-49	Small
I-11	Single family member	Single family member	Owner-managed Mittelstand	50-99	Medium
I-12	Single family member	Single family member	Owner-managed Mittelstand	50-99	Medium
I-13	Owner-manager(s)	Owner-manager(s)	Owner-managed Mittelstand	50-99	Medium
I-14	Several family members	OM and ext. Managers	Mittelstand with influence of ext. managers	100-249	Medium
I-15	Several family members	Single family member	Mittelständisches family business	500-999	Not SME
I-16	Several family members	OM and ext. Managers	Mittelstand with influence of ext. managers	500-999	Not SME
I-17	Several family members	Single family member	Mittelständisches family business	500-999	Not SME
I-18	Several family members	Several family members	Mittelständisches family business	100-249	Medium
I-19	Several family members	Several family members	Mittelständisches family business	30-49	Small

[189] To protect the anonymity of the companies the size is displayed in terms of a range for the number of employees and not by giving the exact number of employees.

[190] According to European Commission (20.5.2003, Annex Article 2) companies are SMEs when they „employ fewer than 250 persons and .. have an annual turnover not exceeding EUR 50 million, and/or an annual balance sheet total not exceeding EUR 43 million". Within these thresholds companies are regarded as small when they have less than 50 employees and an annual turnover and/or balance sheet total below 10 million Euro.

[191] Interview date was agreed with the owner-manager. He brought an external manager to the interview.

[192] Abbreviation for owner-manager(s).

I-20	Owner-manager(s)	Owner-manager(s)	Owner-managed Mittelstand	100-249	Medium
I-21	Several family members	OM and ext. Managers	Mittelstand with influence of ext. managers	>1.000	Not SME
I-22[193]	Several family members	Several family members	Mittelständisches family business	50-99	Medium
I-23[194]	Owner-manager(s)	Owner-manager(s)	Owner-managed Mittelstand	<30	Small
I-24	Owner-manager(s)	Owner-manager(s)	Owner-managed Mittelstand	50-99	Medium
I-25	Several family members	Several family members	Mittelständisches family business	50-99	Medium
I-26	Several family members	OM and ext. Managers	Mittelstand with influence of ext. managers	500-999	Not SME
I-27	Single family member	Single family member	Owner-managed Mittelstand	50-99	Medium
I-28	Several family members	Single family member	Mittelständisches family business	100-249	Not SME[195]
I-29[196]	Single family member	Single family member	Owner-managed Mittelstand	50-99	Medium
I-30	Several family members	OM and ext. Managers	Mittelstand with influence of ext. managers	500-999	Not SME
I-31	Several family members	Several family members	Mittelständisches family business	100-249	Medium
I-32	Single family member	Single family member	Owner-managed Mittelstand	100-249	Medium
I-33	Several family members	Several family members	Mittelständisches family business	250-499	Not SME
I-34	Several family members	OM and ext. Managers	Mittelstand with influence of ext. managers	500-999	Not SME
I-35	Several family members	OM and ext. Managers	Mittelstand with influence of ext. managers	>1.000	Not SME

[193]Excluded from the sample as the interview has shown that the company is not a manufacturing company but trades manufactured goods. This has not been evident from the publicly available information used to identify potential participants.

[194]Excluded from the sample as the interview has shown that the company has less than 30 employees. Based on the publicly available information the researcher assumed that the company is slightly above this lower limit. Furthermore the owner-manager was too busy to keep the appointment and the commercial manager showed up for the interview. The commercial manager is not registered as authorised representative.

[195]Turnover exceeds the threshold of the definition of the European Commission (20.5.2003).

[196]Interview date was agreed with the owner-manager. He brought the company's authorised representative to the interview.

Appendices-Figure 15: Overview of the characteristics of the interviewees in the sample

Interviewee number	Gender of the interviewee	Age of the interviewee	Position of the interviewee	Educational background	Abbreviation used
I-5	Male	>=65	Owner-manager	University education, business and technical/engineering	I-5
I-6	Male	25-34	Authorised representative	University education, business	I-6-EM
I-8	Male	45-54	Owner-manager	Vocational training, technical/engineering	I-8
I-9-1	Male	>=65	Owner-manager	University education, business and technical/engineering	I-9
I-9-2	Male	55-64	External Manager	University education, business	I-9-EM
I-10	Male	55-64	Owner-manager	Vocational training, business	I-10
I-11	Male	45-54	Owner-manager	University education, business	I-11
I-12	Male	25-34	Owner-manager	University education, business	I-12
I-13	Male	45-54	Owner-manager	Vocational training, technical/engineering	I-13
I-14	Male	45-54	Owner-manager	University education, business and technical/engineering	I-14
I-15	Male	55-64	Owner-manager	University education, technical/engineering	I-15
I-16	Male	45-54	Owner-manager	Vocational training, technical/engineering	I-16
I-17	Male	55-64	Owner-manager	University education, technical/engineering	I-17
I-18	Male	45-54	Owner-manager	University education, business and technical/engineering	I-18
I-19	Female	45-54	Owner-manager	University education, business and technical/engineering	I-19
I-20	Male	55-64	Owner-manager	University education, technical/engineering	I-20
I-21	Male	45-54	Owner-manager	University education, technical/engineering	I-21
I-22	Male	55-64	Owner-manager	Excluded from the sample	-

I-23	Male	-	Commercial manager	Excluded from the sample	-
I-24	Male	55-64	Owner-manager	Vocational training, technical/engineering	I-24
I-25	Male	45-54	Owner-manager	Vocational training, business	I-25
I-26	Male	45-54	Owner-manager	University education, business and technical/engineering	I-26
I-27	Male	35-44	Owner-manager	Vocational training, business and technical/engineering	I-27
I-28	Male	45-54	Owner-manager	University education, business	I-28
I-29-1	Male	>=65	Owner-manager	No information provided	I-29
I-29-2	Male	35-44	Authorised representative	University education, business	I-29-EM
I-30	Male	55-64	External Manager	University education, technical/engineering	I-30-EM
I-31	Male	45-54	Owner-manager	University education, business and technical/engineering	I-31
I-32	Male	25-34	Owner-manager (indirect)	Vocational training, business and technical/engineering	I-32
I-33	Male	45-54	Owner-manager	University education, business and technical/engineering	I-33
I-34	Male	45-54	External Manager	University education, business	I-34-EM
I-35	Male	45-54	Owner-manager	University education, business	I-35

Appendices-Figure 16: Extract of findings for the use of relevant methods of investment appraisal in existing empirical studies

empirical study (column) management tool (line)	Britzelmaier et al. (2018), p. 10	Krol (2009c), p. 192	Piontkowski (2009), p. 360	Schlegel et al. (2016), pp. 73, 75-76	Wenzel (2014), p. 147
RoI	RoI: used by 71% of the respondents (SMEs), second most common capital budgeting technique	Rate of return: "(very) often" used by 60 % of the respondents, second most common basis for investment decisions	Net present value method/rate of return: "very often" or "many times" used by 55,9 % of the respondents	RoI: relevant for 52 % of all respondents, no significant size differences for SMEs reported	RoI: 1 interviewee uses RoI, 3 interviewees use a combination of RoI and static procedures of investment appraisal
Profit comparison	Earnings comparison: applied by nearly 50 % of the respondents (exact value of 49 % named by one of the authors via e-mail on request)	Tool not included in study	Tool not included in study	Earnings comparison: relevant for 66,7 % of the SMEs in the sample	Not specifically addressed by the interviewees
Cost comparison	Cost comparison: applied by 73 % of the respondents	Tool not included in study	Tool not included in study	Cost comparison: relevant for 100 % of the SMEs in the sample	Not specifically addressed by the interviewees

Most important methods	Cost comparison most common (applied by 73 % of the respondents)	Experience: "(very) often" used by 83 % of the respondents	Experience: "very often" or "many times" used by 78 % of the respondents	All respondents: net present value (63 %) and qualitative assessments (58 %), significantly higher relevance of cost comparison (100 %) and earnings comparison (66,7 %) for the SMEs in the sample	Net present value method used by 7 interviewees and aditional 6 interviewees use a combination of the net present value and other static/ dynamic procedures of investment appraisal
NPV	NPV: used by 15 % of the respondents	NPV: "(very) often" used by 35 % of the respondents	Net present value method/rate of return: "very often" or "many times" used by 55,9 % of the respondents	NPV: relevant for 63 % of the sample and 40 % of the SMEs in the sample	Net present value method used by 7 interviewees and aditional 6 interviewees use a combination of the net present value and other static/ dynamic procedures of investment appraisal

References

Achleitner, A.-K., & Bassen, A. (2000). Shareholder Value in Klein- und Mittelständischen Unternehmen (KMU). In H. Siegwart (Ed.), *Jahrbuch zum Finanz- und Rechnungswesen* (pp. 145–173).

Achleitner, A.-K., Bock, C., Braun, R., Schraml, S., & Welter, J. (2010). Goal Structures in Family Firms: Empirical Evidence on the Relationship between Firm and Family Goals. *ZfKE – Zeitschrift für KMU und Entrepreneurship, 58*(3), 1–265. doi:10.3790/zfke.58.3.1

Arbeitskreis "Wertorientierte Führung in mittelständischen Unternehmen" der Schmalenbach-Gesellschaft für Betriebswirtschaft e.V. (2003a). Wert(e)orientierte Führung in mittelständischen Unternehmen. *Finanz Betrieb, 5*(9), 525–533.

Arbeitskreis "Wertorientierte Führung in mittelständischen Unternehmen" der Schmalenbach-Gesellschaft für Betriebswirtschaft e.V. (2004b). Möglichkeiten zur Ermittlung periodischer Erfolgsgrößen in Kompatibilität zum Unternehmenswert. *Finanz Betrieb, 6*(4), 241–253.

Arbeitskreis "Wertorientierte Führung in mittelständischen Unternehmen" der Schmalenbach-Gesellschaft für Betriebswirtschaft e.V. (2006). Gestaltung wertorientierter Vergütungssysteme für mittelständische Unternehmen. *Betriebs-Berater (BB), 61*(38), 2066–2076.

Artinger, F., Petersen, M., Gigerenzer, G., & Weibler, J. (2015). Heuristics as adaptive decision strategies in management. *Journal of Organizational Behavior, 36*(1), 33–52. doi:10.1002/job.1950

Astor, M., Rammer, C., Klaus, C., & Klose, G. (2016). *Endbericht: Innovativer Mittelstand 2025 - Herausforderungen, Trends und Handlungsempfehlungen für Wirtschaft und Politik*. Berlin. Retrieved from Zentrum für europäische Wirtschaftsforschung GmbH, prognos AG website: https://www.bmwi.de/Redaktion/DE/Publikationen/Studien/studie-endbericht-innovativer-mittelstand-2025.pdf?__blob=publicationFile&v=14

Astrachan, J. H., & Shanker, M. C. (2003). Family Businesses' Contribution to the U.S. Economy: A Closer Look. *Family Business Review, 16*(3), 211–219. doi:10.1177/08944865030160030601

Bahri, M., St-Pierre, J., & Sakka, O. (2011). Economic value added: a useful tool for SME performance management. *International Journal of Productivity and Performance Management, 60*(6), 603–621.

Baxendale, S. J., & Bowen, L. (2001). Economic Value Added for new ventures and small business. *Journal of Small Business Strategy, 12*(2), 41–51.

Bea, F. X., & Thissen, S. (1997). Institutionalisierung des Shareholder-Value-Konzepts bei der GmbH. *Der Betrieb, 50*(16), 787–792.

Beck, V., & Britzelmaier, B. (2010). VALUE BASED MANAGEMENT IN SMALL AND MEDIUM-SIZED COMPANIES - THREATS AND OPPORTUNITIES. *International Journal of Management Cases, 12*(2), 14–23. doi:10.5848/APBJ.2010.00034

© Springer Fachmedien Wiesbaden GmbH, part of Springer Nature 2020

C. Normann-Tschampel, *Value-Based Management in Mittelstand, Familienunternehmen und KMU*, https://doi.org/10.1007/978-3-658-29228-7

Becker, W. (2000). *Wertorientierte Unternehmensführung. Bamberger Betriebswirtschaftliche Beiträge: Vol. 125.* Bamberg. Retrieved from http://www.uni-bamberg.de/fileadmin/uni/fakultaeten/sowi_lehrstuehle/unternehmensfuehrung/Download-Bereich/Becker_2000_Wertorientierte_Unternehmensfuehrung_BBB_125.pdf

Becker, W., Fischer, S., Staffel, M., & Ulrich, P. (2008). *Implementierungsstand von Unternehmensführung und Controlling in mittelständischen Unternehmen: Ergebnisbericht einer empirischen Untersuchung. Bamberger Betriebswirtschaftliche Beiträge: Vol. 149.* Bamberg. Retrieved from http://www.uni-bamberg.de/fileadmin/uni/fakultaeten/sowi_lehrstuehle/unternehmensfuehrung/Download-Bereich/Becker_2008_Implementierungsstand_BBB_149.pdf

Becker, W., Staffel, M., & Ulrich, P. (2008). *Mittelstand und Mittelstandsforschung. Bamberger Betriebswirtschaftliche Beiträge: Vol. 153.* Retrieved from http://www.uni-bamberg.de/fileadmin/uni/fakultaeten/sowi_lehrstuehle/unternehmensfuehrung/Download-Bereich/Becker_2008_Mittelstand_und_Mittelstandsforschung_BBB_153.pdf

Becker, W., Staffel, M., & Ulrich, P. (2009). Wertmanagement als Instrument der strategischen Führung im Mittelstand: Konzepte. Modifikationen und Empfehlungen. In J.-A. Meyer (Ed.), *Management-Instrumente in kleinen und mittleren Unternehmen* (pp. 257–282). Lohmar, Köln: JOSEF EUL VERLAG GmbH.

Becker, W., Staffel, M., & Ulrich, P. (2010). Elemente von Controllingsystemen im Mittelstand: Empirische Analyse und Ableitung von Handlungsempfehlungen. *Controlling, 22*(3), 195–203.

Becker, W., & Ulrich, P. (2009a). Mittelstand, KMU und Familienunternehmen in der Betriebswirtschaftslehre. *WiSt Wirtschaftswissenschaftliches Studium, 38*(1), 2–7.

Becker, W., & Ulrich, P. (2015b). Begriffsabgrenzung und volkswirtschaftliche Bedeutung. In W. Becker & P. Ulrich (Eds.), *BWL im Mittelstand. Grundlagen, Besonderheiten, Entwicklungen* (1st ed., pp. 19–37). Stuttgart: Verlag W. Kohlhammer.

Becker, W., Ulrich, P., & Ebner, R. (2010a). Wertorientierte Steuerung einer Produktionsgesellschaft in Osteuropa. *WiSt Wirtschaftswissenschaftliches Studium, 39*(3), 164–168.

Becker, W., Ulrich, P., & Ebner, R. (2010b). Wertorientierte Unternehmensführung im Mittelstand. *WiSt Wirtschaftswissenschaftliches Studium, 39*(3), 114–120.

Berrone, P., Cruz, C., & Gomez-Mejia, L. R. (2012). Socioemotional Wealth in Family Firms. *Family Business Review, 25*(3), 258–279. doi:10.1177/0894486511435355

Blackburn, R., & Kovalainen, A. (2009). Researching small firms and entrepreneurship: Past, present and future. *International Journal of Management Reviews, 11*(2), 127–148. doi:10.1111/j.1468-2370.2008.00254.x

Blackburn, R. A., & Curran, J. (2001). *Researching the small enterprise*. London, Thousand Oaks, Calif: Sage Publications.

Blackburn, R. A., & Smallbone, D. (2008). Researching Small Firms and Entrepreneurship in the U.K.: Developments and Distinctiveness. *Entrepreneurship Theory and Practice, 32*(2), 267–288. doi:10.1111/j.1540-6520.2007.00226.x

Bluhm, K., & Martens, B. (2009). Recomposed institutions: smaller firms' strategies, shareholder-value orientation and bank relationships in Germany. *Socio-Economic Review, 7*(4), 585–604. doi:10.1093/ser/mwp011

Blume, K. H. (2016). Value-based management as a tailor-made management practice? A literature review. *Journal of Management & Governance, 20*(3), 553–590. doi:10.1007/s10997-015-9315-3

Bornheim, S. P. (2000). *The organizational form of family business*. Boston: Kluwer Academic.

Braun, V., & Clarke, V. (2006). Using thematic analysis in psychology. *Qualitative Research in Psychology, 3*(2), 77–101. doi:10.1191/1478088706qp063oa

Breuer, G., & Peyerl, H. (2006). Shareholder Value as a basis for strategic business decision making in family firms. *Die Bodenkultur, 57*(4), 185–196.

Britzelmaier, B. (2013). *Wertorientierte Unternehmensführung* (2. Aufl.). *Kompakt-Training praktische Betriebswirtschaft*. Herne: Kiehl.

Britzelmaier, B., Pöpplow, U., & Andraschko, L. (2018). Capital budgeting practices of SME in Baden-Württemberg: Findings of an empirical study. *International Journal of Business and Globalisation, in press.*

Brockhaus, R. H. (1994). Entrepreneurship and Family Business Research: Comparisons, Critique, and Lessons. *Entrepreneurship Theory and Practice, 19*(1), 25–38. doi:10.1177/104225879401900102

Brouthers, K. D., Andriessen, F., & Nicolaes, I. (1998). Driving blind: Strategic decisionmaking in small companies. *Long Range Planning, 31*(1), 130–138. doi:10.1016/S0024-6301(97)00099-X

Bryman, A., & Bell, E. (2011). *Business research methods* (3rd ed). Cambridge, New York, NY: Oxford University Press.

Bundesministerium für Wirtschaft und Energie. (2018). *Erfolgsmodell Mittelstand*. Retrieved from https://www.bmwi.de/Redaktion/DE/Dossier/politik-fuer-den-mittelstand.html

Carraher, S., & van Auken, H. (2013). The use of financial statements for decision making by small firms. *Journal of Small Business & Entrepreneurship, 26*(3), 323–336. doi:10.1080/08276331.2013.803676

Chrisman, J. J., Chua, J. H., Pearson, A. W., & Barnett, T. (2012). Family Involvement, Family Influence, and Family-Centered Non-Economic Goals in Small Firms. *Entrepreneurship Theory and Practice, 36*(2), 267–293. doi:10.1111/j.1540-6520.2010.00407.x

Chua, J. H., Chrisman, J. J., & Sharma, P. (1999). Defining the family business by behavior. *Entrepreneurship Theory and Practice, 23*(4), 19–39.

Copeland, T., Koller, T., & Murrin, J. (1996). *Valuation: Measuring and managing the value of companies* (2nd ed.). *Wiley frontiers in finance*. New York, NY: Wiley.

Creswell, J. W. (2007). *Qualitative inquiry and research design: Choosing among five approaches* (2nd edition). Thousand Oaks, CA: Sage Publications.

Creswell, J. W. (2013). *Qualitative inquiry and research design: Choosing among five approaches* (3rd ed.). Los Angeles: Sage Publications.

Crotty, M. (1998). *The foundations of social research: Meaning and perspective in the research process*. London, Thousand Oaks, Calif: Sage Publications.

Curseu, P. L., & Vermeulen, P. A. (2008). Conclusions: an outline of ESDM research. In P. A. Vermeulen & P. L. Curseu (Eds.), *Entrepreneurial strategic decision-making. A cognitive perspective* (pp. 190–199). Cheltenham, UK, Northampton, MA: Edward Elgar.

Curşeu, P. L., & Vermeulen, P. A. (2008). Entrepreneurs and strategic decisions. In P. A. Vermeulen & P. L. Curseu (Eds.), *Entrepreneurial strategic decision-making. A cognitive perspective* (pp. 1–8). Cheltenham, UK, Northampton, MA: Edward Elgar.

Deloitte & Touche GmbH Wirtschaftsprüfungsgesellschaft (Ed.). (2015). *Optimale Gewinnverwendung im Mittelstand* ("Erfolgsfaktoren im Mittelstand"). Retrieved from https://www2.deloitte.com/content/dam/Deloitte/de/Documents/Mittelstand/Gewinnverwendung_komplett_safe.pdf

Dixit, B. K. (2011). *Do Indian Acquireres Create Shareholder Value? The Effect of Affiliation to a Family Business Group*. Bangalore. Retrieved from Indian Institute of Management Bangalore website: https://www.academia.edu/1867111/Do_Indian_Acquirers_Create_Shareholder_Value_The_Effect_of_Affiliation_to_a_Family_Business_Group

Dresing, T., & Pehl, T. (2013). *Praxisbuch Transkription: Regelsysteme, Software und praktische Anleitungen für qualitative ForscherInnen* (5th ed.). Marburg: Eigenverlag.

Easterby-Smith, M., Thorpe, R., & Jackson, P. (2012). *Management research* (4th ed). Los Angeles, London: Sage.

Eriksson, P., & Kovalainen, A. (2008). *Qualitative methods in business research. Introducing qualitative methods*. Los Angeles, London: Sage.

European Commission. (2003). *Commission Recommendation of 6 May 2003 concerning the definition of micro, small and medium-sized enterprises: 2003/361/EC* (Official Journal of the European Union). Retrieved from https://eur-lex.europa.eu/LexUriServ/LexUriServ.do?uri=OJ:L:2003:124:0036:0041:en:PDF

European Commission. (2005). *The new SME definition: User guide and model declaration. Enterprise and industry publications*. Luxembourg: Off. for Off. Publ. of the Europ. Communities. Retrieved from http://ec.europa.eu/enterprise/policies/sme/files/sme_definition/sme_user_guide_en.pdf

European Commission. (2015). *User guide to the SME definition*. Luxembourg: Publications Office. Retrieved from https://eda.europa.eu/docs/default-source/documents/smedefinitionguide_en.pdf

Firk, S., Schmidt, T., & Wolff, M. (2016). Wertorientierte Unternehmenssteuerung in der Praxis. In W. Becker & P. Ulrich (Eds.), *Handbuch Controlling* (pp. 365–384). Wiesbaden: Springer Fachmedien Wiesbaden.

Firk, S., Schrapp, S., & Wolff, M. (2016). Drivers of value creation—The role of value-based management and underlying institutions. *Management Accounting Research, 33,* 42–60. doi:10.1016/j.mar.2016.04.002

García-Pérez-de-Lema, D., & Duréndez, A. (2007). Managerial behaviour of small and medium-sized family businesses: an empirical study. *International Journal of Entrepreneurial Behavior & Research, 13*(3), 151–172. doi:10.1108/13552550710751030

Gibcus, P., & van Hoesel, P. (2004). *Transforming an idea into a strategic decision in SMEs: The underlying decision-making process* (Research report No. H200311). Zoetermeer.

Gibcus, P., & van Hoesel, P. (2008). Strategic decision-making processes in SMEs: an exploratory study. In P. A. Vermeulen & P. L. Curseu (Eds.), *Entrepreneurial strategic decision-making. A cognitive perspective* (pp. 89–104). Cheltenham, UK, Northampton, MA: Edward Elgar.

Gibcus, P., Vermeulen, P. A., & de Jong, J. P. (2009). Strategic decision making in small firms: a taxonomy of small business owners. *International Journal of Entrepreneurship and Small Business, 7*(1), 74–91. doi:10.1504/IJESB.2009.021610

Gibcus, P., Vermeulen, P. A., & Radulova, E. (2008). The decision-making entrepreneur: a literature review. In P. A. Vermeulen & P. L. Curseu (Eds.), *Entrepreneurial strategic decision-making. A cognitive perspective* (pp. 11–40). Cheltenham, UK, Northampton, MA: Edward Elgar.

Golsner, C. (2012). *Effektives Wertmanagement im Mittelstand - eine systemische Perspektive.* Bamberg: Difo Druck GmbH.

Gonschorek, T. (2009a). *Einflussfaktoren der Anwendung wertorientierter Unternehmensführung im deutschen Mittelstand: Ergebnisse einer empirischen Studie.* Dresden: TUDpress.

Gonschorek, T. (2015b). Wertorientierte Unternehmensführung im Mittelstand. In W. Becker & P. Ulrich (Eds.), *BWL im Mittelstand. Grundlagen, Besonderheiten, Entwicklungen* (1st ed., pp. 495–510). Stuttgart: Verlag W. Kohlhammer.

Gonschorek, T. (2016c). Wert(e)orientierte Unternehmensführung im Mittelstand. In I. Gestring, T. Gonschorek, A.-K. Haubold, R. Sonntag, & R. von der Weth (Eds.), *Ethik im Mittelstand* (pp. 141–153). Wiesbaden: Springer Fachmedien Wiesbaden.

Gonschorek, T. & Günther, T. (2006a). *Wert(e)orientierte Unternehmensführung im Mittelstand: Erste Ergebnisse einer empirischen Untersuchung.* Retrieved from http://nbn-resolving.de/urn:nbn:de:swb:14-1155120256369-88190

Gonschorek, T., & Günther, T. (2011b). Wertorientierte Unternehmensführung im deutschen Mittelstand - Ergebnisse einer empirischen Studie. *Controlling - Zeitschrift für erfolgsorientierte Unternehmenssteuerung, 23*(1), 18–27.

Guba, E. G., & Lincoln, Y. S. (1994). Competing paradigms in qualitative research. In N. K. Denzin & Y. S. Lincoln (Eds.), *Handbook of qualitative research* (pp. 105–117). Thousand Oaks: Sage Publications.

Günther, T. (2014a). Planungs- und Kontrollinstrumente zur unternehmenswertorientierten Führung in mittelständischen Unternehmen. *Controlling - Zeitschrift für erfolgsorientierte Unternehmenssteuerung, 26*(4/5), 220–227.

Günther, T. (2015b). Wertorientierte Steuerung im Mittelstand. In W. Becker & P. Ulrich (Eds.), *BWL im Mittelstand. Grundlagen, Besonderheiten, Entwicklungen* (1st ed., pp. 481–495). Stuttgart: Verlag W. Kohlhammer.

Günther, T., & Gonschorek, T. (2008). Wert(e)orientierte Unternehmensführung im Mittelstand. Ausgewählte Ergebnisse einer empirischen Untersuchung. In V. Lingnau (Ed.), *Reihe: Controlling: Bd. 8. Die Rolle des Controllers im Mittelstand. Funktionale, institutionale und instrumentelle Ausgestaltung* (1st ed., pp. 49–70). Lohmar, Köln: Eul.

Halabi, A. K., Barrett, R., & Dyt, R. (2010). Understanding financial information used to assess small firm performance. *Qualitative Research in Accounting & Management, 7*(2), 163–179. doi:10.1108/11766091011050840

Hallebone, E., & Priest, J. (2009). *Business and management research: Paradigms & practices.* Basingstoke [England], New York: Palgrave Macmillan.

Haunschild, L., & Wolter, H.-J. (2010). *Volkswirtschaftliche Bedeutung von Familien- und Frauenunternehmen* (IfM-Materialien No. 199). Bonn. Retrieved from Institut für Mittelstandsforschung Bonn website: https://www.ifm-bonn.org//uploads/tx_ifmstudies/IfM-Materialien-199_2010.pdf

Hausch, K. T. (2004). *Corporate Governance im deutschen Mittelstand.* Wiesbaden: Deutscher Universitätsverlag.

Heinen, E. (1966). *Das Zielsystem der Unternehmung: Grundlagen betriebswirtschaftlicher Entscheidungen.* Wiesbaden: Betriebswirtschaftlicher Verlag Dr. Th. Gabler.

Helfferich, C. (2011). *Die Qualität qualitativer Daten: Manual für die Durchführung qualitativer Interviews* (4th ed.). *Lehrbuch.* Wiesbaden: VS, Verl. für Sozialwiss.

Ihlau, S., Duscha, H., & Gödecke, S. (2013). *Besonderheiten bei der Bewertung von KMU: Planungsplausibilisierung, Steuern, Kapitalisierung.* Dordrecht: Springer.

Institut für Mittelstandsforschung Bonn. (2018a). *Familienunternehmen-Definition des IfM Bonn.* Retrieved from https://www.ifm-bonn.org/definitionen/familienunternehmen-definition/

Institut für Mittelstandsforschung Bonn. (2018b). *KMU-Definition des IfM Bonn.* Retrieved from https://www.ifm-bonn.org/definitionen/kmu-definition-des-ifm-bonn/

Institut für Mittelstandsforschung Bonn. (2018a). *Mittelstand im Überblick.* Retrieved from https://www.ifm-bonn.org/statistiken/mittelstand-im-ueberblick/

Institut für Mittelstandsforschung Bonn. (2018b). *Mittelstandsdefinition des IfM Bonn.* Retrieved from https://www.ifm-bonn.org/definitionen/mittelstandsdefinition-des-ifm-bonn/

Jocumsen, G. (2004). How do small business managers make strategic marketing decisions?: A model of process. *European Journal of Marketing, 38*(5/6), 659–674. doi:10.1108/03090560410529277

Kammerlander, N., Sieger, P., Voordeckers, W., & Zellweger, T. (2015). Value creation in family firms: A model of fit. *Journal of Family Business Strategy, 6*(2), 63–72. doi:10.1016/j.jfbs.2015.04.001

KfW Bankengruppe (Ed.). (2017). *KfW-Mittelstandspanel 2017: Rekordjagd im Inland geht ungebremst weiter - neue Herausforderungen durch sektoralen Wandel.* Frankfurt am Main. Retrieved from https://www.kfw.de/PDF/Download-

Center/Konzernthemen/Research/PDF-Dokumente-KfW-Mittelstandspanel/KfW-Mittelstandspanel-2017.pdf

Khadjavi, K. (2005). *Wertmanagement im Mittelstand*. Eschen: digiprint AG.

Khadjavi, K., & Volery, T. (2009). Wertmanagement in mittelständischen Unternehmen. *ZfKE – Zeitschrift für KMU und Entrepreneurship, 57*(1), 27–52. doi:10.3790/zfke.57.1.27

King, N. (2012). Doing template analysis. In G. Symon & C. Cassell (Eds.), *Qualitative organizational research. Core methods and current challenges* (pp. 426–450). London: Sage.

King, N., & Horrocks, C. (2010). *Interviews in qualitative research*. Los Angeles: Sage.

Klein, S. B. (2010). *Familienunternehmen: Theoretische und empirische Grundlagen* (3rd ed.). *Family Business: Vol. 1*. Lohmar, Köln: Eul.

Klein, S. B., Astrachan, J. H., & Smyrnios, K. X. (2005). The F-PEC Scale of Family Influence: Construction, Validation, and Further Implication for Theory. *Entrepreneurship Theory and Practice, 29*(3), 321–339.

Kosmider, A. (1994). *Controlling im Mittelstand: Eine Untersuchung der Gestaltung und Anwendung des Controllings in mittelständischen Industrieunternehmen* (2nd ed.). *Schriftenreihe der Wissenschaftlichen Hochschule für Unternehmensführung Koblenz. Forschung: Vol. 5*. Stuttgart: Schäffer-Poeschel.

Kraus, S., Harms, R., & Fink, M. (2011). Family firm research: sketching a research field. *International Journal of Entrepreneurship and Innovation Management, 13*(1), 32. doi:10.1504/IJEIM.2011.038446

Krol, F. (2007a). *Value Based Management in Small and Medium Enterprises: Analysis of internal and external impulses and possibilities of implementation*. Retrieved from http://www.wiwi.uni-muenster.de/ctrl/md/content/publikationen/Arbeitspapier_9_1.pdf

Krol, F. (2009b). *Wertorientierte Unternehmensführung im Mittelstand - Ergebnisse einer empirischen Studie*. Retrieved from http://www.wiwi.uni-muenster.de/ctrl/md/content/publikationen/Arbeitspapapier_10_1.pdf

Krol, F. (2009c). *Wertorientierte Unternehmensführung im Mittelstand: Eine empirische Analyse von Einfluss- und Wirkungsfaktoren*. Westfälische Wilhelms-Univ., Diss.--Münster, 2009. *Schriftenreihe Schriften zum Betrieblichen Rechnungswesen und Controlling: Vol. 75*. Hamburg: Kovac. Retrieved from http://www.verlagdrkovac.de/978-3-8300-4698-1.htm / http://www.gbv.de/dms/zbw/60736758X.pdf

Krol, F., & Wömpener, A. (2009). Wertorientiertes Controlling im Mittelstand: Status quo, Promotoren und Nutzungspotenziale. *Controller-Magazin, 34*(5), 197–203.

Kvale, S. (1996). *InterViews: An Introduction to Qualitative Research Interviewing*. London: Sage Publications.

Landström, H. (2010). *Pioneers in entrepreneurship and small business research*. New York: Springer.

Lavia López, O., & Hiebl, M. R. (2015). Management Accounting in Small and Medium-Sized Enterprises: Current Knowledge and Avenues for Further Research. *Journal of Management Accounting Research, 27*(1), 81–119. doi:10.2308/jmar-50915

Legenhausen, C. (1998). *Controllinginstrumente für den Mittelstand*. Wiesbaden: Deutscher Universitätsverlag.

Lehmann, G. (2012). *Wertorientiertes Management mittelständischer Unternehmungen: Potenziale der Ermittlung von Eigenkapitalkosten sowie Herleitung von Konzeptanforderungen im Rahmen eines Delphi-Verfahrens. Schriften zum Management: Bd. 38*. München: Rainer Hampp.

Leyherr, M. (2000). *Die Situation von Familienunternehmen in Österreich*. Stuttgart.

Lincoln, Y. S., Lynham, S. A., & Guba, E. G. (2011). Paradigmatic Controversies, Contradictions, and Emerging Confluences, Revisited. In N. K. Denzin & Y. S. Lincoln (Eds.), *The Sage handbook of qualitative research* (4th ed., pp. 97–128). Thousand Oaks: Sage.

Litz, R. A. (1995). The Family Business: Toward Definitional Clarity. *Family Business Review, 8*(2), 71–81.

Lohr, M. (2012). Specificities of Managerial Accounting at SMEs: Case Studies from the German Industrial Sector. *Journal of Small Business & Entrepreneurship, 25*(1), 35–55. doi:10.1080/08276331.2012.10593558

Low, M. B. (2001). The Adolescence of Entrepreneurship Research: Specification of Purpose. *Entrepreneurship Theory and Practice, 25*(4), 17–26. doi:10.1177/104225870102500402

Lucas, G. J., Vermeulen, P. A., & Curşeu, P. L. (2008). Entrepreneurial decision styles and cognition in SMEs. In P. A. Vermeulen & P. L. Curseu (Eds.), *Entrepreneurial strategic decision-making. A cognitive perspective* (pp. 105–122). Cheltenham, UK, Northampton, MA: Edward Elgar.

Mafirowanda, R. M. (2015). *Measuring the understanding of value-based management in small businesses in Gauteng*. Retrieved from Potchefstroom Business School, North-West University website: https://dspace.nwu.ac.za/bitstream/handle/10394/18936/Mafirowanda_RM_2015.pdf?sequence=1&isAllowed=y

Mäkeläinen, E., & Roztocki, N. (1998). *Economic Value Added (EVA) for Small Business*. Retrieved from http://www.evanomics.com/presenta/evaspres.pdf

March, J. G. (1991). Exploration and Exploitation in Organizational Learning. *Organization Science, 2*(1), 71–87. doi:10.1287/orsc.2.1.71

Martens, B., & Bluhm, K. (2007). "Shareholder Value" ohne Aktionäre?: Diffusion und mögliche Folgen wertorientierter Unternehmenssteuerung im industriellen Mittelstand. *Working Papers: Economic Sociology Jena, 2007*(2), 1–31.

Nathani, N., Rathod, S., & Rohira, S. (2016). Association between EVA and CSR: A Study of Family Owned Business Companies in India. In S. S. Bhakar, C. Gulati, G. Mathur, & R. Pathak (Eds.), *Global advancements in HRM-innovation and practices* (pp. 79–88). New Delhi: Bharti Publications.

Neubauer, H. (1992). Unternehmensnachfolge in Familienunternehmen. In H. J. Pleitner (Ed.), *Die veränderte Welt. Einwirkung auf die Klein- und Mittelunternehmen* (pp. 168–197). St. Gallen.

Oliveira, C. G. d. (2014). *Economic Value Addedd assessment applied to the portuguese SME during the crisis period*. Retrieved from ISCTE Business School Lisbon University Institute website: https://repositorio.iscte-iul.pt/bitstream/10071/8924/1/cgo_final_mscthesis.pdf

Piontkowski, J. O. (2009). Wertorientierte Unternehmensführung in mittelständischen Unternehmen: Empirische Hinweise auf Anwendung. *Controlling - Zeitschrift für erfolgsorientierte Unternehmenssteuerung, 21*(7), 357–363.

Posch, A., & Speckbacher, G. (2012). Führung in Familienunternehmen: Besonderheiten der Entscheidungsfindung und Verhaltenssteuerung und deren Auswirkung auf den Unternehmenserfolg. *Zeitschrift für Betriebswirtschaft, 82*(S3), 5–23. doi:10.1007/s11573-012-0566-z

PricewaterhouseCoopers AG Wirtschaftsprüfungsgesellschaft (Ed.). (2014). *Nutzt der Mittelstand seine Chancen im internationalen Markt?* (BDI/PwC-Mittelstandspanel No. Frühjahr 2014). Retrieved from https://www.bdi-panel.emnid.de/pdf/BDI-Ergebnisse-Fruehjahr-2014.pdf

Print, C. F., & Reynolds, J. (2011). Family-controlled businesses and shareholder value. *Journal of Family Business Management, 1*(1), 47–64. doi:10.1108/20436231111122281

Rappaport, A. (1986). *Creating shareholder value: The new standard for business performance*. New York: The Free Press.

Reinemann, H., & Ludwig, D. (2015). Die qualitative Dimension des Mittelstandsbegriffs. In W. Becker & P. Ulrich (Eds.), *BWL im Mittelstand. Grundlagen, Besonderheiten, Entwicklungen* (1st ed., pp. 38–52). Stuttgart: Verlag W. Kohlhammer.

Roztocki, N., & Needy, K. L. (1999). *EVA for Small Manufacturing Companies*. Las Vegas, Nevada March 28-30, 1999: Society for Advancement of Management (SAM) 1999 International Management Conference.

Rubin, H. J., & Rubin, I. (2012). *Qualitative interviewing: The art of hearing data* (3rd ed.). Thousand Oaks, Calif: Sage.

Saunders, M., Lewis, P., & Thornhill, A. (2009). *Research methods for business students* (5th ed.). Harlow: Pearson Education.

Schauf, M. (2009). Grundlagen der Unternehmensführung im Mittelstand. In M. Schauf (Ed.), *Unternehmensführung im Mittelstand. Rollenwandel kleiner und mittlerer Unternehmen in der Globalisierung* (2nd ed., pp. 3–30). München: Hampp.

Scheiber, F., Wruk, D., Huppertz, S., Oberg, A., & Woywode, M. (2012). Die Verbreitung moderner Managementkonzepte im Mittelstand. *Zeitschrift für Betriebswirtschaft, 82*(S3), 25–69. doi:10.1007/s11573-012-0567-y

Schlegel, D., Frank, F., & Britzelmaier, B. (2016). Investment decisions and capital budgeting practices in German manufacturing companies. *International Journal of Business and Globalisation, 16*(1), 66–78. doi:10.1504/IJBG.2016.073626

Schlepphorst, S., & Schlömer-Laufen, N. (2016). *Schnell wachsende Unternehmen in Deutschland: Charakteristika und Determinanten ihres Wachstums* (IfM-Materialien No. 246). Retrieved from http://www.ifm-bonn.org//uploads/tx_ifmstudies/IfM-Materialien-246_2016.pdf

Schlüchtermann, J., & Pointner, A. M. (2004). Unternehmensplanung und Mittelstand: Strategieumsetzung mit Hilfe der Balanced Score Card. In J. Schlüchtermann & H.-J. Tebroke (Eds.), *Schriftenreihe des Betriebswirtschaftlichen Forschungszentrums für Fragen der Mittelständischen Wirtschaft an der Universität Bayreuth. Mittelstand im Fokus. 25 Jahre BF/M-Bayreuth* (1st ed.). Wiesbaden: Deutscher Universitäts-Verlag.

Schomaker, M., & Günther, T. (2006). Wertorientiertes Management für den Mittelstand. In N. Schweickart & A. Töpfer (Eds.), *Wertorientiertes Management. Werterhaltung - Wertsteuerung - Wertsteigerung ganzheitlich gestalten* (pp. 215–237). Berlin, Heidelberg: Springer-Verlag Berlin Heidelberg.

Schön, D. (2012). *Planung und Reporting im Mittelstand: Grundlagen, Business Intelligence und Mobile Computing*. Wiesbaden: Springer Gabler.

Simon, H. (1992). Lessons from Germany's midsize giants. *Harvard Business Review, 1992*(March-April), 115–123.

Statistisches Bundesamt Deutschland (Ed.). (2018). *48121-0002 Statistik für kleine und mittlere Unternehmen: Bruttowertschöpfung: Deutschland, Jahre, Unternehmensgröße, Wirtschaftsbereiche*. Retrieved from https://www-genesis.destatis.de/genesis/online/link/tabelleErgebnis/48121-0002

Statistisches Landesamt Baden-Württemberg (Ed.). (2018a). *Eckdaten seit 2008 nach Beschäftigungsgrößenklassen*. Retrieved from https://www.statistik-bw.de/Industrie/Struktur/VG-GK-BBEU.jsp

Statistisches Landesamt Baden-Württemberg (Ed.). (2018b). *Unternehmen und Betriebe seit 2006 nach Wirtschaftsabschnitten*. Retrieved from https://www.statistik-bw.de/GesamtwBranchen/UnternehmBetriebe/040231xx.tab?R=LA

Steinhübel, V. (2006). Strategisches Controlling in mittelständischen Unternehmen. *Controlling*, (4/5), 205–214.

Stokes, P. (2011). *Key concepts in business and management research methods*. *Palgrave key concepts*. Houndmills, Basingstoke, Hampshire, New York: Palgrave Macmillan.

Stokes, P., & Wall, T. (2014). *Research methods*. *Palgrave business briefing*. London, New York: Palgrave, Palgrave Macmillan.

Tappe, R. (2009). *Wertorientierte Unternehmensführung im Mittelstand: Eine Überprüfung der Anwendbarkeit*. Techn. Univ., Diss.--Dortmund, 2009. *Controlling and Management: Vol. 38*. Frankfurt am Main: Lang.

Ulrich, P. (2011). *Corporate Governance in mittelständischen Familienunternehmen: Theoretische und empirische Analyse unter besonderer Berücksichtigung der Wechselwirkungen zwischen Corporate Governance und Controlling* (1st ed.). *Unternehmensführung & Controlling*. Wiesbaden: Betriebswirtschaftlicher Verlag Gabler.

University of Chester. (2016). *Research Governance Handbook*. Chester.

van Auken, H., & Yang, K. (2014). CHINESE SMEs' USES OF FINANCIAL STATEMENTS IN DECISION MAKING. *Journal of Developmental Entrepreneurship, 19*(04), 1450027/1-1450027/16. doi:10.1142/S1084946714500277

Walther, S. (2004). *Erfolgsfaktoren von Innovationen in mittelständischen Unternehmen: Eine empirische Untersuchung*. *Europäische Hochschulschriften : Reihe 5, Volks- und Betriebswirtschaft: Vol. 3050*. Frankfurt am Main: P. Lang.

Weber, J., Bramsemann, U., Heineke, C., & Hirsch, B. (2017). *Wertorientierte Unternehmenssteuerung: Konzepte - Implementierung - Praxis-Statement* (2nd ed.). Wiesbaden: Springer Gabler.

Welge, M. K., Al-Laham, A., & Eulerich, M. (2017). *Strategisches Management: Grundlagen - Prozess - Implementierung* (7th ed.). Wiesbaden: Springer Gabler.

Welge, M. K., & Witt, P. (2013). Corporate Governance in kleinen und mittleren Unternehmen. In M. K. Welge & P. Witt (Eds.), *ZfB : special issue: Vol. 2013,2. Corporate Governance in mittelständischen Unternehmen* (pp. 185–205). Wiesbaden: Springer Gabler.

Welter, F., & Lasch, F. (2008). Entrepreneurship Research in Europe: Taking Stock and Looking Forward. *Entrepreneurship Theory and Practice, 32*(2), 241–248. doi:10.1111/j.1540-6520.2007.00224.x

Welter, F., Levering, B., & May-Strobl, E. (2016). *Mittelstandspolitik im Wandel* (IfM-Materialien No. 247). Bonn. Retrieved from Institut für Mittelstandsforschung Bonn website: https://www.ifm-bonn.org//uploads/tx_ifmstudies/IfM-Materialien-247_2016.pdf

Wenzel, A. E. (2014). *Wertmanagement in grossen Familienunternehmen*. St. Gallen: D-Druck Spescha.

Wolter, H.-J., & Hauser, H.-E. (2001). Die Bedeutung des Eigentümerunternehmens in Deutschland - EIne Auseinandersetzung mit der qualitativen und quantitativen Definition des Mittelstands. In Institut für Mittelstandsforschung Bonn (Ed.), *Schriften zur Mittelstandsforschung: N.F., Nr. 90. Jahrbuch zur Mittelstandsforschung 1/2001* (pp. 25–77). Wiesbaden: Gabler, GWV-Fachverl. Retrieved from http://www.ifm-bonn.org//uploads/tx_ifmstudies/90_nf_2.pdf

Yin, R. K. (2003). *Case study research: Design and methods* (Fifth edition). Thousand Oaks, Calif.: Sage Publ.

The manufacturer's authorised representative in the EU is Springer Nature Customer Service Centre GmbH, Europaplatz 3, 69115 Heidelberg, Germany. If you have any concerns regarding our products, please contact ProductSafety@springernature.com

Printed and bound by CPI Group (UK) Ltd, Croydon, CR0 4YY
30/09/2026
02225597-0005